MARIE ANTOINETTE

MARIE
ANTOINETTE

•

JOAN HASLIP

•

WEIDENFELD & NICOLSON
NEW YORK

Published by Weidenfeld & Nicolson, New York
A Division of Wheatland Corporation
10 East 53rd Street
New York, NY 10022

First published in Great Britain in 1987
by George Weidenfeld & Nicolson Ltd.

Library of Congress Cataloging-in-Publication Data

Haslip, Joan, 1912–
   Marie Antoinette.
   Bibliography: p.
   Includes index
   1. Marie Antoinette, Queen, consort of Louis XVI,
King of France, 1755–1793. 2. France—History—Louis
XVI, 1774–1793. 3. France—Queens—Biography.
                I. Title.
   DC137.1.H37 1988 944′.035′0924 [B] 87-34031
           ISBN 1-55584-183-X

Manufactured in the United States of America

First American Edition, 1988

10 9 8 7 6 5 4 3 2 1

To Liliane de Rothschild and
Bernard Minoret in gratitude for
their encouragement and help

CONTENTS

ILLUSTRATIONS

ACKNOWLEDGEMENTS

When my publisher Lord Weidenfeld suggested I should write a life of Marie Antoinette of France, my first instinct was to refuse to add yet another volume to those which already fill the shelves of public libraries, ranging from the violent diatribes of a Michelet to the panegyrics of the Goncourts. But I was told that in every generation there are certain characters who require a reassessment. And in spite of all the books on the subject which have come out in recent years, the most popular and the most widely read is still that of Stefan Zweig, written half a century ago. Zweig describes Marie Antoinette as an 'average woman' who only found greatness with the guillotine. But had she been given a proper education (and her mother cannot be blamed entirely for negligence in this direction), and had she been married to a man of character and determination who commanded her respect, Marie Antoinette might have been a remarkable queen. I was tempted to find out why she failed and perhaps to find excuses for her failures. Her life can be divided into two parts, broken by the affair of the diamond necklace by which time she was already doomed. There is little that can be added to the second part, and I have written at greater length on the earlier years. In the enormous mass of material contained in the Vienna archives, one comes across early letters from Marie Antoinette to her mother, letters from the ambassador Count Mercy d'Argenteau to the Empress Maria Theresa, and even letters between Marie Antoinette's two brothers, the Emperor Joseph II and the Grand Duke Leopold of Tuscany, all of which pay tribute to her intrinsic goodness and frankness in a world where honesty was regarded as a crime.

In gaining access to the Vienna archives, and in particular to the family archives, I wish to thank His Imperial Highness, the Archduke Michael Hapsburg-Salvator for putting me in touch with Frau-Doktor Benha, director of the Haus und Stadts Archiv. In France my thanks go to Monsieur Jean Lemoyne, until recently *conservateur en chef* of the Château of Versailles, who was kind enough to impart some of his invaluable knowledge and to show me those areas of Versailles and of Trianon which are still closed to the public. I also want to thank Monsieur Prevost Marcyl-Hacys of the Département des Monuments Historiques for obtaining permission for me to visit the Chambre de la Réserve of the Bibliothèque Nationale to read the obscene pamphlets and calumnies of which Marie Antoinette was the victim, almost from the day of her arrival in France. My deepest gratitude goes to Baroness

Elie de Rothschild who, with a lifelong devotion for Marie Antoinette, has not only amassed a unique collection of objects which belonged to her, but a superb knowledge of everything that concerned her; while in Monsieur Bernard Minoret I found a friend who, steeped in the eighteenth century, showed me a Paris I would never have discovered on my own, and was also kind enough to check the French names in my book. Others who were kind enough to help were Mr Nigel Nicolson, who invited me to Sissinghurst Castle to consult the documents concerning his ancestor, the Duke of Dorset; Sir Harold Acton, who took the trouble to read the manuscript and make some valuable corrections; Mr Joseph Baillie who allowed me to reproduce an unpublished drawing by Vigée-Lebrun in his possession; and the directors of Christie's who let me read the secret correspondence of Marie Antoinette and Axel Fersen in the collection of letters from the estates of the Baroness Thyra Klinckowström.

Lastly I would like to thank my friends Claude and Marion Puzenat for the hospitality they offered me when I was doing my researches in Paris, my editor Candida Brazil, and Maria Ellis who achieves wonders in deciphering my handwriting.

PROLOGUE

On All Souls' Day, 2 November 1755, the Empress Maria Theresa gave birth to her fifteenth child, a daughter named Maria Antonia. Austria was at the time enjoying a brief period of prosperity and peace, but the christening celebration was shadowed by the terrible earthquake which devastated three-quarters of the town of Lisbon and prevented Maria Antonia's godfather, the King of Portugal, from attending the ceremony. In later years the tragedy of Lisbon was often referred to as the first portent of disaster in a life which began under the happiest of auspices in the midst of a loving and united family.

As Maria Theresa's youngest daughter with seven older sisters to be married off before her, Maria Antonia seemed destined to a quiet, uneventful life as the wife of one of the innumerable Wittelsbach or Hapsburg cousins. But typhus and smallpox, those two fatal diseases of the eighteenth century, carried off two of her sisters within a year, leaving a third, the most beautiful of all, as a disfigured invalid. By 1767, when Maria Antonia was barely twelve years old, she had become a candidate for the richest matrimonial prize in Europe, to be offered in marriage to a grandson of the King of France.

Ten years had gone by since the Westminster Convention signed between England and Prussia had caused a diplomatic revolution, changing the whole balance of power in Europe and throwing those two hereditary enemies, France and Austria, into each other's arms. Neither trusted the other, but France needed a strong continental ally in her struggle for maritime supremacy against England, who was now threatening both her overseas empire and her trade. Austria, as represented by Maria Theresa and her chancellor Count, later Prince, Kaunitz, had only one object in view: to win back from Prussia the lost province of Silesia. The disasters of the Seven Years' War, in which France lost nearly the whole of her colonial empire and Austria failed to retrieve Silesia, have often been attributed to the Marquise de Pompadour, who is said to have influenced King Louis XV. Against his better judgement, he committed himself to an unpopular alliance, bitterly opposed both by his family and his court, an alliance which might never have survived the humiliating Peace of Paris had it not been for the diplomatic talents of two statesmen, Kaunitz in Austria and Choiseul in France. The latter, who owed his meteoric career to the favour of Madame de Pompadour, had become foreign minister at the end of the war. One of the few Frenchmen to uphold the Austrian alliance, he became the principal architect of the royal wedding so ardently desired by Maria Theresa, so warily approached by King Louis – a wedding which would never have taken place had not the Dauphin and his wife, both of whom hated Choiseul, died within a few years of one another, closely followed by their eldest son, and left Louis Auguste, a shy, awkward boy of fourteen, as heir to the French throne.

Meanwhile no attempt had been made to prepare the little Maria Antonia for her role as future Queen. She was allowed to remain happily playing in the gardens of Schönbrunn while one by one her elder sisters were married off, Caroline to the King of Naples, Amelia to the Infante of Parma, yet another of King Louis's grandsons. Amiable letters continued to be exchanged between King and Empress. But it was not until 1768 that the marriage plans began to crystallize into fact, and not until the summer of 1769 that Maria Theresa received an official letter from the King of France asking for the hand of her daughter Maria Antonia to be given in marriage to his grandson Louis Auguste.

Political pawns in the game of statecraft, the one as naive and ignorant as the other, Maria Antonia and Louis Auguste were to be sacrificed to the ill-fated Franco-Austrian alliance.

The Empress was already in her carriage; the postilion had been given the signal to depart when the Emperor, who was on horseback, suddenly dismounted, calling out, 'Where is my Toinette? I want to give her a last kiss,' and a little girl, who had been fighting back her tears at being left behind while her elder sisters were accompanying their parents to their brother Leopold's wedding in Innsbruck, ran forward suddenly all light and laughter to be caught up in her father's arms. He held her tightly as if afraid to let her go. And to her surprise she felt that his cheeks were wet with tears. Riding away with his gentlemen, the Emperor turned to one of them saying, 'God knows how much I longed to kiss that child,' as if some strange premonition warned him that he might never see her again.

In later years as Queen of France, Marie Antoinette often recalled that August day at Laxenburg and the sadness of her father's last goodbye. With remorse she remembered the written instructions he had left behind, which in her young and heedless days she had barely taken the trouble to read, and which if taken to heart might well have changed her life. Did he foresee the hordes of flatterers and place-seekers at Versailles when he wrote, 'The companions we select are of great importance, for frequently we are drawn by them in spite of ourselves into temptations, which without them would never have assailed us. Friendship is one of the joys of life. Only we must choose our friends wisely and not lavish affection carelessly'?

No one was ready to love the world as carelessly and as indiscriminately as Maria Antonia, the youngest and most spoilt of all the royal children at Schönbrunn. It was a large and happy family and the person responsible for their happiness was their father, Stephen Francis of Lorraine, who had introduced into the arid atmosphere of the Hapsburg court some of the gaiety and warmth of his former court of Lunéville.

But neither the inheritance of the Medicis nor later the Imperial crown had compensated Stephen Francis for the loss of his homelands, the price demanded by France in accordance with the pragmatic sanction for accepting the young Maria Theresa as heiress to the Hapsburg throne. Even as Emperor, Stephen Francis had never been more than the consort of his wife, fathering sixteen children of whom only ten grew to maturity and giving to each in turn the affection and understanding for which their mother could not spare the time. His favourite was Maria Antonia – a pretty, sparkling little girl with no wish to learn her lessons and an incorrigible flightiness, which Maria Theresa had to admit was one of the dangerous qualities her beloved husband had transmitted to their offspring. But for all his faults and his weaknesses both as a statesman and a military leader, Stephen Francis, with his masculine virility and kindly disposition, was eminently satisfactory both as a husband and a father.

There is a charming gouache painted by one of the elder girls, which shows us the Imperial family at breakfast at Schönbrunn with the Empress pouring out the coffee and her husband sitting in dressing gown and slippers with a towel wrapped round his head, while three of the younger children are playing in the foreground. Maria Antonia is holding her favourite doll, looking herself like an animated doll, dressed in her best clothes, waiting to accompany her parents to mass. So she must have looked on that August day of 1765 when her father bade her his sad goodbye.

A week later he was dead, struck down by a stroke in the midst of the brilliant wedding festivities at Innsbruck, of which till now he had been the life and soul. The Empress was only forty-seven at the time, a strong, passionate woman in the prime of life. She had been in love with Stephen Francis since the age of sixteen and his death left an irreplaceable void which brought her to the verge of suicide. In the first bleakness of despair she could not even bear to see her younger children, and summer had turned to autumn before she returned to the Imperial schoolroom at Schönbrunn. Little Maria Antonia, who had shed bitter tears over the death of her beloved papa, had with a child's resilience already regained her usual gaiety and it was a shock to find her mama so cruelly changed. Gone was the lovely golden hair, now cut short under a widow's cap; gone were the laughing eyes, now red-rimmed with tears. The mother who had seemed so dazzling in her coloured silks and satins was a severe, almost frightening figure in her thick mourning robes.

Maria Theresa was fond of her children, but the woman who had fought against every kind of opposition to marry the young Duke of Lorraine had no compunction in making her sons and daughters contract loveless dynastic marriages. There is an extraordinary callousness in her treatment of even her eldest son, Joseph. Only a few months after losing a wife whom he adored, she made him marry a Wittelsbach princess who was physically repellent to him, but whose Bavarian inheritance might one day be added to the Hapsburg Empire. The only person who was kind to poor ugly Josepha was her father-in-law, Stephen Francis, whom she survived by two years before succumbing to the outbreak of smallpox which swept Vienna in the spring of 1767. Maria Theresa herself fell critically ill, and even little Maria Antonia was not immune, but in her case the illness was so slight that it hardly marked the brilliant, transparent complexion which was later to be one of the greatest of her assets. She had barely recovered before the court artists were painting portraits and miniatures to be sent to the court of France.

Stephen Francis was still alive when there was just talk of a royal marriage to cement the French alliance. The alliance, having survived the disasters of the Seven Years' War, was in danger of falling apart, largely owing to the inertia of King Louis XV and the opposition of his son and daughter-in-law. Two brilliant statesmen, Choiseul in France and Kaunitz in Austria, were determined to maintain the alliance, and fate played into their hands with the death first of the Dauphin and shortly after, of his wife – deaths so providential that in court, where calumny was rife, Choiseul's enemies did not hesitate to say they had been poisoned on his orders. By 1768 the chief obstacles had been removed and the Empress, who had been marrying off her daughters into various Bourbon courts – Maria Amelia in Parma and Maria Caroline in Naples – was now in the hope of securing for Maria Antonia the most brilliant matrimonial prize in Europe.

But the girl who had been growing up at Schönbrunn in the charge of loving and indulgent governesses was in no way prepared to be a dauphine of France. Though the educational curriculum sounded impressive on paper – there was Metastasio to teach her Italian and Glück to instruct her in music – Maria Antonia remained gay, high-spirited and totally uneducated, except for a certain talent for dancing. The Emperor Francis, who had been a lover of the arts, had enjoyed seeing his children perform, and amateur concerts and theatricals were a feature of court life in Vienna. Some of the Empress's ministers, and in particular the Lord High Chamberlain, the austere Count Khevenhüller, considered 'there was far too much of play-acting, singing and dancing and dressing up, which might end in turning their Imperial Highnesses into conceited popinjays'. The general opinion was that the children were spoilt. All of them, and above all Maria Antonia, loved to go sleighing in winter, and if there was not sufficient snow at Schönbrunn it would be specially brought down from the mountains. Such extravagances had been encouraged by Stephen Francis, and Maria Theresa would never have taken it upon herself to countermand any of her late husband's wishes.

In 1768 as plans for the French marriage were about to materialize, the Empress, who until now had taken little notice of her youngest daughter, was suddenly made aware of her deficiencies. Her French and even her German were faulty; her spelling was atrocious, and her writing childish and ill-formed. It was not that she was stupid – on the contrary, she was quick-witted and amusing with a desire to please and a natural grace which had won the praise of no less a person than Madame Geoffrin, when the celebrated French *salonière* passed through Vienna on her way to visit the King of Poland. But these qualities were hardly sufficient for a girl who would have to face the critical eyes of the courtiers of Versailles and meet with the approval of the blasé old King, whose first question on hearing the reports of his ambassador to Vienna was to ask whether the Archduchess had good breasts. Whereupon the Marquis de Durfort replied that her Imperial

Highness was enchantingly pretty, but was not yet fully grown and was young, almost childish in her ways.

There was so much to be done in so little time. The most important thing of all was for Maria Antonia to perfect her French, and the Empress considered that no one was more qualified to teach her daughter the language of Racine and Molière than two French actors who happened to be performing in Vienna at the time. But there was a horrified protest from the court of France at the idea of a future dauphine taking lessons from strolling players. And Maria Theresa, who regarded the Hapsburgs in every way as grand as the Bourbons, had to conceal her irritation and instruct her ambassador, Count Mercy d'Argenteau, to consult with the Duc de Choiseul on the choice of a suitable ecclesiastic to act as tutor to the young Archduchess. Other vital matters were her deportment and appearance. Again Choiseul was consulted and his sister, the Comtesse de Grammont, sent her own hairdresser to Vienna to dress Maria Antonia's red-blonde hair in the latest Parisian styles, and if possible hide the high, somewhat bulging forehead which marred the charming oval of her face. Noverre, the most famous of all French dancing masters, was invited by the Empress to instruct her daughter in the latest minuets as danced at Versailles and in the various bows and curtseys decreed by court etiquette – one for the King, another for princes of the blood; one for a duke, another for ordinary mortals. By 15 August, the feast of the Assumption, 1769, when the Empress held a ball in her honour at Laxenburg, Maria Antonia had been transformed from a romping, jolly little tomboy into an exquisite young woman who had a gracious word for each one of her mother's guests.

Her new tutor, the middle-aged Abbé who was already half in love with her, was only echoing the general opinion when he wrote: 'There are other faces more beautiful with more regular features, but I doubt whether you will ever find a more charming one. No one who has not seen her can have any idea of the goodness, the sweetness, and at the same time the gaiety which radiates from her face.' Even her imperfections – the heavy Hapsburg lower lip – turned into a pretty pout on a mouth which was always ready to smile.

The choice of the Abbé Vermond for a post which was to bring him into the closest contact with the future Queen of France was in every sense a surprising one. He was a man of obscure, almost humble origin, who owed his advancement entirely to the patronage of Loménie de Brienne, Archbishop of Toulouse, an intimate friend of Choiseul. In character and morals he was the very opposite of the cynical statesman and the still more cynical prelate, for he was fundamentally honest, a quality which won him the confidence of Maria Theresa and the friendship of her daughter.

Bigots and pedants might disapprove of an abbé who was a friend of the philosophers, an admirer of Voltaire, and whose conversation, light and bantering in tone, never burdened his pupil with heavy dogma and religious treatises. He had been quick to realize that the only way to hold Maria Antonia's attention was in appealing to her imagination, and we read in one of his first reports:

> She has more imagination than she has been given credit for. Unfortunately no effort has ever been made to train her mind, and a certain amount of laziness and a great deal of frivolity makes my task more difficult. She will listen when a subject is clearly explained to her and has a very good judgement. But she will not make the slightest effort to expound any idea of her own, though I feel she would be perfectly capable of doing so.

Fortunately Vermond was a charming, witty, eighteenth-century abbé, who could turn the dullest lesson into a delightful *causerie* – the lives of the various queens of France, the genealogy of the House of Bourbon, the names and titles of the leading families became part of a glowing tapestry to attract an imaginative child. And before long he was reporting with pride,

> My little Archduchess is beginning to take an interest in military affairs. I am sure that soon after her marriage she will know every colonel by his name, and distinguish every regiment by its colour.... As for her French, it will perfect itself as soon as she gets away from hearing German and, what is even worse, the bad French spoken by the Vienna court.

It must have been a bewildering experience for a provincial French abbé suddenly to find himself in the Vienna of the Hapsburgs. His rare visits to Versailles, waiting in the antechambers of the all-powerful Choiseul, surrounded by sycophants and place-seekers, had not prepared him either for the family life of Schönbrunn or the Spanish etiquette of the Hofburg – the curious mixture of *gemütlichkeit* and grandeur, where the aristocracy lived on their country estates as semi-independent sovereigns. In many cases they were as rich or even richer than the Hapsburgs, yet in their town palaces had to conform to the laws of the realm and, owing to the housing shortage, rent out rooms to the court servants. There were the formal magnificence of the Hofburg halls, where the jewels of the Hungarian magnates glittered with an Eastern splendour, and the extravagant summer fêtes at Laxenburg and Schönbrunn, contrasting with the almost spartan simplicity of the intimate family gatherings, to which the Empress was gracious enough to invite her daughter's tutor. Here Vermond became acquainted with the twenty-five-year-old Emperor, whose progressive opinions were in direct opposition to his mother's, and who would take him by the arm and talk to him of French literature and, when out of hearing of the Empress, profess an admiration for Voltaire. Here he met the great Prince Kaunitz, a spoilt and pampered hypochondriac, indulged by the Empress, looked up to by her son. As the principal architect of the Franco-Austrian alliance, conceived at a time when, as ambassador in Paris, he had won the favour of the Marquise de Pompadour, Prince Kaunitz was ready to be amiable to the French Abbé recommended by

Choiseul. All this amiability from the highest in the land was accepted by the Abbé as a tribute to his position, and all his energies were devoted to the task of transforming an archduchess into a dauphine, teaching her to act and think as a Frenchwoman.

His influence on the Queen was later to make him many enemies at Versailles, ranging from the envious Madame Campan, who would have liked to see her husband in his place, to the avid Polignacs, who resented the lowly abbé who dared to criticize them to the Queen. But Maria Antonia never deviated in the affection she had shown her tutor from the time when her mother first introduced him into the family circle at Schönbrunn.

Maria Antonia had become Marie Antoinette. No one was any longer allowed to speak German in her presence. Twice a week she had to take her place at the Empress's card table to learn the fashionable game of *cavagnole*, and twice a week the Emperor, who until now had taken no notice of his little sister, came to visit her in her apartments to talk of subjects which, if they had not been talked of by her handsome brother, would have bored her to tears, for what did a frivolous little girl care about the historical relations between France and Austria and the balance of power in Europe? What could she understand of the importance of the Austrian Netherlands, to whom the French alliance spelt peace after centuries of war? But Joseph, who could be so cold and harsh with some of his mother's courtiers, knew also how to fascinate and charm. The hero-worship he inspired and which she retained long after she became Queen of France dates back to those evening visits at Schönbrunn.

Meanwhile, both in France and Austria, lawyers and diplomats were arguing over every detail in the marriage contract, learned professors were searching in historical records for the exact rules of precedence followed in former royal weddings. In spite of the appalling state of their finances, for neither had recovered from the effects of the Seven Years' War, both countries were determined to outdo the other in expenditure on what was to be the grandest of all royal marriages. Maria Theresa had allotted 400,000 ducats for her daughter's trousseau, all of which was to be made in France, with the exception of the laces from Brussels and Malines. By October 1769 orders had been given to repair all the roads over which the Archduchess was to travel on her way to France. At Versailles the minister of works, together with his colleague from *les menus plaisirs*, were in consultation with the architect Gabriel over the new theatre at Versailles, which was to be inaugurated with the wedding banquet but where works had been delayed because of lack of money. Now new taxes were to be levied which would supply King Louis with sufficient funds not only to complete the Opera House, but to astonish the world with the size and magnificence of the escort which was to travel half-way across Europe to fetch a Hapsburg bride. It was estimated that the cortège of horses, carriages – including the two bridal coaches built by Francieu, the most famous coachbuilder in France – bodyguards and lackeys – of which there were to be no less than 117, all wearing new liveries – would cost over 300,000 ducats.

On 16 April 1770, the ambassadors were already on their way when Maria Theresa, in an eleventh-hour attempt to prepare her daughter for her duties as a wife and as a queen, took her to sleep in her own room, where the tired, nervous girl had to submit to continual religious homilies interspersed with intimate advice based on the Empress's own marital experiences with a husband who was renowned for his sexual prowess; advice pathetically unsuited to what awaited poor Marie Antoinette at Versailles.

But a royal bride was given no time for either nerves or fears in a sequence of official ceremonies culminating with the French ambassador's state entry into Vienna, when the whole of the town came out into the streets to cheer the glittering cortège, the forty-eight carriages each drawn by six snow-white horses; the splendid bodyguards in their blue uniforms embroidered with golden *fleurs-de-lis*, preceding the bridal coaches lined in satin, shining with glass, carved and painted with the gilded crowns of France and of Navarre. That same evening, at a Hofburg reception, Marie Antoinette received from the hands of the French ambassador the first letter addressed to her by her future bridegroom, while the mistress of her household pinned on to her gala dress the Dauphin's miniature set in diamonds. It was a flattering portrait in which the court artist had done his best to accentuate the slight resemblance between the Dauphin and his handsome grandfather: the same aquiline Bourbon nose; the same heavy-lidded eyes, which in the King were deep and blue, in the grandson pale and myopic. But none of his defects was apparent in a miniature sufficiently romanticized to foster the illusions of an adolescent girl.

The next day the Archduchess, following in the traditions of the House of Hapsburg, had to appear in front of the Empress, the Emperor and all the assembled ministers, to solemnly renounce her hereditary rights both on the maternal and paternal sides. In the evening a masked ball was held at the Palace of the Belvedere, to which the Emperor Joseph had invited 3,000 guests and at which Marie Antoinette looked so exquisitely pretty that he told his mother the following morning that if she would only find him a princess as lovely as his sister, then he might consider marrying again. But though her daughter was now word-perfect in her part and everyone praised her affability and charm, the Empress knew that the frivolous, thoughtless little girl was in no way prepared for responsibilities. Maria Theresa had finally achieved all she had worked for in the past years to put an end once and for all to Prussia's plans of aggrandizement. But just when she should have been feeling satisfied and at peace, she was miserable and afraid. She was seen to have been crying when on 19 April she led her daughter up to the high altar of the church of the Augustinians to be married by proxy to the French Dauphin with her brother Ferdinand standing in for the bridegroom. The Papal Nuncio gave the benediction and blessed the nuptial rings; the church choir sang a Te Deum while a roar of cannon, a salvo of musketry and the ringing of all the church bells announced the joyful event.

Two days later on a lovely spring day, the fourteen-year-old girl bade farewell to the mother she would never see again and, escorted by the ambassadors of France and Austria and followed by a cavalcade of 340 horses, drove out of the Wienerwald and up the Danube valley to the great Benedictine monastery of Melk, where the Emperor was waiting to receive her with all the honours due to a future Queen of France.

A wooden pavilion on an uninhabited island on the Rhine, where the waters divide at Kehl, had been for many months the subject of controversy between the rival heads of protocol of France and Germany. For it was here that Marie Antoinette was to shed her Austrian identity and be transformed into a French princess. Every effort had been made not to offend the susceptibilities of either court. The only one whose susceptibilities were not taken into account was the young bride, who had arrived at Kehl after an exhausting twelve-day journey up the Danube, through Bavaria and across Germany to the Rhine, with every prince and margrave vying with the other in the splendour of their reception. The rococo palaces of southern Germany with their painted stucco ceilings were the perfect setting for the blonde, blue-eyed girl with porcelain skin and a radiant smile, who responded so warmly to the admiration of the crowds. In Munich the Wittelsbachs had lodged her in the Amalienburg, loveliest of all the Nymphenburg pavilions; at Augsburg one can still see the exquisitely painted rooms which were specially decorated for her visit by the master craftsmen of the town.

Here at Kehl the poor little Princess had to part with everything that reminded her of her own country. The pavilion consisted of five rooms, two facing east and two facing west, and in the middle a large hall where the official ceremony of the handing over was to take place. The rich burghers of the town had been proud to lend their grandest furniture; magnificent Gobelin tapestries from the church treasury of Strasbourg covered the walls, but only a young German called Wolfgang von Goethe, who together with a group of fellow students had been permitted to visit the pavilion, noticed that the superb tapestries depicted the most tragic and ill-fated of all marriages – the story of Jason and Medea – and, seeing it with the sensitive eyes of a poet, felt a premonition of disaster.

The weather had changed. The sunshine, which till now had accompanied the bride on her journey, had turned to a bitter cold, and the wind which crept through the wooden crevices chilled the rooms in which Marie Antoinette had to discard her Austrian garments. Shivering, she was quickly redressed in the embroidered shifts and petticoats of her French trousseau, the silk stockings from Lyons, the diamond-buckled shoes from the court shoemaker of Versailles. Her Austrian attendants, many of whom she had known since childhood, came forward to bid her a last tearful goodbye. Not one of them, with the exception of Prince Starhemberg, the Empress's envoy extraordinary to the court of France, was to accompany her beyond this sandbank on the Rhine. As formally as in a minuet, in which every gesture has been carefully rehearsed, Marie Antoinette was now handed over to her new country. Prince Starhemberg led her up to a raised dais in the central hall, in front of which was a long table representing the symbolic frontier between France and Germany. Here waiting for her were the French envoys with the official documents to which she offered her signature in the round, childish hand which was ever her mother's despair. The familiar figures of her Austrian youth receded into the background and she was engulfed in a world of strangers asserting their rights and privileges.

The Comte de Noailles had the honour of presenting the members of her new court, first of all his wife, her chief lady-in-waiting, cold-eyed, thin-lipped, with no word or gesture to reassure a timid, nervous girl. One after another they came, gentlemen- and ladies-in-waiting, equerries and pages, officers of her personal bodyguard, followed by all the town officials of Strasbourg and the governor of Alsace; until the little Dauphine, who up to now had had a smile and word for everyone, suddenly broke down and in a flood of tears flung herself into the arms of the scandalized Comtesse de Noailles.

There is no word of this unfortunate incident in the reports sent back to Versailles, and the lack of sympathy displayed by her new lady-in-waiting may have helped Marie Antoinette to regain her self-control. For within an hour she was again smiling and serene, ready to face the rapturous crowds of Strasbourg and the ordeal of a civic reception at which a kindly magistrate, hoping to please her, addressed her in German, to which she tactfully replied that from now on she wanted to hear nothing but French, a happy phrase which was greeted with a storm of applause.

Though royal princesses are trained in endurance and self-control, one marvels at the stamina displayed by Marie Antoinette during her first twenty-four hours in France. As the guest of the eighty-year-old Cardinal de Rohan, lodged in the episcopal palace, she had to submit for the first time to what was known as 'Le Grand Couvert', to dine alone in state waited on by the gentlemen of her household, while the leading citizens of the town were privileged to stand by and watch her eat. This unnerving experience was followed by a gala performance at the theatre and a ball attended by all the local nobility, while out in the illuminated streets the fountains ran with wine and whole oxen were roasted in the public squares. Seeing all this show of wealth and abundance and the enthusiasm of the crowds, the new Dauphine would have found it hard to believe that there had recently been rioting in the streets of Paris, where bread was at famine prices.

On the following morning, Marie Antoinette attended mass in the cathedral, where she was met by the Cardinal's coadjutor and nephew, Prince

Louis de Rohan, a handsome, somewhat effeminate-looking young man, who wore his priestly vestments as if they were fancy dress. In words calculated to appeal to Maria Theresa's daughter, he praised 'the great Empress who for many years has been the admiration of Europe and will be the glory of posterity'. Who could have foreseen that within a few years Louis de Rohan, as ambassador to Vienna, would incur the Empress's bitter enmity and later contribute to the downfall of her daughter?

At Nancy, where Marie Antoinette prayed at the tombs of her Lorraine paternal ancestors, she found herself again among relatives and friends. The people who still remembered their beloved Duke welcomed her as her father's daughter rather than as the French Dauphine. But when she showed what the Comtesse de Noailles considered to be too great a familiarity towards her Lorraine cousins, she was gently but firmly reminded that subjects of the King of France could not be regarded as her equals. The little Dauphine enchanted all with her natural amiability, her sweetness to the children who lined the route carrying bouquets of flowers, the unaffected pleasure she took in the fêtes and masquerades. Reports which kept arriving at Versailles brought one long paean of praise. Whatever might be the opposition at court, the country as a whole was ready to welcome the Austrian bride, who came as a harbinger of peace.

Even King Louis, who for the past months had been completely taken up with his infatuation for his latest mistress, the notorious Comtesse du Barry, and the thorny problem of persuading an arrogant nobility to accept her at court, was beginning to show a certain amount of interest in his grandson's bride. He was under no illusion that it was a popular marriage, either at court or in his immediate family circle, and it would probably never have taken place except for the persistence of Choiseul. The dead Dauphin, his elder son, had hated the vainglorious minister and his wife. His Saxon daughter-in-law, whom the King had loved as much and perhaps more than his own children, had been bitterly opposed to an Austrian marriage. The unmarried princesses had shared their brother's prejudices. The King himself remembered being brought as a child of five to his great grandfather's deathbed, when the old King had whispered as his last injunction, 'Love your wife and ask God to give you one who suits you, but not an Austrian.' Now Choiseul had succeeded in convincing him that an Austrian alliance spelt peace and security for the future, and he was ready to welcome Maria Theresa's daughter as a beloved grandchild.

On the afternoon of 14 May 1770, King Louis set out from the Castle of Compiègne accompanied by his grandson and his three unmarried daughters to meet the bride on the outskirts of the forest. The spring sun shone on the brilliant scene of what was supposed to be an intimate family gathering, but which by the time of the bride's arrival had swelled to several hundred people. Choiseul had been given the honour of meeting the

Dauphine before her arrival at Compiègne, and Marie Antoinette's first words in greeting the minister were to thank him for having contributed to her good fortune, to which he gallantly replied, 'Madame, the good fortune is that of France.'

A fanfare of bugles and of trumpets heralded the bride's approach. The King descended from his coach with an ease and agility which belied his sixty years. In contrast to his elegance and grace, the sixteen-year-old Dauphin presented a sorry spectacle. He was slow and cumbrous in his movements and his excessive timidity appeared to have an almost paralysing effect on his reactions. Whereas his grandfather's eyes brightened with pleasure at the sight of the pretty little girl who stepped so lightly from her carriage, running the few steps towards him to drop a graceful curtsey at his feet, the bridegroom looked on with a cold myopic stare, and the formal embrace he bestowed on his future wife chilled even the optimism of Marie Antoinette. She must have found him sadly different from the handsome young man of the miniature around whom she had woven so many childish dreams on the long journey through Europe.

Seated in the royal coach beside the King, the cynosure of a thousand eyes, greeted by spontaneous cheers, cheers such as King Louis had not heard for many a year, Marie Antoinette was ready to love both her new family and her new country. She did not know that the very courtiers who welcomed her with such enthusiasm, the aunts who embraced her with so much affection, were those who but a year ago had caballed against the Austrian marriage and that their change of heart was due only to their hatred of Madame du Barry and the fear that her growing ascendancy over the old King would undermine still further an already descredited monarchy. The arrival of a pretty young dauphine at a court where for the past hundred years the queens had been no more than shadows, the King's obvious delight in his new granddaughter, brought fresh hope to those who still believed Louis xv to be capable of mastering his passions and remembering his duties as King. This fourteen-year-old girl was to be the chief pawn in the court intrigues to get rid of Madame du Barry, in the hope that her artless prattle, her innocent gaiety could act as an antidote to the erotic wiles and talents of the most accomplished of courtesans.

Waiting for her at the Castle of Compiègne were the royal cousins, the so-called princes of the blood. It was the time to remember the elaborate curtseys taught her by Noverre, the lessons in etiquette learnt from Madame de Noailles, for the slightest mistake would irrevocably offend those who were only too ready to find fault with a Hapsburg bride. First in precedence was the Duc d'Orléans with his son, the newly married Duc de Chartres, a tall, handsome young man with a dissipated look and bold, appraising eyes. Next came the Princes of Condé and Conti with their sons and the Duc de Penthièvre, with his daughter-in-law, the blonde and fragile Princesse de

Lamballe, widowed at eighteen of a husband who had died the victim of his own excesses. Hers was the only kind and friendly face among all those cold Bourbons, divided in their family jealousies, envious of each other's privileges, nevertheless united in their dislike of the Austrian marriage.

No sooner had they left than the royal party set out for La Muette, the castle on the outskirts of Paris at the edge of the Bois de Boulogne where, according to tradition, the royal brides of France spent the night before their wedding. All that remains today of what must have been the most enchanting of summer palaces are the bare walls of a municipal building in a busy Passy street.

On the way to La Muette lay the Carmelite convent of St Denis, where Marie Antoinette was to meet the King's youngest daughter, who in the previous month had caused consternation at court by becoming a Carmelite nun. The general opinion was that she had taken the vows in order to expiate her father's sins. The King, who was embarrassed but also touched, respected her decision and paid regular visits to the convent, giving large donations out of his privy purse. But the Dauphine, who with her pious mother had visited many a country shrine and convent and met many a worthy abbess, found none of their sweetness and resignation in Sister Thérèse des Augustins, who in the vestments of a Carmelite nun had still the haughtiness of a Bourbon princess.

It was already evening when Marie Antoinette arrived at La Muette, which for the next nineteen years was to be one of her favourite summer houses, smaller and more intimate than either Choisy or Marly, allowing her more freedom than Compiègne or Fontainebleau. Here, laid out in her apartments, were the royal wedding gifts, the King's personal present of a magnificent diamond parure, as well as all the jewels which had belonged to the late Dauphine. Marie Antoinette was the last to notice the sullen look that came over the bridegroom's face when she wore for the first time the pearls that had belonged to his beloved mother. Louis Auguste – she had barely learnt his name – had spent all day beside her without addressing her a single word, while his two younger brothers, the Comte de Provence and Comte d'Artois, were both amiable and talkative. But what pleased her most was that waiting at La Muette was the Empress's ambassador, with a letter from her mother.

Comte Mercy d'Argenteau, whose letters to Vienna help us to reconstruct every detail of Marie Antoinette's first years in France, was a typical product of the Holy Roman Empire: a native of Liège, yet passionately devoted to his Austrian Empress; an able disciple of Prince Kaunitz, who had hoped to make him his successor but found him too attached to France and to his Parisian mistress ever to transfer himself to Vienna. This middle-aged diplomat, whom Maria Theresa now appointed as nurse and mentor to her young daughter, was to carry out his mission with tact and zeal, never hesitating when the Empress added to his duties the more unpleasant one of spy.

In the following years, the Dauphine's every word and action were to be faithfully reported to her mother in Vienna, and Marie Antoinette was too naïve ever to suspect that it was this charming, fatherly ambassador who noted every fault and registered every complaint, whether she neglected her religious duties or omitted to wear her corset. For at fourteen the future queen of fashion was still something of a romping tomboy who was careless in her appearance and, according to Madame de Noailles, did not always brush her teeth.

But this evening Mercy had more important matters to worry about. A rumour had been circulating at Versailles that the King had the intention of including Madame du Barry among the guests invited to the family supper party at La Muette. At first no one could believe that Louis xv would outrage public opinion to the extent of including the former Jeanne Bécu, a girl dragged up in the streets of Paris and later hostess at one of the city's most notorious gambling dens, to sup at the royal table at the most exclusive of all the wedding festivities, to which only forty ladies bearing the greatest names in France had been invited. But gradually rumour had hardened into fact, putting an end to the short-lived hope that the Dauphine's arrival would introduce a new era in France. Once again King Louis had refused to allow either court or family to question his actions. King since the age of five, he had never had any criteria to consider other than his own desires. Yet at heart no one despised his court more than Louis himself, for he had been heard to say that he wondered how any decent man could survive there. But at the same time he was so weak, so obsessed by his physical passion for Madame du Barry that to please her, he was ready to insult both his family and his court by deliberately inviting her on an occasion when the first appearance of the new Dauphine would force both his daughters and the ladies of their household to control their indignation.

In her letter to Marie Antoinette the Empress had written so admiringly and so affectionately of King Louis as 'a tender father, who if you deserve it will become your confidant and friend,' that even an experienced diplomat like Mercy felt a certain embarrassment at having to explain the situation to someone as innocent as the Dauphine. He must have felt that this time the insincerity of his Empress was such that her daughter's disillusionment would only be the greater when she finally discovered the truth. The King's decision left the diplomat with no other choice than to enlighten Marie Antoinette on what her mother had chosen to ignore.

Amongst the last of the guests to arrive in the grandest and most ostentatious of carriages, blazing with diamonds, triumphantly beautiful, was Madame du Barry. Years of living in the intimacy of some of the most brilliant men in France had prepared her for tonight. Both manners and bearing were impeccable. Outwardly she appeared to be as indifferent to the studied rudeness of the women as to the admiring glances of the men. Seated on the King's right hand, the Dauphine noted how his face lit up at the sight of the woman seated at the far end of the table, and guilelessly she asked him her name. 'The Comtesse du Barry,' he replied. Showing no sign of anger or resentment, speaking in a light, almost indifferent voice, Marie Antoinette remarked, 'She is very pretty.' Mercy had already taught her her first lessons in diplomacy.

3

By the following morning, Marie Antoinette had forgotten all about the Comtesse du Barry, for this day belonged to her and to her alone. The whole of Paris had converged on the roads leading to Versailles, leaving behind them a deserted city. Everyone who could find a carriage, horse or cart was on the way to the royal wedding. Carriages were being hired at the astronomical sum of three louis a day; a horse fetched no less than two louis. Six thousand tickets had been issued to those who were privileged to enter the palace to watch the bridal procession. But thousands more had come to bivouac in the courtyards and garden, which for today had been thrown open to the public.

In one of her letters to her daughter, Maria Theresa had written, 'If it depends on a great position in the world, then you are the most fortunate of all your sisters and of all the princesses of Europe.' Marie Antoinette must have believed this to be true when she saw Versailles for the first time, pink and gold glittering in the sunlight, an epic poem in stone dedicated to one man's glory. Even to a girl reared in palaces, Versailles was at once breathtaking and awe inspiring. Schönbrunn with its 1,100 rooms, the Vienna Hofburg slowly growing through the centuries in the heart of the old city, faded into insignificance beside the arrogant splendour of Versailles; an isolated world of privilege and pomp, in which the grandest of courtiers was ready to perform the most menial of tasks if it brought him into the presence of the King, and duchesses fought for the honour of sitting for hours on hard stools in the royal antechamber.

The whole of this artificial world now revolved round the fourteen-year-old girl who drove through the gilded gates of Versailles on her wedding day, 16 May 1770. The King and Dauphin, who had left La Muette in the early hours of the morning, were waiting to receive her with her two little sisters-in-law, Mesdames Clothilde and Elisabeth, children only a little younger than herself and still confined to the schoolroom. In her apartments were the ladies of her household who had been presented to her at Strasbourg, together with the maids, milliners and hairdressers ready to dress her for her wedding, while Madame de Noailles reserved to herself the honour of adjusting the final touches to the huge panniers of white brocade and the long train of cloth of silver which was to be carried by one of the King's pages.

But Marie Antoinette looked neither hesitant nor intimidated when she took her place at the head of the cortège which, starting from the King's apartments, passed through the Gallery of Mirrors and across the staterooms till it finally reached the royal chapel. A murmur of admiration went through the crowd of spectators as she advanced towards them with her light and lilting walk, her head held high in pride, her blue eyes shining, her pouting mouth parted in a smile. With her brilliant complexion barely touched by rouge, her blonde hair only lightly powdered, she looked so young and fragile, still so unmarked by life, that even King Louis felt a fleeting compassion for this pretty child who was to become the wife of his heavy, boorish grandson – someone who in his opinion 'was not as other men'. Was this the fault of the late Dauphin, who before his death chose the cold, hypocritical Duc de la Vauguyon as tutor to his son? When his parents died, the lonely boy who had little in common with his younger brothers turned for affection to his aunts, but four middle-aged women were hardly in a position to initiate a backward boy into the joys of matrimony.

There would have been plenty of women at court only too ready to complete the Dauphin's education. But he had been as blind to their attractions as he now appeared to be indifferent to his charming bride. His splendid suit of cloth of gold encrusted with diamonds only served to emphasize his thick and graceless figure; the jewelled collar of the Saint Esprit showed up his short and heavy neck. Even the courtiers despised this Bourbon prince who was so awkward in his movements, he did not even know how to handle his sword.

Louis Auguste and Marie Antoinette, two strangers who until now had addressed no more than a few words to one another, knelt at the high altar of the magnificent royal chapel dedicated by the Sun King to God and to himself. The Archbishop of Rheims, grand almoner of France, performed the ceremony, blessing the couple and anointing the golden rings which the Dauphin nearly dropped in his clumsiness. Then came the signing of the Marriage Act, when, according to an age-old tradition, a humble *curé* from the church of Versailles presented the King with the register which he and the immediate members of his family had to sign. Marie Antoinette's signature is still to be seen with the uneven, sloping handwriting disfigured by a blotch of ink, the only sign of nerves she betrayed throughout the day, in which she was not given an hour to rest between one exhausting ceremony and the other.

The official festivities opened at six o'clock and were to continue for nine days. First of these entertainments was the royal card game, at which the newly married bride had to take her place beside the King at a round green table placed in the Gallery of Mirrors. Large crowds behind a marble balustrade passed by in a long and respectful queue. Marshalled by the Swiss Guards, they were allowed no more than a few seconds in which to gaze reverentially at the royal family disporting themselves at the games of *lansquenet* and *cavagnole*, games so boring that they are decried by Voltaire in one of his most celebrated epigrams:

On croirait que le jeu console,	You might think that games console,
Mais l'ennui vient à pas comptés	But boredom comes with measured steps
A la table d'un cavagnole	Toward the game called *cavagnole*,
S'asseoir entre deux majestés.	And sits between two majesties.

So it must have seemed to a fourteen-year-old girl who longed to be outside in the gardens where there was merriment and dancing by the fountains. The rays of the setting sun streamed through the windows reflecting on the mirrored walls, showing up the lines on the tired and raddled faces of the older courtiers. Bride and bridegroom could barely suppress their yawns, but there were over two hours still to be endured before it was time for the wedding banquet.

In Vienna the weddings of Marie Antoinette's brothers and sisters had been happy, carefree occasions on which the imperial family shared with the people in the general rejoicing. But here at Versailles the Bourbon kings remained inviolate and aloof, out of touch with their subjects, but constantly in the public eye, whether they were dressing, eating, playing cards or going to mass. In her nineteen years at Versailles Marie Antoinette could never become accustomed to the imposition of the *Grand Couvert*, where on certain days not only those who had the *entrée* to court, but any distinguished foreigner could satisfy his curiosity and watch the royal family dine.

It was characteristic of Versailles that the wedding banquet took place in a new theatre commissioned from Gabriel – a show as theatrical in every way as any court performance. Of all the recent work carried out at Versailles, the reconstruction of Gabriel's Theatre has been the most successful, and can be seen today in all its exquisite beauty with every detail faithfully reproduced from the gildings of the Payous sculpture to the brocaded velvets and damasks woven in Lyons. Here in all its elegance and grace is the very quintessence of the rococo, the final flowering of the old regime – King Louis's tribute to the Austrian bride who was to become Queen of France.

Only the immediate royal family, twenty-two in number, partook of the banquet, which was served on the stage, while the more favoured of their courtiers were allowed to watch from the gallery and boxes, having to satisfy their appetites with sweetmeats and cooling drinks, while delicious aromas of a Lucullan feast wafted from below. The rest of the guests jostled and struggled for places in the crowded auditorium, ruining their gala dresses and crushing their plumes. Less fortunate still were the people outside in the gardens, for a sudden storm sent them running for shelter into the courtyards where they overwhelmed the guards and invaded some of the lower rooms. The fireworks which were to crown the festivities had to be postponed, and the evening ended with the hungry and disappointed crowds, worn out and soaked to the skin, struggling back to Paris. But no echo of this storm penetrated to the theatre, where with a true Bourbon appetite the princes of the blood royal did full justice to the gastronomic delicacies prepared by the greatest chefs in France. Only the Dauphine had no thought of food as she looked around with wonder and delight. Her husband on the contrary devoted himself to the pleasures of the table, looking happy and contented for the first time in the day, until the King reminded him with an indulgent smile, 'Go easy, my son, there is work for you to do tonight,' to which came the celebrated reply, 'I always sleep better after a good meal.' When at last the meal was over, the princes, replete and flushed with wine, staggered to their feet and followed the King in the procession to the bridal chamber, which no one was allowed to enter before the Archbishop of Rheims had sprinkled the sheets with holy water. The King himself handed his grandson his embroidered chemise; the recently married Duchesse de Chartres helped the Dauphine into her nightgown. The curtains of the great fourposter bed closed then reopened on the young couple sitting up in bed, and with all due ceremony the King and his court wished them goodnight.

However young, however uninitiated, this must have been the moment when Marie Antoinette expected some show of affection, a loving kiss or a warm embrace. The sweating body in her bed, which in a few moments was sound asleep, was so very different to what her mother had led her to expect. In a letter dictated by sentimental memories of her beloved Stephen Francis, the Empress had written, 'I will say nothing about the Dauphin. You know how fastidious I am about such matters. A woman should be in all things obedient to her husband and have no other thought than to please him and carry out his wishes. The only real happiness in this world is a successful marriage. I know what I am talking about. All depends on the woman, if she is willing, loving and amusing.' Lying on her side of the great double bed, Marie Antoinette must have wondered how her mother would have reacted to someone as cold and reserved as Louis Auguste. But before long she had also fallen asleep in the heavy, dreamless sleep of childhood. When she woke it was a brilliant spring day, her husband had already left and there was only Madame de Noailles with her tight-lipped smile, deferentially enquiring as to whether she had slept well. She had barely risen when the maids fluttering round her bed were already reporting to whatever ambassador they were in the pay of, that the nuptial sheets were still unstained. By midday the news was already circulating in the 'Oeil de Bœuf', and at his levee Louis Auguste could already sense the whispered malicious comments of his courtiers.

While the gentlemen paid homage to the Dauphin, the ladies preceded by the royal princesses invaded the Dauphine's apartments for her first levee. Situated on the ground floor, giving out on the inner courtyards, the rooms which had satisfied the modest Polish Queen must have seemed very dark and cramped to a girl used to the large airy spaces of Schönbrunn. Here the doors were so narrow that the ladies in their big panniers could hardly pass and often fainted with the heat. On leaving the confusion was so great that many used to lose their way in the maze of corridors and courtyards.

After *Le Grand Lever* came the midday mass, followed by the official entertainment of the day, Lully's *Perseus*, an opera of interminable length and unutterable boredom, in spite of the efforts to enliven it with ballets and *divertissements*. Devised for the formal court of the Sun King, it was in no way suited to the more frivolous tastes of his successor. The King looked bored, the ladies yawned behind their fans and the poor little Dauphine was seen to be wilting from fatigue.

There was no court on the following day, and the Abbé Vermond, who had arrived at Versailles after travelling from Strasbourg at his own expense, gives a pathetic account of the three-day bride left alone in her apartments, with Madame de Noailles for company, while the Dauphin went out hunting with the King. Before leaving he had paid a perfunctory visit to his wife to enquire as to how she had slept. But she had barely replied before he had already gone. And the girl who at home had had so many brothers and sisters to play with had now to dine by herself watched by the curious courtiers, some of whom were heard to murmur, 'It's rather soon to be left alone.' The Abbé commiserated, 'Madame la Dauphine amuses herself with her little dog, who may serve to distract her for the moment. But then she relapses into reverie and looks so sad that it nearly breaks my heart.'

Her spirits brightened with the visit of her mother's ambassador. Mercy was an accomplished diplomat who knew how to charm and entertain, and he may have taken this opportunity of enlightening Marie Antoinette on the political situation at the French court and the reason for the Dauphin's strange behaviour. From boyhood Louis Auguste had grown up with a hatred of Choiseul, the all-powerful minister who had always kept his father in the background and never allowed him to have a share in the government. After his parents' death, his tutors and his aunts had contrived to keep that hatred alive. His mother's last wish had been that he should marry a Saxon princess. And in the eyes of Louis Auguste the Austrian marriage represented the triumph of Choiseul. Marie Antoinette with her frivolity and charm, her essential femininity, was all that his Jesuit teachers had taught him to distrust and to fear. It would take time and practice to break down his reserve and conquer his prejudices. Meanwhile the most important thing of all was to win the affection of the King and persuade him to dismiss the Duc de la Vauguyon, who as long as he remained attached to the Dauphin would influence him against her.

Marie Antoinette, who was of a sanguine and cheerful temperament and very sure of her powers to please, never doubted of her ability to win her husband's love. Mercy was less hopeful. There were rumours going round the Oeil de Boeuf that the Dauphin had a physical defect. His Spanish colleague, the Marquis d'Aranda, was particularly well informed on the subject and full of clinical details, which for the moment Mercy chose to ignore. He had sufficient problems to cope with. That very day his beloved Empress had inadvertently stirred up a hornets' nest by asking as a favour of the King that her husband's relatives, the princes of Lorraine, should have pride of place at tomorrow's court ball. That those who at Versailles were referred to with distrust as '*les princes étrangers*' (the foreign princes) should presume to take precedence over the dukes and peers of France, outraged families of ancient descent like the Rohans and the Mortemarts. While Marie Antoinette remained quietly in her apartments in happy ignorance of what was going on outside, the rest of Versailles was in a state of mutiny. Great ladies maintained they would prefer to miss the ball rather than follow a Mademoiselle de Lorraine in a minuet. Matters reached a pitch when a letter of protest was sent to the King who, both irritated and embarrassed, admitted that the demand came from Vienna and called on the loyalty and affection of his subjects to abide by his decision and on this one occasion to give precedence to the bride's relations.

None of her ladies, and not even Mercy, told Marie Antoinette of her mother's somewhat tactless behaviour, which cast a cloud on what was to be the most brilliant of all the festivities. Never since the great days of the Sun King had Versailles seen such an extravagant ball. Enormous sums were spent in transforming the theatre for one night into a ballroom with decorations in gold and silver representing the lilies of France and the eagles of Austria with dolphins disporting themselves among cupids. Only fifteen couples had been chosen to dance in the formal *bal paré*, where the Dauphin and Dauphine led a minuet watched by the entire court, she light and delicate as a Sèvres figurine, he overcome by shyness, struggling as best he could with the complicated steps. Among those who had been chosen to dance was Mademoiselle de Lorraine, whose innocent presence accounted for several absences. Only Marie Antoinette, who was enjoying every moment of the ball, remained happily unaware of all the quarrels and dissensions, and even her critics had nothing but praise for the faultless grace she displayed in a German quadrille partnered by the young Duc de Chartres, in which both of them danced with such verve and spirit as to bring a smile to the lips of the old King.

Far removed from the formality and protocol of the state ball was the *bal champêtre* held in the gardens, where over 200,000 people had come from Paris and the surrounding villages to watch the fireworks, which were on an even grander scale than those spoilt by the rain on the night of the wedding. The immense gardens were given over to the public. There was dancing on the lawns and musicians played from boats on the Grand Canal. There were orchestras in every grove and the King's troupe of clowns and jugglers to spread laughter among the crowds. After the fireworks came the illuminations with effigies of the royal couple glittering in the night sky and a temple dedicated to the Sun God bursting into flame on the Grand Canal. A hundred and sixty thousand Chinese lanterns reflected in bouquets of light on the pools and fountains forming long shining ribbons on the trees. As the night wore on, the courtiers drifted out into the gardens to flirt and gossip in the shadows. Only the Dauphine, who would have loved to join in the fun, had to content herself with standing by the King and watching the fireworks from a window in the Gallery of Mirrors. King Louis, who suffered from hypochondria, thought that the night air would be injurious to her health. He was continually telling Madame de Noailles that 'la Dauphine must on no account get tired', and Marie Antoinette was finding that her chief lady-in-waiting was more like a governess than any she had ever known as a child.

The most delightful of all the wedding festivities was the masked ball held in the state apartments, at which the stiffest and most formal of courts discarded all rules of protocol and allowed anyone in domino and mask to come in from outside. The only measure of control taken at the gates was that one person in every group was made to unmask and establish his identity. The Dauphine was just beginning to savour the fun of a masked ball, the excitement and mystification, the pleasure of dancing unrecognized, of accosting any handsome stranger, when on the King's orders she was made to retire at the stroke of midnight.

Louis Auguste, who took no pleasure either in masked balls or *bals parés*, was always the first to leave. The only part of the festivities he enjoyed was the programme of classical drama, performed in the new theatre by the greatest actors of the Théâtre Français. Racine was his favourite dramatist and he knew the whole of *Athalie* by heart. But for his frivolous little Austrian wife it was all too much like hard work. Several years were to elapse before she could appreciate the cadences of French verse and become a discerning patron of the theatre.

This year the festival of spring held in Paris on the last day of May was to be even more brilliant than usual. To celebrate the wedding there were to be orchestras and fountains of wine with distributions of bread and meat in all the poorer quarters of the town. The centre of attraction was in the Place Louis XV, where from the recently completed colonnades the privileged guests of the city of Paris could watch Ruggièri's fireworks by the river. Neither the King, who was on bad terms with the city authorities, nor the Dauphin planned to attend, but the Dauphine was to arrive accompanied by her husband's aunts at nightfall in time for the illuminations. The honours of the evening went to the Orléans family, whose gardens in the Palais Royal were thrown open to the public, while the Duchesse de Chartres as the queen of the festival gave the signal for the fireworks to begin. But all these glittering festivities were to end in tragedy.

Fifty years later, as an old man, Philippe de Ségur could still remember the horror of an evening which began so joyously and ended with a total of 600 dead. He was a young boy at the time and he and his brother had been taken by their tutor to view the fireworks from the scaffolding erected in the Place Louis XV. He writes:

> After the fireworks, the immense crowd which filled the square and the Champs Elysées tried all at the same time to reach the boulevards where there were to be further illuminations. By a combination of negligence and an appalling mistake on the part of the workers who had completed the colonnades, deep trenches had been left uncovered at the entrance to the Rue Royale, and the carriages converging in both directions from the Rue St Honoré obstructed the passage leading out of the square. There were not sufficient watchmen to control the crowds and the city authorities had been too mean to pay the 1,000 *écus* it would have cost to bring out the Gardes Français to keep order. Gangs of thieves and pickpockets, quick to profit by the situation, robbed the wretched people trying to force their way to the Rue Royale. In the midst of the confusion rapidly turning into panic, people fell into the open trenches and were crushed by others falling on top of them. The crowds came in waves, pushing and struggling to find a way out of the square. Many were thrown to the ground and trampled to death. Others clawed and fought one another to escape. Among the victims were the very scoundrels who had caused most of the disorder, now dying with their pockets disgorging loot rifled from their victims. I can still remember the screams of the women and the cries of the old men and children dying in the trenches, the bodies piled one on top of the other.

These were the screams heard by the Dauphine when she arrived with her aunts to see the illuminations – these anguished cries for help instead of the cheers and *vivat* she had expected on her first entry to Paris. The illuminated temple to Hymen, erected in her honour, still blazed in the Place Louis XV, on the very spot where twenty-three years later she was to mount the guillotine.

When the Dauphine returned in tears to Versailles the first person she encountered was her husband, who had just heard of the disaster, and received her with a tenderness and solicitude she would never have suspected of him. The young couple, who until now had seldom spoken to one another, came together in this hour of tragedy. Without taking advice either from his governor or his aunts, the Dauphin sent a page to the Minister of Police with a casket of gold containing the whole of his monthly allowance and a letter in which he wrote, 'This is all I have to dispose of. Use it as best you can. Help those who need it most.' The minister was so touched by the warmth and humanity of this gesture that he showed the letter round, and by morning the people of Paris had learnt that there was someone behind the gilded gates of Versailles who really cared. A large sum sent by the King, who only heard the news on the following day, having spent the night with his mistress at the castle of Bellevue, had little effect on the general population. The monarch who in his youth had been known as Louis the Well-beloved had long since forfeited the respect and affection of his subjects.

But at Versailles Louis xv – or rather his mistress – ruled supreme and for the next four years a proud Austrian archduchess was to find that it was not she but Madame du Barry whom the master of ceremonies consulted as to what plays and operas were to be given, which actresses to be chosen. Before long the Countess was mixing into politics, making and unmaking ministers, sending into exile anyone who dared to offend her, until even the position of the hitherto all-powerful Choiseul, who had refused to pay her homage, was beginning to be undermined.

Six weeks after her wedding, Marie Antoinette was writing to the Empress: 'My dear husband has changed very much for the better. He is very friendly towards me and beginning to confide in me. Also the King could not be kinder and is full of attentions. I love him dearly, but it is pathetic to see how weak he is with Madame du Barry, who is the silliest and most impertinent creature imaginable.' The shrewd old Empress realized at once that Marie Antoinette was merely quoting the opinion of her husband's aunts, and she foresaw the danger of her daughter allowing herself to be influenced by the embittered old maids living in the shadow of their father's throne.

History has in many ways been unfair to Louis xv's four unmarried daughters, known collectively as 'Mesdames de France'. In Horace

Walpole's much quoted and malicious description they appear in the light of Cinderella's ugly sisters: 'The four Mesdames who are clumsy, plump old wenches with a bad likeness to their father stand in a row with black cloaks and knitting bags, looking good humoured, not knowing what to say and wriggling as if they wanted to make water.' On the other hand there are Nattier's charming allegorical portraits of Mesdames Adelaide and Victoire painted as Diana and as Flora which, even allowing for the flattery of a court painter, show them in their youth to have been pretty, healthy young girls. This was not the case with their younger sisters, for Sophie was repellently ugly with a nervous twitch, while the Carmelite Louise had a slight hunchback.

The dice were loaded against these princesses from their earliest childhood, when in an attempt at economy Cardinal Fleury sent them to be brought up in a convent, where they learnt nothing and where the nuns were unable to curb Adelaide's violent and headstrong character. She was the only one of the King's daughters who was really intelligent, with a passionate desire to learn. She would have made a good queen or even empress, had there been any reigning prince available when she returned to Versailles at the age of fourteen to find her Polish mother relegated to the background and the Marquise de Pompadour as the uncrowned queen of France.

Louis XV was an affectionate father who would have liked to see all his daughters happily married. But only one of them, Marie Elisabeth, had secured a husband, and she had died at the age of thirty-two. Her husband was the second son of the King of Spain who had succeeded to the Duchy of Parma, and Marie Elisabeth, known as Madame Infanta, had done nothing but complain of life in a provincial capital. For someone as haughty as Adelaide it was infinitely preferable to remain a Madame de France at Versailles. There was a time when it looked as if she might play a leading role at court. When la Pompadour's health began to fail, the King took to going out hunting with his daughters. Adelaide was an excellent horsewoman and a gay and amusing companion. Before long the more scurrilous of the courtiers were whispering that the King, like his uncle the regent, was indulging in incestuous relations with his daughter. The gossip persisted with the years, casting doubts on the identity of Louis de Narbonne, who was said to be the son of Adelaide's favourite lady-in-waiting, but who bore a striking resemblance to the King.

Whatever may have been the gossip, the limitations of a convent education and a lack of knowledge of the world made it impossible for Adelaide to hold the attention of the bored and restless King, who before long had drifted back to the illicit delights of the Parc aux Cerfs. Both she and her sisters had to settle down to the narrow, frustrated lives of royal spinsters, Victoire indulging in the pleasures of the table and rapidly running to fat, and Louise finding consolation in religion. Only Adelaide continued to cherish the dream of playing a political role, first through her brother, the older Dauphin, and later through her nephew. Though she hated Choiseul and was opposed to the Austrian marriage, the advent of Madame du Barry forced her to change her tactics and to recognize in her niece the only hope of rescuing her father from the clutches of the 'whore'. Taking advantage of Marie Antoinette's youth and inexperience and her reluctance to hold court, she encouraged her under the cloak of friendship to let her and her sisters do the entertaining in her honour and thereby attract the presence of the King. The old man enjoyed the company of his little granddaughter, he liked taking her on his knees and kissing her pretty hands, and she for her part treated him with the natural confidence of a child. But the aunts instilled the first drops of poison by telling her that whatever letter she might write the King – and he was a man who had such a horror of argument that the smallest request had to be put in writing – she must always remember that every word was read by his mistress. Marie Antoinette confessed to her mother's ambassador, 'I am frightened of writing to the King, when I know that that creature reads all his letters.'

'That creature' was everywhere, sitting beside her at the royal gaming table, accompanying the King on what were called '*les petits voyages*' – visits to the royal pleasure houses of Marly and of Choisy which lasted no longer than a few days, entailed enormous sums of money, and involved the transportation of the entire court. The lackeys of Madame du Barry were more extravagantly dressed than those of the royal household. Even her little blackamoor, Zamore, glittered in jewels. But Marie Antoinette had only been a few weeks at Versailles when she heard that none of her ladies had been paid their salaries since the day of their appointment, and that she would have to follow the example of her aunts and go herself to the Royal Controller to solicit the payment of her servants.

There were hundreds of gardeners at Versailles and the parterres were ablaze with flowers. But some of the trees were dying from neglect, and on one occasion, when she went out walking with the King, they came across a pile of stones and, in helping her across, he said with a certain sadness, 'Forgive me, Madame, but I remember that here there used to be a handsome flight of steps.' Marie Antoinette saw only the crumbling steps in the gardens of Versailles, but in these very years one of the King's ministers wrote: 'Everything is falling to pieces. All is in decay. If we prop up the building on the one side, it crumbles on the other.... We are approaching the ultimate period of decadence.'

There was political unrest in the provinces and bread riots in the towns, where a demagogue had only to talk of hunger to stir up revolt. Choiseul with his superficial brilliance, his love of '*grandezza*', was not prepared to make himself unpopular in advocating economic reform. To compensate for the ignominious disaster of the Seven Years' War, he had made the expensive gesture of conquering Corsica. But the people were tired of expensive gestures, of a rich and bigoted clergy, a privileged nobility. They wanted food for their families and careers for their sons unhampered by the shackles of the caste system. But none of these complaints penetrated the precincts of Versailles to be heard by a king who cared for nothing but his comfort and by courtiers who cared for nothing but money.

The King's quarrels with the city authorities had isolated him from Paris, and three years were to pass before Louis Auguste and Marie Antoinette were allowed to make their official entry into the capital. Meanwhile no attempt was made to prepare the Dauphin in the art of kingship. Virtually unoccupied, he indulged the passion for hunting he had inherited from his grandfather, and in the first months of their marriage his young wife depended almost exclusively for company on the aunts.

In a letter to her mother Marie Antoinette describes the daily routine at Versailles: 'I get up between nine and ten o'clock, and having dressed say my morning prayers, then have breakfast and go to visit my aunts, where I usually find the King. This lasts till about ten thirty. At eleven I have my hair dressed. After which everyone is allowed to come in – that is everyone who has the right of entry. I put on my rouge and wash my hands in front of them all. Then the gentlemen go away, while the ladies stay and I put on my formal dress. Mass is at midday, and if the King is at Versailles I go with the King and my husband. If he is not there I go alone with the Dauphin. After mass the two of us dine alone, but anyone who cares to can come and watch us. As we both eat very quickly we have finished by half past one, and I go back with the Dauphin to his apartments, but if he is busy I go back to my own where I read or write or work, for I am embroidering a waistcoat for the King, which is not making much progress, but by the grace of God I hope to get it finished in a few years. At three o'clock I go again to my aunts, where I usually find the King. At four the Abbé [Vermond] comes to see me and at five there is the music master, who stays till six when I either return to my aunts or go for a walk. I must tell you that my husband almost always comes with me to visit the aunts. At seven we sit down to cards, but if it's fine I go again for a walk. At nine we have supper and if the King is not there the aunts come and have supper with us. Otherwise we go to them where after supper we wait for the King, who usually appears at about a quarter to eleven. But while waiting I put myself onto a comfortable sofa and sleep till he arrives. When he is not there we go to bed at eleven.'

It is a pathetic letter to be written by a young bride, but the Dauphine does not complain. With her sanguine temperament she accepts the monotony of the routine, the continual visits to the aunts who were probably better company than Madame de Noailles, for they arranged with their ladies-in-waiting to give small dances to amuse her. In her letter Marie Antoinette stresses the fact that her husband usually accompanies her on her visits to the aunts, but she lets it transpire that they rarely if ever keep one another company after dinner. She was left alone to read or write, neither of which she enjoyed, but which she did not dare neglect for fear of losing the Abbé Vermond, whom her enemy, the Duc de la Vauguyon, was trying to get dismissed on the grounds that it was useless for the Dauphine to have an official reader if she never opened a book. From the very beginning the Duke and the royal governess Madame de Marsan, a member of the powerful Rohan family, had been intriguing to destroy the marriage promoted by Choiseul. The Duke had even gone so far as to encourage the Dauphin to ask his grandfather's permission to take part in the hunting suppers of St Hubert, where Madame du Barry acted as hostess and behaviour and conversation were both ribald and relaxed. Much to the annoyance of his young wife, the Dauphin rather enjoyed these evenings, till his aunts enlightened him as to the origins and reputation of the charming hostess who was on such easy terms with the King. From that moment Louis Auguste conceived a violent dislike of Madame du Barry and a growing distrust of his governor. Marie Antoinette wrote to her mother, 'The Dauphin certainly does not like Monsieur de la Vauguyon, but he is frightened of him. A curious incident happened the other day. I was alone with my husband, when Monsieur Vauguyon was at the door in order to listen. A footman, who was either very silly or very honest, opened the door and there was the Duke fixed like a pikestaff, unable to move, whereupon I observed to my husband on the inconvenience of allowing people to listen at doors, and he took it very well.'

None of these letters written in the early months at Versailles was calculated to reassure a mother of her daughter's happiness, or, what was of far more importance to the Empress, on the political success of an alliance where everything depended on the birth of a son and heir. Mercy might report that the Dauphin had told his aunts he was very pleased with his bride, that he liked her looks and her way of expressing herself, and that from all accounts he was now paying regular visits to his wife's room. But as a good German who had shared her husband's bed for every night of their married life, Maria Theresa deplored the custom at Versailles of husband and wife having separate rooms. After four months of marriage Marie Antoinette informed her mother with the frankness that runs through their correspondence that 'though the *générale* [her periods] have not come for the past four months, there is no good reason for this'. The Empress was beginning to be impatient with her ambassador, who with true diplomatic tact kept telling her that, 'in view of the extreme youth of the young couple, the fact that so far there has been no real intimacy between them is nothing to worry about, for a relationship which develops slowly is often the most lasting'.

Even King Louis was beginning to be concerned, and in July overcame his aversion to straightforward talks with his family sufficiently to approach his grandson on the subject of the non-consummation of his marriage. Whereupon the Dauphin assured him that he had every intention of doing his duty as a husband and was waiting for the summer holidays at Compiègne where life was more peaceful and relaxed than at Versailles. But when the court moved to Compiègne the Dauphin had a bad cold and was confined to his bed for a fortnight. At Versailles, outside influences seemed to be at work to keep the young couple apart. That autumn at Fontainebleau Marie Antoinette discovered that the works on the Dauphin's apartments adjacent to her own had been deliberately delayed so that he had to sleep at the other end of the castle. This time she plucked up her courage and complained directly to the King, who for once took action and ordered the works to be finished in two days.

In a court where everyone lived in a close and oppressive intimacy, a girl still little more than a child had to fight her way through a jungle of intrigue without a single friend to guide her other than her mother's ambassador, who was also her mother's spy. Even the aunts, outwardly so benevolent, so ready to spoil her, and pander to her, were deadly jealous of her youth and charm and only too ready to repeat her slightest indiscretion. Her instinctive dislike of Madame du Barry was encouraged and her every slighting remark repeated either by Mesdames or their ladies-in-waiting. Her carelessness in dress – a carelessness natural to her age – her refusal to wear the heavy boned corset advocated by Madame de Noailles, was condoned by the aunts, who had become so neglectful of their appearance that they spent most of the day in *déshabillé* and only dressed in formal clothes when meeting the King. Then they would put an elaborate panniered skirt over their dress, adjust a train around their waist, and cover the rest with the short black taffeta mantelet. But even when it was only to visit the King for the short ceremony of what was known as '*Le Débotté du Roi*', when his majesty came in from hunting, etiquette required that Mesdames had to be escorted by a suite of ushers, pages and gentlemen-in-waiting from one part of the palace to another. Back in their own rooms they would discard their finery, take up their knitting and embroidery and resume the gossip and the tittle-tattle which gave some spice to the long empty days.

The fastidious Comte Mercy, who disapproved of Mesdames, deplored their influence on the impressionable Dauphine. And before long Marie Theresa was writing to her daughter:

> I beg of you not to neglect your appearance. It is very wrong to do so at your age, and even worse when you are in your position.... Which is why I keep pestering you on the subject, to warn you against letting yourself go and ending up like the French royal family, who have no idea how to present themselves or to set the tone, or even to amuse themselves in an honest way. Which is why so many of their rulers, not finding any resources at home, have gone in search of distraction elsewhere.... It is possible to be virtuous and at the same time to be gay and sociable. But if one keeps too much to oneself and sees only a few people one

ends by offending the other and having nothing but discontent and trouble all round.

I beg of you as a friend and as a loving mother who speaks from experience, do not neglect either your looks or your manners. If you do, you will regret it when it is too late. So please do not follow the example or advice of the family. It is up to you to set the tone at Versailles and so far you have succeeded admirably.

It was not very easy for Marie Antoinette to act on her mother's advice, as every month saw the King falling more and more under the influence of Madame du Barry, so that the only way of pleasing him was by pleasing a favourite with whom she could hardly bear to be in the same room.

At the end of the first year of marriage – a marriage which for some inexplicable reason was still unconsummated – Marie Antoinette's position at the court of France was sufficiently vulnerable for the King's favourite to allow herself several petty triumphs. The King was still attentive towards his grandson's wife, but there was already talk of hurrying on the marriage between the Comte de Provence and a Piedmontese princess. In Vienna Maria Theresa was consulting doctors as to what could be wrong with a son-in-law who remained so indifferent to someone as charming as her daughter. To add to her worries, Marie Antoinette had taken up riding, which her mother considered to be bad for the health, and which had not only been encouraged by the aunts, but approved of both by the King and the Dauphin:

> You are right in thinking that I disapprove. You quote your aunts, but they were thirty when they started to ride, not fifteen. Also they were Mesdames and not the Dauphine. I have a slight grudge against them for having encouraged you. But as you say the King approves and also the Dauphin – that is what counts for it is they who have charge of you now. To ride on horseback spoils the complexion and in the long run spoils the figure. Should you ride astride, which I don't doubt, it is even dangerous with a view to child bearing. For after all that is what you are there for and that is what is going to bring you happiness.

In letter after letter the Empress harps on the same theme – the one thing on which the whole fragile structure of the Austro-French alliance depended. Then in the New Year of 1771 came the staggering news that the Duc de Choiseul, the architect of that alliance and for the past eleven years the most important man in France, had been dismissed from his post.

5

The man chosen to succeed the Duc de Choiseul was the Duc d'Aiguillon, one of the most hated men in France, whose corrupt administration as governor of Brittany had been at the root of the King's quarrels with his *parlements*. His relationship to the old Maréchal de Richelieu, First Gentleman of the Bedchamber and a close friend of the King's, and his intimacy with Madame du Barry, said to have been his mistress, had made him a leading member of the cabal which was out to destroy the Duc de Choiseul.

The minister had been too long in power and was too confident of his influence over the King to take heed of the gathering storm. He had dared to criticize the favourite in public and to support the *parlements* against a governor chosen by the King. But even so, Louis, who hated change, might have kept him in power had it not been for the constant nagging of a woman who could not forgive the minister who would not allow her to forget that she had once been Jeanne Bécu.

The fall of Choiseul, followed by the sudden reassertion of royal authority, the suppression of the *parlements*, the exile of the magistrates and the summoning by the King of a *lit de justice** to instal a new *parlement* created by the Chancellor Maupeou were measures so violent and so unpopular that even the Princes of the Blood abstained from appearing.

In a lame little letter describing a situation she did not begin to understand, Marie Antoinette wrote to her mother: 'There is a lot going on here. Last Saturday there was a *lit de justice* to confirm the suppression of the old *parlements* and the creation of a new one. The Princes of the Blood refused to appear and have protested against the will of the King who has banished them all and for the present none of them are allowed to appear at court. A few of the dukes have also protested and I am told that about twelve of them have been exiled.'

The Dauphine does not write of the nobles, who of their own accord had deserted Versailles to make a pilgrimage to the Choiseuls in exile in Touraine. She did not hear the verses in praise of the fallen minister which were circulating round the salons of Paris, or read the scurrilous pamphlets against the King and his mistress, which were on sale in the precincts of Versailles itself. Brought up to believe in the divine right of princes, she

*A ceremonial session of the Parlement of Paris to register, in the King's presence, decrees he had himself proclaimed.

would never have dared to question the decisions of the King. But she recognized that the dismissal of Choiseul was a blow to herself and to her family and a dangerous threat to the Franco–Austrian alliance.

In Vienna the Empress made no secret of her displeasure at the dismissal of a loyal ally. But at the same time she warned her daughter not to compromise herself in any way: 'I admit I am very upset, but whatever reasons the King may have had, it is none of my affair, still less of yours. But never forget that your marriage was made by Choiseul and that you must always be grateful to him. Knowing you to be so straightforward and honest, I fear that this blow is going to hit you very hard. But do not let yourself be involved in any faction and above all remain neutral.'

Marie Antoinette's position after a year of marriage was not an enviable one. Though the Dauphin was beginning to show some affection towards her, even going so far as to attend the weekly balls she held during the winter, and taking dancing lessons in order to please her, there was as yet no sign of any real intimacy between them, and neither she nor Comte Mercy had anything to report to the Empress, who wrote to her devoted ambassador: 'I am glad to hear that the Dauphin has changed for the better, but I cannot begin to understand his behaviour towards his wife. Is it all the fault of his education? Does not the King's indulgence go too far in not having dismissed the Duc de Vauguyon?' Far from being dismissed, the Duke, though stricken by a mortal disease, was actively intriguing to supplant the Dauphin by his younger brother. The Comte de Provence's forthcoming marriage to a princess of Piedmont-Sardinia was interpreted by the Austrian ambassador as a further threat to his Archduchess.

Stanislas Xavier, the Comte de Provence, only a year younger than Louis Auguste, was both cleverer and more cultivated and from his earliest childhood had resented taking second place to a brother he despised. With a handsome face, fine eyes and a regal bearing, though somewhat marred by the precocious obesity which afflicted so many of the later Bourbons, he presented a far more impressive figure than the timid and clumsy Dauphin. But all the efforts of the ruling cabal to stage a wedding as grand if not grander than that of the Dauphin failed on account of the bride, who was too unattractive to be any kind of rival to the Dauphine. Marie Josephine of Savoy, with her long nose, beady eyes and leathery skin, was too unprepossessing to find favour with either the public or the King. And all the money spent on the lavish festivities which drained an already depleted treasury resulted in nothing more than the apotheosis of Madame du Barry, who appeared opulently and triumphantly beautiful with seven million francs' worth of diamonds round her throat, the cynosure of all eyes, the object of the doting admiration of the King. Beside her the Dauphine looked little more than a child, but a child who, under all the gaiety and sweetness, was beginning to develop a hard core of pride, a dangerous obstinacy.

Her brother-in-law's marriage and the introduction of a new princess into the family had made Marie Antoinette less dependent on the aunts and more ready to assert her position as Dauphine. Until now she had never had a library in her apartments, nor had she ever asked for one. But no sooner did she see that Marie Josephine, who was extremely well read, had been provided with beautifully sculpted bookcases than she immediately ordered Madame de Noailles to commission Gabriel to make her a library. The lady-in-waiting, who knew how little time was devoted to reading, economized by ordering the cheapest and plainest of bookcases. Marie Antoinette was furious. The offending bookcase had to be destroyed and replaced with an elaborately sculpted and gilded rococo library which she insisted had to be ready by the end of the summer. She, who until now had shown so little interest in fashion, tearing her dresses while happily playing with the children of her maidservants, was beginning to emulate the Comtesse du Barry in her elegance and extravagance. The first to advise her in these matters was her brother-in-law Provence, who had superb taste and with whom she was outwardly on excellent terms while recognizing the underlying slyness of a character only too ready to denigrate and slander.

Though the Dauphin and his brother thoroughly disliked one another, life at Versailles was so closely knit that the two young couples were constantly in one another's company, and Marie Antoinette wrote to her mother of her new sister-in-law: 'She is very sweet and very gay. She is very fond of me and not at all on the side of Madame du Barry.' It is doubtful whether their relations were as warm and as straightforward as she would have had the Empress believe, for the Italian princess was as versed in the art of dissimulation as her husband, and far better equipped than Marie Antoinette at steering through the rival factions of Versailles.

The Dauphine's obstinacy in refusing to come to terms with the King's mistress was beginning to have international repercussions. Comte Mercy went so far as to inform Prince Kaunitz in Vienna that the Dauphine's attitude might seriously affect the French reaction to the secret treaty regarding the partition of Poland. Forced by her unscrupulous minister and her ambitious son, Maria Theresa was being led against her will into becoming the partner in crime of the two people she disliked the most, the Empress of Russia and the King of Prussia. Though her religious principles and intrinsic honesty revolted against the unjust spoliation of an innocent people, the statesman in conflict with the woman drove her to put her signature to a pact which would give Austria the rich province of Galicia. All these nefarious negotiations were being conducted without France, who was Austria's ally, having been informed, and Comte Mercy, who had good reason to dread King Louis's reaction to the news, was more than ever exasperated by his silly, rebellious little charge for refusing to say Good Evening to Madame du Barry. After repeated admonitions and exhortations, reminding her of her duty to her mother and her country, the ambassador finally persuaded Marie Antoinette that on a certain summer's evening at Compiègne she would address a word to the royal favourite. The stage was set, but unfortunately the Dauphine confided in Madame Adelaide, and the vindictive princess, who hated Marie Antoinette only a little less than she hated Madame du Barry, was determined to thwart Comte Mercy's carefully laid plans.

The royal card game was finished and the Dauphine was holding court, moving with ease and grace across the hall, exchanging pleasantries with the favoured few, curtseying to the ladies. Only a slight flush, a quickened step betrayed a certain tension as she came to where Comte Mercy was talking to Madame du Barry. But just as she was about to utter the eagerly awaited words, Madame Adelaide appeared at her side and, in the harsh, commanding tones which always succeeded in unnerving her, called out, 'We are late. It is time for us to go to my sister Victoire and await the King.' Flustered and taken by surprise, the Dauphine lost her head and, forgetting the promises made to Mercy, turned on her heels and almost ran out of the room, leaving the discomfited Countess with an expectant smile dying on her lips, and the ambassador controlling his mortification.

King Louis was in a rage. The favourite had been publicly humiliated. Even Madame Adelaide realized she had gone too far when the Dauphin, asserting himself for the first time, told her it was wrong of her to have interfered and prevented his wife from doing what would have pleased the King. Matters became still more critical when it became known that the Comtesse de Provence had entertained the favourite to supper and that the Duc d'Aiguillon was courting her husband. Comte Mercy had no choice but to inform the Empress of the dangers of her daughter's subservience to her ill-intentioned aunt. His dislike of the meddlesome princesses, and in particular of Madame Adelaide, led the ambassador to hold them responsible for all Marie Antoinette's mistakes. But it was not so much the influence of her aunts as her own almost pathological dislike and jealousy of Madame du Barry, which made it so hard for Marie Antoinette to extend her the barest courtesy.

It was only her mother's scoldings which finally cowed her into submission. This time the Empress did not mince her words. Harassed by the importunities of a son bent on conquest and the aggrandizement of his empire, Maria Theresa was not in a mood to be patient with a tiresome and refractory daughter.

What is all this fuss and bother, this fear of speaking to the King who is the best of fathers, of addressing as much as a word to people whom you have been advised to speak to, the inability to say good morning, or make a compliment or exchange some other triviality. All these tiresome caprices for no other reason than that you have allowed yourself to become so enslaved by your aunts that you have forgotten both reason and sense of duty. I cannot remain silent about your failure to obey Comte Mercy after the conversation in which he told you explicitly of the wishes of the King. What excuse have you got to behave in this way – none whatsoever! You are only required to know Madame du Barry as a lady who has an entrée at court and who is admitted to the society of the King of whom you are the first subject. It is the King to whom you owe obedience and submission, as an example to the court and to see that his orders are carried out. No one has asked you to become intimate or to indulge in any kind of familiarity, all that is required is an impartial word, a certain regard not for the lady herself but for your grandfather, your master and your benefactor, whom you have let down on the first occasion when you could have obliged him and shown him your attachment. And for what reason? Because of a shameful subservience to people who have completely subjugated you by treating you like a child, in providing you with horseback and donkey rides, and dogs and children to play with. If these things are more important in your life than to please your master, then you will end in making yourself ridiculous and in forfeiting all affection and esteem.

It was a long letter all on the same subject, and even the Empress wondered whether it was not too hard, leaving it to her ambassador's discretion as to whether to hand it over to the Dauphine. But Mercy considered that it was only the Empress who had sufficient authority to counteract the pernicious influence of Madame Adelaide.

Contrary to Comte Mercy's expectations, it took several months for Marie Antoinette to give in. Her first reaction to her mother's scoldings was to protest that she had no reason to believe the King wished her to speak to Madame du Barry. 'He has never mentioned it to me and is more amiable than ever. If you could only see what goes on here, you would realize that that woman and her clique will never be satisfied with a few words. No sooner spoken, than it will start all over again. You may rest assured that I do not need to be told what to do when it is a matter of my conscience.'

It was a proud, defiant reply, but neither Mercy nor her mother seem to have taken into account her loneliness and unhappiness in a court where she had not a single friend. With tears in her eyes she told the ambassador, 'If only the Empress could see all that goes on here I am sure she would forgive me, for one has to have the patience of an angel to put up with it.' She might tell her mother that the Dauphin slept with her every night and was the best of husbands – that there was no truth in the wicked rumours which said that he was impotent, that it was only a question of time before everything would be all right. But she said nothing of the humiliation of going to bed night after night with a fumbling, inept husband who, after a few unsuccessful attempts at lovemaking, would collapse sweating and snoring at her side. She never wrote of the family quarrels; of a certain incident described by Mercy when, at a supper party held by the Comte de Provence, the Dauphin, who enjoyed irritating his brother by playing with the precious objects in his collection, ended in breaking an exquisite Meissen vase. In a fit of fury Stanislas Xavier fell upon Louis Auguste and the two princes rolled fighting on the floor till they were separated by Marie Antoinette, who received several scratches for her pains. Bourbon family life was certainly very different from that at Schönbrunn.

Despite her deficiencies, which the Empress never let her forget, writing, 'You have to be doubly amiable as you have no natural talents of your own,' Marie Antoinette, by the time of her sixteenth birthday, had succeeded in making her shy, reserved young husband fall in love with her – and her enemies were beginning to fear the day when an Austrian queen would rule the country.

It was not until New Year's Day of 1772 that Marie Antoinette finally capitulated and consented to speak to Madame du Barry. It was a day when Versailles was crowded with courtiers come to offer their congratulations, when the Dauphine's apartments were so full that there was a long queue of ladies waiting to file past in strict order of precedence; among them Madame du Barry, who was accompanied by the Duchesse d'Aiguillon. When she passed in front of the Dauphine all eyes turned in her direction to see whether she was to suffer yet another humiliation. But this time Marie Antoinette looked her full in the face and in a loud, clear voice which could be heard all over the room said, 'There are a lot of people today at Versailles.' The Countess flushed with pleasure as she made a profound and graceful curtsey. But the Dauphine's face was frozen, and when her mother's ambassador congratulated her on her behaviour she replied in the mutinous tones he had learnt to know so well: 'I have spoken to her once, but that is as far as I will go. That woman will never hear my voice again.'

Neither Comte Mercy nor the Empress would ever understand the wrong they had inflicted on her integrity and pride, and there is a new element of boldness in Marie Antoinette's letters to her mother: 'Madame, my very dear mother. I do not doubt but that Mercy must have told you of my behaviour on New Year's Day. I hope you were pleased. You can rest assured that I will always be ready to sacrifice my own prejudices and dislikes, provided I am not asked to do anything which conflicts with my sense of honour.' The Empress, who was both angry and amazed by this attitude on the part of her youngest and hitherto most docile child, retorted:

> You make me laugh if you imagine that either I or my minister would ever want to make you act contrary to your sense of honour or do anything in the least unworthy. This makes me see how much you have been influenced by prejudice and by bad advice. It really worries me that you should work yourself up into such a state over a few words and declare that you will never speak to Madame du Barry again. What interest should I have other than your own good and your and the Dauphin's mutual happiness. Who can advise you better or deserve your confidence more than my minister who knows your country and the various factions with which one has to deal?

But it was not only her mother and her ambassador who shocked Marie Antoinette. More than anything else it was the attitude of the King. Until now she had always believed the aunts when they assured her that their father had no wish for his family to be on friendly terms with his mistress. But now, for the price of a few words he was radiant, welcoming her with open arms, showering her with presents and, as the crowning mark of favour, visiting her for breakfast and bringing along his own coffee machine, for one of the last pleasures left to this bored old man was to make his own coffee in the morning. But for the proud little Hapsburg Archduchess all these favours counted for nothing when it was ransom paid to Madame du Barry.

It was only when the Empress, half against her will, was forced to take her daughter into her confidence and to treat her as an adult human being that Marie Antoinette submitted with good grace to the advice of her mother's ambassador. By the summer of 1772 the forthcoming partition of Poland was no longer a secret. Louis XV had been the first to know through the '*Cabinet Noir*', the secret diplomacy he had subsidized for years without the know-ledge of his government. When news of the partition became known in France, public opinion was universally hostile. Maria Theresa, who began to fear for the future of the Austro-French alliance, wrote to her ambassador, 'One must employ all possible measures to put an end to this hostility. And there is only my daughter, assisted by your knowledge and advice, who can render this service to her family and her country. Above all she must cultivate the good graces of the King and not upset him in any way; to be amiable to the favourite, not so much for her sake as out of consideration for her grand-father and master and in view of the good it will do to our two countries.'

It was a heavy commitment for a girl of barely sixteen. When Mercy showed Marie Antoinette the letter from her mother her first reaction was to ask him what influence she could possibly have on the King when she never saw him alone, and to wonder what role a woman like Madame du Barry could play in international politics. The ambassador informed her that La du Barry could interfere in everything, that in order to carry out the wishes of her mother and to preserve the alliance between their two courts it was absolutely necessary for her to do all in her power to captivate the King and to be on good terms both with the favourite and his ministers. This time he even went so far as to remind Marie Antoinette of the vulnerability of a dauphine who had not yet produced an heir. It was a subject he was loath to dwell on, for Madame de Noailles, who had grown fond of her young mistress, now told him that the Dauphine had lately been suffering from bouts of depression brought on by her husband's incomprehensible behaviour; for though the Dauphin appeared to be genuinely attached to his wife he had not yet shown any sign of physical tenderness. When Marie Antoinette assured the ambas-sador that she would do her best to contribute to the good relations between their two countries – 'for where would I be if matters came to a break' – she was voicing the fear of a woman frightened of the insecurity of her own position.

During the summer at Compiègne when the Dauphin spent his days out hunting with the King, he would come back in the evening in such a state of exhaustion that he usually slept in his own room, and his wife would hardly have seen him had she not joined in these expeditions. She loved riding and driving out into the forests, wearing the smart blue and red riding habit and plumed hat which became her so well, escorted by her admiring courtiers, forgetting in the excitement of the hunt all the tedium of Versailles. Even the Dauphin, who was usually so dull and lifeless at court, became another man when he was on a horse. He was a superb rider, dashing and courageous, always in the midst of the fray, the first at the kill, and for once her scolding mother could not complain for she was sharing in the pleasures of her husband and of the King. 'I have nothing to say on the subject, so long as the King and the Dauphin approve,' was Maria Theresa's somewhat acid comment.

Beset by ill health, at loggerheads with her son, painfully aware of the unworthy role he and Prince Kaunitz had forced her to play in Poland, the aging Empress Maria Theresa had neither patience nor understanding of a daughter to whom she was frequently unkind. Ever since she had left Austria, Marie Antoinette had been in regular correspondence with her former governess, who wrote to her once a month giving her all the gossip of Vienna. She looked forward to those letters which came through the regular post. When they failed to appear she complained to Comte Mercy, who had the unpleasant task of informing her that the Empress had given orders that the correspondence was to cease for fear that Countess Brandeiss's harmless chat might contain some indiscretion. Marie Antoinette, who loved her old governess, wept bitter tears at this news and was in no way consoled to be told by her mother that from now on her two unmarried sisters would write to her regularly giving her all the family news. Unmarried archduchesses still living under their mother's yoke were hardly in a position to supply amusing descriptions of Viennese life as lived outside the precincts of the Hofburg. Even Comte Mercy felt that in this instance his imperial mistress had been unduly hard, and that with a character like the Dauphine's gentleness sometimes achieved more than severity. She had confessed to him once that though she feared and respected her mother she could never really feel at ease with her.

At the French court there was no one she could love, far less respect, for the ambassador was amazed to see with what a clear and dispassionate eye the sixteen-year-old Dauphine judged the King, as a man who 'had neither warmth nor feeling' and was indifferent to everything but his own comfort and his own pleasure – a king who went out hunting when Europe was in crisis and in exchange for her politeness to his mistress was ready to accept the treaty of St Petersburg, the dismemberment of one of France's oldest allies. The subject of Poland was raised one evening at Compiègne when the King, taking her on his knees, said in a light, bantering tone, 'We must not talk of Poland in front of you, for we and your relations are not of the same opinion. If we began to quarrel we would have to send you back to Austria,' and he embraced her with the utmost affection. This was the attitude of a king who had been married to a Polish queen and whose grandchildren had Polish blood in their veins.

Maria Theresa had not taken the trouble to initiate her daughter into the political motives which dictated her conduct, but there were plenty of people at Versailles only too ready to show the Dauphine the scurrilous pamphlets and broadsheets which were being sold in Paris, while the brilliant young courtiers who attended her balls, the Lauzuns, the Coignys and Ségurs, all of them ardent adherents of the Duc de Choiseul, were loud in their indignation at the despicable part which France was being made to play under the leadership of the Duc d'Aiguillon.

But only someone very near the throne would have dared to tell the Dauphine of a supper party held by the Comtesse du Barry at which the Duc d'Aiguillon regaled the guests with a ribald letter he had received from his ambassador to Vienna, in which Prince Louis de Rohan made fun of the tribulations of the pious Empress '*qui prenait en pleurant*' – who wept while allocating to herself the largest share of the spoils. That her mother should have been mocked and ridiculed in front of Madame du Barry and her friends roused Marie Antoinette to such a state of fury that Comte Mercy had the greatest difficulty in persuading her ever to speak to the Duc d'Aiguillon again. From now on began Marie Antoinette's hatred of the future Cardinal de Rohan, which was to have disastrous consequences for her reign.

Mercy suspected the Comte de Provence, who of late had become very assiduous in his visits to the Dauphine. Neither the ambassador nor the Empress approved of these visits but they had to be accepted as part of the closely knit family life. Stanislas Xavier was witty and amusing and excelled in the kind of light-hearted gossip which delighted Marie Antoinette. They also shared a love of play acting which for her recalled those happy days in Vienna spent in amateur theatricals. Now with the help of Monsieur Campan, who bore the highsounding title of '*Secrétaire du Cabinet de la Dauphine*' but who in reality had little to do, and of his son who happened to be an accomplished actor, the Dauphine and her brothers-in-law began to put on plays for their own amusement. Their repertory was ambitious, including plays of Molière and Goldoni staged in one of the disused mezzanines of Versailles where a collapsible set could be hidden in a cupboard. The necessity for secrecy, lest it should reach the ears of Madame de Noailles or of the disapproving aunts, gave an added spice to the entertainment. The Dauphin, who was too timid to perform, was the enthusiastic audience, for he loved the theatre and in particular the Italian comedies. He had a retentive memory and on more than one occasion would act as prompter to his younger brother Artois, who could never be bothered to learn his lines. Artois, who had just graduated from the school-room, was an attractive, mischievous boy, the only one of King Louis's grandsons to have inherited his elegant, graceful figure.

Endless trouble was taken over the costumes to make up for the lack of talent, for Provence was the only one of the family who was a really good actor. He was particularly successful in the role of Molière's Tartuffe, which led the Dauphin to comment with a certain acidity, 'The part was not difficult for him as he was only acting himself!' Marie Josephine, who in real life could dissimulate as well as her husband, was nevertheless deplorable on the stage, and even the Dauphine, for all her enthusiasm, was a very indifferent actress. But their common interest in the theatre had the advantage of bringing Dauphin and Dauphine together and of taking Louis Auguste away from the locksmith's and carpenter's shop where he practised his two favourite hobbies and from where, to his wife's despair, he would emerge with dirty hands and stained clothes. These hobbies of Louis Auguste, which were so despised by the courtiers, were far more intelligent and worthwhile than the fatuities which took up so much of the time at Versailles and which caused the Comtesse de Provence to complain to her parents in Turin that 'There were so many balls she could not stand any more'.

It was extraordinary that for three years the future King and Queen of France lived in this closed, artificial world of Versailles without ever visiting Paris. Louis Auguste does not appear to have shown any curiosity to see his capital. When he had been king for three years he shocked his brother-in-law the Emperor Joseph by admitting he had never visited Les Invalides. Marie Antoinette's terrible experience on the night of the disaster in the Place Louis XV had for many months given her a fear of returning to a place where she too might be crushed by the crowds. But in the past year she had longed to escape from Versailles and to explore a town so near and at the same time so unattainable. It seemed that everything and everyone conspired to keep her away, beginning with the jealousy of her aunts and Madame du Barry, who did not dare to ride through the streets for fear of being attacked by the mob, and ending with a government, weak and frightened lest the still powerful Choiseul party might exploit the growing popularity of the young couple to provoke another Fronde. There had been a clandestine expedition into the city in the last week of carnival when the Dauphine, taking advantage of King Louis's love of secrecy, cajoled him into allowing her and the Dauphin and the Comte and Comtesse de Provence to pay an incognito visit to the opera ball. Bubbling over with excitement, Marie Antoinette wrote to her mother: 'Last Thursday the Dauphin, the Comte and Comtess de Provence and I went to the opera ball. It was done in the greatest secrecy, and we were all masked. But after half an hour we were recognized. ... We returned to Versailles at seven in the morning, where we heard mass before going to bed. Everyone appears to be delighted by the fact that Monsieur le Dauphin should have consented to come to the ball, for he usually has an aversion to this kind of party.'

The childish delight with which she related her experiences must have warmed the old King's heart, for now that his sexual powers were failing he was beginning to be bored by Madame du Barry with her affected lisp and continual demands for money, and the Dauphine's endless prattle was a refreshing contrast. 'I try to please the King and I think I sometimes manage to succeed,' she wrote. 'It is not always easy, for his entourage are always trying to make him change his mind. But, unless I am mistaken, I really think he quite likes me.'

Her enemies were beginning to realize that the Dauphine was a power to be reckoned with, and that it was only a question of time before she obtained a complete ascendancy over her husband. That he should have been ready to accompany her to the masked ball was already proof of his affection. For once even the Empress was delighted. 'Your excursion to Paris seems to have been the greatest success,' she wrote. As a loving mother she was happy to think that her laggard and incomprehensible son-in-law was beginning to behave like a normal young man.

King Louis was also beginning to be seriously concerned that neither of his two elder grandsons had fathered an heir. The King could sympathize with Provence, for there was nothing very tempting about Marie Josephine who was so careless about her person that she actually smelt, and a tactful letter had to be sent to their Sardinian majesties to find out whether their daughter could be made to brush her teeth. But with someone as charming as the Dauphine the situation was more difficult to understand. At the beginning of March 1773 Marie Antoinette wrote to her mother with characteristic frankness: 'The King has been talking to Dr Lassone. He seems to think there is nothing wrong with me and the Dauphin other than clumsiness and ignorance. He discussed with the Dauphin very seriously as to what was to be done and in the end he ordered him to instruct us separately. The Dauphin came and visited the doctor in my apartments, as he did not want him to be seen in his own. He spoke to him very sensibly and without any embarrassment. Lassone was very pleased and seems to be optimistic.' A month later Marie Antoinette wrote again: 'Monsieur le Dauphin's talks with Lassone have been very satisfactory. There is nothing wrong with his constitution. Unfortunately he is incredibly listless and lazy and this laziness never leaves him except when he is out hunting.'

What she refers to as 'listlessness' may have been a lymphatic condition, a kind of glandular disturbance which afflicted not only the Dauphin and his brother Provence, but also the elder of their two sisters, Madame Clothilde, who was so enormously fat that she was known as '*Grosse Madame*' and so slow and apathetic that she appeared to be completely devoid of feelings. This did not apply to the Dauphin, but unfortunately his timidity, allied to an acute inferiority complex, often made him unable to show his affection so that he could be gruff and almost rude towards the very people he felt fondest of. Even the best-intentioned of courtiers found it almost impossible to hold a conversation with him and the palace ladies complained that when he addressed them he never looked them in the face. But the Prince, who lumbered so heavily across the polished floors of Versailles, looking, as the Duc de Croy described, 'more like a ploughman than a Bourbon', was a revelation to his wife when they made their '*Joyeuse Entrée*' – their state entry into the capital – and he came into contact for the first time with the ordinary people of Paris.

'What pleased me most in the whole of this wonderful day was the behaviour of Monsieur le Dauphin. He replied perfectly to all the speeches and addresses and responded warmly to the acclamations of the crowds,' wrote Marie Antoinette in triumph to her mother.

It was eleven o'clock on 8 June, a perfect summer's day, when the booming of the cannon from the Bastille and the Hôtel de Ville announced the arrival of the royal princes. The Duc de Brissac, governor of Paris, was at the city gates to present them with the keys of the city. Six state coaches escorted by detachments of the Town Guards and preceded by the Household Cavalry drove them through cheering crowds along the quays from the Tuileries to Notre Dame. They came in hundreds and thousands, pouring out of the mean streets which huddled behind the quays, out of the splendid palaces reflected in the river, out of the churches, the hospitals and schools – people in every walk of life, merchants, shopkeepers and students, from the town marshals and the heads of the corporations to the market women in their best clothes pelting them with flowers. There was a special welcome for the Dauphine from the prioress and the nuns of the hospital of the Hôtel Dieu, which a few months previously had been devastated by fire, and Marie Antoinette had been the only member of the royal family to send a large donation from her privy purse.

The Archbishop was waiting to receive them on the steps of Notre Dame where they attended mass, then returned to the Tuileries, stopping at the university and the church of Ste Geneviève. By now the crowds had grown to such enormous proportions that they could proceed at no more than a snail's pace. But throughout the long hot drive Marie Antoinette sat proud and erect in her carriage, with flushed cheeks which had no need of rouge and eyes shining with delight. 'How beautiful she is,' was the general refrain. 'How kind he looks,' said the women, for the Dauphin with his broad and honest face was beaming with pleasure.

In the palace of the Tuileries the royal couple dined alone with the ladies in attendance, but an open gallery overlooking the dining hall allowed a continual chain of people to witness the feast, while in an adjoining room fifty women from the Paris market had been invited to dine as the King's guests. Their noisy toasts and raucous laughter echoed through the palace, and Marie Antoinette heard for the first time a question she was to hear so often in the next few years: 'When are you going to give us an heir, Madame la Dauphine?'

The Duc de Brissac led them out on to a balcony overlooking a terrace seething with people, all throwing their hats in the air and shouting in joyful acclamation, *'Vive Monsieur le Dauphin! Vive Madame la Dauphine!'* For a second Marie Antoinette hesitated as if overwhelmed by the roar of welcome. 'There are so many of them,' she whispered to the Duc de Brissac, and the gallant old Duke made his celebrated reply: 'Madame, I hope Monsieur le Dauphin won't be jealous if I say you have two hundred thousand lovers waiting below.'

All her nervous hesitation had gone. Nothing would satisfy her but to go down into the gardens and, arm in arm with the Dauphin, mingle with the crowds, sharing in their laughter and their love. 'Let them come as close as they want to. The guards must not push them away, and above all no one must be hurt.' 'The Dauphin gave these orders,' she writes, 'which had a very good effect, for in spite of the huge crowds no one was hurt.' They were orders characteristic of the future Louis XVI, who throughout his martyred life would never allow any of his guards to raise a hand against the mob.

Marie Antoinette's letter to her mother is written in a mood of euphoria, but one senses the presence of the liberal-minded Abbé Vermond when she writes: 'What touched me most of all was the warmth and eagerness of the welcome from these poor people who, in spite of being crushed by taxation, nevertheless seemed to be so happy to see us. How fortunate we are in our position to have been able to win with so little the love of our people. There is nothing more precious and I shall never forget it.' Marie Antoinette had no need of prompting from either Mercy or Vermond when, on returning that evening to Versailles, she said to King Louis, 'Your Majesty must be very much loved otherwise we would never have received such a welcome.' The King, who was under no illusion as to the feelings of his subjects, thanked her for the pretty compliment.

In the spring of 1770, when Marie Antoinette was already on her way to
France, Prince Kaunitz had written to Comte Mercy: 'Our little Arch-
duchess will be all right provided they don't spoil her in France.' But the
spoiling began the day of the *Joyeuse Entrée* in 1773. Two days later the
Dauphine and the Dauphin were at the Opera House, followed by the
Comédie Française, and finally the Italian Theatre to see the popular play *Le
Déserteur*, when the whole of the pit joined in the chorus of 'Long Live the
King' and the comic actor Clairval, playing the part of a drunkard, came
reeling on to the stage, throwing his bonnet in the air and crying out, 'Long
live the King and also his dear children.'

The enthusiasm of these audiences combined with the adulation of the
crowds made Marie Antoinette realize for the first time the potential of her
future role. And aglow with gratitude she wrote to her mother: 'To think that
I who was the youngest of us all should have been treated by you as if I had
been the oldest. What have I done to deserve it?' But before long she grew
used to the cheers and the admiration, accepting them as her due, distribu-
ting her easy smiles, ready to charm and to be charmed by everything. There
were official visits to the ministries and the museums, to the manufacturers of
Gobelin tapestries, of Sèvres and of Savonnerie; expeditions on which she
would be accompanied by either her aunts or her sister-in-law of Provence.
Learned professors who showed her round the royal library with its collec-
tions of manuscripts and medals, the artists whom she honoured by a visit to
the Salon du Louvre – all fell under the spell of the young Dauphine. But
what she enjoyed most of all was to visit the popular fêtes and fairgrounds
and to watch the people dancing under the trees and buy from the open air
boutiques. These excursions were thoroughly disapproved of by Mesdames,
who in the whole of their sheltered lives had never been in touch with the
ordinary people and who would sit proud and stiff in their carriage, uncomfortable and also a little afraid of any popular demonstration.

It was not long before the aunts were left behind and younger and more
congenial companions took their place: the charming Princesse de Lamballe
and her sister-in-law the Duchesse de Chartres. These innocent young
women had been brought by marriage at an early age into the raffish,
dissipated set of the Palais Royal, the Orléans stronghold in the heart of
Paris. When its gardens were thrown open to the public the whole of Paris
met under the chestnut trees: gallants in search of adventure and prostitutes

in search of trade; news vendors hawking their wares of pornography and slander and young lawyers from the provinces airing their oratory in the open-air cafés. While the old Duc d'Orléans, the richest man in France, lived in retirement with his morganatic wife, his son, the dissolute and ambitious Duc de Chartres, reigned at the Palais Royal. The Orléans were the only princes of the blood royal who had not yet made their peace with the King and who still refused to sit in Maupeou's parliament, a gesture of defiance to Versailles which won them immense popularity in Paris.

Though neither the Dauphin nor the Dauphine frequented the Palais Royal, both Marie Thérèse de Lamballe, born a princess of Savoie-Carignan, and her sister-in-law the Duchesse de Chartres had the right to the *petites entrées* at Versailles. And it was these two women who unwittingly encouraged Marie Antoinette in those wilful absurdities and extravagances for which she was later to be blamed. Both of them had limitless money at their disposal and limitless time on their hands in which to indulge the latest craze, whether it was gambling for high stakes at the dangerous game of faro, which as yet had never been played at Versailles, or launching the towering headdresses which had taken Paris by storm. It was the Duchesse de Chartres who first put Marie Antoinette in touch with Mademoiselle Bertin, the milliner from Abbeville whose genius in creating topical coiffures reflecting the mood of the day was to win her the favour of the Queen.

It was the time when the whole town was discussing the 'Goezman' case – the quarrel between Pierre Augustin Caron de Beaumarchais, watchmaker, playwright and pamphleteer of brilliant talent and dubious reputation, and Goezman, a corrupt magistrate; when Beaumarchais' famous *Memorials* written in his own defence were being sold on every street corner and the playwright condemned by the courts had become the idol of Paris. '*Ques a co*?' ('What is up?' The theme song of the *Memorials*, a catchword in provincial patois) was on everybody's lips. Mademoiselle Bertin created a new model: a '*Ques a co*' – a bunch of feathers in the form of a questionmark to be worn at the back of the head, impudent, diverting and wholly original, sported by the Dauphine at Versailles.

But the versatile adventurer condemned by the courts who made mock of his parliament was not unknown to the King or to his daughters. The son of a humble watchmaker had played many parts in his rise to fame, and one of the most anomalous of all had been that of music master to Mesdames de France. His talents as a harpist combined with a handsome presence and distinguished manners had won him the patronage and favour of three bored and lonely women, who had been only too ready to further his career till their jealousy was aroused by his marriage to a rich widow, whose mysterious death only six months after the wedding attached the first scandal to his name.

Since then his career had gone through many vicissitudes of poverty alternating with wealth when, as agent to the well-known financier Paris-Duverney, he had been entrusted with large sums to further far-reaching schemes in the French colonies. His troubles began with the death of Duverney, when the bankers' heirs contested a document produced by Beaumarchais claiming a large part of the inheritance. And then began the series of court cases with corrupt magistrates and bribed judges. No one came out of the trial unscathed. With his biting satire Beaumarchais had dealt a blow to an already weak and importunate government. But at Versailles, where Madame du Barry still ruled supreme, the royal favourite was so amused by the *Memorials* that she ordered part of them to be dramatized for performance in her private theatre, a performance at which the King was said to have been present.

Even the Dauphine, who rarely shared the opinions of Madame du Barry and hardly ever read a book, was so delighted by the *Memorials* that she gave them to her husband to read and was angry and surprised to see him throw into the fire what he described as 'a seditious and obscene publication'. It was a curious gesture on the part of a young prince who was usually considered to be so slow and obtuse. But of all the royal family he appears to have been the only one who understood the danger of men like Beaumarchais, whose light-hearted mockery covered an underlying bitterness ready to denigrate any form of authority. Louis Auguste was one of those unfortunate people whose first instincts were always right but who rarely had the courage to stand by his decisions.

Beaumarchais was famous, but nevertheless down and out. The judgement of the courts prevented the Comédie Française from performing *Le Barbier de Séville*. The cost of the trial had lost him the whole of his fortune and the sentence which divested him of his civil rights precluded him from holding any court appointment. But at the court of Louis xv clever adventurers rarely remained unemployed.

Monsieur de Sartines, the current minister of police, could always find jobs for outlaws of society. In England one of Madame du Barry's former lovers had just published a lurid and highly detailed account of the Countess's early beginnings in a Parisian whore house. They were hardly the kind of revelations to be appreciated by a woman striving after respectability who still hoped for a morganatic marriage to the King. Madame du Barry had gone in tears to Monsieur de Sartines imploring him to have the libellous pamphlet suppressed and the miscreant brought to justice. But the English government had refused to interfere and attempts at abduction had ended in ignominious failure. Only two weeks after his condemnation by the court, Beaumarchais was entrusted by the King with a secret mission to England to secure the incriminating documents by any means in his power. It was a sordid mission for a man who, on the publication of his *Memorials*, had been acclaimed as '*L'homme de la nation*' and might well have become a revolutionary leader. But Beaumarchais was too money-loving by nature, too attached to the life and habits of a class he fundamentally despised. He was the mockingbird who heralded the downfall of the old regime rather than the carrion crow who devoured the remains. So he accepted King Louis's offer – an outlaw hunting an outlaw. But by the time he had successfully concluded his mission the old King was dead and no one cared any longer about the reputation of a former prostitute. Sartines, who could have refunded his expenses, did not wish to include in the accounts to be presented to the young King a large sum paid out in the service of Madame du Barry. And he was cynical enough to suggest to Beaumarchais that his only chance of being paid was if another case of the same kind came along – another pamphlet which had to be suppressed. It was a dangerous thing to say to a man in desperate need of money, for what could be easier for someone of Beaumarchais' imagination than to fabricate himself a libel against the innocent young Queen, who wore the coiffure *à la Ques a co* with such panache and laughed so gaily at his satires?

Beaumarchais' trial coincided with the last weeks of the Paris carnival of 1774, a carnival which had never been more brilliant with the opera balls honoured by the presence of the royal princes. The Dauphine in particular was known to have a passion for masked balls and was under the illusion that no one ever recognized her, whereas everybody always did. She revelled in the anonymity of the incognito, when in domino and mask she was free to flirt and tease the charming young foreigners who, when presented by their ambassadors at Versailles, could only be given the most formal of curtseys, the briefest of smiles or at the most be invited to one of those small, exclusive balls held every week in her private apartments from five in the afternoon to the stroke of nine.

At the opera balls she could dance all night, only retiring when the crowds became too great and their attentions too intrusive. Access to the opera was made easy by a passageway which connected the Duchesse de Chartres' apartments in the Palais Royal directly to the first balcony boxes at the opera – and dancing took place on a raised platform at a level with these boxes.

The masked ball held on the night of 30 January 1774 was one of the great social events of the season. All the royal princes including the Dauphin were known to be present, though many would have had difficulty in recognizing the shy, retiring Prince in the rollicking masked figure who laughed so loudly with his companions and joked with any stranger. The Dauphine was more recognizable and there was a stir in the hall from the moment she appeared. But there was one young foreigner present who failed to recognize the graceful figure in the grey velvet domino and mask who addressed him by name and teased him so gaily about the various ladies pursuing him. The eighteen-year-old Count Fersen, on his first visit to Paris, was handsome enough to attract the attention of any woman. His tall, elegant figure, his perfect features and vivid blue eyes framed by long black lashes had already earned him the name of 'le beau Fersen', and an air of cool reserve gave him an added fascination. The Swedish ambassador, Count Creutz, reported to King Gustavus: 'Of all the Swedes who have passed through Paris since I have been here, no one has been so well received as young Count Fersen nor behaved with a greater modesty and discretion.'

Axel Fersen was certainly discreet. One senses it already in the journal in which he describes his meeting with the Dauphine at the opera ball: 'It was one o'clock in the morning when I left Madame d'Anville to go on to the opera ball. It was a great social event since Madame la Dauphine, Monsieur le Dauphin and the Comte de Provence came and were at the ball for half an hour before anyone recognized them. The Dauphine spoke to me at length without my knowing who she was. When at last she identified herself everyone rushed to her side and she withdrew to her box. At three I left the ball.' That was all he wrote of a meeting which was to change the whole course of his life. And this discretion was maintained throughout his relationship with a woman whose indiscretion was to be among the worst of her faults.

They were to meet in the next two months at the balls and receptions at Versailles where Marie Antoinette, surrounded by her retinue, could accord him no more than a few formal words, a fleeting smile. But even this was sufficient to arouse the jealousy and envy of those who had nothing else to do but to spy on the 'hated Austrian'. The Swedish ambassador, who had spent sufficient years in Paris to recognize the crosscurrents of intrigue directed against the Dauphine, warned his young protégé against becoming involved in 'the bees' nest' of Versailles.

Count Creutz was a clever diplomat. Axel Fersen belonged to one of the oldest families in Sweden and was a favourite of the young King Gustavus, and it would be unwise for him to become involved at a court where the French would always be ready to turn against a foreigner. The Dauphine was very pretty and seductive with a natural innocence and sweetness: all one could reproach her for was her frivolity and that was understandable at her age, especially as she was tied to a man who, in spite of his apparent devotion, was unable to satisfy her as a husband. In later years Axel Fersen was to be grateful for the advice given him by his ambassador, not to listen to those who tried to belittle the Dauphin. Though neither brilliant nor attractive, Louis Auguste was far from being stupid and had a lot of common sense, a love of justice and a real wish to do good. Unfortunately he lacked the strength of character either to influence or stand up to his young wife who was envied, spied on and betrayed at every turn.

Axel Fersen left Paris in the spring of 1774, at a time when the nineteen-year-old Louis Auguste and the eighteen-year-old Marie Antoinette represented the hopes of the majority of the nation. Four years were to pass before he returned. They were years during which, dazzled by her position and intoxicated by the incense of continual flattery, Marie Antoinette listened less and less to the admonishments of her mother and the advice of the imperial ambassador. From the very beginning Comte Mercy had deplored in the young Dauphine her readiness to poke fun at whatever she regarded as ridiculous, a humour which was typically Viennese and which all unwittingly offended those whom she should have been at pains to conciliate.

In the first months of her marriage, her lady-in-waiting Madame de Noailles had already been nicknamed 'Madame l'Etiquette', and once, when she fell off a donkey in the forest of Compiègne, Marie Antoinette had laughingly called out to her companions, 'Run and get Madame l'Etiquette and ask her what is the correct procedure when a dauphine of France falls off a donkey.' A young maid who had incurred Madame de Noailles' disapproval for failing to have the lapels of her bonnet or the ribbons of her apron tied in the correct manner would be comforted by a conspiratorial smile or even a wink from her royal mistress. The members of her household, from the humblest of servants to the youngest of pages, adored the Dauphine. But the stiff-necked dowagers who considered themselves ignored and the pompous old gentlemen whose prosy speeches reduced her to yawns were only too ready to listen to the barbed remarks and acid comments of the Dauphin's loving aunts.

The first occasion on which Marie Antoinette asserted her position and tested her influence was in her championship of her former music teacher, the celebrated composer Gluck, when his opera *Iphigenia in Aulis* was performed at the Paris Opera House on 19 April 1774. A German had dared not only to produce an opera in French, but to produce one that was based on one of the greatest classics in the language, Racine's *Iphigénie*. The whole town talked of nothing else – as if a German could possibly supplant the familiar airs of Rameau and Lully! His opera claimed to pioneer music suited to the demands of dramatic action, music which relied on the inexhaustible resources of harmony and the close ties between human emotions and sensations, music which belonged to the world and was native to no country. But would Gluck, for all his genius, ever have succeeded in breaking down the opposition he encountered without the support of Marie Antoinette who, having been the most mediocre of his pupils at Schönbrunn, was now the most powerful of his protectors? The directors of the Royal Opera House who complained of his intransigence and the spoilt divas who were reduced to tears by the violence of his temper, found themselves forced to submit to this bullying, hectoring composer, so obsessed with his own work that he refused to make allowances for either weaknesses or caprices.

On the morning of 19 April the queues hoping to gain admission to the Opera House stretched as far as the Tuileries; tickets were being hawked at three times the original cost. It did not matter if one was a lover of music or tone deaf; everyone who was anyone wanted to be present at the greatest musical event of the season. At half past five in the afternoon the Dauphin and Dauphine arrived, with the Counts and Countesses of Provence and Artois,* followed by a galaxy of state coaches from Versailles. The Princesse de Lamballe, the Duchesses of Chartres and Bourbon were already in their boxes. Even the ministers were present: the Duc d'Aiguillon and the Chancellor Maupeou, ministers who no longer dared to antagonize a princess who might so soon be queen. According to one account, the majority of the audience remained unreceptive, disconcerted and unable to comprehend a music so completely alien to what they had been taught to admire: 'Admittedly some of it was sublime, but a great deal of it was boring; the ballet, so essential a part of French opera, was almost non-existent and the décor was mediocre.' But the Dauphine's enthusiasm and her constant applause, an applause which the rest of the royal party was obliged to emulate, turned the evening into a triumph, and among that fashionable Parisian audience there were a few who were reduced to tears 'by that unique musical experience' and who, like Julie de Lespinasse, filled pages in praise of a 'music which can raise one to the heights of joy and plunge one into the depths of despair'. A message which meant more to Gluck than all the applause of Versailles was a letter handed him by an errand boy at the end of the performance – and signed by Jean Jacques Rousseau.

Monsieur le Chevalier Gluck, I have just come from your opera *Iphigenia*. I find it delightful. You have achieved what till now I believed to be impossible. *Iphigenia* changes all my ideas. It proves that the French language is as adaptable as any other to a musical style at once strong, touching and sensitive.

Inadvertently Marie Antoinette had been responsible in bringing together two of the greatest geniuses of the century.

* The Comte d'Artois married Marie-Thérèse, sister of the Comtesse de Provence, in November 1773.

8

'Sire, one must be ill at Versailles.' The royal surgeon was not a man to mince his words and when the King fell ill at Le Petit Trianon he insisted that the King be brought in his dressing gown by carriage to the palace. Lately King Louis had been spending more and more time in the classical pavilion built by Gabriel in the middle of those famous botanic gardens which had given him so much pleasure in his youth. But now he had lost interest in the rare plants and flowers which celebrated botanists had brought back from the Indies and Antilles – the forty varieties of strawberries, the enormous pineapples he sent as gifts to his fellow monarchs. The only attraction of Le Petit Trianon lay in its privacy, for it was a place where he could relax with his mistress and a few chosen companions and escape from the cabals and dissentions of his court. None of his relations ever attended the intimate little supper parties at Trianon where the royal mistress set the tone.

On 27 April the King had insisted on going out hunting though he had already felt ill on the previous evening. After a few hours sitting huddled in a carriage, he had returned to his room shivering with a high fever. But his entourage still tried to keep his illness a secret from Versailles, and it was not until the morning of 28 April that the news reached the palace and the ears of Madame Adelaide, who for the first time in the whole of her frustrated life found herself in control at Versailles. The King was brought to her apartments while his rooms were being prepared. But no sooner was he installed in his own bed than he made it clear that he wanted Madame du Barry to keep him company, and neither the doctors nor his daughters dared to send away the one woman through whom he maintained his hold on life.

Two days later it was confirmed that His Majesty was afflicted with a particularly virulent form of smallpox, the dread disease which in the past hundred years had proved so fatal to the ruling house of France. No sooner was it known than the Dauphin and Dauphine and the Counts of Provence and Artois were banished from the vicinity of the sick room, though Marie Antoinette, who had had the illness as a child, begged to be allowed to stay with her grandfather, a gesture which even her enemies could not fail to admire. But it fell to the King's daughters, none of whom had had smallpox, to make the heroic decision of remaining to nurse their father, a decision which was not entirely appreciated by the King who, in spite of the terrible risk of contagion, still wanted his mistress by his bedside. The poor Comtesse was involuntarily forced into the role of heroine, not only by the King, who with sublime egotism kept asking her to feel his forehead, but also by the Duc d'Aiguillon and the so-called Dévot Party, who were doing all in their power to keep the King alive and postpone the dreaded day of the public confession. In his journal the Duc de Croy, one of the few brave and devoted courtiers who carried on his duties to the end, describes the unedifying spectacle of the rival parties disputing the King's soul; how the old Archbishop of Paris was kept from approaching the King's bed and the Duc de Fronsac threatened to throw a humble little *curé* from Versailles out of the window if he dared talk of confession. By the evening of 4 May the King knew that he was dying, and with admirable lucidity he summoned the Duc d'Aiguillon to make plans for the Comtesse's departure. The Duke, who now realized that he had nothing further to lose, made a generous gesture and offered her the hospitality of his house, which was no more than a few miles from Versailles – not far enough to satisfy the priests and the general public who had been clamouring for her dismissal.

The Comtesse, who really loved the King, left in a flood of tears, travelling simply in a hired carriage so as not to expose herself to the insults of the crowds who in the past days had been gathering round the palace, drawn not by their affection or love for the King, but out of idle curiosity. Those who like the Duc de Croy were really fond of their master were disgusted by the indifference of the majority of his subjects. The town of Versailles was crowded with holidaymakers, enjoying the first spring sunshine without giving a thought to the man dying in the palace. Forty hours of prayer had been ordered throughout the country, but the churches remained empty. And only a handful of courtiers, held by the privileges of their position, were forced to remain on duty in the infected sick room and put up with the pestilential smell emanating from the suppurating pustules of a body which was already beginning to decay.

Stoically the three princesses remained by the bedside of their father who, with his mistress's departure, had given himself up to death and repentance. Finally the priests were satisfied that the King was ready for the confession he had not made for well over thirty years. And early on the morning of 7 May the solemn procession of the holy sacraments, borne by the Grand Almoner of France, attended by courtiers in full regalia and preceded by a galaxy of priests and bishops, passed from the chapel, along the galleries lined with troops of the Household Cavalry and Swiss Guards, up the so-called staircase of the Dauphine which led to the royal apartments. Behind the host walked the Dauphin, the Dauphine and the rest of the royal princes, followed by all the ministers of state. By order of the King none of them was allowed to proceed beyond the council chamber. Only two princes of the blood royal, Orléans and Condé, both of whom had already had the disease, were allowed to come near the King's bed and hold the napkin of the dying communicant – and as a crowning irony they were the two princes who hated him most. Those who were praying in the council chamber could see through a vista of rooms the terrifying spectacle of the King lying on a camp bed, his head swollen to twice its natural size and black with encrusted scabs, while the priests hovered round waiting for him to make the public confession demanded as the price of his repentance. The Archbishop came to the threshold of the royal apartments to read aloud the words to the assembled court: 'Gentlemen, His Majesty desires me to tell you that he begs pardon of God for having transgressed and brought scandal on his name. Should God in his mercy give him back his health, he promises that henceforth he will try to uphold the faith and his religion and dedicate himself entirely to the welfare of his people.'

King Louis, who remained lucid throughout this declaration, was heard to say, 'If only I had the strength to say these words myself.' For two days he lingered on, conscious almost to the last, while the stench became so over-powering that loyal servants were carried fainting from the room and the courtiers on duty huddled by the door, in deadly peril of their lives.

The end came at a quarter past three of the afternoon of 10 May when an usher threw open the doors of the Oeil de Bœuf and called out, 'Gentlemen, the King is dead.' There followed a general stampede with ambitious courtiers pushing and clawing their way to be among the first to congratulate the new King.

Struggling to hold back their tears, the royal couple appeared on the threshold of the Dauphine's apartments, both of them looking pathetically young and inexperienced. In the past week, while ministers had continued to attend dinners and receptions, Louis Auguste had spent most of the time in prayer. Two days before the end he had sent 200,000 francs out of his privy purse to be distributed to the poor of Paris, and now the first act of his reign was to renounce the money voted to him on his accession. The Queen followed his example by giving up the *Droit de Ceinture*, a medieval tribute dating from the days of the jewelled belt and chasuble, and it was charac-teristic of Marie Antoinette to make light of her action by saying that anyway belts were not being worn any more.

By four in the afternoon the sixteen state coaches, each of them drawn by eight horses which had been waiting all day outside the palace, were already under way to take the royal family out of the contaminated atmosphere of Versailles. It was agreed that for the first nine days they were to remain in seclusion at Choisy, without seeing any of the ministers who had been in contact with the late King. Seventeen people who had been on duty at the palace were already known to have died, and such was the fear of contagion that none of the courtiers who came to pay homage to Louis Auguste were permitted to kiss his hands. The young King had loved his grandfather and was shattered by his death and by the appalling burden which had fallen on his shoulders. His first words on hearing the news had been, 'I am the most unhappy man in the world.' Only his strong religious feelings and sense of duty kept him from giving way and his first written orders were clear and concise. He was to be known as Louis – Louis x v i – and all the ministers, governors and administrative officers who had served under his grandfather were to remain for the present at their posts. But everyone knew that d'Aiguillon's days were numbered and everyone hoped for a clean sweep of the corrupt and unpopular government. Choiseul's supporters were already gathering strength, relying on the backing of the young Queen.

Marie Antoinette, who ever since the King's illness had been forced to assume responsibilities foreign to her nature, was on the verge of a nervous breakdown. The uncongenial company of her Piedmontese sisters-in-law with whom she had partaken every meal in the past weeks and the continual exhortations of her mother's ambassador had combined to undermine her morale. But she was far from being the sentimental, frightened girl described in the memoirs of Madame Campan, and her tears for King Louis did not go very deep.

In one of her first letters as Queen to the Empress she was already writing, 'The public expect a lot of changes from the new regime. The King has already dispatched the "creature" to a convent and banished all her relatives from court. He owed this to the people of Versailles who, when the late King was dying, had attacked the carriage of Madame de Mazarin, one of the favourite's most intimate friends.' Maria Theresa was shocked by her daughter's vehemence towards Madame du Barry when 'the unfortunate creature had lost everything and was more in need of pity than anyone else'. Actually the terms of the banishment were mild as the Comtesse was the first to admit, for she was allowed to retain all the property and jewellery given her by her royal lover and within a year was allowed to return to her pavilion at Louveciennes.

While Louis x v i drove off to Choisy through miles of cheering crowds, the death of a monarch who had reigned for some sixty years passed unregretted by his subjects. The whole country was plunged into mourning, but the few who had really loved King Louis were shocked by the indifference of the majority of the people. On the day after his death there appeared the first of a series of popular ditties besmirching his memory:

> *Louis a rempli sa carrière*
> *et fini ses tristes destins.*
> *Tremblez voleurs, fuyez putains,*
> *vous avez perdu votre père.*

Louis has brought his career to an end
and accomplished his sad fate.
Tremble all robbers and flee all harlots
for now you have lost your father.

Only the priests remained in the stinking room of the deserted palace, where no one dared to approach the corpse till ordinary labourers from the town of Versailles were summoned by force to place the body in a leaden casket packed with aromatic herbs. Secretly by night, escorted by bodyguards, the remains of the king who in his youth had been known as 'Louis the Well-beloved' were conveyed in a coach and six to his last resting place in St Denis.

The King is dead. Long live the King! The joy of the Parisians was almost indecent. So much was expected of the new reign and of that timid young man who had nothing more to offer than his good intentions. 'What is certain,' wrote Marie Antoinette to her mother, 'is that the King has a real taste for economy and the greatest desire to make his people happy. He needs and wants to learn and I only hope that God will reward his good will.' But already there was intriguing in the background. Madame Adelaide and her sisters had been sent in quarantine to a small house in the grounds of Choisy. People questioned, 'Why so near?' 'Why expose the King to such a risk?' But Madame Adelaide was now determined to play the role she had been waiting for for so long. Before she and her sisters all succumbed to smallpox, she succeeded in conveying a letter to the King containing a list of reliable ministers compiled by his father, the late Dauphin. The two top names were Machault and Maurepas, excellent men in their youth, who had incurred the resentment of la Pompadour and been sent into exile for twenty-five years while Louis xv forgot their existence. Both of them were now seventy-three and somewhat old to advise a twenty-year-old king. But most of the younger men available belonged to the party of Choiseul, and Choiseul was the one person Louis Auguste was determined never to have in his government. His first public statement, in which he promised to protect religion, which was sadly in need of protection, to avoid corrupt and wicked men and look after his people, made it sufficiently clear that he would never appoint a man who had been responsible for the outlawing of the Jesuits and who was known to be a friend of Voltaire. Madame Adelaide had won her first battle over Marie Antoinette, who had counted on bringing back Choiseul. Many of the ex-minister's friends regretted that none of the King's aunts had died of the smallpox. By the end of May they were out of danger and Madame du Deffand, a courtier who had no love for Mesdames, wrote, 'The avenging angel has sheathed his sword. Once again we shall find the three spinsters installed at the new court, weaving their petty intrigues.'

The outbreak of smallpox at Choisy sent the royal family to La Muette. And in the smallest and most delightful of all the summer palaces was spent what was described as the 'honeymoon of the new reign'. The Bois de Boulogne, which had previously been closed when the court was in residence there, was now thrown open to the public and, unattended by guards, the young King and Queen could be seen walking arm in arm like any bourgeois couple. The Duc de Croy describes 'those first summer days when the charming little Queen went riding in the woods, together with her great friend the Princesse de Lamballe, as attractive and as graceful as she was. It was delicious – all Paris came out and it was like one continual fête. Everyone looked happy and there were shouts of joy, and even clapping of hands.'

Once when the Queen was out riding she came across the King who was walking alone, whereupon she dismounted and ran towards him and he took her up into his arms and, to the delight of the public, 'planted two good kisses on her cheeks'. On other occasions Marie Antoinette and her sisters-in-law would be seen sitting on a bench in the forest picnicking off strawberries and milk. Small wonder that the romantic Duke described such scenes of arcadian simplicity as 'delicious'.

But for all his good intentions towards the Queen, Louis made her understand from the very beginning that he wanted neither suggestions nor advice. The very mention of Choiseul was sufficient to reduce him to silence, and two days after his accession the seventy-three-year-old Comte de Maurepas, a witty and amiable gentleman, did after all receive a flattering letter from the young King, asking him to act as his mentor and adviser: 'I am only twenty years old and lack both knowledge and experience.... I have always heard of your probity and of the great reputation you have acquired in the handling of affairs, which is why I beg of you to give me your valuable help and advice.' In a sense it was a wise choice, for it offended no one except the Queen who, however angry, did not dare to question her husband's choice. Maurepas was a man who was known to be without ambition, who had no desire for the post of prime minister and was content to be no more than the confidential adviser of the King.

In Vienna, Maria Theresa, who was more sceptical about the new adviser's shortcomings, wrote to her daughter: 'I am only astonished at the choice of Maurepas, for which I presume Mesdames are responsible. How unwise to have let them come to Choisy and at what a risk.' Unlike Marie Antoinette, neither she nor her minister Prince Kaunitz had wanted the return of Choiseul, who was far too jealous of French prestige to countenance Austria's expansionist policy. Both would have preferred a weak, accommodating minister like d'Aiguillon. But d'Aiguillon had not only earned the hatred of the Queen but of the greater part of the French nation, and not even the fact that Maurepas' wife was his aunt could save him from dismissal. It was a dismissal accompanied by a golden handshake of no less than 500,000 francs, a sum which in view of his general unpopularity was sufficient to arouse the fear that the young King, of whom so much was expected, would end by being as weak as his predecessor. Maria Theresa was the first to disapprove of her son-in-law's generosity 'which has aroused considerable comment not of admiration for his kindness, but of fear that he is going to allow himself to be led by others and end in having favourites'.

In a letter unusually mature for an eighteen-year-old girl, Marie Antoinette replied to her mother's criticism:

For the moment there is nothing but praise and admiration for the King, which he thoroughly deserves because he is so honest and so anxious to do good. But I am worried as to how long the enthusiasm of the French will last. From the little I understand of politics, it seems that things are very difficult at present, and that the late King has left the country in a very bad state. It is impossible to please everybody in a country where the people are so volatile and impatient that they want to have everything done at once. But the King will never be as weak as his grandfather, nor I hope will he ever have favourites.... Though I fear he may be too gentle and easygoing, as in letting Monsieur de Maurepas give 500,000 francs to Monsieur d'Aiguillon.

Marie Antoinette had every right to resent the enormous sum being given to a minister who had done nothing but intrigue against her in the past years, when it was only after tears and pleading that she had succeeded in obtaining the recall of the Duc de Choiseul from banishment.

The court had barely returned to Versailles when the ex-minister appeared to pay homage to the King. While Marie Antoinette was at her most gracious and most charming towards 'the man who was responsible for making her the happiest woman in the world', Louis was rude and almost offensive. 'You have aged a lot, Monsieur de Choiseul. You have put on a lot of weight and lost a lot of hair.' And before the Duke could reply he had already turned his back. The Comte de Provence, who was now known as 'Monsieur', had the politeness to ask after the Duchess. But by now Choiseul had realized that the support of the young Queen was not sufficient to destroy the enmity the older Dauphin had transmitted from the grave through his three sisters to his eldest son. Choiseul left Versailles still wearing the mask of smiling indifference he adopted throughout his life. In Paris there were cheering crowds outside his house, but he was elegant in defeat and, having no wish to make trouble for the young King, he went back to his estates in Touraine.

Would history have been different had Choiseul come back to power and been in a position to advise the young Queen in those first dangerous years? He alone might have made an Austrian princess into a really French queen, something which, for all his good intentions, Comte Mercy could never do. The ambassador would always act first and foremost in the interests of the Empress, and in spite of her wisdom Maria Theresa made many mistakes. Her intense dislike of Prince Louis de Rohan and her determination to have him recalled from Vienna, thereby offending one of the most important families in France, was hardly calculated to win her daughter friends among the Rohans. Nor were her continual demands in favour of the Lorraines, who were both envied and disliked in France, likely to enhance her popularity. But perhaps unwisest of all was her insistence on the Abbé Vermond retaining his post as reader to the Queen. Neither Comte Mercy nor the Empress appear to have taken into account that the Abbé was so disliked by the young King, who looked on him as a creature of Choiseul's, that he never addressed him a word. A stronger man would have dismissed Vermond, but the Queen's devotion to her servant prevented Louis from making a decision which would have caused endless scenes and tears of the kind that he had already learnt to dread.

The only decision taken by the King that was said to have been influenced by his wife was over his inoculation against smallpox. So far none of the Bourbons had followed the example of the northern courts where inoculation had been practised for the past twenty years. The news that the King and both his brothers, neither of whom as yet had any heirs, were to be vaccinated at the same time was generally considered to be both dangerous and foolhardy. As Louis was known to be against any form of operation and had been heard to say that he would rather die than be inoculated, Marie Antoinette, whose six brothers and sisters had been inoculated in Vienna, was generally held to be responsible. The whole country, and in particular the provinces, was in a state of suspense. Shares on the stock exchange fell to their lowest level. Numberless petitions were presented to the King begging him not to undergo such a dangerous operation and all those who were against the Austrian Queen were loud in their denunciations. Not even the successful outcome of the inoculations spared her from the accusation of being a dangerous influence on the King. Only Marie Antoinette knew how little she counted in her husband's life and how lonely and friendless it could be in the thousand-room palace of Versailles.

The age of favourites was over. After over a hundred years the country had at last a Queen of whom every Frenchman could be proud. But Marie Antoinette had only been a year upon the throne before she was subjected to calumny and libel, which came not from the Parisians who adored her, but from the salons of Versailles, enabling an unscrupulous adventurer like Beaumarchais, at the lowest ebb of his fortunes, to profit by the situation. The minister of police who had been willing to pay thousands of livres to suppress a libellous pamphlet against the King's mistress was ready to pay still more to suppress a libel against the innocent young Queen. The terrible pamphlet – which Beaumarchais claimed to have discovered in London in the possession of a wealthy Jew – contained all the inflammatory ingredients calculated to excite a minister such as Monsieur de Sartines, who was anxious to prove himself to the new government. Entitled *Advice to the Spanish line of Bourbon*, the publication was in the form of a letter and dwelt on the King's impotence and the Queen's adulterous intentions. Beaumarchais informed Monsieur de Sartines that it would need a clever agent with large funds at his disposal to obtain possession of a pamphlet which was due to appear both in London and Amsterdam. Whether or not Sartines realized that the whole story was a hoax, it nevertheless provided a useful opportunity of proving his efficiency. He suggested to King Louis that Beaumarchais, who had so many useful connections in England, would be the most suitable person to employ on such a delicate mission. At first the King was reluctant to give authorization to a man whom he trusted as little as Beaumarchais, but under pressure from Sartines he finally consented to supply the official credentials.

In Beaumarchais, this man of many parts, the artist now took over from the swindler. Allowing his imagination to run riot, he pursued the mythical Jew from England to Holland and from Holland into Germany, where he staged a bogus assault on his person in a forest outside Nuremberg and claimed to have finally overpowered him, seized the manuscript, and to be now on his way to Vienna. Even Sartines must have found it hard to accept this fantastic story as the truth, but he did not dare to disavow his own actions or throw suspicions on a man he himself had supplied with a letter from the King.

Beaumarchais hoped to find in Vienna new victims for his talents, but neither the Empress nor her ministers were as gullible or as cynical as their French counterparts, and Beaumarchais was given a frigid reception at the

Hofburg, where his official credentials obtained him an Imperial audience. But his arts of persuasion had no effect on the Empress who was disgusted by the libellous accusations brought against her daughter. The pamphlet was handed over to Prince Kaunitz, who had no hesitation in declaring it to be a fake, and Beaumarchais was placed under house arrest while the whole of his fantastic story was investigated by the police. In custody he appears to have completely lost his head, constantly contradicting his own story, and at the end of several weeks he was released and ignominiously expelled from the country. But such was the corruption in France that Sartines refused to accept Prince Kaunitz's judgement, while Maurepas was so amused by Beaumarchais' description of his fictitious adventures that he persuaded the young King that he was no more than a harmless lunatic who should not be taken seriously. This lenient attitude surprised even Beaumarchais, and shocked Prince Kaunitz, leading him to wonder whether Sartines himself had been part of the conspiracy or whether France was so rotten that her ministers and even the King were amused by imposters.

Prince Kaunitz kept his opinion to himself, but Maria Theresa gave full vent to her indignation in writing to her ambassador.

> I never imagined that the inveterate hatred against the Austrians, my own person and that of the poor innocent Queen was still so deeply ingrained in the French. Is this what all the adulation, the love they profess to have for my daughter comes to in the end? Nothing could be more revolting, more calculated to make me despise a nation which possesses neither religion, morals nor sentiment. I am not going into the details of the whole story, but I am annoyed we had the man arrested. It would have been better to have treated him from the first as an imposter and dispatched him within hours across the frontier, letting him understand that one was in no way his dupe and only let him go out of charity. I can foresee that we will still have a lot of trouble from him. Sometimes it is better to know too little than too much. Prince Kaunitz's interest and curiosity was aroused by the name of this miserable scoundrel who appears to have been the leading figure in the celebrated Goezman trial and the author of those *Memorials* which were so popular and which everyone here was reading last winter – everyone except me for I take no pleasure in that kind of thing. It only saddens me to think that someone can waste his time and talents in making fun of matters which should be taken seriously. But by now you have had enough of listening to my grievances. I am absolutely outraged and am only curious to know what will be the reactions in France. I am not saying much to my daughter as I do not want her to realize by what knaves and traitors she is surrounded – And as yet no hope of an heir.

Marie Antoinette, who secretly resented the casual attitude taken by the King, nevertheless upheld him in writing to her mother: 'I had forgotten to tell you about Beaumarchais. The King informed me himself. This is again an occasion on which he has shown me his confidence and friendship. He looks upon the man as a harmless lunatic and I think he is right.' Comte Mercy however wrote to his mistress that the Queen had no sooner heard the story, than she summoned him to Versailles and demanded to know why he had kept it a secret from her for so long. The King had now spoken to her of the libel, but in such a way as to make her suspect that he had never read it, treating it as if it were a matter of no consequence, which only upset him because it was distressing to the Empress. The Queen had declared that it was far more distressing for her than for her mother, and she requested him to make every effort to unravel the truth of the whole extraordinary story and to prevent any fresh copies of the libel from being circulated in France.

The ambassador was of the same opinion as Prince Kaunitz in considering Beaumarchais to be a dangerous scoundrel whose talents in some way were useful to his government. Neither Sartines nor Count Maurepas was ready to prove the story fictitious and both defended Beaumarchais as someone who might on occasion be careless and unscrupulous but had never until now been definitely dishonest. The result was that the man who had returned to his country as an outcast was now daring to complain of the outrageous treatment he had received in Vienna, and Prince Kaunitz thought it wisest to put an end to the affair by paying him the sum of a thousand ducats to compensate for his imprisonment. Playing the part of an offended gentleman, Beaumarchais refused to accept the money and the Imperial Ambassador was forced to swallow his indignation and present him with a handsome diamond ring.

This incident gave Maria Theresa an insight into what her daughter had to expect in a country where the King was too weak and his ministers too cynical to defend the honour of their Queen and where the Queen herself was too young and lighthearted to recognize the dangers which lay ahead. Marie Antoinette was not as lighthearted as she had led her mother to believe. Her four years in France had taught her to adapt herself to the people among whom she had to live and to content herself with a husband who was neither a lover nor a companion, and who since his accession had been so taken up with the formation of the new government that his visits to her apartments were even less frequent than before. The rooms communicating directly with the King's apartments, which had formerly been those of Madame du Barry, were now occupied by Comte Maurepas, who had access to Louis at all hours of the day and who in his fear of being supplanted by Choiseul was doing everything in his power to estrange Louis from the Queen.

In his cold undemonstrative fashion Louis was devoted to his young wife. But there were times when her overbubbling spirits and noisy laughter got on his nerves, when her explosive temper and sudden tears embarrassed him. He tried to make up for his inadequacies as a husband with an unfailing generosity, and Marie Antoinette wrote in triumph to her mother of the King's largesse, that her personal allowance had been doubled to the sum of 200,000 livres a year and that she had been given the pavilion and gardens of Le Petit Trianon where now even the King was to be her guest.

Comte Mercy painted a less rosy picture of life in the palace of Versailles, of the jealousy of the Piedmontese sisters-in-law who refused to pay the young King and Queen the ceremonial morning visit they had always paid to their grandfather, of the youthful impertinences of the seventeen-year-old Comte d'Artois who disregarded etiquette to the extent of passing in front of the King and even on occasion interrupting him in speech. Still worse was his familiarity towards the Queen, who was seen far too much in his company. The Comte de Provence was more circumspect in his behaviour and always treated the King and Queen with the greatest deference. But on looking through his grandfather's papers, Louis had come across some letters which proved his brother to have been intriguing against him with the Duc d'Aiguillon, a discovery which cost the ambitious Stanislas Xavier his seat in the Council of State. Nevertheless the King was determined there were to be no quarrels in the family and that they were all to live on the same terms of intimacy as before. Artois' indiscretions were invariably condoned and 'Monsieur' was never curbed in his extravagant tastes in building and in collecting works of art.

Louis was still more indulgent in his treatment of his aunts. Mesdames Victoire and Sophie, who had been sharing a household, now demanded separate establishments – a matter which entailed considerable expense. When the princesses went on their yearly cure to Vichy, a watering place they had recently brought into fashion, they never travelled with a retinue of less than three hundred people. And no minister, not even the new controller-general Monsieur Turgot, who was pledged to a policy of economic reform, dared to suggest that the expenditure could be reduced. Madame Adelaide was still a power to be reckoned with and Comte Maurepas, the minister she had brought to power, was a constant visitor to her salon, where her former music master, that 'charming, witty Monsieur de Beaumarchais', was back in favour entertaining her guests with his brilliant imitations of Prince Kaunitz and of the Empress Maria Theresa, and his scathing accounts of life in the Hapsburg Empire. Among those who paid court to Madame Adelaide were her cousins the Princes of Condé and Conti, both of them bitter opponents of Choiseul and of the Austrian alliance. In Comte Mercy's opinion, those elegant apartments giving out on the gardens of Versailles were a hotbed of intrigue directed against the Queen, where charming little ditties spiced with malice would be heard by Mesdames with deprecating smiles.

The ambassador's reports brought little cheer to the ageing Empress. When Comte Mercy described the King as being 'too good' she knew that he meant 'too weak', and what would happen to her daughter with a husband who was too weak and too indifferent to give her either counsel or advice? 'You are both so young and the burden is so heavy. I am worried – terribly worried as to what is going to happen,' wrote Maria Theresa.

But at nineteen the Queen was only too ready to make light of her burdens and to rejoice in the fact that she was no longer under the tutelage of her aunts. 'No one can say any longer that they rule me. As for Monsieur and Madame, I have no choice other than to accept them for what they are and though the Comte d'Artois can be very thoughtless at times, I know when it is necessary to put him in his place.'

Marie Antoinette was still so young, so ready to enjoy herself, and d'Artois was the only member of the family who enabled her to escape from the ennui of Versailles. But d'Artois had dangerous companions, and the most dangerous of all was his cousin, Philippe d'Orléans, Duc de Chartres, who attracted to the Palais Royal all the most dissipated elements of Paris. There the gambling stakes were high, the drinking excessive and the prostitutes the prettiest and most expensive in Paris. Artois admired his older cousin for his immense wealth, his sartorial elegance and fashionable anglomania. The first horse races held on the Plaine des Sablons, organized by Chartres and Artois, were attended by the Queen, whose presence in the company of her brother-in-law and a group of dashing young sportsmen all betting for enormous stakes was immediately reported back to a disapproving mother. Nor was it appreciated by the older courtiers of Versailles when her majesty was seen driving out alone with her brother-in-law in a little open cabriolet known as '*un diable*'. Still more criticized was her attendance at a fancy dress ball given in her honour by the Duc de Chartres. Till now no Queen of France had ever attended a ball at the Palais Royal. And it was significant that the King, who disliked his Orléans cousin, had declined to be present.

The Queen's presence at the Palais Royal was due not so much to Artois as to the Princess de Lamballe who in the past year had become her 'dearest and closest friend'. Marie Antoinette, who was loving and affectionate by nature, craved for friendship and in this fragile, unhappy young woman with the huge blue eyes and long blonde curls, she hoped to have found the ideal companion with whom to share the delights of Le Trianon and exchange mutual confidences of matrimonial experiences which for the one had been so tragic and the other so frustrating. It was the age of sentimental friendships, when women who had little to do would exchange long and soulful letters, addressing one another as 'Dearest Heart'. And Marie Thérèse de Lamballe, clinging, delicate and abnormally sensitive, was the very person likely to attract someone as lonely as Marie Antoinette.

For all her sensitivity and easy tears, Madame de Lamballe was as much a place seeker as anyone else at Versailles, and she had barely established herself in the Queen's favour before she had begun to solicit favours not only for herself but for her relations. Her brother, the Prince de Savoie-Carignan, for whom his cousins, the Piedmontese Princes, had already solicited in vain, wanted to be given the command of a French regiment, an appointment calculated to arouse jealousy and opposition both in the army and at court. But his sister was more determined and persistent than his cousins. By pleading her loneliness, her longing to have her brother living in France, she succeeded in persuading the Queen into espousing his cause. And the King ended in giving way against the advice of his minister of war.

One of the Princess's most irritating traits was her excessive pride and hauteur. Regarding herself as being of royal rank, she resented the fact that as a childless widow she had no official status at Versailles. She was financially dependent largely on the generosity of her father-in-law, the immensely wealthy Duc de Penthièvre, with whom she spent many months of the year isolated in the country. In her obsession for her new-found friend, Marie Antoinette was determined to procure for her a position which would keep her permanently at Versailles. The post of *'superintendant* of the Queen's household', which the late Queen had wisely suppressed as being costly, unnecessary and calculated to make trouble with the other ladies-in-waiting, was now revived for the benefit of a woman who was both too delicate and too inefficient to carry out duties which required infinite tact and great knowledge of the world. The King and his ministers were against the revival of the appointment. Monsieur Turgot, the controller-general, was particularly outspoken on the subject, refusing to consider it unless it was re-established on a more economical basis than in the past. But the Duc de Penthièvre, Louis XIV's last surviving natural grandson, declared that his daughter-in-law could only accept the position if it retained all its ancient prerogatives and rights. The Princess came in tears to the Queen, and the Queen came in tears to the King, and Comte Maurepas, who for the moment found it useful to ingratiate himself with Marie Antoinette, advised Louis to give way.

Marie Thérèse de Lamballe was now established at court in complete control of the Queen's household, with the enormous salary of 150,000 francs a year. Madame de Noailles was the first to be offended and lost no time in tendering her unregretted resignation. The lady of honour, the Princesse de Chimay, only consented to remain if her father the Duc de Fitz-James was created a marshal, for which he had so few qualifications that five other marshals had to be appointed in order to justify his promotion. When Comte Mercy ventured to upbraid the Queen on having given Madame de Lamballe such an unnecessary honour, she replied, 'I wanted to make my dear friend happy'.

There is no doubt that the Princess loved the Queen, as she was later to prove so heroically. But in Paris she lived in the world of the Palais Royal and had accepted both its habits and extravagances. Her salon, frequented by Marie Antoinette, was an Orléanist centre of which the Duc de Chartres and his friends were *habitués*. Among these was the young Duc de Lauzun, the most fascinating and accomplished of roués, who had dissipated a vast fortune by the time he was twenty-five and could claim mistresses in all the capitals of Europe. In memoirs which are largely apocryphal, Lauzun boasts of his conquest of the Queen. Madame Campan, the faithful woman of the bedchamber, admitted that there was a time when the handsome Duke was high in the Queen's favour and she records one occasion when Marie Antoinette was sufficiently unwise to admire and accept the gift of a beautiful heron feather he wore in his hat and even to appear wearing it at a ball. However, the Queen's natural modesty and purity – there were those who called it frigidity – prevented her from succumbing to libertines like Lauzun, and he was never forgiven when he abused the right to a private audience by attempting to make love to her.

Madame de Lamballe who was already in her middle twenties should have warned the young Queen of the Duc de Chartres and his friends. But she only cared about who or what was the fashion, '*le bon ton*', whether it was the masonic lodges of which Chartres was the grand master, or the modes of Mademoiselle Bertin. The little milliner from Abbeville who was now at the height of her fame dictated the fashions of Europe, and Marie Antoinette's towering head-dresses of gauze and plumes were copied by every elegant young woman from London to St Petersburg. No subject was too recondite or too bizarre to provide material for the milliner's fertile imagination. The funeral of Louis XV inspired the model of a cypress tree and of a rising sun which announced the new reign. The King's inoculation made a charming coiffure, with the serpent of Aesculapius twined round the olive tree of wisdom. Some of the would-be leaders of fashion went to the lengths of having reproductions of mountains, rivers and prairies on their heads. The Duchesse de Chartres, who was a particularly stupid woman, commemorated the birth of her first son with the scene of an *accouchement* made of gauze and horsehair. Bad taste went so far as to record the bread riots of the early months of 1775 with a bonnet called '*coiffure à la Révolte*'.

Though Marie Antoinette never went in for these extravagances, her coiffures of plumes and flowers rose to such dizzy heights that she could barely get into her carriage. From Vienna, the Empress wrote scolding letters deploring such outlandish fashions.

> I read in the gazettes that your head-dresses of ribbons and feathers get higher every day. You know that I have always been of the opinion that one should follow the fashions in moderation. A pretty young queen with natural attractions has no need to indulge in such follies. On the contrary a simple head-dress should only serve to enhance her charms and is also more suited to her rank. It is for her to set the fashion and everyone will follow whatever she chooses to do.

'It is true that I am interested in clothes,' replied Marie Antoinette, 'but as for feathers, everyone wears them and I would look extraordinary if I was the only one to appear without them.' It was not just her daughter's head-dresses that worried the Empress. The foreign gazettes gave long accounts of the brilliant and costly festivities of Versailles, of the Queen's incognito visits to the opera balls, 'in the company of her brother-in-law but never with the King'.

The Queen's life was one of constant dissipation and the Abbé Vermond reported that she did not open a single book. In the role of tutor rather than of ambassador, Comte Mercy went so far as to remonstrate with the Queen on the subject of her flightiness and her late hours which were estranging her more and more from the King, who was always in bed before eleven. Marie Antoinette was sufficiently good-natured to hear him to the end. Then dropping her usual smiling mask she defended herself on the grounds that her abnormal married life left her no other choice than to be frivolous, adding, 'You see, I am so terrified of being bored.'

Having obtained the dismissal of the Duc d'Aiguillon and failed in the attempt to restore Choiseul, the Queen lost most of her interest in politics, though she was at pains to listen on the rare occasions when the King spoke to her of his new government. The choice of Maurepas had on the whole been a wise one. A man without either prejudices or convictions, he had succeeded in reconciling widely divergent elements. Most surprising of all was the appointment of Jacques Turgot, a former *intendant* (administrator) of Limoges, to the post of controller-general. Turgot, a leader of the *Philosophes* (free-thinkers), was generally recognized to be one of the most enlightened men in France. As *intendant* of Limoges, he had brought order and prosperity to one of the poorest and most heavily taxed districts in the country. But though he was a man of enormous intelligence and culture, he was totally lacking both in common sense and humanity, determined to abide by his principles against all opposition. The King had no liking for the *Philosophes* or for the intellectual salons of Paris, which acclaimed Turgot as an oracle, uncorruptible, totally committed to an economic policy of free trade in corn and the doing away of the closed corporations and monopolies, a policy which was bound to come up against all the vested interests in the country, and in particular those among the higher ranks of the nobility. But the country needed to be swept with a new broom, and Turgot, admired by the young, championed by the encyclopaedists, was a minister deliberately appointed to please Paris rather than Versailles.

In February 1775, the Empress' youngest son, Archduke Maximilian, a seventeen-year-old boy with nothing to recommend him beyond a certain vapid amiability, arrived in Paris on a visit to his sister. Maria Theresa had no illusions about the talents of her youngest born. In a letter of instructions for him, she wrote, 'Your utter indifference is what so often leads you to voluntary forgetfulness. Your "gauche" replies sometimes give you the air of an imbecile, while your banal remarks and bored expression are hardly calculated to stimulate those who are trying to interest you.'

Neither Kaunitz nor Mercy was in favour of the visit of this raw young man who would do nothing to enhance the reputation of the Hapsburgs and would cut a very poor figure at his sister's court. But for Marie Antoinette, Maximilian, only two years younger than she, was the little brother who had shared her games in their happy, carefree childhood at Schönbrunn. And she looked forward to his arrival with a touching eagerness. But the young Archduke was certainly not worth the trouble his sister took over his visit. The sights of Paris, the museums and the academies, Les Invalides and the Jardin du Roi, the celebrated botanical gardens, all left him indifferent. When the famous naturalist Buffon presented him with beautifully bound copies of his works, he committed the gaffe of refusing to accept them, saying he did not wish to deprive him of such valuable books. This remark went the rounds of Paris and the Hapsburg prince was labelled an idiot.

Travelling incognito under the name of the Count of Burgau, a form of travel always favoured by the Emperor, but one which required considerable tact and knowledge of the world, the Archduke had the arrogance to presume that the princes of the blood royal should treat the Count of Burgau as a Hapsburg prince and pay him the first courtesy visit. The princes, who for once were in the right, refused to comply and all the anti-Austrian elements at court upheld their decision. The Queen was sufficiently unwise to support her brother's pretensions, going so far as to upbraid the proud old Duc d'Orléans in public for having failed in his manners towards a member of her family whom the King had treated as a brother and invited to have supper alone with him in his private apartments, 'an honour I presume to which you have never dared to pretend'. Even Comte Mercy was shocked at this outburst, and he did his best to remedy the harm by inviting all the oldest and most important people at court, including the Queen's enemy the Duc d'Aiguillon, to meet the Archduke at a series of sumptuous soirées at the Austrian Embassy. But Marie Antoinette's popularity was on the wane and as yet there was no sign of an heir. A malicious little ditty circulated round the town reminding the Queen of her vulnerability.

Petite reine de vingt ans,	Little twenty-year-old Queen,
Vous qui traitez si mal les gens,	You who treat people so badly,
Vous repasserez la Barrière.	You will be sent packing
	across the frontier.

Lairela Lairela

In his kindly and chivalrous fashion the King stood by the Queen, and the princes were forbidden to appear at Versailles for the next fortnight. By then Marie Antoinette had listened to reason and wrote to her mother: 'When the Prince de Condé and his son came to a supper party at court, I treated them as if nothing had happened.' But the harm had already been done.

Marie Antoinette was among the first to realize that the Archduke's visit had been a failure. 'My little brother's departure made me very unhappy. For me it is terrible to feel I may never see him again. He was admired for his good manners and his attentions for everyone. Unfortunately he was very much criticized for the lack of interest he showed in all the places he visited. Perhaps it would have been better to have waited till he was older.'

It is curious that a woman as intelligent as Maria Theresa should have sponsored this visit. And it can only be explained by the fact that travelling with the Archduke, as his tutor or rather mentor, was a Count Rosenberg, who had been the Empress' friend and confidant for over forty years, and who could be counted on to give her an exact and detailed account of her daughter's life at the court of France. Maria Theresa was beginning to suspect that her ambassador was too partial, too much under the spell of the pretty young Queen and too inclined to blame the King for the failure of a marriage which in its fifth year was still unconsummated. The news of the pregnancy of the Comtesse d'Artois gave the Empress fresh fears for the future. Marie Antoinette was still loved in Paris, but when she drove through the streets, the fishwives hailed her with their raucous cries of 'Madame, when are you going to give us a dauphin?' Many a time she had come home in tears.

Mercy was one of the few who knew that underlying the gaiety and laughter was a streak of sadness, the growing melancholy of an unsatisfied and frustrated woman. Maria Theresa, who lacked her ambassador's subtlety and understanding, put it all down to the fact that 'they don't have our good German habit of sharing a double bed,' and she had been shocked to hear of the distance which separated the King's apartments from those of the Queen. Mercy had been instructed to see that her daughter had a secret passage and staircase made, which by passing through the inner apartments gave her closer access to the King.

However, Count Rosenberg told the Empress that neither husband nor wife took much advantage of this passage and that weeks went by without Louis visiting his Queen's room. As the mother of sixteen children, Maria Theresa was unable to reconcile herself to the idea that her daughter might be frigid, or if not frigid, indifferent, incapable of adapting herself to the King's habits and way of life. Rosenberg blamed it on her entourage of beautiful vapid women and wild young men who dragged her into a vortex of pleasure and made her feel it was more important to be the queen of fashion than to be Queen of France. Yet in spite of all her giddiness Marie Antoinette remained essentially pure.

The Prince de Ligne, one of the most charming noblemen of the 'St Empire' and the Queen's most fervent admirer, wrote, 'The love affairs she was accused of were never more than friendships for which she singled out a few, her behaviour the coquettishness of a woman, or rather of a queen, who wants to please the world. Even in the days of her youth, when her lack of experience might have encouraged us to be too much at our ease in her company, there was not one of us who would ever have abused her condescension. She always remained the Queen and we adored her without dreaming of being in love with her.'

In an immoral and corrupt society where there was not a woman without a lover, not a man who was free of debt, where the great ladies went to mass with pornographic novels hidden under their breviaries and where every job at Versailles was bought, where in the words of the Vicomte de Ségur, 'the courtiers cared for nothing but money and the young nobles walked on a carpet of flowers which covered an abyss,' the King and Queen remained the most honest members of their court.

Count Rosenberg did not hesitate to tell the Empress that Marie Antoinette was not in the least in love with her husband. A letter he had received from her after his departure left him under no illusions. Writing in a flippant vein, very different from the letters she addressed to her mother, she confessed, 'My tastes are not those of the King, who only enjoys hunting and making mechanical contraptions. You must agree I would look somewhat out of place in a forge. I could not be a Vulcan and if I took on the role of Venus, he would dislike it far more than my present dissipations, of which he in no way disapproves.'

Marie Antoinette never suspected that the wily old Maurepas was deliberately encouraging the King to tolerate the frivolities which would keep her out of meddling in politics. In the first years of his reign Louis had far too many problems to deal with to devote much time to his wife. But he took part in the court festivities and we hear of him appearing at a carnival ball, wearing the costume of King Henry IV, in a tableau representing a shooting party of the period; a happy idea on the part of the Queen of getting her husband to appear in the role of the most popular of monarchs. But he made no more than a perfunctory appearance at the balls which Marie Antoinette held twice a week in her private apartments and where he never stayed later than eleven o'clock. It was even said that the Queen and her friends sometimes put forward the clock to rid themselves of his awkward and unwanted presence.

But on the whole Marie Antoinette made genuine efforts to tame her 'Savage', to overcome his natural timidity and to get him more used to the society of women. The first of her reforms at court, and one which came up against the opposition of Mesdames, was to introduce little supper parties at which she and the King could entertain those whom they wanted to single out for favour. Until now etiquette had forbidden the Queen and the royal princesses from eating in the company of men other than their husbands. At these supper parties, the King would invite the gentlemen and the Queen the ladies. When she first broached the idea to the King, his immediate reaction was to refuse to commit himself without consulting the aunts. But this time Marie Antoinette was determined to have her own way and not to be bullied, and after an angry scene Louis ended by giving in. The first of these supper parties was deliberately arranged at a time when Madame Adelaide was confined to bed with a cold, and by the time she was well enough to reappear at court, the Queen's supper parties had become an accepted and welcome institution. On these occasions Marie Antoinette appears to have behaved with exemplary discretion in including older and distinguished courtiers among her guests, and the Duc de Croy was one of the many who were charmed by her affability.

For once the Empress was delighted. 'I find these supper parties an admirable idea. I would have preferred to have had them three times rather than once a week. But once a week is better than not at all, especially if the nights are better employed than they have been up to the present.' How tired Marie Antoinette must have been of her mother always harping back to the same subject, a subject which even the women in the Halles would not let her forget, which was talked of in every drawing-room and was of interest to every European court. In the old King's day her matrimonial problems had been openly discussed by her husband and his grandfather. Doctors had been consulted and remedies suggested. There was even question of an operation. But Louis had recoiled at the thought of a knife and ever since his accession the subject had been completely ignored. Marie Antoinette never knew how much her husband minded the ribald songs and scurrilous pamphlets which were circulating round Versailles and of which one of the most popular was:

Chacun se demand tout bas	Everyone asks in a whisper
Le Roi peut-il, ne peut-il pas?	The King – can he or can't he?
La triste Reine se desespère.	The sad Queen is in despair.

Lerela

L'un dit, il ne peut l'eriger,	One says he can't get it up,
L'autre, il ne peut y nìcher,	Another – he can't get it in,
L'autre, il est fluté traversière.	The other says he is crossed.

Lerela

Ce n'est pas là que le mal gît	It is not there that the trouble lies
Dit le Royal Clitoris	Says the Royal Clitoris
Mais il vient que l'eau claire.	But nothing comes out but clear water.

Lerela

The Comte de Maurepas, who was himself reported to be impotent, did his best to prevent these obscenities from reaching the King who, in the first years of his reign was too overwhelmed by work to pay much attention to the gossip and slander of Versailles. His grandfather had left behind him a sad heritage of debt, misery and discontent. And throughout the country from the princes of the blood to the families of the exiled magistrates who pleaded poverty and hardship, the people were demonstrating for the return of the old *parlements*. To quell this dangerous spirit Maurepas chose new ministers from among the '*Philosophes*' rather than from the nobles of Versailles. Apart from Turgot, there was Vergennes at the foreign office, St Germain at the war office and Malesherbes as secretary of state of the Maison de Roi, a position of enormous responsibility giving him power over the police, ecclesiastical affairs, and a large part of the provincial government. Of all these ministers Vergennes was the only one who remained in office till his death in the mid eighties. He was an accomplished diplomat who had done much to further French interests in Stockholm and in Constantinople where he had fallen out of favour with Choiseul by marrying somewhat injudiciously the Greek widow of a Phanariot merchant, an act which at the time lost him his post. Madame de Vergennes had not been received at Versailles until now, when at her mother's instigation Marie Antoinette persuaded the King to allow her to be presented at court, and she wrote, 'When I announced this to her husband he was touched almost to tears.'

The most surprising of the appointments was that of the seventy-year-old Comte de St Germain who succeeded to the war office on the death of the Comte de Muy. He was a brilliant and uncompromising soldier, who having quarrelled with his superiors had spent most of his life fighting abroad. But his reforms were no more popular with the soldiers than with the officers. His draconian measures of maintaining discipline and his attempt to introduce the Prussian form of corporal punishment with the flat end of the sword aroused such violent opposition throughout the ranks that he remained in office no more than a year.

Louis had not been many months upon the throne before Maurepas advised him to recall the old *parlements*. Both the King and his minister were fully aware of the danger of recreating an institution in which the revolutionary elements were always ready to make trouble. In a speech introducing the *lit de justice* which took place in the Grand Chamber of the Louvre King Louis said, 'Gentlemen, the King my honoured Lord and ancestor, was forced by your continued resistance to his authority to suspend your duties. Today I recall you to resume the functions which you should never have left. Be grateful for my clemency and never forget it.' But in spite of flowery speeches and graceful tributes to their young King and the adorable Queen, how many were really loyal in that assembly which nurtured so many future Jacobins, ambitious men only waiting for the tide of popular opinion to change in order to display their demagogic oratory?

Even the Queen who understood so little of politics was concerned over the outcome of the *lit de justice*. Until now she had always refused to allow Comte Mercy to talk to her of subjects too difficult for her to understand. But she was proud and delighted when on the evening before the opening of the *lit de justice* the King brought her a paper explaining the functions of the old *parlements*. And she lost no time in writing to her mother,

The chief business of the day, that of the parliament, is at last concluded. Though I did not want to interfere or to ask questions, I was very pleased at the confidence which the King has shown in me. My dear mother can judge this by the paper I am including. It is in the King's own handwriting and he gave it to me on the evening of the *lit de justice*. Everything went off perfectly and the princes of the blood came to see us the next day. I am so happy at the thought that there is no one any longer in exile or unhappy. When they suspended the *parlements* many of the princes and peers were in opposition. Today everything is settled. And yet it seems to me that if the King is able to maintain his authority, the monarchy will be greater and stronger than in the past.

So wrote the Queen with the optimism of her twenty years. But by the spring Turgot's reform for free trade in corn had met with bitter opposition and there were bread riots throughout the country, riots which in many cases had been maliciously provoked by a prince of the blood royal.

The most erroneous and also the most persistent of all the accusations brought against Marie Antoinette is that at the time of the bread riots of 1775, she is reported to have said, 'If they have not got bread, then let them eat cake.' It is a remark completely out of character in a woman whose chief fault lay in being too soft-hearted, too ready to solicit favours for her friends and obtain promotions for her servants. As a young dauphine she had been warned by Comte Mercy of the dangers of allowing herself to be exploited. Her kind heart showed itself in a hundred different ways. When out hunting she would be the only member of the royal family who even in the excitement of the kill would never drive or ride across a peasant's field of wheat. Should a groom or postilion meet with an accident, she would always be the first to stop and see that he was given proper medical treatment.

When Turgot's drastic reforms came up against the vested interests of the wealthy bourgeoisie and of the higher nobility, the Queen was far more concerned over the hardships of the poor than frightened by the bandits converging on Versailles. The King behaved with an admirable calm, refusing to submit to the rebellious parliamentarians who after being recalled in the name of liberty were doing all in their power to obstruct the liberal and far-reaching reforms put forward by Turgot. Loudest of all in his protests was the Prince de Conti, the cleverest but also the most mischievous of all the royal princes, to whom the suppression of the monopolies and the introduction of free trade meant the loss of a large part of his income derived from the business premises rented out in the precincts of his palace of the Temple. The King, acting largely on his own initiative, cowed the rebellious magistrates into submission by summoning a *lit de justice* in which he stood by Turgot's policies and accused certain mutinous elements in their midst of deliberately trying to starve the country by intercepting the grain ships and holding up transport to prevent the stocks from reaching the towns. The Prince de Conti whose age and position gave him the greatest licence to speak was the only one who dared to reply for the opposition. But Louis closed the session before he had finished his discourse.

Troops were called out. Bakeries were guarded and military convoys escorted the grain supplies to the capital. Within less than a fortnight complete order had been restored both in Paris and the provinces. Turgot and the King had triumphed. But now they had come to a parting of the ways. While Louis advocated clemency, his minister showed an unnecessary harshness in stamping out the mutiny, and in over-ruling the wishes both of the monarch and of the Grand Council. Two of the rioters, one of them a hairdresser, the other a workman caught pillaging a baker's shop, were summarily hanged and both of them went to the scaffold shouting: 'We die for the people.' At Versailles the young Queen wept on being told of their death and blamed the Abbé Vermond, a friend of Turgot's, for supporting such a brute. By now the greater part of the country had lost faith in Turgot. He had forfeited the friendship of his colleagues and the King was beginning to wonder if his controller-general was not too much of a theorist, too obstinately attached to a system.

The forthcoming coronation brought a further parting of the ways. For over twelve centuries the kings of France had been consecrated at Rheims, an act which had a tremendous spiritual significance for a man as deeply religious as King Louis. But for a free-thinker such as Turgot, the hierarchic ceremonies and costly pageantry of Rheims meant only unnecessary expense. To be crowned in Paris would not only give immense satisfaction to the people, but would attract far greater crowds and encourage commerce by bringing a large number of visitors to the capital. A change of tradition would also provide the opportunity to alter the archaic and by now obsolete oath in which the King had to swear 'to exterminate all heretics'. Louis listened patiently to every argument in favour and against the coronation at Rheims. But in his mind he was fully decided to follow in the steps of his ancestors and to be girt with the sword and invested with the crown of Charlemagne in the holy city of Rheims.

In the Queen's court there had been much whispering and speculation as to whether Her Majesty was to be included in the ceremony. In Vienna the Empress Maria Theresa appears to have had her doubts, for she wrote to her ambassador: 'I do not think they are going to accord the Queen the honour of being crowned with the King. You are quite right to have kept out of the affair and not to have let my daughter become involved in any intrigue.' Despite her attitude of smiling indifference, Marie Antoinette must have suffered at being relegated to the role of onlooker. Over two centuries had gone by since a Queen had been crowned at Rheims. The last three Kings, Louis XIII, XIV and XV, had all been unmarried at the time of their coronation, and there was no law of precedence to prevent Marie Antoinette from being crowned as Queen of France. In his subtle unobtrusive fashion Comte Mercy had done his best to carry out what, in spite of her instructions, he knew to be the secret wishes of his royal mistress. But he had come up against both Turgot and Maurepas who for once were united in their opposition; the former because he was anxious to avoid any further expenditure, the latter because he was determined to combat the growing influence of Choiseul, who since his return to Paris had been actively intriguing with the Queen and her friends. The very name of Choiseul was sufficient to decide the King, who in spite of his genuine affection for his wife had not yet lost his initial distrust of the Austrian archduchess who had been chosen for him by Choiseul.

Marie Antoinette had no part in the historic ceremony of Rheims, no place in the great procession which entered the city on the afternoon of 9 June 1775, in which the King sat alone in his painted gilded coach with the four white plumes on the roof and the horses harnessed in silver and gold, followed by sixteen other coaches carrying the princes of the blood royal, the ministers of state and the grand officers of the crown. Two detachments of cavalry, all wearing their gala uniforms, escorted him on a journey for which no less than 20,000 horses had been commandeered.

The Queen, who travelled with the King's young sisters, her sister-in-law, the Comtesse de Provence, and brother-in-law, the Comte d'Artois, had preceded her husband by several hours, arriving at Rheims on a clear moon-lit night. Despite the lateness of the hour the crowds still lined the roads to cheer the glittering procession of young and smiling faces, the exquisite court ladies in their flowered and feathered hats, the elegant young officers in the blue and gold uniforms of the Queen's household, the Comte de Provence, large and magnificent, bemedalled and bejewelled, and the Comte d'Artois, a dashing and brilliant figure on horseback, gaily responding to the greetings of the peasants of Champagne. Last in the procession came the Queen, a radiant vision in the moonlight making a brave effort to smile and to fight back the tears over the good wishes called out to Artois for the pregnant wife he had left behind at Versailles.

A few days later Marie Antoinette was writing to her mother, 'I do my best to respond to the enthusiasm of the people, and in spite of the heat and the enormous crowds, the fatigue I experience does not at all affect my health. For it is wonderful and at the same time astonishing to receive such a welcome only two months after the riots and with the price of bread which continues to be terribly dear. The extraordinary thing about the French character is how they let themselves be carried away by agitations and then almost at once come back to the right way of thinking. What is certain is that where one is so well treated by people who have so little to be grateful for, one feels oneself more than ever obliged to try to make them happy.'

It was a sincere letter reflecting the emotions she had experienced at Rheims after witnessing ceremonies in which she had seen her husband elevated to an almost superhuman height, ceremonies which free-thinkers such as Turgot and Condorcet might decry as 'out-dated and absurd', but which for the King and his people confirmed his divine right to rule. No one was more moved than the Queen at seeing the shy young man who cut such a poor figure in the drawing-rooms of Versailles transformed at Rheims into a godlike being, sanctified by the bishops when they anointed him with the holy oil from the miraculous phial of St Rémy, girded him with the sword and crowned him with the crown of Charlemagne. 'The sacred ceremony was perfect in every way,' she wrote. 'Everyone was delighted with the King, and rightly so. From the grandest to the humblest of his subjects all were equally enthusiastic. There was even a moment during the coronation when the ceremony was interrupted by an outburst of spontaneous acclamations. It was so touching that however much I tried I was unable to restrain my tears.' And for the assembled congregation, perhaps the most moving moment of the day was when the young King on noting his wife's tears gave her a look of beatific content.

For all the ceremony and pomp, Louis and Marie Antoinette had never been closer to their people than at Rheims. Though the Queen had no part in the ceremony, they were both lodged in the Archbishop's palace and on the evening of the coronation they could be seen walking arm in arm through the streets with no escort other than a captain of the guards. No effort was made to keep back the crowds who invaded the gallery of gilded wood which had been constructed to join the Archbishop's palace to the cathedral and for over an hour the royal couple mingled with the rapturous crowds.

The festivities lasted for four days with one ceremony following on the other. After the coronation came the solemn mass at St Rémy where, according to an age-old tradition, the King had to ride through the town on horseback and afterwards go out into the gardens to give the healing touch to thousands afflicted with scrofula, the so-called 'King's Evil'.

The Duc de Croy wrote that 'though the young King was lacking in the late monarch's majesty and beauty, his air of ineffable goodness more than compensated for his defects'. But it was the Queen who drew the loudest acclamations from the crowds, winning all hearts by her sweetness and her charm. The old Duke noted the presence of the Duc de Choiseul who had come to attend the ceremonies as a Knight of the 'Order of the Holy Ghost' and the absence of the Duc d'Aiguillon who, as the hereditary commander of the King's Regiment of Light Horse, was on his way to Rheims when he received an order to stay away, followed by a letter from the King instructing him to retire to his estates in Gascony.

No one doubted that d'Aiguillon's sudden exile was the direct work of the Queen. She herself boasts of it in a letter written to her mother's confidant, Count Rosenberg. 'The departure of that horrid man is entirely due to me. He had really overreached himself in spying and intriguing.' The tone of this letter is very different from the one she was writing to her mother in which she gives no hint of the political role she had been playing in the past months and which was so disturbing to the King's ministers.

For the past years the trial of the Comte de Guines had been one of those '*causes célèbres*' dividing society between his champions and his detractors. The Count, a friend and nominee of Choiseul and a popular figure at Versailles, was ambassador in London when he was accused of taking advantage of his position to smuggle contraband and speculate on the London

Stock Exchange. The accuser was one of his secretaries who had been used as a cover but whom he had refused to pay when some of his speculations had failed. It was an ugly case and both the *parlement* of Paris and the Grand Council had no hesitation in condemning him and in recalling him from his post. But by now it had developed into a political struggle between the followers of Choiseul and those of d'Aiguillon and the 'Dévots'. In appealing against the verdict, the ambassador accused d'Aiguillon of defaming his character. And the latter responded with a counter accusation.

The letters and memoirs of the day are full of nothing but this case, which dragged on for several years. Madame du Deffand, a friend of Choiseul's and a passionate defender of de Guines, writes of it at length in her correspondence with Horace Walpole. And all the Queen's set from the Comte d'Artois and the Duc de Chartres to the Princesse de Lamballe and the Princesse de Chimay looked upon the Count as the victim of the nefarious intrigues of the 'Dévots'. The Queen, who knew nothing about de Guines beyond the fact of his being a good dancer and an excellent flute player, espoused his cause with her customary enthusiasm. When the ambassador in preparing his defence wanted to make use of some secret documents in his ministerial files, the demand was quite rightly refused by Vergennes as encroaching on diplomatic privilege. But Marie Antoinette, worked on by his friends, made such a scene with the King, accusing Vergennes of deliberately favouring her enemies, that Louis ended in giving way and in over-ruling the decision of his minister. A letter and a memoir of the Comte de Guines were suppressed by the Grand Council for their libellous attack on the Duc d'Aiguillon, and again the Queen came to his defence in persuading the King to write to the ambassador, allowing him to make use of the material.

Marie Antoinette had no difficulty in influencing King Louis who had always been prejudiced against d'Aiguillon for his friendship and support of Madame du Barry. And in the end when de Guines was eventually acquitted and recalled to his post it was she who insisted on the Duc d'Aiguillon being sent into exile, a foolish action which won her many enemies, in particular the Comtesse de Maurepas of whom he was the favourite nephew.

The part played by Marie Antoinette in the trial of the Comte de Guines brought out both the best and the worst of her character, a passionate loyalty towards her friends, in this case Choiseul, and a childish rancour towards her enemies. A dangerous quality for a Queen was the fact that she was unable to forgive or to forget. Small wonder if a man like Maurepas considered that the young King had to be protected from his wife and in particular from Choiseul, whose secret manoeuvres in favour of his former ambassador had won him his acquittal.

D'Aiguillon was on his way to his estates in Gascony and Choiseul was at Rheims going around 'as always with his nose in the air', giving no hint of his impending ruin, the enormous debts which had already forced him to sell his

horses and his silver. The loss of the large revenues through the vindictiveness of Madame du Barry, in particular the income derived from the
commandership of the Swiss Guards which had reverted to the young Comte
d'Artois, had now brought him to the verge of bankruptcy. But the Queen was
determined that the ex-minister's presence at Rheims should not be entirely
ignored. And in a letter to Count Rosenberg so foolish and indiscreet as to
arouse the imperial thunders in Vienna she boasted of how cleverly she had
managed for the King himself to set the hour of her interview with Choiseul.

> You may have heard of an interview I gave to the Duc de Choiseul at Rheims. It
> has been so much spoken about that I would not be surprised if old Maurepas felt
> uneasy in bed. Naturally I was not going to see the Duke without first speaking to
> the King. But you will never guess how cleverly I managed so as not to give the
> impression of deliberately asking permission. All I said was that I desired to see
> Monsieur de Choiseul, but I did not know what day to choose. I did it so
> well that the *poor man* arranged himself the hour in which it would be most
> convenient for me to see him. You must admit that on this occasion, I displayed
> considerable feminine guile.

Count Rosenberg was so shocked at the way in which the Queen of France
referred to her husband as 'the poor man' that he felt in duty bound to show
the letter to the Empress. Maria Theresa was furious but her son the Emperor
was outraged. That cold, strange man, who was fonder of his little sister
than of any other member of his family, nevertheless looked upon her first
and foremost as a political pawn in an alliance, which was vital to his future
policies of aggrandizement in Bavaria and the Low Countries. Both he and
Prince Kaunitz were beginning to suspect that it was not only Louis who was
to blame for the failure of the marriage. Stories of her dissipation, exaggerated a hundred fold, had reached Vienna, circulated by the friends of Prince
Louis de Rohan. And Joseph was planning to come to France to judge for
himself of a situation which if allowed to continue could have deplorable
consequences. He wrote a scathing letter which the Empress was sufficiently
wise to intercept, knowing that Marie Antoinette would accept from a mother
what she would not tolerate from a brother:

> Can one write anything more impudent, more unreasonable and more unsuitable
> than what you wrote to Count Rosenberg regarding the way in which you
> arranged your meeting with the Duc de Choiseul? If ever such a letter went
> astray; if ever, and I don't doubt it, you should have used that kind of language
> with your intimates, then I can only foresee the gloomiest future for you, which
> on account of the affection I have for you would cause me infinite pain. Those
> who influence you in such behaviour are not your friends but your enemies.
> Believe me. Listen to the voice of a real friend, of a man whom you know loves
> you; to the only person who can tell you the truth. Do not meddle in public
> affairs. Try to gain the king's friendship and respect. First of all it is your duty,
> the only interest you should have at heart. Try to be with him as much as
> possible, but never be importunate and win his confidence through your affection
> and your discretion.

But Joseph's chilly censure could not wound Marie Antoinette like the letter which Maria Theresa saw fit to write to her wayward daughter and which Comte Mercy was the first to deplore.

I cannot hide from you the fact that the letter you wrote to Rosenberg absolutely horrified me. What a style! What flippancy. What has happened to the kind heart and generous nature of my Archduchess Antoinette? All I see here is intrigue, petty hatred, a persecution mania and an attempt at irony – the kind of intrigue that might have suited a Pompadour or a du Barry, but certainly not worthy of a Queen, a great princess, a decent good princess coming from the House of Austria and Lorraine. Your superficial successes and your flatterers have made me fear for you, seeing you indulge in a constant round of frivolity, wearing those ridiculous coiffures, going on constant pleasure trips with or without the King, knowing that he neither enjoys nor approves of them and only consents to them out of his goodness of heart. All my recent fears are more than confirmed by this letter. What language! 'The poor man'. Where is the respect and gratitude due in thanks for so much kindess and amiability? I leave you to your reflections and won't say anything more, though there is a lot more I could say.

In Comte Mercy's opinion she had already said too much. He, who knew Marie Antoinette far better than either Joseph or Maria Theresa, realized that she would never forgive being compared to a Pompadour or a du Barry. Her reply was the coldest letter she had ever written to her mother.

I would never dare to write to my revered mother if I thought myself half as guilty as she appears to believe me to be. To be compared to a Pompadour or a du Barry and branded with the most terrible epithets hardly applies to your daughter. I wrote a letter to a friend of yours and who I also believed to be a friend of mine. As he knows this country, he knows how easily one speaks. And I thought I did nothing wrong. But you seem to think differently. And in that case there is nothing for me to do but to bow my head and hope that in other circumstances you may think more kindly of me and judge me as I think I deserve.

To Comte Mercy she confessed, 'I could not write anything more. I was too upset. All I could show her was my respect.' But the ambassador noted that for the first time there was no word of love.

The festivities at Versailles continued throughout the summer, combining the celebrations in honour of the marriage of the King's sister Clothilde to the Prince de Piedmont, and the birth of a son and heir to the Comtesse d'Artois. The Queen's behaviour on these occasions was exemplary. She displayed an affectionate solicitude for fat, unattractive Clothilde, who showed very little feeling on leaving a court where she had no friend other than the royal governess, the Comtesse de Marsan, the most fascinating but also the most dangerous of all the Rohans, who had done nothing but intrigue against Marie Antoinette from the time of her arrival in France. The Countess was due to retire, but the Rohans had hereditary right to what was one of the most important positions at court and the post of governess to '*Les Enfants de France*' passed to her niece, the equally fascinating Princesse de Guéménée, daughter to the Prince de Soubise and married to yet another Rohan, whose friendship for the Queen was to prove as dangerous as the enmity of her aunt. Madame Elisabeth, the King's younger sister, a sensitive little girl of eleven, now came into the charge of this delightful but totally amoral woman who might well have had a corrupting influence had not the Queen watched over her young sister-in-law as tenderly as any mother, taking endless trouble to win the affection of a girl who had been prejudiced against her from her earliest childhood. 'She is a charming child, very sensitive and in despair over her sister leaving,' wrote Marie Antoinette. 'I am afraid I may grow too attached to her.'

The Queen showed even greater kindness in her treatment of the young Comtesse d'Artois at the time of her confinement, spending the last hours before the birth in her room, though she confessed to Mercy how much it cost her to see an heir to the throne who was not her own son. She even persuaded the Comte d'Artois to concentrate for a while on his wife and child and to stay away from the dissipations of the Palais Royal.

According to Comte Mercy, the festivities at Versailles were not as extravagant or as brilliant as usual. In an attempt at economy to please the King, Marie Antoinette had forbidden her ladies to have gold or silver ornaments on their gowns. Horace Walpole, who was a guest at one of these balls and not usually a generous critic, describes Marie Antoinette in glowing terms when writing to a friend. 'One had eyes only for the Queen. The Hebes and the Floras, the Helens and the Graces are nothing but streetwalkers in comparison. Whether sitting or standing she is the statue of beauty. When she moves she is the very personification of grace. She wore a silver gown garlanded with roses, very few diamonds and feathers on her head. I noted no other beauties, but perhaps that was because the Queen eclipsed them all.'

Horace Walpole may not have noticed, but in that crowd of lovely young women was one whose enchanting looks and simple dress attracted the notice of the Queen. Yolande Gabrielle de Polignac was rarely seen at court, where she had been introduced by her unmarried sister-in-law, the Comtesse Diane, newly appointed lady-in-waiting to the Comtesse d'Artois. The Queen, who was always drawn to beauty, asked her why she had not seen her before and was given the ingenuous reply that she and her husband had not sufficient means to reside at Versailles. It was a reply calculated to appeal to Marie Antoinette who was touched at meeting someone so lovely and apparently so unspoilt.

Madame de Polignac, who came from a good but not particularly distinguished family, crossed the Queen's path at a time when the King's ministers were beginning to show concern at her growing ascendancy over her weak young husband and in particular at the dominating role she had played in securing the acquittal of the Comte de Guines. The *jeunesse dorée* who surrounded the Queen and who were all supporters of Choiseul despised Maurepas as a man of neither honour nor conviction. But Maurepas was clever enough to know that none of these brilliant young courtiers with whom the Queen went racing and hunting and danced at her weekly balls had any more than an ephemeral hold on her affections. Her confidences and intimacies were reserved for her women friends, those she admitted into '*les petits cabinets*', women such as Marie Thérèse de Lamballe and the exquisite Lucie Dillon of partly Irish extraction, married to a cousin, the hereditary colonel-in-chief of the famous Irish regiment which had fought with the French at Fontenoy. The Queen's fondness for the lovely young Irish woman had procured her a place in her household and the position of a lady-in-waiting, thereby causing more jealousy at court where the absurd pretensions of Marie de Lamballe were already causing trouble. But neither the Princesse de Lamballe, who was affiliated to the Palais Royal, nor Lucie Dillon, who depended entirely on her uncle, the immensely wealthy Archbishop of Narbonne, were of any interest to Maurepas. What he needed was an ally in the Queen's circle, someone who could be relied on to influence her in his favour and reveal her confidences.

When the Austrian ambassador began to make enquiries about the Comtesse de Polignac, he was told she was a niece of Maurepas and that the old minister was responsible for having got the Countess's sister-in-law the position of lady-in-waiting to the Comtesse d'Artois – disturbing news for a diplomat who was in constant fear of the young Queen's indiscretions.

There must have been something extraordinarily appealing about Yolande de Polignac. For in all the memoirs of the time from the gush of Madame

Campan to the more stringent comments of the Duc de Levis, it is one long paean of praise, 'of the serenity of her beauty, the magic of her smile'. Middle-aged roués like Besenval, the commander-in-chief of the Swiss Guards, adored her, and elderly courtiers like the Duc de Croy were equally enchanted by her; intelligent young men like Philippe de Ségur came under the influence of the Polignac circle and maintained that 'the Countess's influence was only for the good'. Even the King, who was usually so cold and distant with the ladies of his court, was willing to attend the parties of the Comtesse de Polignac. Yet almost all are agreed in saying that she was neither clever nor brilliant, being quiet and rather indolent by nature; a woman who did not give the impression of being ambitious or of having any desire to shine, but who nevertheless must have possessed some secret quality which enabled her to be anything to any man or any woman and which fascinated and enthralled the Queen from the day of their first meeting.

Marie Antoinette's passionate friendships with women had already caused a great deal of malicious gossip. The tenacity with which she had fought to secure for Marie de Lamballe the totally unnecessary post of superintendent of her household had been bitterly criticized at court where the fashion for satirical songs spared neither the King nor Queen. 'They have been liberal enough to accuse me of having a taste for both women and lovers,' wrote Marie Antoinette in the last days of 1775. But a few weeks later she was writing:

> My dear mother is right when she talks of the fickle character of the French, but I would be really upset if she conceived an aversion for them. Their character is inconsequential, but not bad. Their pens and their tongues write and say a lot of things they do not mean. The proof that they do not hate us is that given the occasion they will praise one much more than one deserves. I have just had that kind of experience. There was a terrible fire at the Palais de Justice the same day I was due to go to the opera. Naturally I did not go, but sent 200 louis to help the victims. From that moment the very people who were spreading calumnies against me began praising me to the skies.

But the Empress could not reconcile herself to the fact that her innocent daughter should have been labelled a lesbian and that Marie Antoinette herself had become so cynical and French that she dismissed the accusation as being a matter of no importance.

The Queen's friendship with the Princesse de Lamballe and the Princesse de Guéménée, who together encouraged her extravagances, her love of gambling, her growing passion for jewels and inordinate interest in clothes, was not as dangerous as her friendship with the gentle insinuating Comtesse de Polignac, who gradually succeeded in isolating her from court life, enclosing her in her own little coterie made up almost entirely of her relations and her friends. Behind Yolande was her sister-in-law, Diane, whom the young Talleyrand described as being 'as ugly as a raw skinned bird with a beaky nose and beady eyes', but of such sparkling wit, so versed in ridiculing the airs and pretensions of her rivals that she was the most fascinating company and for all her ugliness could count more lovers than many an acknowledged beauty.

Still more important was Yolande's aunt, the Comtesse d'Andlau, banished from Versailles for a thoughtless jest twenty years previously, when she had lent the young Princess Adelaide a pornographic novel. This book had made such an impression on the fourteen-year-old girl just out of a convent-school, that she gave it to her brother, the strait-laced and bigoted Dauphin, who went immediately to the King and demanded that the Countess should be dismissed. King Louis, who was secretly amused, had no choice but to comply. The Countess never set foot again in Versailles and Marie Antoinette did not meet her until she appeared with the Polignacs as their favourite aunt. According to Comte Mercy she was a very bad influence on her niece, who emulated her indifference to public opinion by openly flaunting her liaison with the Comte de Vaudreuil. The female members of the Polignac circle consisted solely of relations; Madame d'Andlau's pretty daughter the Comtesse de Chalons and her sister-in-law Yvonne de Polastron, whose langorous beauty was later to win the life-long devotion of the Comte d'Artois.

The men belonging to this coterie were all *habitués* of the Queen's set, Besenval, de Ligne, Coigny, Ségur, a Hungarian Esterhazy and that amiable nonentity, Yolande's husband, Jules de Polignac. The most intelligent and by far the most dangerous member of the coterie was Yolande de Polignac's official lover, the Comte de Vaudreuil, a cultured man of great taste, immense charm and fascination, irresistibly attractive to women, but with a character marred by a violent and uncontrollable temper, which prevented him from playing any active part in public life, but at the same time enabled him to dominate and terrorize an adoring mistress.

The Comte de Vaudreuil was a force to reckon with in those years when the Queen was subjugated by Yolande de Polignac, and the Countess was subjugated by her lover. But it was only gradually that the Polignac coterie succeeded in dominating the Queen. Madame de Lamballe was still her favourite companion during the winter of 1775-6, the coldest in living memory, when the snow lay on the ground for months and Marie Antoinette reverted to the pleasures of her Austrian childhood, getting old sledges out of the royal stables and organizing sledging parties in the park. Madame Campan rhapsodizes over the beauty of the Queen and the Princesse de Lamballe wrapped in their furs of ermine and of sable, 'their fresh young faces giving a hint of spring, gliding across the snow in their gilded sledges with the plumed horses and the tinkling sleigh bells'.

A charming spectacle this may have been, but the winter was too hard and too many people were cold and hungry to appreciate the sight of the Queen disporting herself in the snow. When the Comte d'Artois arranged for a convoy of sledges to drive into Paris, Marie Antoinette for once had the good sense to stay away. She wrote to her mother, 'I would love to have gone but I do not want to encourage any more gossip.' The King disapproved of these sledging parties and never took part in them. On one occasion when the Comte d'Artois and his friends were setting out from the palace, Louis pointed to stacks of wood cut down in the royal forests on his orders for distribution among the poor and said with a smile, 'These, my dear gentlemen, are my sledges.'

But the sledging parties were among the more harmless amusements in that endless round of pleasure with which the Queen tried to fill the emptiness of her life. Her frequent incognito visits to the opera halls with her brothers-in-law, and almost always without the King, gave rise to a lot of unfavourable comment. Artois' behaviour was usually noisy and indiscreet and there was also an unpleasant incident with Monsieur, who having been rudely jostled by a fellow reveller, responded by punching him in the face, whereupon he was arrested by one of the guards, unmasked and recognized as the King's brother. There was also the famous occasion when the Queen's carriage broke down on the way to the ball and she and her lady-in-waiting had to shelter in a shop before they succeeded in hailing a hackney carriage. The story would never have been divulged had it not been for the Queen herself, who delighted in her adventure and repeated it all over Versailles: 'Think of me driving in a hackney carriage!' This was one of the times when even an admirer like the Prince de Ligne remarked that 'the charming Queen could sometimes be very tiresome with her endless stories about her adventures at the masked balls'.

Those occasions when she would return to Versailles in the early hours of the morning and attend mass before going to bed, or sometimes not go to bed, but rush straight off to a race meeting with Artois, estranged the Queen still further from the King. She loved dancing and was one of the few who could manipulate with grace the heavy whalebone panniers when performing a minuet.

In her memoirs Madame de la Tour du Pin writes that the fashions of the day made dancing into a form of torture 'with the narrow heels three inches high which kept the foot in the same position, constantly on tip toe; a pannier of stiff heavy whalebone spreading on either side; hair dressed at least a foot high, sprinkled with a pound of powder and pomade which the slightest movement shook down on the shoulders and crowned by a coronet known as a *pouf* on which feathers, flowers and diamonds were piled pell-mell – an erection which quite spoilt the pleasure of dancing'. But Marie Antoinette enjoyed every form of dancing, whether it was the stately minuet of the court balls, or the *bals champêtres* of Trianon. She even took lessons in English country dances from the popular British ambassador Lord Stormont. But what she enjoyed most of all was arranging quadrilles over which hours would be spent in rehearsing and in consulting with Mademoiselle Bertin over the theme and colours of the costumes.

Thanks to the patronage of Marie Antoinette, the little milliner had become an important personage at Versailles where her pretensions and insolence were bitterly resented by the Queen's household. She regarded herself as a minister of fashion and would talk of her 'work with the Queen'. Every month a new shape or colour emerged from her inventive brain. In 1776 both men and women wore a brownish purple known as *couleur de puce* 'colour of the flea'. A subtler tone of the same colour was called 'stomach of the flea'. Elegant ladies preferred soft and tender colours, the most popular of which was a pale gold known as *couleur des cheveux de la Reine* ('colour of the Queen's hair'). These clothes were ravishing, impractical and extravagant; husbands and lovers complained that women were spending twice as much on their clothes as before. The Queen ordered twelve gala dresses every winter, twelve simple dresses and twelve formal dresses to be worn over panniers. This did not include the linen and muslin dresses for summer, the exquisite *déshabillés*, the countless accessories and ornaments which were changed every season.

Madame Campan describes the etiquette by which every morning before the Queen's levee the first women of the bedchamber would present her with a book of patterns, from which to choose her dresses for the day – the formal dress for mass, the *déshabillé* for the hours of intimacy in *les petits cabinets*, the gala dress for the evening. Though the number of dresses ordered from Mademoiselle Bertin sounds comparatively modest, one must remember that every gala gown, usually covered with embroidery of gold or pearls, cost well over 1,000 francs.

Madame de Lamballe was chiefly responsible for the Queen's extravagant fashions, but it was the Princesse de Guéménée who encouraged her growing passion for jewels, inciting her to buy on credit and to exchange some of her own diamonds in order to acquire a pair of chandelier diamond earrings for which the fashionable jeweller Boehmer was asking the fantastic sum of 400,000 francs. Six months later when her debts had already mounted to over double her yearly allowance, Marie Antoinette bought a pair of bracelets for 200,000 francs and finding herself unable to pay for them, went to the King and asked him to lend her the money. However much he disapproved, the good-natured Louis ended by giving way. When the Empress remonstrated over her daughter's foolish extravagance, Marie Antoinette's only reply was to say that she was surprised her dear mother bothered herself over such a 'bagatelle'.

As *gouvernante des Enfants de France* with no children to attend to other than the twelve-year-old Elisabeth, who was soon to pass out of the hands of governesses, Madame de Guéménée set out to amuse the Queen by reviving the weekly balls given by Madame de Noailles for the young Dauphine. But the balls held in the Guéménées' apartments in the Tuileries, where the Prince had his own private theatre, were very different from the decorous little parties given by Madame de Noailles, which always ended on the stroke of nine. At Madame de Guéménée's one could dance and gamble all night. Court card games like *cavagnole* and *lansquenet* were discarded for the more fashionable game of faro where huge sums were lost in one night, and where Marie Antoinette, who was not a gambler by nature, was carried away by her friends and encouraged to play for large stakes. Within a year faro had became the favourite game with which to while away the boredom of '*les petits voyages*' – the visits to Choisy and Fontainebleau.

It was at one of these parties when play was at its height that the hostess came into the gaming room with a look of consternation on her face, making the dramatic announcement that the Comte de Guines had been recalled from the London Embassy. The news was received with loud-voiced indignation by the guests, all of whom were friends of de Guines. It was all put down to Vergennes having vented his spite on a friend of Choiseul. In the past months he had been represented to Marie Antoinette as a man who would eventually undermine the monarchy although it was generally agreed that Vergennes would never have dared to act without the support of Turgot.

Had Marie Antoinette been the mother of a dauphin, she might have succeeded in having a minister of her choice appointed, but for the present, she could only hope to subjugate the King by sexual wiles for which she had neither the knowledge nor the inclination or to dominate him through fear. Choiseul advised the latter, the easier course to adopt for a young woman who was feeling particularly frustrated by the fact that her Artois sister-in-law was again reported to be pregnant. Surrounded by the most attractive young men in France, she could only have seen her husband at a disadvantage. His unsuccessful attempts in bed must long since have grown distasteful to her. Mercy reports that her nerves were beginning to feel the strain of her unnatural married life. 'There are fits of the vapours, tears and tantrums, and though she has no natural affection for de Guines she allows herself to be so worked upon by his friends that she makes scene after scene to the poor King.' Louis might have had the courage to resist her if he had had the full support of Maurepas, but failing that support he ended in sacrificing Turgot to her childish rancour.

Maurepas, who looked upon himself as being the King's mentor, was quite pleased to let the Queen take on the onerous task of getting rid of a man who had long since become a burden to him. But it was Turgot who signed his own death warrant by addressing a letter to Louis which no absolute monarch could have accepted. Enraged by Maurepas' decision to replace Malesherbes by a complete nonentity, he implored the King not to allow himself to be overruled by Maurepas and not to forget that weakness had brought Charles I to the scaffold – hardly a letter to appeal to even the most modest of Bourbons. After this it did not require much effort on the part of the Queen to bring about his downfall. She was now in such a state of hysteria over the recall of de Guines that it needed the combined efforts of both the Abbé Vermond and Comte Mercy to prevent her from demanding that Turgot should be sent to the Bastille.

It was only later that Marie Antoinette was to be blamed for the fall of Turgot. At the time her opinion was that of the majority of the upper classes of France, and she was admired rather than condemned for the ability with which she succeeded in obtaining the dismissal of a man who was disliked by all except the ordinary people, the voiceless masses, who dimly felt that he was trying to do some good. Abroad he was almost universally admired. And blind Madame du Deffand, whose pen was still as tart and astringent as ever, upbraids Horace Walpole for making a hero of a man 'who would have upset everything if he had stayed in power'. But Horace Walpole's was the opinion not only of the English but of almost the whole of Europe. In Tuscany Marie Antoinette's brother the Archduke Leopold was such an admirer of Turgot that he had adopted his system in the administration of his country and even the Emperor professed to admire his reforms. The Queen herself appears to have regretted her behaviour, for she informed her mother that though she was not sorry over the change of ministers, she had had nothing to do with it. She had nevertheless forced Louis to reward an incompetent ambassador, a diplomat who had been sufficiently foolish as to inform the British government that Louis would never come to the help of the American insurgents, with the honour of a dukedom. This was in the spring of 1776, when all the young officers were afire with enthusiasm to volunteer and fight with the American rebels and the King was reading with interest a report on conditions in Britain's American colonies, written somewhat surprisingly by the author of *Le Barbier de Séville*.

Caron de Beaumarchais had undergone yet another metamorphosis in his extraordinary career. Though still deprived of his civil rights, his success at the Théâtre Français, when *Figaro* made its first immortal appearance, had brought him the fame and prestige he had enjoyed in the days of the Goezman trial. Gone was the time when he had to eke out a livelihood in composing libellous songs and pamphlets at the bidding of the three embittered princesses who had been his first patrons, or frequent the underworld of discredited spies and informers who had fed the sources of the old King's secret diplomacy. The last and most successful of his missions to England had been in order to contact and pay off the cleverest and most dangerous of these spies, the celebrated Chevalier d'Eon, half man, half woman, who started life as an officer in the dragoons and was one of the most deadly swordsmen of the day. He was equally successful as a spy, when, dressed in women's clothes, he was employed as reader at the court of the Tsarina Elisabeth of Russia; or when he served as a diplomat at the English court. Brilliant, brave and unscrupulous, rewarded for his valour with the Cross of St Louis and yet too much of an adventurer to succeed, he ended as the victim of his own duplicity.

It was a brilliant stroke on the part of the French government to pit one adventurer against another. 'We met,' wrote d'Eon, 'compelled no doubt by the natural curiosity of two rare animals to examine one another.' But Beaumarchais was the cleverer and subtler of the two. For him d'Eon was no more than a character in a play, a character more extraordinary than any he would have dared to invent. The late King's compromising papers were handed over by d'Eon in return for a small pension, a free pardon and immunity against his enemies. But from now on the most successful of Louis xv's undercover agents had to vanish and to be replaced by the Chevalière d'Eon, a lady living on the government's bounty, furnished with a trousseau paid for by the King. Actually she received two trousseaux. For no sooner had the story reached Versailles, the very kind of story to appeal to the Queen's friends, than Marie Antoinette insisted on giving the Chevalière the gift of 24,000 francs to buy herself 'some pretty gowns', adding the personal present of a painted fan to compensate for the loss of her sword.

Beaumarchais was still in London negotiating with d'Eon when his imagination was attracted to a vaster stage than any he had hitherto envisaged. In the clubs and coffee houses of London, he listened to Whigs and Tories discussing the rights and wrongs of British colonial rule. He made contact with American agents working in the city of London and listened to their grievances over unjustified taxation, their determination to fight rather than to be ruled from Whitehall. By the end of February 1776 Beaumarchais, who was still legally an outlaw deprived of his civil rights, was writing to Vergennes, 'We must come to the aid of the Americans. They require both arms and ammunition and would be ready to offer France, as the price of her aid, a secret commercial treaty, which would favour her exclusively.'

Preferential treatment for French goods; a new overseas market hitherto controlled by England; a peaceful ally in the north to protect the French islands in the Caribbean. Beaumarchais' enthusiasm infected even someone as cautious as the Comte de Vergennes. But this time it was the King who influenced his foreign minister rather than the foreign minister who influenced the King. For once it was Louis, usually so slow and so obtuse, who was the first to envisage the potential of an independent America. For all his initial distrust of Beaumarchais, whom he had always looked upon as an unscrupulous madman, he nevertheless recognized the streak of genius in the letters and articles stressing the urgent need to help the American rebels. By June 1776, a month before the Declaration of American Independence, Beaumarchais was already accredited as a secret agent acting for the government to furnish arms and ammunition for the American insurgents. All that Beaumarchais had learnt at the time of his apprenticeship to the great banker Paris Duverney was now put to good effect. The first of his ships laden with ammunition had already set sail when at the end of September 1776, the seventy-year-old Benjamin Franklin, America's most illustrious son, landed at Le Havre as the first unofficial ambassador to France.

Franklin conquered the salons of Paris and was one of the most popular figures in the capital, but it was nearly two years before King Louis could conquer his natural disinclination to profit by England's difficulties and forget his Bourbon heritage sufficiently to receive a republican ambassador at Versailles.

The Queen had no sympathy with the American insurgents. It was only later when her favourite courtiers had left Versailles to volunteer in Washington's armies, when America had become so much the fashion that Parisian tailors copied Mr Franklin's suits and Mademoiselle Bertin created a fur bonnet *à la Franklin*, that Marie Antoinette was ready to give a hero's welcome to young officers who returned to Versailles proudly displaying the oak leaves of the Order of Cincinnatus.

Throughout the years of 1776 and 1777, it was still considered *bon ton* to be anglophile. The British ambassador, Lord Stormont, was a favourite guest at Versailles and visitors from across the Channel brought over their horses and their jockeys to race at the Bois de Boulogne and at Fontainebleau, where a race course was laid out in a clearing in the forest. The Queen had a pavilion built here with a revolving stage, where she could watch the races and where a cold buffet was served to a crowd of noisy young racegoers, most of them friends of Chartres or of Artois, who to the horror of Comte Mercy and some of the older courtiers would appear before the Queen in sporting clothes and muddy boots, shouting and arguing over their various bets. The fact that the King was known to dislike racing and that many of the Englishmen present were of notoriously bad reputation made horse-racing unpopular with the majority of Frenchmen and reflected badly on the Queen.

Comte Mercy's reports became more and more gloomy. 'If the Queen persists in her dissipations she will forfeit all the good will she acquired as Dauphine.' The Abbé Vermond wrote a despairing letter to the Empress:

> The Queen's friends take up the whole of her time and prevent her from paying the slightest attention to me. I have swallowed all my bitterness and disappointment as long as it only depended on me for I still live in the hope that I will again be able to be useful to the Queen. For over a year she has barely listened to me, but she still confides in me and I still think there are certain things she tells no one else but me. My own character and what I believe to be my duty never prevent me from telling her the truth.... But I am consumed with worry at the thought of all the unhappiness she is preparing for herself.

At the end of 1776, after spending an unhappy month at Fontainebleau in which days passed without his even seeing the Queen, Vermond finally decided to hand in his resignation. Marie Antoinette refused to accept it, saying that there was no one she trusted as much as him, that no one was more necessary to her and she would never consent to have him leave her. But the arrogance and rudeness with which he was treated by the Queen's new friends, in particular by the two favourites Marie de Lamballe and Yolande de Polignac, who recognized in the honest plain-spoken Abbé an incorruptible opponent, made life so unpleasant for him at Versailles that it was only with the greatest difficulty that Mercy was able to persuade him to spend a fortnight a month in attendance on the Queen.

The Empress was in despair. 'This good man threatens to leave my daughter when she is at the most critical stage, having lost all sense and heading straight for disaster.' The ambassador kept writing of the growing trouble at court – how the first of the weekly balls at Versailles, which were to continue throughout the winter, had been practically empty with no more than ten or twelve ladies dancing. This, he said, was certainly the fault of the Queen, who for the sake of her other amusements had cut down on the number of formal receptions which in the time of the late King had always been held regularly on specific days of the week. Parisians were losing the habit of going to Versailles, as they never knew when they would have a chance of being received at court. The small intimate supper parties at which the young King and Queen had entertained the older and more distinguished of their courtiers and where Marie Antoinette had won all hearts, had ended in boring them both. The King preferred the hunting suppers of St Hubert. The Queen was only happy in what she called her '*société*', with the result that those who had the right of *Les Grandes Entrées* at court and were used to playing an important role at Versailles felt themselves humiliated and neglected.

It was the duty of the Princesse de Lamballe, as mistress of the Queen's household, to keep open house and entertain to supper all the ladies who were invited to the Queen's balls. But such were her pretentions, her insistence on being treated as royalty, and the delicacy of her health, which always served as an excuse to avoid entertaining, that the ladies would arrive from Paris, hang around in their gala dresses for several hours without being given a bite of food and return hungry to Paris at midnight. As Mercy wrote to the Empress, 'All this effort and fatigue brings them no particular honour or distinction such as a supper in the private apartments, so whenever it is possible they avoid going to Versailles.'

Marie Antoinette learnt her lesson and after the failure of her first ball took the Princesse de Lamballe to task, telling her that in view of her enormous salary it was her duty to hold open house and invite the guests to supper after the balls. As usual there were tears and protestations, pleas of being too delicate to entertain, accusations against those who were trying to undermine their friendship, all of which was beginning to get on the Queen's nerves.

By the beginning of 1777 the Polignacs were installed at court. To please the Queen and suit his own purposes, Maurepas prevailed on the King to pay the Countess' debts and though the Queen had asked for no more than 200,000 francs, Maurepas doubled the amount, thereby showing all too clearly the interest he had in keeping in with the Polignacs. The Countess appears to have told the Queen that it would be impossible for her to remain at Versailles unless her husband was given a suitable appointment at court. One of the most important positions in the Queen's household was that of master of the horse, an appointment which for three generations had passed from father to son of the Comtes de Tessé. The present Count, a respected and familiar figure at court, was forty years old and childless. As he was married to a Noailles, it was generally assumed that the post would revert to one of the family and all the Noailles were up in arms when the Queen suddenly announced that the twenty-eight-year-old Comte Jules de Polignac had been chosen.

To offend the Noailles, as she had already offended the Rohans by refusing to include Prince Louis de Rohan in her parties either at Versailles or at Trianon, meant antagonizing two of the most powerful families in France. And all on account of an adolescent crush on a young woman who had little to commend her beyond her great blue eyes and her angelic smile. 'A friend of whom I am infinitely fond', she wrote to her mother – words calculated to shock the Empress, whose ambassador's reports told of a growing estrangement between the young King and Queen and of the many nights they spent apart. It was not only the Empress who was shocked, but also her son, and by the early spring of 1777, Joseph had come to the conclusion that it was time for him to make the journey to France which he had been planning for several years. To bring his young sister to reason and force her to realize the vulnerability of her position, to establish personal contact with his brother-in-law and help an ignorant couple with his knowledge and experience were things which the young Emperor, who was supremely sure of himself, hoped to accomplish on a journey on which as usual he would be travelling incognito to enable him to visit places and meet people whom he would have no opportunity of seeing on a royal visit.

Maria Theresa had little faith in his journey. 'One of two things will happen. Either my daughter will win over her brother with her sweet words and smiles. Or else he will be too harsh and get on her nerves by preaching to her.'

It was a cold rainy afternoon on 18 April 1777 and the streets of Paris were deserted when an open German travelling carriage drove up in front of the Austrian Embassy in the Palace of Le Petit Luxembourg. The Duc de Croy, who happened to be passing that way and had heard that the Emperor's servants had already arrived at the neighbouring Hôtel de Treville where rooms had been booked in the name of Count Falkenstein, sent a footman to make enquiries. The man returned agog with excitement, to say that not only had the Emperor arrived, but he had seen him. He was one of the young men in the carriage. It was difficult for the old Duc de Croy, born in the reign of Louis XIV and brought up in the splendour of Versailles, to conceive that this young man in his wet overcoat with no other retinue than the two servants on the carriage box was in reality the Emperor of Germany and brother of the Queen of France.

This was only the first of many shocks which Joseph was to give the French aristocracy during his month's visit to France. But this carefully studied incognito, which annoyed his sister, irritated the King and brought tears of frustration to the master of ceremonies at Versailles, enchanted the Parisians who in their love of novelty welcomed the democratic Emperor who refused to sleep at Versailles and went everywhere without either guards or attendants. No one could be more charming than Joseph when he wanted. Knowing that both his mother and Comte Mercy had been against his visit, he put himself out to be simple and sympathetic, showing an interest in everything he saw and in everyone he met, so that by the end of the month he was writing to his brother Leopold, the only person he ever took into his confidence, 'You are worth more than me, but I am more of a charlatan, and in this country it is necessary to be one. I go in for being modest and understanding, perhaps exaggeratedly so, for it seems to have excited an enthusiasm which is beginning to be embarrassing.'

When the Emperor arrived in Paris Comte Mercy was confined to his bed with a bad attack of gout, but the fact that he was unable to be in attendance distressed him far more than it distressed his Imperial master, who had always looked upon him as his mother's spy and resented the secret correspondence they carried on behind his back. Outwardly Joseph was at his most gracious, sitting at his bedside, listening to the endless exhortations and advice as to how to avoid the pitfalls of Versailles.

The magnificent hospitality offered by an ambassador famous for his table and superb cellar of fifteen thousand bottles of rare wines, a fact hardly likely to be appreciated by an emperor who drank nothing but water, was accepted only on condition that he was given the simplest of rooms and was left free to dine with his suite in the neighbouring hotel. Mercy's illness was an unexpected blessing for Joseph, leaving him free to explore Paris in the company of Count Belgiojoso, his ambassador to England who was now on his way to Spain and was a young man of his own age.

Of all the Hapsburgs, Joseph was one of the most intelligent and the most misunderstood. He lived under the shadow of his formidable mother, sharing in the burden of running a huge and cumbrous Empire, constantly frustrated and straining at the maternal leash. Maria Theresa might profess to love her difficult and wayward son, who from his earliest childhood 'had never known how to obey', but it was she who was partly responsible for the cold cruel streak in Joseph's character. Forcing him to marry Josepha and sending his most charming mistress, the beautiful Eleanor Franchi, packing across the frontier, were calculated to enrage a man who since the death of his first wife had only found sexual satisfaction with women of a lower class. As an experienced sensualist, Joseph now felt himself to be fully qualified to give marital direction to the little sister who was so sadly in need of advice.

It was still raining when early on the morning of 19 April the Emperor, accompanied by Count Belgiojoso, drove up to a side entrance of Versailles where the Abbé Vermond was waiting to conduct him up a private staircase leading directly into the apartments of the Queen. Wearing one of the most charming of *déshabillés*, with her hair unpowdered, her face unrouged, disregarding all etiquette in her excitement, Marie Antoinette ran forward to embrace her brother. At first sight of the lovely young woman he had last seen as a fourteen-year-old girl, Joseph, who was usually so cool and self-possessed, felt a surge of affection such as he had not known for years. Overcome with emotion they fell into one another's arms and for a moment neither of them spoke, till half laughing, half crying Marie Antoinette began to pour out everything she had stored up to tell her brother whom she loved so much, but of whose criticism she was so afraid – so afraid that in a way she had dreaded his coming, wondering how he would react to those strange apathetic Bourbons, whether he would accept her friends and make allowances for her dissipations. She would have liked to impress Versailles with the grandeur of the Hapsburgs, to have her stiffnecked courtiers genuflecting before the Emperor of Germany, instead of which he had insisted on masquerading as Count Falkenstein, wearing a plain dark suit with neither orders nor decorations, yet looking so elegant and so unconsciously arrogant that no one could be deceived.

It is said that in the first hour Marie Antoinette gave Joseph a frank account of her marital situation, telling him that she was still a virgin '*encore grande fille*'. He is supposed to have replied, 'Well, it is high time your husband became *un grand garçon*.' But there were no harsh words, no hint of criticism of her behaviour towards the King. Listening to her pathetic tale of seven years of failure, of her loneliness and of her longing to be loved, Joseph felt nothing but pity for his pretty little sister being tied to a man whom in private he dismissed 'as a wet slab of fish'. Gallantly he told her, 'If I could only meet someone half as charming as you, I would be ready to marry tomorrow.' Marie Antoinette, who was so used to adulation, blushed like a young girl at the unexpected compliment.

The time had come for the Queen to take her brother to the King's apartments; she wondered how someone as timid and reserved as Louis would react to the prospect of discussing the most intimate and humiliating details of his marriage with a brother-in-law to whom he was instinctively inimical. Louis knew that his reputed impotence was common knowledge in the courts of Europe. But he and perhaps Joseph were the only ones to know that Marie Antoinette was also partly to blame, ready to seize on any pretext such as the slightest indisposition to avoid having to share his bed. For this reason he welcomed Joseph as the person most competent to deal with the situation, pandering to his foibles and allowing him to wander round Paris as plain Count Falkenstein.

From all accounts, beginning with that of the Duc de Croy, one of the most observant and truthful of chroniclers, the King behaved admirably throughout the Emperor's visit, dealing quite naturally with the difficult problem of an incognito which gave so many headaches to his gentlemen-in-waiting. The Duke gives a curious picture of the first royal dinner at Versailles, partaken of by the King, the Queen and Count Falkenstein, and which, in a palace of 1,400 rooms, took place in the Queen's bedchamber, with a grandly laid table pushed up against the bed. To solve the question of the incognito, Louis, Marie Antoinette and Joseph all sat or rather perched uncomfortably on folding stools of exactly the same size. In spite of the draughts on a chilly spring day, the doors were left open, so that some of the more favoured courtiers could have a view of this extraordinary spectacle. It was noted that of the three, the King was the one who was most at his ease, talking and laughing a lot and appearing to derive some amusement from the horrified faces of his courtiers. The Queen on the contrary looked nervous and embarrassed, while Count Falkenstein adopted the air of a deferential stranger. When dinner was over, the two brothers-in-law had a long talk, while the Queen, still looking nervous as if she regretted leaving them together, retired to have her hair dressed.

The Duc de Croy writes that in the course of his long life he had never witnessed anything so curious as the Emperor's arrival at Versailles. Yet no one could have carried it off with greater elegance and poise. Monsieur, Madame, the Comte and Comtesse d'Artois, Mesdames de France, the princes of the blood royal, the ministers and their wives were all visited in turn. Joseph even made the graceful gesture of asking to see the little Duc d'Angoulême while the haughty Madame Adelaide was so charmed by his manners that she insisted on giving him 'a kiss from an old aunt'.

The one person who took an instantaneous dislike to him was Monsieur, a dislike largely motivated by the jealousy of a man intensely vain, physically handicapped by an ever increasing obesity, condemned to play a secondary role in a court where he longed to shine. Both Louis and Marie Antoinette were too frank and open by nature to conceal their dislike of the brother who in the days of the old King had actively intrigued against them with the Duc d'Aiguillon and who in the Luxembourg Palace presided over a circle of poetasters and *beaux esprits* ready to reward his generosity with malicious verses at the expense of the Queen and her court. Writing to his friend the King of Sweden whose tastes were somewhat akin to his own, Monsieur describes the Emperor as being 'very cajoling in manner, profuse in his protestations of friendship, till one discovers that underlying the apparent frankness is a wish to worm out information. But in this he is very maladroit, for with a little flattery, of which he cannot have enough, he ends in being the one who is taken in and in giving himself away. He is also excessively vain and his knowledge is superficial.' But it was Monsieur who was the more superficial of the two, and who was far too hasty in his judgement of someone as complicated and as devious as the Emperor. For his part Joseph seems to have found him even more unattractive than the King, 'an indefinable being, mortally cold, his wife ugly and vulgar, not a Piedmontese for nothing – a mass of intrigue'. Artois he dismisses as an 'amiable fop, his wife the only one who produces children but is otherwise a complete imbecile'.

However much Bourbons and Hapsburgs might dislike one another, and however careful the Emperor might be to preserve his incognito, etiquette decreed that following the Queen's Sunday concert at which Count Falkenstein mingled with the court, a family supper had to be given by Madame, of which Comte Mercy, in his sick-bed, appears to have heard every detail through the efficiency of his spies. The fact that Joseph never ate supper or drank any wine was hardly likely to ingratiate him with his brothers-in-law all of whom ate and drank copiously. Whether out of boredom or in a deliberate attempt to denigrate the King, Monsieur plied his brothers with so many rare wines that they staggered up from table in a state of drunken euphoria, indulging in the most childish pranks, chasing one another round the room and falling over the sofas in such a way as to make the Queen and the princesses angry and ashamed of their husbands. Joseph behaved impeccably, taking no notice of them and going on quietly talking to the princesses, till Madame, having noted that the Queen was on the verge of tears, called on her husband to put an end to this tomfoolery and the evening ended quite amicably with the Emperor still treating the King with a deferential politeness.

Brother and sister spent the following day at Trianon, with only two of the palace ladies in attendance, one of them the Duchesse de Duras, whose intelligence intimidated the Queen, but whom she probably thought would be more appreciated by her brother than some of her more intimate friends. The Emperor had lost no time in telling her that he found the Princesse de Lamballe 'an intolerable bore not worth the quarter of her salary'. And the Queen, who was beginning to be irritated by the Princess, admitted that she had made a mistake in making her *superintendant* of her household. Nor did she attempt to defend the Princesse de Guémenée when her brother upbraided her for visiting a woman 'whose salon was nothing but a gambling den'. But not even Joseph dared to be too harsh in his judgement of the Comtesse de Polignac. His sister needed someone she could love and a sentimental friendship for a rather stupid woman was less dangerous than having a lover. It was only later that the Emperor's ambassador enlightened him on the morals of the men and women who belonged to the 'Société Polignac', to all of whom the pretty Countess appeared to be so devoted that hardly a month passed without some lucrative court appointment falling into their hands.

But on a fine spring morning in the gardens of Trianon, even an older brother found it difficult to resist the charming Queen, showing off with a childish delight her newly completed English garden. The herbaceous borders had been planted with flowers from all over the world: thousands of daffodils, tulips and hyacinths, a hundred different species of iris, and every variety of flowering bush from the lilacs cultivated by Artois at Bagatelle to the rare shrubs sent by ambassadors and travellers as a tribute to the Queen. 'And what of the botanical gardens, the famous hothouses which were the old King's pride and joy?' It was typical of Joseph to have asked such a tactless question. Marie Antoinette, who had no interest in botany, had had these all destroyed and the exotic plants sent to the Jardin du Roi in Paris. In place of 'those boring old hothouses' were green lawns and a flowing stream, which meandered by artificial rocks and caves, and a Chinese pagoda designed by Mique, who had become her favourite architect. She had kept the little temple of love and it was here that she and Joseph partook of their frugal dinner of chicken, strawberries and milk. What setting could be more suitable for intimate confidences and still more intimate advice? As a crude and experienced amorist, Joseph had to choose his words, so as not to shock the little sister of whom he wrote to his brother Leopold, 'She is somewhat childish and essentially decent and virtuous.'

Blushing and embarrassed, Marie Antoinette had confessed all that was wrong with her marriage, information which Joseph did not hesitate to repeat to Leopold in language which would have horrified their sister. 'This is the secret – in bed he has good hard erections. The organ remains there motionless for two minutes or so, then withdraws, still stiff without discharging and he goes off to sleep. It makes no sense as from time to time he has night-time ejaculations. He never completes the act himself, yet is content, saying himself that he does it out of duty and without the slightest enjoyment. If only I had been there once I could have fixed things. He needs to be beaten like an ass to make him discharge his spunk. With all this my sister has little appetite for the whole business and together they make a hopelessly clumsy couple.'

It would have amused the old King, who in his temple of love had spent his last happy hours with Madame du Barry, to hear the young Emperor instructing his sister in the arts of love with Marie Antoinette listening obediently like a child at school. For Joseph had been at pains to stress the vulnerability of her position, the choice between remaining a Queen or being repudiated, with the horrifying possibility of a convent. 'Don't try to drive your husband; be tender, be warm, above all be patient. Get him to bed with you in the afternoon. It's no good waiting till after supper, when he is already sunk in a state of apathy.' The advice was good, but it was not going to be easy, for as Joseph told Leopold, 'She is not in the least in love with him. Her relation to her husband is altogether peculiar. She drives him by force to make him do things he does not want to do. As for the King, he is a little weak but not an imbecile. He has ideas and a sound judgement. But in mind and body he is apathetic. He converses reasonably but he has neither curiosity nor desire to learn. In fact the *fiat lux* has not yet come. The matter is there, but completely without form.' Would Marie Antoinette ever be capable of firing the missing spark?

Joseph was conscientious by nature and determined to do his best by devoting many hours during his first weeks in France to winning the young King's confidence, until gradually Louis overcame his timidity and began to speak frankly and openly of his longing to have children and to lead the life of a normal married man. He was too chivalrous to blame his wife, who was always talking of the necessity for an operation. But Joseph does not appear to have thought it was a malformation of which the Spanish ambassador had already spoken in the first months of the marriage. As he told Leopold, he considered it to be nothing more than a question of ignorance, clumsiness and partly the fault of their sister.

Most of Louis' latest biographers refute the theory that Joseph got his brother-in-law to undergo an operation, for according to his diaries, the King hardly ever missed a day's hunting. But we read of him going out hunting with the Emperor in a carriage, and the question as to whether or not he had an operation remains disputable. But whatever Joseph may have recommended appears to be have been eminently successful.

That the brothers-in-law should have come to an understanding did not entirely please Marie Antoinette, who confessed to Comte Mercy that she was afraid her brother might advise the king against paying her debts and giving in to her solicitations on behalf of her friends. She did everything she could to discourage their tête-à-têtes and was furious when Joseph, talking to the King in front of her ladies, remarked that it was a lucky thing for France that Choiseul was not in power, as 'with his restlessness and overweening ambition he would have already involved the country in a war,' to which the King heartily agreed.

In the role of Count Falkenstein the Emperor was present at all the official ceremonies at Versailles, *La Messe du Roi*, *Le Grand Couvert*, *Le Débotté du Roi*, where courtiers fought for the honour of holding a candle for the King. But at times the Emperor forgot to play the role of a deferential courtier, as when he returned from a visit to Les Invalides, genuinely enthusiastic about what he considered to be one of the finest buildings in Europe, and was horrified to hear that the King had never even seen it or had the slightest intention of going there. The Emperor, who had visited every province of his vast dominions, could not understand Louis' lack of curiosity, the fact that he showed no desire to venture beyond the Ile de France and took no interest in the wonderful treasures housed in the royal storerooms at the corner of the Rue Royale and in the Place Louis xv. There were rooms full of exquisite furniture and rare tapestries only occasionally seen by some privileged visitor, which in Joseph's opinion should be placed in a museum open to the public. But what shocked him most of all was that tradesmen were allowed to sell their wares outside the royal palaces and in the inner courtyards of Versailles.

Joseph's sarcastic tongue was not always appreciated by his sister. On attending her levees he would criticize her either for wearing too much rouge or for spending too much on clothes, to which she would reply that it was her duty to dress in expensive satins and brocades as half of the silk manufacturers of France would close down if she led the fashion in dressing more simply. When she asked him to admire some ravishing and elaborate coiffure he somewhat brutally remarked that 'it might be charming on an actress but was too fragile to support a crown'. It is not surprising if Marie Antoinette, in spite of her love and admiration for her brother, sometimes resented his criticisms, especially when made in front of her ladies. He would scold her for not being sufficiently considerate with her husband, for keeping him waiting for his supper on fast days when he had not dined; of ignoring his tastes and forcing him to share in her pleasures, saying openly in front of Comte Mercy that if she were his wife he would know how to make her behave and do as he wanted.

Nevertheless, he put himself out to please her, departing from his incognito to attend a fête given in his honour in the illuminated gardens of Trianon, at which he charmed the guests from Madame Adelaide and the Comtesse de Noailles to the youngest of the palace ladies. Here the King was in his most jovial mood, chatting and laughing with his brother-in-law, whom he always referred to as the Emperor.

By now Joseph's incognito was becoming somewhat of a farce. He attended a military review with the King and a race meeting with the Queen, where he openly disapproved of the familiarity with which Artois and his friends treated his sister and the high betting which took place in her presence. He and Marie Antoinette went together to the theatre and the opera where they received a standing ovation from the audience and on one occasion she even succeeded in dragging him to a party at the Princesse de Guéménée's; he disliked the Princess intensely and refused to sit down at a card table, saying that he was not rich enough to play with such experienced players. That same evening a vapid beauty, hoping to ingratiate herself with the democratic Emperor, asked him whether he sympathized with the American insurgents and received the cutting reply, 'Madame, it is my trade to be a Royalist.'

'One talks of nothing here but of the Emperor,' writes Madame du Deffand. 'He speaks our language very well and with great facility and is of a charming simplicity. He is surprised one is surprised. He says that the natural state is not to be a King, but to be a man. There is nothing he does not want to see or know.' When free from his duties at Versailles, Joseph was determined to see as much of Paris as possible, starting at eight in the morning without telling either his ambassador or anyone else of his plans. The gentlemen of his suite never knew to the last moment where they might be going, whether to the hospital of Saint Dieu or the prisons of Bicêtre and of Salpêtrière; to the factories of Gobelins and of Sèvres or to the ministry of works, where he paid homage to the genius of Monsieur Perronet, whose bridge at Neuilly he considered to be one of the finest sights of Paris. When visiting the Jardin du Roi quite near to his hotel, he called on the veteran naturalist Buffon and paid him the charming compliment of saying he had come to fetch the books his brother had inadvertently left behind, thereby retrieving the gaffe made by the Archduke Maximilian. At the Académie Française he listened for over an hour to flattering rhetorical addresses from Marmontel, La Harpe and d'Alembert, all of which secretly bored him to death, for in reality he had as little interest in literature as his sister. He was far happier discussing finance with Laborde, a banker and minister, and one of the richest men in France, or with Jacques Necker, the brilliant Swiss banker whom the King had just made his director of finance, a brave appointment in view of the fact that Louis never really trusted a Protestant. A long visit was paid to Turgot, whose economic policies had been adopted by his brother Leopold in Tuscany, and another to the scientist Lavoisier.

In spite of his incognito, rapturous crowds followed him wherever he went. But some of the Emperor's visits were of a strictly private nature, which his tactful ambassador abstained from mentioning in his letters to Maria Theresa. There were certain intimate supper parties in the company of the delightful actresses he had admired on the stage, for Joseph loved the theatre and many evenings were spent in a private box at the Théâtre des Italiens or the Comédie Française. Of all the Emperor's visits, the one which gave the greatest umbrage to the Queen came when he set out to examine the water-works at Marly, and finding himself in the neighbourhood of Louveciennes stopped to call on Madame du Barry, who by royal clemency had been allowed to return to her old home, where she still reigned over a court of admiring suitors. The pavilion of Louveciennes, a masterpiece by Ledoux, smaller and more intimate than the Trianon, where every picture and piece of furniture down to the great gilded bed evoked some memory of her royal lover, was the perfect setting for Madame du Barry, whose mature, voluptuous beauty, unimpaired by age, was far more to the Emperor's taste than the langorous, delicate beauty of a Yolande de Polignac. Whether by accident or design, Joseph wandered into the gardens, introducing himself as Count Falkenstein and deceiving no one, least of all the Countess, who received him with royal honours in a part she had learnt to play so well. For an hour they stayed together, a pleasant interlude in which the Emperor and the Countess were equally charmed with one another, but when the news of their meeting reached Versailles it was not appreciated by either the King or Queen. It was even less appreciated in Vienna, from where Maria Theresa complained to her ambassador that she considered it quite unnecessary of her son to have visited 'that dreadful woman'.

In spite of their occasional quarrels, Marie Antoinette enjoyed her brother's visit and did everything in her power to make him prolong his stay, while half against his will, Joseph allowed himself to succumb to 'her sweetness and her charm and the pleasures of a life I thought I had given up, but for which I find I have not lost the taste. I spent hours and hours in her company, without noticing how the hours flew by.' But now the time had come for him to set out on his planned tour of the French provinces. 'I was unwilling to leave Versailles, for I had really become attached to my sister. She is sweet and good and it needed all my strength to tear myself away.' Marie Antoinette was miserable and had difficulty in restraining her grief in front of the court. They parted at midnight, equally sad to say goodbye. But Joseph was conscious of having done some good, for it was noted that the Queen was now gentler and more considerate in her treatment of the King. Louis, by now deeply in love with his wife, said to her, 'We have seen much more of one another during the Emperor's visit. And for that I am very grateful to him.'

Two weeks after the Emperor's departure, Marie Antoinette wrote to her mother, 'I was so happy during the time he was here. But now it all seems like a dream. What remains of the dream is the good advice he gave me and which is for ever graven in my heart. What gave me the greatest pleasure of all were the written instructions he left for me and which I had asked him for. Should I ever forget what he said, which I doubt, I shall always have those instructions in front of me to remind me of my duty.'

Yet according to Comte Mercy, the Queen did not entirely appreciate the tone of her brother's instructions, which were in many ways unfair, being too harsh and too often reminiscent of the angry letter intercepted by his mother, in which he had upbraided her for her indiscretions in her letter to Count Rosenberg. Joseph was too much of a preacher and a pedant to make allowance for his sister's weaknesses, and his instructions were often written at the end of a tiring day, when he had been irritated at a party of the Princesse de Guéménée or by the behaviour of the Comte d'Artois. He had been genuinely shocked by Marie Antoinette's attitude towards her husband and in his long and repetitive instructions he begged her to make more efforts to please the King, to think of his glory rather than of her own and never to want to shine at his expense. He implored her to be softer and kinder and to confide more in her husband. The Emperor, who affected simplicity and despised all etiquette and pomp, reproached his sister for neglecting her duties as a Queen, for having a coterie rather than a court and for choosing companions who alienated all the more decent elements of society. Joseph's instructions were deliberately exaggerated, being intended to frighten Marie Antoinette into adopting a more sensible way of life. He foresaw the dangers which lay ahead, the animosity she was arousing by her heedlessness and selfishness. 'I tremble when I think of your happiness because things cannot go on like this indefinitely. The Revolution if it comes will be a cruel one and probably caused by you yourself.'

Travelling through the provinces of western France, visiting the Atlantic ports, Joseph had been as much impressed by the natural prosperity of the country and by the industry of the people as he had been appalled by the incapacity of the government, the lack of cooperation in the various departments and the fractious parliaments which blocked all attempts at reform. His advice to his brother-in-law to visit some of his provincial cities resulted only in the King's brothers being sent on useless and extravagant journeys involving enormous expense, straining the resources of the countryside and shocking the local population with their arrogant and ostentatious style.

There could have been no greater contrast between their royal progress and that of His Imperial Majesty the Emperor of Germany, who dashed across France in a simple travelling carriage, putting up at the local inns and, when passing through Touraine, deliberately avoided Chanteloup, where the Duc de Choiseul had prepared elaborate festivities in his honour, an act which pleased the King, but annoyed Maria Theresa and his sister. Given the dearth of experienced statesmen in France, Maria Theresa felt it was unwise to offend a man who might still return to power. But Joseph knew King Louis sufficiently to realize that in no circumstances would he ever restore Choiseul. It was even more surprising that the Emperor passed within a few kilometres of Ferney without stopping to call on Voltaire. But Joseph was always unpredictable and this may have been one of the occasions when he preferred to please his mother rather than the philosophers of the Parisian salons.

Contrary to her expectations, the Empress was delighted with the success of her son's visit to France. Back in his own country he had forgotten the irritations of Versailles and spoke lovingly of the 'charming little Queen, who would be quite perfect, if only she listened less to the place-seekers and toadies by whom she was surrounded'. Neither brother nor sister was entirely honest with their mother, who was never shown the instructions for which Marie Antoinette expressed such an extravagant gratitude, but at which, according to Comte Mercy, she barely glanced after the first months. In all those repetitive pages of instructions there was no advice as wise as that which Francis de Lorraine had written in the testament left to his children, warning them against the pitfalls which surrounded a throne, 'the companions who should be carefully chosen, the affection which should never be carelessly lavished'. For all his brilliance, Joseph lacked his father's subtlety and understanding and could never help his sister in the way their father might have done. But he had given her a lot of useful advice, and Mercy reported to the Empress that during the summer months the Queen was far more attentive towards her husband, foregoing her own amusements to accompany him to the suppers of St Hubert and showing the utmost sympathy on an occasion when he wounded himself with a knife during a hunting expedition at Compiègne.

Finally in the month of August came a cry of triumph from the Queen: 'This is a very joyful occasion for me, for I have at last achieved the most essential happiness of all. Eight days ago my marriage was finally consummated, and yesterday again and even more completely than the first time. I wanted to send a special courier to let my darling mother know at once. But I felt it might cause too much of a stir. I don't think I am pregnant as yet, but at least I have now the satisfaction of knowing it could happen from one moment to another. Loving me as she does, I can picture my dearest mother's joy, almost as if it were my own.'

But Maria Theresa had to wait many months before she had the satisfaction of hearing that her daughter was pregnant. The autumn, during which the King devoted himself to hunting and the Queen reverted to her usual dissipations, appeared to have dampened their matrimonial ardour. Marie Antoinette complained to her mother that the King had no liking for the double bed. 'I do my best to prevent him from getting into the habit of sleeping apart and he sometimes spends the night with me. I feel it is wiser not to worry him too much on this account, as he always comes to visit me in the morning and is kinder and more affectionate than ever.' Mercy on the contrary told the Empress that, if the King abstained from going to bed with his wife, it was chiefly in order not to disturb her, as she sat up half the night playing cards and did not want to be woken up in the morning. It could only be wished that the Queen would change her habits so as to suit those of her husband. Unfortunately her disappointment at not finding herself pregnant, while the Comtesse d'Artois was expecting her third child, had resulted in her resuming her usual dissipated life. Gambling had never been for such high stakes as that autumn at Fontainebleau, and those who could not afford to lose a hundred louis a night kept away from the Queen's card table. The Comte d'Artois, back from his tour of the western provinces, was once more in favour and his inseparable companion, the Baron de Besenval, was one of the Queen's intimates. Marie Antoinette was sufficiently foolish to think that his grey hairs entitled him to her confidences, and one of the popular rhymes circulating round Versailles dealt with the Queen and the middle-aged colonel of the Swiss Guards.

La Reine dit imprudemment	The Queen says imprudently
A Besenval, son confident,	To Besenval, her confidant,
Le Roi est un pauvre sire.	The King is a poor sire.
L'autre répond d'un ton léger	The other replies in a casual tone,
Tout le monde le pense sans y dire.	Everyone thinks so, without saying so.
Vous le dites sans y penser.	You say so without thinking.

Besenval's friendship with the Queen gave him access to the Polignac coterie, where he became one of the Countess's most fervent admirers. Much of his popularity depended on the fact that he was a rich bachelor who wanted neither honours nor rewards for himself and cared only for the illusion of power, the promoting of army appointments and the making and unmaking of ministers. But Besenval was not the only one to worship at the rising sun of Yolande de Polignac. Every place-seeker in Versailles aspired to an invitation to her drawing-room, which was beginning to assume the proportions of a court, where it amused the Queen to appear as a guest. The older courtiers were horrified to see the Queen passing through the Gallery of Mirrors linked arm in arm with the Comtesse de Polignac. By the end of 1777 the power of the coterie was such that the foreign minister had to cancel his brother's appointment as minister to Switzerland, one of the most remunerative posts in the foreign service, in favour of the father of Comte Jules de Polignac, who had no qualifications other than being related to the royal favourite.

Curiously enough, the Countess's lover, Monsieur de Vaudreuil, was the only member of the set who never succeeded in getting any appointment more important than that of royal falconer, hardly a position to satisfy the ambition of a man who dreamt of becoming minister of the King's household. Whether from jealousy or good sense, Marie Antoinette never liked Vaudreuil, and she listened to the advice of the Abbé Vermond, who succeeded in keeping that dangerous man out of public office. As a result all the Polignacs hated Vermond and did all in their power to encourage the King in his dislike of a man who had been chosen by Choiseul.

While Versailles was given over to dissension and intrigue, Benjamin Franklin from his headquarters in Passy was waging a successful publicity campaign in favour of the American insurgents. The Quaker from Philadelphia had become the fashion, and the *jeunesse dorée* of France, who had been so slavishly imitating the English, were now longing to fight them overseas. In the spring of 1777 an event occurred which at the time was overshadowed by the Emperor's visit, but which nevertheless caused considerable excitement both in Paris and Versailles. The nineteen-year-old Marquis de Lafayette, married into the powerful family of Noailles, had disobeyed the orders both of his father-in-law and the King and sailed off to America to fight in Washington's armies. At an age when most young men of his world were still dependent on their families, Gilbert de Lafayette was in the fortunate position of having inherited a fortune sufficiently large to win him a Noailles for a bride. His marriage brought Gilbert into the charmed circle of young men such as his brother-in-law Louis de Noailles and Philippe de Ségur, friends of the Comte d'Artois and dancing partners of the Queen. Tall and gangling with bright red hair that no amount of powder could hide, a bad horseman and an indifferent dancer, he cut a poor figure at Versailles. On one occasion when dancing in one of the Queen's quadrilles, he stumbled and fell and Marie Antoinette, so prone to mockery, could not help but laugh. In spite of the royal welcome she was to give him when he returned in triumph from America, the proud young man was never to forget her laughter, and from that moment he disliked Versailles and all it stood for.

The Noailles were kind to their awkward young relative and he had a sweet and loving young wife. But having to be fashionable, he courted the beautiful mistress of the Duc de Chartres only to find that even his large fortune could not compete with that of the richest of the royal princes. Frustrated, restless and dissatisfied, Lafayette found in the American war the opportunity of becoming a hero in the New World. He was the only one of his friends who could afford to be independent by chartering a ship at his own expense and, defying government orders, set sail for America. Later they came in droves – the Noailles, the Lauzuns, the Ségurs, romantic Swedes like young Count Stedynk and Axel Fersen, deserting the pleasures of Versailles to share the hardships of Washington's armies. But to Lafayette came the glory of being the first of the volunteers to land on American soil, the only one who was to become known and loved as the American Marquis.

For the Noailles, their young relative's departure was not only an embarrassment but an outrage, particularly as one of their cousins was ambassador to England, a country still officially at peace with France. Though public opinion as a whole was in favour of the American insurgents and bored young men kicking their heels in garrison towns were thirsting for a battle, though Beaumarchais was secretly dispatching arms and ammunition to American ports by way of the West Indies, Maurepas, the King's mentor, was still unwilling to commit himself to a full-scale war. Necker, the prudent Swiss banker who was now director of finance, was of the same opinion and, like Turgot, believed that it would be madness for France to embark on a war which would drain her resources and make it impossible to carry out the necessary reforms.

Both Vergennes and the King were on the side of the insurgents and recognized that England's difficulties gave France the chance of taking her revenge for the humiliating defeats of the Seven Years' War. But Louis was both too honest and too convinced of the divine right of kings to support armed rebellion against a crown. And it was not until French shipping had suffered depredations from British piracy at sea that, in the early months of 1778, he was finally persuaded to conclude an alliance with the thirteen states of America. On 8 February, at the beginning of carnival, the British ambassador Lord Stormont was attending one of the Queen's balls at Versailles when the Comte de Provence came in from a meeting of the Grand Council to announce the news, which was greeted with acclamations of joy by the same young men who only a few nights previously had been Stormont's guests at the British Embassy.

Six weeks later, on 20 March 1778, Benjamin Franklin and Silas Dean, the former wearing neither sword nor powdered wig, were officially received at Versailles as the accredited envoys of republican America, welcomed as allies by the Bourbon King and his Hapsburg Queen. Gay, unheeding and athirst for glory, France embarked on a war which was to have incalculable consequences. It was both a splendid and a foolhardy action which was to empty her treasury and introduce a new and dangerous spirit in a class which until now had accepted the restrictions and shibboleths of the old regime. But it was strangest of all that this most reckless and unselfish of wars took place in the reign of the most timorous of kings, who on this occasion displayed an energy and a tenacity all the more surprising at a time when the Emperor Joseph was threatening to engulf all central Europe in a war.

The death of the childless Elector of Bavaria had given Joseph the chance of staking his claim to a part of southern Bavaria, which he had always coveted and to which he maintained that the Hapsburgs had a right through a treaty which dated back to the fifteenth century. The Elector Palatine, who was the rightful heir, was willing to come to an agreement. But Austria's old enemy the King of Prussia had no intention of letting the Hapsburgs extend their hegemony in Germany. Poor and ill and old, Frederick still had the finest army in Europe, and Joseph found himself confronted by Prussian and Saxon troops advancing into Bohemia. Maria Theresa was in despair, Prince Kaunitz disapproved of an action he judged to be both unwise and unjust. But Joseph, who saw himself as a great military leader, was prepared to fight, counting on the support of his brother-in-law and ally the King of France. Neither King Louis nor his foreign minister however had any intention of helping Joseph to pull his chestnuts out of the fire. Even Marie Antoinette, who was usually so loyal to her Hapsburg relatives, complained to her beloved Yolande de Polignac that Joseph was as usual only thinking of himself. Nevertheless she was ready to defend her brother when her husband told her, 'The ambitions of your family are going to upset everything. They started with Poland and now it is Bavaria. I am annoyed on your account.' As Queen of France Marie Antoinette was both angry and ashamed to hear that all French diplomats accredited to the German courts had been told to adopt the line that the Emperor's policy in Bavaria was contrary to the interests of France.

More important than any political event of 1778 was the Queen's pregnancy. On 19 April, Marie Antoinette wrote to her mother in joyful trepidation, still half afraid that something might go wrong. 'Already eight days ago I wanted to tell you of my hopes but did not dare to do so, for fear of how upset you would be if they failed to materialize.' By May the news was confirmed, giving the unhappy and harassed Maria Theresa the only consolation of the year. 'What wonderful and unexpected news. Let God be praised, that now my beloved Antoinette will be able to affirm her brilliant position by giving heirs to France.' It was the head of state speaking rather than the mother; the Empress now saw her daughter more powerful and influential, more able to dominate her husband into supporting Austrian claims. Her country counted more for Maria Theresa than any of her children. However much she might disapprove of Joseph's unconsidered actions, he was nevertheless the Emperor who dictated Austria's foreign policy, and Marie Antoinette was no more than a political pawn to serve the interests of the Hapsburgs and their empire.

This year of 1778, which was one of pride and achievement both for Louis and Marie Antoinette, was disturbed by political strife and divided loyalties because of the American war. Marie Antoinette was heart and soul a patriotic Frenchwoman, discarding her English sympathies at the outbreak of hostilities, forgetting her aristocratic prejudices in favour of the Republican allies, 'those dear Americans'. She shared the cult for Franklin, whose plain spectacles and grey, unpowdered hair were considered the height of *bon ton*, sympathizing with his infirmities and putting one of the royal litters at his disposal for the journey from Passy to Versailles.

She cut down on her expenses, cancelling a fête at Trianon, refusing the gift of a costly necklace, telling the King she would prefer to spend the money on a battleship. No Queen deserved to be more popular. If only her family could have left her alone and not harassed her to support their claims in Bavaria. Playing on every emotional cord, Maria Theresa appealed to her daughter's affections, loyalties and her love of her native country. Despairing and hysterical she referred to her 'two brothers in danger', for the Emperor had dragged the unwilling Maximilian with him to the front. Did France want Europe to be divided between Prussia and Russia? Did not the King understand that peace depended on the strength of the Franco-Austrian alliance? But Louis and Vergennes were firm in refusing to become involved, and all Marie Antoinette's tearful scenes were to no avail. Her failure only made her mother the more insistent, never stopping to consider that her pregnant daughter required rest and peace of mind. While the Empress played on her affections, the Emperor indulged in heroics. 'If you don't want to stop this war, then at least, my dear sister, you will find that we are brave and in whatever circumstances you will never have to be ashamed of a brother who will always deserve your esteem.' It would have needed a stronger character than Marie Antoinette to stand up to this barrage of emotion. But, in supporting her family's claims, she aroused the antagonism of her husband's ministers and the distrust of his subjects. From now on she was labelled 'l'Autrichienne'.

In 1778 came the return of Count Axel Fersen, who arrived in Paris after four years' absence in Sweden, where he had lived under the tutelage of an exacting father and a still more exacting king. Senator Fersen, one of the most important men in his country both as a soldier and a statesman, was a fierce old disciplinarian, who thought that it was time for his twenty-three-year-old spoilt and handsome son to settle down and marry a wealthy heiress. King Gustavus had other plans for Axel, reserving for him the role of a court favourite, a boon companion to share in his diversions and accompany him on his travels. Neither role appealed to a young man who, on his first visit to France, had fallen under the spell of the *douceur de vivre* which existed nowhere but in Paris. The rich heiress chosen by his father lived in England. A half-hearted and unsuccessful attempt to press his suit brought him back to Paris, where he arrived to find the court still installed at Versailles, having cancelled the annual visits to Compiègne and Fontainebleau.

The gay young Dauphine in the grey velvet mask, who had enchanted him one night at the opera ball, had settled down to a quiet domestic life, absorbed in the joys of impending motherhood. The Dresden figurine had become a large, stately woman who took pride in her increasing girth, measuring her waist as if to reassure herself that a baby was really on the way. The day when it made its first movement she came laughing to the King. 'I have come to complain, Your Majesty, regarding one of your subjects, who has had the audacity to kick me in the stomach.' And Louis had taken her in his arms and hugged her in a very unroyal fashion, which drew looks of disapproval from the elegant gentlemen of the bedchamber. His newfound manhood had given Louis an added confidence and he showed a touching gratitude towards his wife, telling his aunt Adelaide, hardly the person to appreciate the remark, that he only regretted having missed so much for so long. Marie Antoinette for her part was sweet and loving to the father of her unborn child, and the young couple had never been so united as during this summer of 1778 when Axel Fersen returned to Versailles.

'He is an old acquaintance,' said the Queen in a voice that betrayed her pleasure at seeing again the young Swede to whom she had given little thought in the past four years, but who now came so vividly to mind. The eighteen-year-old boy had matured into a strikingly handsome man, to whom a certain melancholy only lent an added charm. The face itself with its perfect features was impassive, almost cold; only the eyes, the clear light eyes as changeable as a northern sky, betrayed a man who was both reserved and introspective, poetical and passionate – a dangerous person to come into the life of a queen who, at twenty-three, had never been in love, who had flirted and frivolled in her rococo world without knowing romance. And from the day when his ambassador presented him at court, Axel Fersen was given the entry to *les petits appartements* and invited to Trianon. Officially it was his father's position which had opened all doors, for Senator Fersen had fought in the French army under the Maréchal de Saxe and been a leader of the pro-French party, the so-called Chapeaux which had brought King Gustavus into power.

In his letters home, Axel was careful to flatter his father by telling him how much he owed to the Senator's reputation in France. His enthusiasm for the Queen is apparent from his first letter, written on 8 September, when Marie Antoinette, in the sixth month of pregnancy, still preserved the power to fascinate. 'The Queen, who is the prettiest and most amiable princess that I know, has been so good as to enquire after me. She wanted to know why I had not come to her Sunday card parties, and she even went to the lengths of excusing herself when she heard I had been one Sunday and been unable to see her.'

Late summer at Versailles was a season without festivities or balls, when all action seemed to be suspended waiting on the great event of the royal confinement. The weather was hot and humid and the Queen rarely went out until the late evening, when she and the royal princesses would go out onto the terrace and listen to the music played by the bands of the royal guards. At times they would venture out into the gardens and mingle with the crowds – a harmless amusement but, like everything else connected with the Queen, only too apt to be criticized and misinterpreted. The fact that the people of Versailles were allowed to participate in these nocturnal concerts, that the gardens were dimly lit and the figures of the princesses in their light muslin gowns were barely discernible soon led to tales of secret assignations and illicit pleasures, followed by the usual spate of malicious songs on the Queen's nocturnal revelries. Marie Antoinette, who was both hurt and angry, retreated more and more to the privacy of the Trianon and the company of a few chosen friends. Already there was talk of Fersen, for the Polignac circle had been quick to note the Queen's interest in the romantic-looking Swedish count, whom they saw both as a challenge and a danger to their interests.

But Fersen himself was absent. After a few weeks at Versailles he had gone to the coast of Normandy to assist in military preparations for an eventual invasion of England. There was a warlike atmosphere in the country. All his friends were volunteering to fight, and he hoped for a commission in the French army. There had been a time when, in his reluctance to return to Sweden, he had gone so far as to offer his services to the King of Prussia –

something he had omitted to mention to the Queen of France, who would hardly have been pleased to hear that 'le beau Fersen' had been ready to fight in the army of her brother's enemy. Their paths might never have crossed had Frederick accepted Fersen's offer, but the last thing he wanted was a spoilt young Swede introducing an alien element into his spartan army.

His father's connections and his personal success at Versailles gave him the possibility of making a far better career in France. In spite of his dreamy and romantic appearance, Axel Fersen was first and foremost interested in himself, and in his letters home he revealed himself as vain, egotistical and self-satisfied. By the end of October he was back in Versailles from where he wrote to his father, 'the Queen continues to treat me with the greatest kindness. She always makes a point of talking to me when I go to pay her my court. She has heard of our new Swedish uniform and wants me to wear it when I attend her next levee.'

The Swedish uniform of the King's dragoons, with its blue cloak, white tunic, tight chamois breeches and dashing shako with its blue and yellow plumes, had been specially designed by King Gustavus to show off the male figure to the greatest advantage. When worn by Count Fersen at the Queen's levee it attracted the attention of every woman in the room, beginning with the Queen. Those who were close to her noted the sudden blush, the slight trembling of the hand, the look of suppressed excitement, which lasted no more than a moment before she had regained her self-control and the usual smiling mask with which she greeted distinguished foreigners. There followed a few amiable words, a compliment on his country's uniform and on the King's good taste. Perhaps she lingered too long and took too great an interest in the details, for by the end of the day every courtier at Versailles was aware that young Count Fersen was the Queen's new favourite. However, either from discretion or a fastidious reluctance to be present at the Queen's confinement, Axel absented himself from Paris in the last month of her pregnancy.

With his departure, Marie Antoinette relapsed into a state of melancholy beset by anxious fears. All France was praying for a dauphin. From Vienna her mother kept writing of the male child who was vital both for her and for the Austrian alliance. Though the Empress assured her daughter that she did not want her to do anything which would render her importunate to the King, suspect to his ministers and odious to the nation, she could not help comparing the loyalty of Prussia's Russian ally to the cowardly behaviour of France, writing:

> I hate to tell you this for there is very little you can do as matters have gone too far to put them right in time. But a stronger policy would have been of a greater advantage to France, and I must confess that I am profoundly shocked at the way in which the French abandon our interests at a time when your pregnancy

makes them so vital to their country. What can one expect for the future, for no power can survive without the help of a loyal ally.

This letter, dated 2 November, can have reached Versailles only a few weeks before the Queen's confinement and was hardly calculated to calm and comfort a heavily pregnant woman.

Used to incessant movement and excitement, Marie Antoinette was becoming bored with the quiet life, the endless precautions ordered by the doctors. By the beginning of December she was complaining to Louis that this year she would be missing half the fun of carnival, and in order to amuse her the King went to the lengths of staging a masked entertainment in his private apartments at which the oldest of his ministers were persuaded to adopt the most absurd and fantastic disguises. Maurepas, who at seventy-eight was still as gay and sparkling as ever, appeared as a winged cupid with his raddled old wife as Venus. The naval minister Sartines was Neptune, while Vergennes arrived with a globe on his head, a map of America on his stomach and one of England on his back. The most applauded costume was worn by the eighty-six-year-old Maréchal de Richelieu, who was disguised as a Triton and danced a light and graceful minuet with the septuagenarian Marquise de Mireport disguised as Aurora. Only the Austrian ambassador felt a certain embarrassment in reporting to Maria Theresa, feeling that in the present circumstances neither the Empress nor her son would appreciate this brand of Bourbon humour. But Marie Antoinette was enchanted and the courtiers, who were usually as bored and as idle as she, congratulated the King on an original and amusing entertainment, which they had never thought him capable of devising.

A week later the Queen's doctor and male midwife, a brother to the Abbé Vermond, had moved into the rooms adjoining the apartments. Four carefully selected wet nurses were waiting in attendance. Mercy wrote to Vienna that such was the public interest that over two hundred families of quality, usually residing in Paris, had established themselves at Versailles, where there was not a room to be had, either in the palace or the town.

The labour pains began on the morning of 18 December, and at half past one Madame de Lamballe, superintendent to the Queen's household and both temperamentally and physically totally unsuited to assist at a confinement, was called into the Queen's room. At 3 p.m. the King was sent for, after which there was general pandemonium. Everyone had the right to be present. No sooner had the doctors announced that the Queen was about to give birth than there was a general stampede which neither guards nor ushers were able to control.

The child was born shortly before midnight, and to the general disappointment it was a girl. The one exception was the King, who gazed happily on his little daughter when she was handed over to the Princesse de

Guéménée, who carried her off to be washed and dressed, followed by the royal nurses, the King and the gentlemen of his household.

Suddenly there was panic in the Queen's room – a rush to open the windows, an urgent cry for hot water. The Queen had a slight seizure and had to be bled immediately. In spite of the elaborate preparations, not one of the doctors or nurses had thought of providing a bowl of hot water. With immense presence of mind, Vermond ordered the surgeons to bleed the patient without the usual preparations, and his action probably saved the Queen's life. She opened her eyes and a sigh of relief went through the room, followed by an outburst of hysterical joy, with people laughing, crying and embracing one another at the same time. To add to the confusion the Princesse de Lamballe fainted from emotion.

The Austrian ambassador, who very much against his will had been forced to witness the confinement, dictated his first report to Vienna barely an hour after the birth, and in order not to alarm Maria Theresa made light of the whole incident. 'The Queen showed great courage and the effort she made to control her labour pains brought about a convulsive movement of the nerves. It was decided to bleed her and this was entirely successful. At the time of writing she is as well as can be expected.' It was only a few days later that this fastidious, middle-aged bachelor admitted how much he had suffered at having to submit to 'the curious customs of this country' and attend a confinement, an experience which made him feel quite ill.

The Queen, who was never told that her life had been in danger, recovered remarkably quickly. A natural disappointment at having failed to produce an heir was compensated by her husband's radiant happiness, and even the more cynical of courtiers were touched by the charming spectacle of the royal couple together with their child. 'Poor little thing,' said the Queen when she first took her in her arms. 'You were not wanted, but you will be none the less dear to me. You will belong solely to me. You will always be under my care, to share in my joys and lighten my sorrows.'

In Paris the disappointment over the twenty-one cannon shots, instead of the hundred and one which would have announced a dauphin, gave way to rejoicing at the munificence of the royal bounty. Both King and Queen were as generous in their alms as if their child had been a boy. Among the sums distributed to the poor of Paris was the curious gift of 12,000 francs to free the debtors who had been put in prison for failing to pay their wet nurses. A hundred young couples selected by the *curés* of the various parishes were married by the archbishop and provided with trousseaux and dowries at the Queen's expense. To celebrate the royal birth there were fireworks at the Hôtel de Ville, while in all the poor quarters of the city the fountains ran with wine and bread and meat was distributed free. Performances were held at the Comédie Française where, according to an old tradition, the King's box was reserved for the coalmen and the Queen's box for the fishwives.

But there was little sincerity in the celebrations at Versailles or in the congratulations for the royal family. Monsieur, the King's brother, might derive comfort from the fact that the baby was a girl, but now that Louis had proved his manhood, and Marie Antoinette was an exceptionally healthy woman, there was no reason why they should not produce a large family. Artois, whose son was still the heir, was too occupied with his pleasures to give much thought to the future, but his wife and sister-in-law, those embittered Piedmontese princesses, who had never been considered at court, cordially hated Marie Antoinette and resented an event which would enhance her prestige. The aunts on the contrary were genuinely pleased that their nephew had managed to father a child, and for a short while were reconciled to their Austrian niece.

Apart from a small coterie, Marie Antoinette had few real friends at court. Maurepas feared her increasing influence on the King, while his wife had never forgiven the exile of her favourite nephew, the Duc d'Aiguillon. The '*grandes charges*', the great families with a hereditary right to sit in the Queen's room during a royal confinement, were outraged at finding Madame de Polignac installed at the bedside. The Princesse de Lamballe and the Princesse de Guéménée, the two women with the most important positions in the Queen's household, were united in their dislike of the new favourite, without whose company the Queen seemed unable to exist.

From the highest echelons to the lowest spread an atmosphere of jealousy and distrust; an underlying subversiveness sapping at the royal authority. The old Duc de Richelieu, who had lived under three reigns, was once asked by the King to give his impressions of the courts in which he had served, to which he replied, 'Sire, under your great ancestor King Louis XIV no one dared to speak a word; under your grandfather they began to whisper, and now they speak out loud,' at which the King thought fit to laugh. But he did not laugh when, a few days before his wife's confinement, a bundle of papers was thrown through a window of the Oeil de Bœuf, consisting of a series of scurrilous lampoons naming the Queen and various ladies of the court. Orders were immediately given to the police to lay hands on the offender. But no further measures were taken when the author was discovered to be the son of the Marquis de Champenetz, a young man whose witty and salacious ditties made him very popular at court, particularly with the Comte de Maurepas, whose light-hearted humour delighted in comic songs.

With a king who was too weak to assert his will and a minister who was too cynical to care, the abuses multiplied. The most glaring of all was when Madame de Marsan, former governess to the royal princes who had ranked among Marie Antoinette's enemies from the day of her arrival in France, now persuaded the King to promote her profligate nephew, Louis de Rohan, to the post of Grand Almoner of France. It was sufficiently scandalous that someone as debauched as Prince Louis should have been created Cardinal and

Archbishop of Strasbourg in succession of his uncle. But that he should now be given one of the highest church appointments in the kingdom, for no other reason than that the late King had promised it to his aunt, was damaging both to the clergy and to the Crown. No one was more angry than the Queen, but neither tears nor scenes were of any avail against the King's stubborn and misguided loyalty to his grandfather and his governess. On 18 December, the day of her birth, Marie Thérèse Charlotte was solemnly christened in the royal chapel of Versailles by his eminence the Cardinal of Strasbourg, Grand Almoner of France. From now on the young Queen, who would never learn how to forgive or to forget, vowed that even if she had to accept the Cardinal's presence at Versailles he would never gain admittance to her domain at Le Trianon. Marie Antoinette's unflinching pride and Rohan's overwhelming vanity were to prove disastrous to them both.

A t the beginning of February the King and Queen drove into Paris to attend a mass of thanksgiving at Notre Dame, an event which usually took place only for the birth of a dauphin. Marie Antoinette had never looked so lovely as in these first months of motherhood when she radiated happiness and good will. But the crowds were not as large, nor the cheering as loud as had been expected. Neither the public celebrations nor the generosity of the royal gifts could compensate for the high cost of living and the crippling taxes which were paying for a war so far away as to have little meaning for the average Frenchman. The naval battles fought out in the Atlantic brought no gain to the Parisian workman, and in the poorer quarters of St Antoine there were few who had ever heard of Washington. The calumnies of Versailles were spreading to the city, and people whose business it was to trade in filth made sure that the scurrilous rhymes and broadsheets which came out of the private presses of the Palais de Luxembourg and the Palais Royal should find their way into the humblest taverns. Failed writers, out-of-work journalists and penniless poets were ready to sell their wares to the highest bidders. As Beaumarchais wrote in one of his immortal comedies, 'Nothing is as powerful as calumny, which can spread from the first breath to a tempest of scandal.'

Both Monsieur, the King's brother, and the Duc de Chartres were fully aware that Marie Antoinette was almost childishly innocent and intrinsically virtuous, but she was a more vulnerable target than the King, whom the people loved and revered.

Philippe d'Orléans's bitterness against the court was comparatively recent, though the relations between the older and younger branches of the House of Bourbon had always been marred by jealousy and distrust. The young Duc de Chartres, immensely rich and intensely ambitious, aspired to become high admiral in succession to his father-in-law, the Duc de Penthièvre. He was eager to fight and to earn his laurels at sea, and the American war provided a longed-for opportunity. But in true Bourbon tradition Louis XVI had always envied and disliked his more brilliant cousin, and neither he nor his ministers had any intention of allowing an Orléans to become a naval hero. Though his comrades testified to his courage at the battle of Ushant, a mistake in interpreting a signal which led him to retire his ships at a critical moment in the combat gave his Admiral the chance of making him into the scapegoat for a battle which ended in a draw rather than a victory.

As a prince of the blood, Chartres was given the honour of bringing the dispatches back to Paris, where he was accorded a hero's welcome at the Opera House and the Palais Royal. But at Versailles a secret report addressed to the naval minister accused him of negligence and cowardice. When he appeared at court the King barely addressed a word to him and the courtiers, taking their cue from the King, made fun of him behind his back. Seeing his hopes of becoming grand admiral fade in a cloud of opprobrium, Chartres resigned from the navy, and in a letter full of bitterness and pride he wrote to King Louis, 'I hoped to serve Your Majesty at sea and instead I seem to have forfeited the favour of my father-in-law, the future of my children, the happiness of my wife and my own reputation.' All he now wanted was to be transferred to the army and to vindicate his honour. Artois, who was his only friend at court, enlisted the Queen's support in obtaining him some suitable appointment. Marie Antoinette, who loved to please, used all her influence in persuading an unwilling King to create a new command in making him colonel-in-chief of the *Chevau-Légers* (the light horse), a position which in no way satisfied his ambition, and before long the wits of Versailles had dubbed him 'colonel-in-chief of *Les Têtes Légères* (the empty heads), an epigram at which the Queen was sufficiently unwise to laugh with that frank, open laughter, so careless and light-hearted, so utterly devoid of malice, but so dangerous in a country where wit was always barbed and sufficient to turn a vain and angry man into an enemy – an enemy more powerful and more dangerous than Provence, who was too timid and circumspect to come out into the open.

Chartres was now the acknowledged leader of the Fronde, the people's champion against the court, and spokesman for the rebellious parliament. The Palais Royal became the meeting place for all the discontented elements in town, and as grand master of the French freemasons Chartres fell even more under the influence of the secret societies which, under cover of the masonic lodges, worked to disrupt society. The bookshops of the Palais Royal sold libellous broadsheets against the court, and in the gardens the musicians who strummed their guitars beneath the chestnut trees sang of the Queen's secret amours. Shortly before the royal birth the Duke had been heard to say in public, 'Coigny's child will never be my king.' The Duc de Coigny, one of the Queen's coterie, was among those who quite erroneously were believed to be her lovers. The words came back to Marie Antoinette, who with contempt and a certain sadness said, 'I must confess it is not very pleasant for me to have such things said about me.' Then with a flash of humour she added, 'But if it is unkind of people to accuse me of having so many lovers, it is peculiar on my part not to have had even one.' No lover, only a husband who now, when she had barely recovered from her confinement, was more passionate and eager than he had ever shown himself and who was so clumsy and awkward in trying to please his young wife before. But she was happy with her child, happy to be a mother. Her letters to the Empress abound in details of the baby's progress, in which she took far more interest than in the political events. This caused Maria Theresa to complain that her son-in-law had done little to protect the interests of his ally.

Both Louis and Vergennes had remained firmly resolved not to get involved in a war over Bavaria. After a frustrating and unsuccessful campaign, the Emperor had been forced to give in to his mother's desire for peace, a peace which was hard on Maria Theresa as it brought to the council tables of Europe Catherine of Russia, a woman whose character and morals she detested and who, together with her son-in-law, King Louis, was to be one of two mediating powers at the Peace of Teschen.

'Peace is signed at last and I want you to convey my gratitude to the King. And with it goes my gratitude to you, my darling child, for what he has done is because of his tenderness for you,' wrote the Empress to the daughter who in private she did not think had done half enough. But as Marie Antoinette told her mother's ambassador, 'When it comes to politics, I have very little influence over the King.' Both Maurepas and Vergennes did their best to prevent the King from imparting state secrets to his wife, and one can hardly blame them. When Gilbert de Lafayette returned from America in the early spring of 1779, he was warned by Maurepas not to impart details of military preparations to the Queen.

On receiving him at Versailles, she questioned him about the plans for the invasion of England, and he was sufficiently tactless to reply that he had been specially instructed not to discuss such matters. Marie Antoinette was furious. She had not liked Lafayette as a callow adolescent. She liked him even less now that he was full of his own importance, regarding himself as General Washington's spokesman. But at Versailles it was considered *bon ton* to enthuse over the twenty-year-old Marquis who, defying the orders of his King, had gone off to fight for freedom. Such was his popularity that the only punishment for his disobedience had been a week's house arrest at his father-in-law's Paris mansion. He then returned to be fêted at Versailles, where even the Queen had to be gracious and allow him to kiss her hand.

Most of the *jeunesse dorée* had volunteered to fight, some out of ambition, some out of boredom, a few out of idealism, attracted by the simple life in a new world. But there was one among them who had volunteered in the hope of escaping from himself and from the interest he was beginning to arouse in a woman to whom he could never dare to aspire.

In a despatch dated 10 April 1779, the Swedish ambassador Count Creutz wrote to his King,

I want to confide to Your Majesty that Count Fersen has been singled out by the Queen in such a way as to give offence to certain persons. I confess that I can't help thinking that she has a weakness for him, as I have too many proofs of it to doubt. Count Fersen's behaviour on this occasion has been quite admirable, both for its modesty and reserve and because of the decision he has taken to leave for America, thereby avoiding all possible danger. But it needed a strength of character unusual in his age to resist such temptation. In these last days the Queen could not keep her eyes off him. Looking at him they filled with tears. I beg of Your Majesty to keep this a secret both for her sake and for that of Senator Fersen. All the favourites were delighted to hear of his departure. The Duchesse de Fitz-James said to him, 'How is it, monsieur, that you are able to abandon your conquests?' to which he replied, 'Had I made any, madame, I would not have abandoned them. But I leave completely free and unfortunately without regrets.' Your Majesty will agree that such an answer shows a wisdom unusual at that age.

It must have been hard for Axel Fersen to tear himself away from the delights of Versailles and the enchanting Queen. We can see her as she must have appeared to him in the spring of 1779 – the year when Madame Vigée-Lebrun painted her live for the first time in a portrait destined for her brother the Emperor. It is a portrait on which there were to be many variations from the years 1779–87, during which the artist painted the Queen no less than thirty times. She worked with the same two or three formulas, yet each time conveying with a surprising freshness the evanescent charms of a woman who was not strictly beautiful, in some ways barely pretty, with her pouting mouth with the thick Hapsburg lip and high, bulging forehead, but was nevertheless possessed of a radiance which defied all criticism.

Marie Antoinette was not an easy subject to paint. Many had tried and failed, among them established artists like Ducreux and Duplessis. The Empress's letters to her daughter abound in complaints that none of the portraits sent to Vienna ever did her justice. The young Vigée-Lebrun, of the same age as the Queen, was the only one who succeeded in capturing a likeness while minimizing her defects and emphasizing her good points, as in the charming picture with the rose which shows off her beautiful hands. In this picture painted in 1779, she appears as Vigée-Lebrun described her in her memoirs.

Marie Antoinette was tall and admirably built, being somewhat stout but not excessively so. Her arms were superb, her hands small and admirably formed.... She had the best neck of any woman in France, carrying her head high with a dignity which stamped her as a queen in the midst of her whole court. Her majestic mien did not in the least diminish the sweetness and amiability of her face. Her features were not regular; her blue eyes were not large but both merry and kind. The nose was slender, the mouth not too large, though perhaps the lips were rather thick. But the most remarkable thing about her was the splendour of her complexion. I have never seen one so brilliant and transparent.

Vigée-Lebrun sees Marie Antoinette with the eye of a painter, even if it is the uncritical eye of a court painter whose career depended on the patronage of a woman who wished to be immortalized as a queen of fashion rather than as a queen of France.

Marie Antoinette may have been wearing the pale blue satin dress of the painting when Fersen saw her at the end of March at a fête at Trianon. It was their last meeting, for two days later she fell ill with measles. Even her illness gave rise to gossip when it became known that she had caught it from Madame de Polignac, who was confined to bed at her house near La Muette. Separation from her husband, even from her child, meant less to Marie Antoinette than separation from a friend whose company had become essential to her happiness. None of the palace ladies, not even Marie Thérèse de Lamballe, and still less her Italian sisters-in-law who according to etiquette had to be in waiting during her illness, were able to amuse the Queen who, when her fever had gone, was faced with three weeks of quarantine to be spent at Trianon. At least it gave her the chance of sleeping for the first time in the pavilion which had been newly decorated according to her taste. The exquisite furniture was designed by Roentgen and Jacob, and bronzes by Gouthière, marble statuettes by Clodion and the romantic landscapes by Hubert Robert, all chosen by the Queen with the help of the architect Richard Mique. There were gifts from a loving mother: family portraits from Vienna, vases of petrified wood studded with precious stones, rare porcelains, boxes in lapis, quartz and crystal. It was an enchanting pavilion in which everything was light and airy, feminine and frivolous, set in a décor of white and gold with hangings of turquoise and rose-coloured silk and ceilings frescoed by Barthélemy, who had been a pupil of Boucher. Trianon was the Queen's domain, the one place where she felt at home and where life would be so simple and idyllic were it not for the jealousy of Versailles, where her enemies called it 'Little Vienna'.

Giddy and thoughtless, Marie Antoinette had no one to advise her other than her mother's ambassador, who was hardly in a position to disapprove openly of her foolish actions when they were condoned by the King and accepted by his ministers. In those first weeks of quarantine she managed to shock all the more respectable elements at court by selecting four of the most amusing men of her coterie to keep her company at Trianon. None of the four was a suitable *garde malade* for a Queen of France. They were de Guines, who had never been completely absolved from his part in a notorious trial; Coigny, who according to gossip was a lover of the Queen; Esterhazy, a Hungarian serving in the French army; and Besenval, a fifty-year-old bachelor and a well-known libertine. All four were supporters of Choiseul and only too ready to encourage Marie Antoinette in her grievances against Maurepas. All that Mercy could do was to make sure that these 'gentlemen in waiting' were only on duty during the daytime. Even so, 7 a.m. until 11 p.m. were long hours in which to entertain a bored young queen who was missing the company of Yolande de Polignac and kept dreaming of the romantic young Swede who had captured her imagination.

De Guines, with his flute playing, his scathing repartees, and Besenval, with his witty ditties and barbed sallies, knew all too well how to denigrate the King's ministers. In a subtler and more insidious fashion, they denigrated the King himself, by working on Marie Antoinette's vanity and pride and suggesting the names of those she should put forward for ministerial jobs, men on whose loyalty she could count and who would never dare to oppose her will. 'The poison of their language is only moderated by the presence of Madame,' wrote Mercy to Maria Theresa. 'But Madame, and one can hardly blame her, did not spend all day by the couch of the sister-in-law who showed her all too clearly that she was bored by her company.'

Meanwhile there was much mockery and laughter at Versailles as to who in a similar situation would be the four ladies chosen by the King. All the Queen's enemies were longing to find a mistress for King Louis but he showed no inclination in that direction, confessing to Maurepas that he was so much in love with his wife that he found it difficult to refuse her anything, words which in no way pleased his 'mentor', who saw all too clearly the storms which lay ahead.

In France the war was becoming ever more unpopular, for the year 1779, which brought the combined fleets of Spain and France out into the Channel in preparation for an invasion of England, had ended in total failure. The Spanish ships were late in arriving and there was further delay due to quarrels over precedence among the allies. Contrary winds blew the ships off course and the unhygienic conditions on board together with the shortage of food supplies caused outbreaks of scurvy and dysentery among the crews. In a letter dated 13 September, Marie Antoinette wrote to her mother showing for the first time a genuine concern over public discontent: 'The people complain a lot that Monsieur d'Orvilliers, with forces in every way superior to the English, never succeeded in engaging them in battle or managed to prevent any of the merchant ships from returning to port. A great deal of money has been wasted for nothing and I don't think there is the slightest chance of having peace this winter.' A month later she writes again:

> We have given up our visit to Fontainebleau on account of the expense caused by the war and also so as to be in closer touch with news of the army. We have spent five days at Choisy and are off tomorrow for a fortnight in Marly.... It is a lost campaign of enormous expense and, to make matters worse, the illness which broke out in the ships caused a lot of casualties. Also the land troops waiting to invade have been affected by the dysentery which is prevalent all along the coasts of Normandy and Brittany.

By May 1780, the French expeditionary force commanded by Général Rochambeau was finally on its way to America. On board was Count Axel Fersen, who had signed on for the duration of hostilities. His own common-sense rather than the advice of Breteuil (the French ambassador) had told him it was time for him to get away and to forget what he now recognized to be his hopeless love for the Queen. Marie Antoinette shed tears at his departure, but the tears did not last for long. For the illness of Madame de Polignac, culminating in a pregnancy for which either Vaudreuil or d'Adhémer was said to be responsible, drove all other thoughts from her mind. Ignoring the scandal, she announced her intention of assisting at the confinement, and no one dared do more than murmur when the King himself gave orders for the Count de Polignac to be transferred to La Muette so that the Queen could have easier access to her friend who had a house near the Bois de Boulogne. Living in cramped, uncomfortable quarters in a place too small to house a court, the palace ladies nursed their grievances against the Polignacs. At Bellevue the King's aunts made no secret of their disapproval and there were scandalous broadsheets with pictures of the Queen in the role of midwife. With her light-hearted indifference, Marie Antoinette ignored the gossip of her court. No sooner was the Countess recovered from her confinement than her husband was created a duke and, to the fury of all the duchesses and princesses, Yolande de Polignac became '*une dame à tabouret*' with the right of sitting on a stool in the presence of the King. But in writing to the Empress, Comte Mercy describes the Polignacs as a family who were more interested in money than in honours.

To have her daughter, the Queen of France, assisting at the confinement of a woman of dubious morals and tarnished reputation upset the proud old Empress to such a degree as to affect her health, which had been rapidly deteriorating in the past year. One disappointment had followed on the other. On the one hand was her son making overtures of friendship to the Russian Empress, a woman she had always regarded with loathing and contempt. On the other the daughter for whom she had secured the greatest matrimonial prize in Europe was allowing herself to be dominated by what could at best be called a schoolgirl infatuation. Neither Maria Theresa nor Joseph appears to have had any doubts that Marie Antoinette's relationship with Yolande de Polignac was completely innocent. To the end of his life the Emperor persisted in regarding his sister as one of the most virtuous women he had ever known. The Empress, who in private referred to Yolande de Polignac as 'that woman', was irritated to hear the Baron de Breteuil speaking of her in eulogistic terms, dwelling on the 'wonderful influence' she had over the Queen. 'At this I changed the subject,' wrote Maria Theresa with a note of asperity.

The Empress could see little proof of Yolande de Polignac's 'wonderful influence' when her daughter was indulging in a senseless round of dissipation. While Necker was trying to economize on the enormous expenses of the royal household by suppressing hundreds of superfluous jobs in the kitchens and the stables, economies of which the Queen approved, he was too much of a courtier to question her personal expenses. In 1780, when Rochambeau's army was on its way to America, 2,000 men having been left behind owing to a shortage of transport, Marie Antoinette was occupied in giving the last touches to her theatre at Trianon, an exquisite building designed by Mique with a simple classical façade and an interior aglow with gilding, reproducing on a smaller scale the elaborate decor of Gabriel's theatre at Versailles.

On this stage, the Queen and Artois and some of their chosen friends performed in pastoral comedies such as Rousseau's *Le Devin du Village*, comedies extolling the simple life which were the fashion at the time. In a sense they were reverting to the pleasures of their early youth and the plays they had acted in secret in the attics of Versailles, away from the disapproving eyes of the royal aunts. But it would have been better if they could have continued to act in secret. For they were at once too exclusive and too public. All the actors belonged to the Polignac coterie, while the audiences consisted only of the King, Monsieur, the royal princesses, and the men and women belonging to the household staff of Trianon. None of the palace ladies, not even Madame de Lamballe, was admitted, which caused a great deal of offence and recrimination. The first gentleman of the Queen's bedchamber, the Duc de Fronsac, went so far as to send an official complaint claiming his right to be present, to which the Queen replied that no one could claim a court appointment when she was only being an actress, and that Trianon was not a palace but a private house.

When Maria Theresa wrote in alarm over her daughter's unsuitable passion for play acting, Comte Mercy replied that the plays at Trianon at least had the advantage of keeping the royal couple together, that the King never missed a performance and always applauded loudest whenever the Queen was on the stage. In private Mercy may have thought that his imperial mistress had no right to complain when this love of play acting had been ingrained in her children from their earliest youth, and her own ministers had criticized Maria Theresa for allowing her family to appear so often on the stage. The Emperor still had a weakness for play acting, for wandering in disguise through the streets of Vienna in the role of a modern Haroun al-Rashid, a habit of which, in her intolerant old age, his mother thoroughly disapproved.

Of all Maria Theresa's sixteen children, her eldest son and her youngest daughter, the two in whom she had placed the greatest hopes, were the ones who gave her the least satisfaction. All that she still hoped from life was to see the birth of a dauphin of France. There is not a single letter written to Marie Antoinette in which she does not harp on the same theme. 'We must have a dauphin. I am getting impatient. I have not got the time to wait.' Racked by rheumatism, afflicted with chronic catarrh, so obese that she could no longer climb the stairs, her mind still lucid but becoming increasingly forgetful, Maria Theresa struggled on, always hoping to hear the news that never came. In what was to be her last letter to her daughter she was still writing on what had already been discussed a hundred times. 'If only you could have slept together in the German way and enjoyed the intimacy that comes from sleeping in a double bed.' Two days later, on All Souls' Day, she caught a chill paying her customary pilgrimage to the family vault in the Capuchin church. Pneumonia set in and after a fortnight of agonizing pain, of coughing and gasping for breath so that she was unable to stay in bed, the Empress died in full possession of her faculties, announcing herself that the time had come for her to receive the sacraments. Joseph, who was with her till the end, refused to believe that she had to die. When she finally collapsed in his arms, he sobbed like a child.

Maria Theresa died on 29 November 1780, but the news did not reach Versailles till 6 December. The King, who had not the courage to break the news to his wife, entrusted the task to the Abbé Vermond. Marie Antoinette was inconsolable. Genuine unhappiness over the death of a mother she revered, remorse combined with a feeling that she had failed her and been unworthy of her love, reduced her to such a state of misery that for many weeks she refused to appear in public and remained shut up at Trianon, either with Madame de Lamballe or Yolande de Polignac, reminiscing about her mother and father and her childhood at Schönbrunn. In a despairing letter to the Emperor she wrote, 'I am writing to you in tears, overwhelmed with grief – oh my brother, my friend, you are all that is left to me in a country which will always be dear to me. Look after yourself well and preserve your strength. You owe it to the world.... Adieu, for my tears are flowing so fast I can no longer see to write. I embrace you.' Her mother's death had made Joseph all-important to her – a heroic figure in contrast to the husband of whom she was fond and had learnt to esteem but could never look up to. Physically Louis was not improving with the years. In his middle twenties he was already becoming obese with a large stomach and a pronounced double chin. His manners were brusque and very often rude, with a rough and ready humour which sometimes wounded without intent. As Joseph wrote to his brother Leopold, 'It cannot be much fun for our sister to go to bed with Louis.' But in those months of mourning during which the Queen never sat down at a card table, and the courtiers grumbled over the monotony of life at Versailles, Comte Mercy was able to inform the Emperor that the royal couple's conjugal life was such as to give great hopes of the future, and by the end of April 1781 Marie Antoinette was officially reported to be pregnant again.

The hundred and one gunshots which on 22 October 1781 announced the birth of a dauphin heralded what was to be the most glorious year of the reign. Three days before, on the other side of the Atlantic, the English General Cornwallis had surrendered at Yorktown to the Franco-American troops commanded by Rochambeau and Washington. And though the war was to drag on for another year, victory was already in sight. The enthusiasm with which the French people welcomed the birth of her son made it seem as if Marie Antoinette could still regain the popularity she had enjoyed as Dauphine and forfeited as Queen. It had been an easy birth and this time the doctors took the precaution of preventing the crowds of importunate courtiers from invading the Queen's room and, in the case of the child being again a girl, keeping the news from the mother until all danger had passed and she had been moved from *le lit du travail* back into her own bed.

Poor Marie Antoinette was waiting anxiously, prepared for another disappointment, when Louis appeared by her bed, half laughing, half crying, telling her in a voice quivering with excitement, 'Madame, Monsieur le Dauphin asks for permission to enter.' And there was Madame de Guéménée carrying a small bundle smothered in lace – at once her vindication and her triumph.

A dauphin: everything forgotten and everything forgiven – all the years of taunts and humiliations, from her mother's remonstrations and advice to the insolent shouts of the fishwives, 'What we need is a dauphin.' Marie Antoinette felt a jealous, overwhelming love for the son who would belong to the nation rather than to her, and she embraced him as if for the first time and the last before handing him over to Madame de Guéménée, saying, 'Take him back for he belongs not to me but to the country. My daughter, however, is my own.'

From the moment when the gilded doors of the *petits appartements* were thrown open to the sound of trumpets and the birth of a dauphin was announced to the world, Versailles was caught up in an explosion of joy. Everyone wanted to be the first to see, the first to congratulate, when Madame de Guéménée, beaming with pride, holding the baby in her arms, was carried in a chair through the Gallery of Mirrors, acclaimed by a rapturous crowd. Close behind her came King Louis, unable to keep his eyes off the child, friendly and affable with everyone, giving his hand to all – a man who for the first time really felt himself to be a king with his people sharing in his joy. At every moment he could be heard repeating the magic phrase 'my son the Dauphin'.

That same afternoon, in the royal chapel of Versailles, Louis Joseph Xavier François was christened by the Grand Almoner of France. Standing proxy for his godfather, the Emperor, was Monsieur, so that two of Marie Antoinette's bitterest enemies were officiating at the ceremony. Monsieur was as smiling and inscrutable as ever, never betraying either by word or gesture his disappointment at a birth which took him ever further from the throne. Artois cared less, but showed it more. When his son, the little Duc d'Angoulême, remarked that his baby cousin was 'very small', he replied with a rueful humour, 'Don't worry. You will find him quite big enough one day.' But Artois was sufficiently generous to be pleased for the sake of his pretty sister-in-law, whose married life must have been as tedious as his own, though now that he had done his duty and produced three children his ugly wife was rarely honoured by his visits.

Today all criticism was silenced in the joyful excitement which pervaded Versailles, spreading to Paris and across France, where there was dancing and singing in every street and square. There was not a provincial theatre which did not produce some allegory on the royal couple, not a local paper which did not print a eulogistic poem extolling their virtues, poems which in many cases were written by men who, a few years later, were to be the most rabid of Jacobins.

For over a month one celebration followed on the other. But the most exciting of all was the day when the Duc de Lauzun arrived in Paris, bringing the news of Cornwallis's capitulation at Yorktown. Rochambeau had honoured Lauzun as an officer whom he considered to be one of the bravest of the brave, a man who practically single-handed had captured Senegal and at his own expense had raised the regiment he had commanded with valour in America. But Lauzun was no longer *persona grata* at Versailles. Marie Antoinette had not forgotten his insolence in having dared to make love to a queen. It was an incident for which her innocent coquetry had been largely responsible, and which could so easily have been forgiven, had it not been magnified a hundredfold by the Polignac coterie, who saw in the fascinating Lauzun someone it was wiser to destroy. Every effort had been made to belittle him in the eyes of the Queen, and the Duke arrived at Versailles to be officially welcomed by the King and his ministers, but to be deliberately snubbed by Marie Antoinette, who made her convalescence an excuse to refuse him an audience, another mistake so carelessly made and later to be so bitterly regretted. By her treatment of Lauzun the Queen lost a friend who would have defended her to the end.

Curiously enough, Axel Fersen was among those who recognized the chivalrous qualities of a man who was worshipped by his soldiers and in wartime had refused the luxuries denied to his men. Seated round the camp-fire in America, far removed from the intrigues of Versailles, the young Swede listened entranced to Lauzun recounting his amatory exploits, telling of the beautiful women he had loved in all the capitals of Europe. But a year later, when Fersen returned to France, he found that his friend was sadly changed, having grown hard and embittered, an *habitué* of the Palais Royal who avoided Versailles.

In 1782 all the honours and ovations which celebrated the victory went to the young Marquis de Lafayette, who arrived in Paris on 21 January, the day on which the town was officially fêting the birth of the Dauphin. No one was at home at the Hôtel de Noailles. The Marquise, who in his absence had been appointed *dame de Palais*, was at the Hôtel de Ville in attendance on the Queen. But no sooner did Marie Antoinette hear of his arrival than she made the charming gesture of taking the young Marquise in her carriage and driving her straight to the Hôtel de Noailles, where Adrienne was so over-come at the sight of her beloved husband that she fainted straight into his arms, a sight that delighted the crowds converging from every street and square to acclaim the Queen and the Marquis de Lafayette.

At last he was famous. Even the *poissardes* were familiar with his name, chanting it in chorus as they pelted him with flowers. The Noailles who had looked down on him, the Queen who had mocked at him were welcoming him as the hero of the day. At twenty-five Gilbert de Lafayette had not yet learnt the fickleness of public acclaim. For one season he was the darling of Versailles and Adrienne had to be the patient, submissive wife while the prettiest women at court disputed his favours. At the state ball held in honour of the Russian Tsarevich and the Grand Duchess Maria Feodorovna, travel-ling under the incognito of the Comte and Comtesse du Nord, Lafayette was chosen as a dancing partner by the Queen. And now there was no question of Marie Antoinette making fun of his dancing. But neither was there any need for Madame de Polignac to fear that the young Marquis might impinge on her empire, for Lafayette and the Queen had no real liking for one another. Both were too tactless and both were too vain. At this ball, one of the most splendid ever held at Versailles, Gilbert de Lafayette was heard to say too loudly that the cost of one such fête would feed a regiment in America for a whole year. Marie Antoinette did not appreciate criticism of this kind any more than King Louis had appreciated Necker's presumption when he pub-lished his famous *Compte Rendu* which gave a detailed and optimistic account of the country's finances, omitting to include the huge loans he had borrowed from foreign banks to bolster the economy.

The King's dislike of what he regarded as a piece of self-glorification on the part of a Protestant banker gave Maurepas the opportunity of getting rid of a minister whose popularity with the general public was rendering him too powerful. Such was his reputation that his fall in the summer of 1781 affected

French credit abroad, which the mediocrity of his immediate successors did little to restore. By the end of the year Maurepas himself was dead, in the words of the young Talleyrand, 'more regretted than he deserved to be'. A minister in his early twenties, when he had been dismissed from office for making fun of Madame de Pompadour, Maurepas had reached the age of eighty-one without ever attempting to be serious, still ready to enjoy scurrilous rhymes and witty lampoons even when they were written at his own expense. But King Louis had loved his old mentor, who had given him his first lessons in kingship and had helped him to lose the intolerance and harshness of a narrow-minded and bigoted education. He had also prevented the Queen from interfering in politics. For one of Maurepas' only convictions was that no Queen of France should ever be allowed to have a hand in the running of the country. Comte Mercy had gone so far as to accuse him of deliberately encouraging the Queen in her follies and extravagances and of favouring her friendship with the Polignacs. This was probably true, for Maurepas may well have thought that Marie Antoinette playing the shepherdess at Trianon did less harm than when she tried to meddle in politics. But he never thought that the gentle little creature, the poor relation he had brought to the notice of the Queen, would bring a train of ambitious bloodsuckers in her wake. As his health began to fail he found it increasingly difficult to stand up against the Queen when she finished a sentence with the words '*J'exige*' (I demand).

Pushed by the Polignacs and their coterie to play a role for which she had neither the knowledge nor the understanding, Marie Antoinette interfered increasingly in the making and unmaking of ministers. She does not appear to have had anything to do with Necker's dismissal, for his wife writes in her diary, 'The Queen was so upset over Mr Necker leaving the government that she cried for a whole day.' She and her coterie were, however, directly responsible for the appointment of the Marquis de Castries to the Ministry of the Marine and of the Comte de Ségur to the Ministry of War. The latter was her last victory over Maurepas, who together with the King considered Ségur, the father of one of the Queen's favourite courtiers, to be too old and infirm for the job. But the Queen was so insistent, so determined to have her way, that he had no choice but to comply. Maurepas confessed to a friend that it was the cruellest blow he had suffered in the whole of his political career.

On the day of Ségur's appointment, Marie Antoinette announced with pride to Madame Campan, 'You have just seen a minister of my own choice. I am delighted for the King's sake, because he is a good man. But in a way I am sorry to have played a part in his nomination, because it makes me responsible.' She had every reason to be sorry. Ségur was a brave and honest soldier, but he had the rigid standards of an old man blind to a changing world. To help the sons of the poorer nobility, who had no other career open to them than the army and the Church, he introduced a law by which no commoner, other than those whose fathers had won the Cross of St Louis, could be promoted beyond the rank of captain, thus eliminating by a stroke of the pen all the useful reforms brought in by the Comte de St Germain, who had opened out the army to the rising middle classes. First-class engineers like the future Jacobin Lazare Carnot, brilliant artillery officers like Choderlos de Laclos, found their careers blocked to make way for men who in many cases had nothing to recommend them other than their titles. When Marie Antoinette regretted having helped to obtain the nomination of Ségur, she little knew for how much she was responsible. Nor did she realize that the book which everyone was reading and discussing in that summer of 1782, which she herself was reading in secret from the King, was written by an embittered officer taking his revenge on a society which, because of his lack of quarterings, prevented him from ever holding a command.

Who was this Choderlos de Laclos, who could describe with such a terrifying accuracy the depraved morals of a world to which he had never been admitted? Certain great ladies at Versailles would not have liked to hear that the author had found their counterparts in the provinces, yawning their lives away in cold and draughty châteaux, and that there were just as many 'Madames de Merteuil' in the garrison towns of Grenoble and La Rochelle as in the Parisian palaces of the princes of the blood. The debauched 'Valmont', who by his enemies at Versailles was said to be the portrait of Lauzun, could have been any bored young officer who found pleasure in corrupting the local girls. After two hundred years *Les Liaisons Dangereuses* remains the cruellest and also the most profound of all the indictments against the old regime. But in 1782 the book was no more than a *succès de scandale* forgotten two years later when *Figaro* reappeared on the stage, censored, proscribed but finally triumphant. Like so many other disappointed officers, Laclos found his way to the Palais Royal to become the *âme damnée* of the future Philippe Egalité.

There was already talk of Beaumarchais' *Figaro* at the time of the Russian visit. The Grand Duchess Maria Feodorovna, who wanted to supply her formidable mother-in-law, the Empress Catherine, with the latest scandal of literary Paris, asked the Baron Grimm to arrange for Monsieur de Beaumarchais to read her extracts of his latest play. The King had forbidden *Le Mariage de Figaro* to be performed in public, and Beaumarchais was only too ready to give private renditions of his play, for the more people who heard it, the more people would talk about it and it would become more difficult for King Louis to persist in his veto. Louis was one of the few who had recognized the dynamite underlying the laughter. However much it might amuse his courtiers to be described as 'useless parasites who had done nothing in their lives beyond taking the trouble to be born', he, Louis, was not prepared to have his administration mocked at, his institutions decried by a man who made fun of everything that should be respected in the state. A man like Beaumarchais was particularly dangerous in the present mood of the country, when it was considered *bon ton* to denigrate the government. However, the King's veto did not prevent Monsieur de Beaumarchais from being lionized in every fashionable salon and from delighting the Russian Grand Duchess with a selected reading of his play.

Maria Feodorovna's lady-in-waiting, Madame d'Oberkirch, wrote in her memoirs, 'We found the play most interesting and Monsieur de Beamarchais a most fascinating man.' Both she and her royal mistress were entranced by everyone they met and everything they saw in France, from the splendour of Versailles to the beauty of the summer fêtes given by the Condés at Chantilly, the Duc d'Orléans at Rainey and the Comte d'Artois at Bagatelle, that exquisite pavilion surrounded by rose gardens, built in six weeks as a wager with the Queen. At the fancy dress ball held in Gabriel's theatre at Versailles, where no less than five thousand candles glittered in crystal chandeliers and where on the Queen's orders all the ladies who danced had to wear white satin dominoes with hoops and trains, Marie Antoinette appeared wearing a white plumed hat decorated with the famous Pitt diamond, valued at no less than two million francs.

Never had there been such an orgy of spending as during this year, when the expenses of the American war had brought the country to the verge of bankruptcy. The mistress of the robes had to ask the Treasury to advance an extra 111,000 francs towards the cost of the Queen's wardrobe to pay for all the gala dresses required for the Russian visit. Mademoiselle Bertin had a bumper year, for not only the Queen and her court but all the Russian visitors honoured her with their patronage. Case upon case of Parisian fashions was sent back to St Petersburg, only to meet with the disapproval of the Empress Catherine, who had them all sent back to Paris, telling her poor young daughter-in-law that large women like themselves looked far better in simple and dignified Russian fashions.

During those few brief weeks in Paris, Maria Feodorovna lived in an enchanted world with the Queen in the role of a benevolent fairy godmother, overwhelming her with gifts. However bored Marie Antoinette might be with the heavy and pedantic Grand Duchess, however much she might want to laugh at the ridiculous Tsarevich with his nervous tic and ugly Kalmuck features, they nevertheless represented a new incalculable power to be wooed as an ally for the future.

In her memoirs, Madame d'Oberkirch depicts Marie Antoinette as the most charming and thoughtful of hostesses, treating even the lady-in-waiting as if she were an honoured guest, enquiring as to her tastes and as to what would give her pleasure. There was a visit to the porcelain manufacturers of Sèvres, where the Russian visitors spent over 300,000 francs, only to find at the end of the visit that the most beautiful and extravagant of toilet sets in lapis blue with painted enamel plaques was a personal gift for Maria Feodorovna from the Queen.

Of all the evening entertainments the most memorable was the fête held by the Queen on a fine June night at Trianon, where the illuminations reflected the colour of every flower and Chinese lanterns cast mysterious shadows on the water. Disguised as nymphs and fawns, ballet dancers flitted among the trees, and musicians playing on a raft anchored on the lake sang the latest airs of Grétry. Here there was none of the pompous grandeur of Versailles. The Queen and her ladies had discarded their silks and satins for gowns of diaphanous white gauze and wore flowers rather than diamonds in their hair. Marie Anoinette was receiving the Russian royalty in her own private domain, to which no one was invited other than her friends.

But who was the mysterious figure enveloped in a cloak who spoke to no one and throughout the evening managed to evade the notice of the guards? It was only towards the end, when the royal carriages were already leaving, that someone noted the scarlet stockings emerging from the cloak – a high-ranking prelate, but what prelate would come uninvited to Trianon? Was it possible that the Grand Almoner of France, the Prince de Rohan, whom the Queen had sworn never to invite to Trianon, would abuse his position to the extent of bribing a porter to let him intrude into the gardens on the plea that he only wanted to see the illuminations?

This extraordinary incident gives us the first hint of the distorted mentality of a man so spoilt by fortune, so insanely vain that he refused to admit that he had forfeited the favour of the Queen. It is the prelude to the whole fantastic story of the 'Queen's necklace' which no playwright, however imaginative, could ever have invented.

Marie Antoinette was furious when she heard that the Cardinal had dared to trespass in her gardens, and the unfortunate porter was threatened with dismissal. Madame Campan took upon herself the credit for having persuaded the Queen to forgive him on the grounds that it would give too much publicity to her dislike of the Cardinal. But Louis de Rohan's extraordinary behaviour was soon to be forgotten in the reverberating scandal which overtook his family in the autumn of 1782, when the bankruptcy of his cousin, Prince Rohan de Guéménée, shook the foundations of Versailles.

The debts of the Prince de Guéménée, 33 million livres, were on such a scale that his bankruptcy affected everyone from the Duc de Lauzun to the peasants of Brittany who, regarding the Rohans as the descendants of their kings, had put their savings into the hands of the Prince's fraudulent administrators. Had he been a banker or a tradesman, he would most certainly have gone to prison. But a Rohan, bearing one of the greatest names in France, was merely ordered by the King to retire to his country estates. His notary, who had probably swindled him as much as he had swindled his creditors, was sentenced to jail. The Prince's relatives, many of whom disliked him cordially, nevertheless rallied round to save the family name. His father-in-law, the old Prince de Soubise, sold his horses; his aunt, Madame de Marsan, sold her pictures; his daughter-in-law, and the Princesse de Montbazon, sent back to the jewellers the diamonds given her for her wedding. The general feeling at Versailles was one of sympathy for the Guéménées, who had been among the most popular couples at court, and the Princess was pitied when she had to hand in her resignation as governess to the royal children. Though Marie Antoinette used all her influence to secure her a handsome pension and the King came to her assistance in buying her estate of Montreuil as a present for his sister, the royal family appears to have been on the whole relatively indifferent to the plight of the Guéménées. The extent of the scandal, the thousands of people who had been reduced to penury by the profligacy of a *grand seigneur*, may have made both Louis and Marie Antoinette unwilling to identify themselves too much with a couple who from now on were forbidden to appear at court.

In this case the Queen's behaviour only added to her unpopularity. People spoke of her fickleness in friendship and remembered Lucie Dillon, the lovely young Irishwoman who for a short time had been the Queen's inseparable companion before she fell ill with consumption and could no longer keep up with the dissipations of Versailles. Marie Antoinette continued to visit her and sent daily messengers to enquire after her health, shedding bitter tears when she died at the age of thirty-one. But twenty-four hours later she was already expressing a wish to go to the Théâtre Français and had to be reminded by the Duchesse de Duras, the lady-in-waiting of whom she stood most in awe, that it might be better if she went to the opera, otherwise in passing by St Sulpice she might run into Madame Dillon's funeral procession. The Queen had the grace to blush and stayed at home. But the story went round Versailles to be repeated to Lucie Dillon's daughter, Henrietta, who could never forgive Marie Antoinette for having mourned her mother no longer than a day.

Yolande de Polignac was the only woman who succeeded in maintaining her hold over Marie Antoinette's volatile affections. When the question came up as to who should succeed Madame de Guéménée as governess to the royal children and the favourite's name was first suggested, Monsieur, who was usually so careful not to commit himself, went so far as to tell the King that he would be blamed by the whole of France if he gave the post to the Queen's favourite. Louis, who had always remained attached to his aunts, of whose religious opinions he approved, would have liked to have had Madame Adelaide take care of his children. But he had only to mention her name in front of his wife for Marie Antoinette to burst into tears and accuse him of cruelty in venturing to suggest someone who had poisoned her life from the first day of her marriage. Poor Louis, who could never stand up to her tears, was reduced to a silent acquiescence when the Queen appeared holding the Duchesse de Polignac by the hand and saying, 'Here is my choice.' Yolande prostrated herself in front of him to ask for his blessing, and the sight of the beautiful young woman at his feet was so moving as to reduce also the King to tears.

Left to herself, Madame de Polignac, who had poor health and was indolent by nature, might well have refused an offer which involved such tremendous responsibilities. But her coterie, and in particular Vaudreuil, kept urging her to accept a post which would be so advantageous both for her and her friends. In a palace which housed over 12,000 people, and where even the princes of the blood, when on duty at Versailles, complained of their cramped and uncomfortable quarters, the governess of the royal children was given an apartment of thirteen rooms overlooking the orangerie and adjacent to that of her royal charges. Even this was not sufficiently large in which to entertain all the aspiring place-seekers who came to pay her court, and a wooden conservatory with a piano and a billiard table was built at the far end. Here, three times a week, the Duchess received the whole of the government and the court, and it was generally agreed that no parties were as agreeable as those given by the Polignacs, where all etiquette was banished and the atmosphere was completely relaxed. It was strange to see the Queen of France, who only enjoyed entertaining at Trianon, come as a guest in her own palace of Versailles. There came the day when she ventured to complain of some of the people present and the Duchess had the impertinence to reply that because Her Majesty honoured her with her presence, that was no reason for her to criticize her friends, and if she had had the misfortune to displease Her Majesty, there was only one thing left for her to do, which was to resign from her post.

Besenval, who recounts this incident, writes that Marie Antoinette was so taken aback by this cold and reproachful tone that she tried to make amends, only to find that the Duchess refused to be mollified until she had her begging in tears for her forgiveness. It is difficult to believe this tale, for Besenval was neither truthful nor discreet. But the very fact that he should have dared to recount it shows the extent of the Queen's obsession for Madame de Polignac and how openly their friendship was being discussed. There was an even more damaging story for which the Comte d'Artois was responsible, for on coming unannounced into the Queen's room, he found the two friends embracing one another and, in a loud voice so that everyone could hear, asked to be excused for having disturbed such a loving scene. But this was the age of sentimental friendships and, in view of a growing unpopularity for which she did not understand the reasons, Marie Antoinette felt an ever greater need of sympathy and understanding from the one friend on whom, in spite of all her shortcomings, she still felt she could rely.

Criticism against the Queen was no longer confined to anonymous pamphlets. When a portrait by Vigée-Lebrun, in which she is wearing a simple white muslin gown, was exposed for the first time at the Salon du Louvre, it aroused such a storm of abuse that it had to be removed. Having formerly been condemned for the extravagance of her clothes, she was now accused of 'dressing like a chambermaid' and of deliberately promoting the linen industries of the Austrian Netherlands at the expense of the silk manufacturers of Lyons. The truth was that these white muslin gowns, known as *'gaulles'*, which the Queen had introduced at Trianon, were a fashion imported via Bordeaux from the Creoles of Martinique. And Vigée-Lebrun, the most fashionable painter of the day, was persuading her sitters to wear these plain classical gowns instead of the formal panniers and feathers of court dress.

It seemed that the Queen could do no right. Too proud to fight back, she retreated more and more into the make-believe world of Trianon, where her architect Richard Mique and her favourite artist Hubert Robert were building her a model village by a lake, with eight cottages and a farm complete with bakery and dairy – an arcadian setting worthy of the most imaginative of painters, down to the broken cobblestones and painted cracks in the walls. Here could be found the whitest of lambs and the cleanest of cows, here milk was poured into porcelain jars from the manufacturers of Sèvres and butter was churned by the prettiest of milkmaids. Rousseau and Bernardin de Saint-Pierre had extolled the charms of rural life. Their writings had made it the fashion, even if the Queen had never read a word of Rousseau other than *Le Devin du Village*, which was on the theatrical repertoire of Trianon.

Marie Antoinette was not the only one to have her *'hameau'*. The Prince de Condé had a far more elaborate one at Chantilly, but as usual it was the Queen who was blamed for throwing away money on what was no more than a toy. Even a loyal courtier like the Marquis de Bombelles wrote, 'A lot of money has been spent on giving the Queen's "*hameau*" the aspect of poverty.

By spending a little more, Her Majesty would have been able to improve the conditions of those who are really poor within a radius of twenty miles or so and turn their hovels into decent homes ... to imitate in a place given over to amusements the unfortunate existence of your fellow beings seems a somewhat heartless thing to do.'

In 1783, the year of the peace treaty with England which freed Dunkirk after twenty years from the presence of British commissioners, the year in which the French conquered the skies and the Montgolfiers' balloons floated over the Ile de France, the Queen spent the greater part of the summer in her retreat at Trianon. Her initials were emblazoned on the blue and gold balloons in which Pilâtre de Rozier and François Laurent d'Arpandes made their first ascent into the skies. But King Louis, who had subsidized the inventions of the Montgolfiers and witnessed the launching of the first balloon carrying the cargo of a cock, a hen and a rabbit, disapproved of human lives being risked in such a hazardous undertaking, and had forbidden his wife to be present at the historic event which took place on the terraces of La Muette. The only member of the royal family to watch was the two-year-old Dauphin with his governess and some of her friends. La Muette had now been handed over to the Dauphin, or rather to the Polignacs, and the Duchess presided over what was known as the '*Cour de Monsieur le Dauphin*'.

Ten days later, the King, who was always slow in coming to a decision, was persuaded to give his official sanction to 'men going up in balloons', and on 1 December a crowd of over 100,000 saw two more heroic airmen, Charles and Robert, ascend in a hydrogen balloon from the parterres of the Tuileries, a venture backed by the Duc de Chartres. This time the whole of the royal family was present, and an English traveller who saw the Queen watching from a balcony noted that she was looking unusually serious, perhaps because the Duc de Chartres was more loudly cheered than any other member of the family.

Axel Fersen, who had returned from America in the summer of 1783, was distressed by the Queen's unpopularity and the lack of loyalty from her own courtiers. His years abroad had hardened and matured him. The young Adonis had grown more manly and more fascinating and in his feelings more loving and protective towards a woman who was in such desperate need of friends. Marie Antoinette made no secret of her feelings. Those who were present when he first returned to Versailles and walked into the room where she was sitting playing the harp to some of her ladies saw her face light up with pleasure and, judging by the spontaneous warmth of her welcome, saw that nothing had changed in the past years. Fersen's arrival in Paris may help to explain the Queen's long visits to Trianon, where she could entertain him more freely.

Meanwhile Axel's father was pressing him to marry, saying that he could no longer support his extravagant way of life at the expense of his younger brothers and sisters. Necker's daughter, the richest Protestant heiress in Europe, was of a marriageable age. But Germaine Necker's loquacity and brilliance, her coarse features and massive build held no appeal for a young man who confided to his sister that he would remain a bachelor, as he was unable to belong to the one woman to whom he would have liked to dedicate his life. By now he knew that his feelings for the Queen were reciprocated. But how was he to remain in France when his father refused to pay the 100,000 francs, the cost of remaining with the regiment of the Royal Suédois, one of the most exclusive and expensive of the foreign regiments of France? Fortunately King Gustavus was on his side. Russia's insatiable ambition was such that Sweden, the most vulnerable of her neighbours, required fresh subsidies and a new treaty of alliance with France. A letter from Marie Antoinette extolling 'Senator Fersen and his admirable son' left King Gustavus under no illusion as to Axel's position at Versailles. To have one of his favourite aides-de-camp installed at the French court represented a valuable asset for the King. Even more satisfactory was the fact that young Fersen's 'exemplary behaviour' had won him favour with King Louis, who found the quiet, slow-spoken Swede far more to his liking than the noisy crowd of young men who gathered round the Queen. In the end it was the King of France who enabled Axel Fersen to have his regiment by cancelling the payment of 100,000 francs and giving him an income of 20,000 as colonel of the Royal Suédois.

King Gustavus, however, had no intention of depriving himself of the company of the captain of his guards, with whom he himself was more than a little in love. Fersen, who was not due to take over his regiment till the following year, was about to leave on a visit to his father in Sweden when he was ordered by his King to accompany him on a protracted tour of Italy, which kept him away from Versailles from September 1783 until the following June of 1784 – nine months during which his stabilizing influence might have prevented Marie Antoinette from committing so many foolish actions.

During all this time he was forced to accompany King Gustavus on an endless round of routs and masquerades – a life totally unsuited to someone of his solitary, introspective character. Nevertheless he was sufficiently passionate and sensual by nature to console himself with a series of amatory adventures and, while dreaming of an inaccessible princess, to indulge in sentimental relationships with the charming Englishwomen he encountered on his travels. There was the delightful Emily Cooper, the future Lady Palmerston, and the unhappily married Elizabeth Foster, whom few men were able to resist and who was willing to play the role of a mistress or a confidante. Fersen, who was so discreet in his behaviour at Versailles, appears to have been ready to talk of his infatuation for Marie Antoinette to any woman who was ready to listen.

While Fersen remained in unwilling attendance on his King, Marie Antoinette returned to what she regarded as the bondage of Versailles. One of her pages, the sixteen-year-old Alexandre de Tilly, has left a clear and on the whole a sympathetic portrait of his royal mistress. He wrote: 'She treated us all with a singular sweetness and we all adored her. Her most destructive fault, and one which did a lot of harm, was her dislike of all pomp and formality, the formality which is more necessary in France than anywhere else. She was childish and inconsequential, with no definite ideas except to free herself of the burdensome ties imposed by her rank. When she wanted to, no one could be more royal and dignified. One has never seen anyone curtsey so gracefully, singling out ten persons in one curtsey and giving to each in turn the regard which was their due.' Tilly drew attention to another fault, and a far more dangerous one, her exaggerated likes and dislikes, often taken on the slightest provocation. Once someone had fallen out of favour, he or she was rarely if ever forgiven, and it was all too easy for the troublemakers who abounded at Versailles to profit by this weakness.

So many of Marie Antoinette's critics refer to her childishness and inconsequence. But only the more discerning note the melancholy which underlay the feverish search for amusement. A loving sister-in-law and a still more loving mother, she never succeeded in winning the affection of either Madame Elisabeth or her own daughter. King Louis's youngest sister was a hefty, fresh-complexioned country girl, whom not even the flattering brush of a Vigée-Lebrun could turn into a beauty. Intensely pious, utterly devoted to her brothers, and in particular to the handsome and charming Artois, the shy, rather awkward girl never felt at ease in the artificial world of Trianon. Marie Antoinette found her affection rejected not only by Madame Elisabeth but by her own five-year-old daughter, who already showed the cold, hard character of the future Duchesse d'Angoulême. As a child she was resentful of the beautiful mother who, when visiting her nursery, spent her time chatting to the Duchesse de Polignac. On one occasion when Marie Antoinette had fallen from her horse while out riding and the Abbé Vermond was advising her to be more careful in the future, he turned to the little Princess who happened to be in the room and asked her to speak to the Queen, only to be answered in the coldest of tones that whatever happened to her mother was a matter of complete indifference to her. The Abbé, who felt she did not know what she was saying, persisted: 'But suppose Her Majesty had cracked her head and died. Do you realize what death means?' And in the same cold voice the child replied, 'Yes, Monsieur l'Abbé. I know what death means. It means one does not have to see the people any more once they are dead. If I did not have to see the Queen, I would be left in peace and could do as I liked.'

Poor Marie Antoinette, who had been one of a large and devoted family, could not understand the reactions of her unnatural daughter. A governess who was accused of putting Madame Royale against her mother was instantly dismissed. But no one dared to repeat to Marie Antoinette the remark made by the little Princess who, when she was upbraided for the way in which she had spoken of the Queen, replied, 'No, I do not love my mother. She is always interfering with me and at the same time takes no notice of me. When she brings me to visit the aunts, she walks straight ahead of me and does not even look round to see whether I am following, whereas Papa takes me by the hand and looks after me.'

It was at the beginning of 1784, when Madame Royale was barely five years old, that the Duc de Chartres requested her hand in marriage for his eldest son, the Duc de Valois. The offer was curtly, almost rudely, refused. Not only was the Princess already half promised to Artois' son, the young Duc d'Angoulême, but neither the King nor the Queen was prepared to give their daughter in marriage to one of the hated Orléans. History might have been very different if in 1789 the ten-year-old Princess had been the prospective bride of the Duc d'Orléans' son. For Madame Royale's prospective father-in-law would never have gone the way of Philippe Egalité, and in old age the sad, embittered Princess might have known a few glorious years as Queen of France.

In the autumn of 1783, Marie Antoinette had a miscarriage which affected her health for several months to come. The pregnancy had been a difficult one from the very beginning, and in the first four months she was already so large that the doctors prognosticated twins. Her enemies were quick to say that the miscarriage had been brought about by her carelessness and excessive dissipation, and it was some time before she had regained her usual vitality and strength. During these months of lassitude and melancholy, she relied almost entirely on the company of what she called her '*société*', in which she was ruled by Madame de Polignac, who was in turn ruled by Vaudreuil. This brilliant, unbalanced man, frustrated in his talents and living on debts, was more than anyone else responsible for the appointment of Calonne to the post of Controller General, a disastrous appointment which led France, already on the brink of bankruptcy, into complete insolvency.

As *intendant* of various provincial cities, Calonne had been hoping for many years to become Controller General, only to find the way barred by the innate distrust of Maurepas. But now Maurepas was dead and the King's dislike of Necker and the incompetence of his successors opened the way to Calonne, who promised all things to all men and was as popular in banking circles as he was at court. Women adored him, and the proudest names of the *Noblesse d'Epée* regarded him as the only member of the *Noblesse de Robe* who could be treated as an equal. In his portrait by Vigée-Lebrun, one of the most celebrated of his mistresses, we see him elegant and urbane, a man who must have been the most charming of dinner companions and the most delightful of lovers, but whose talents as a statesman were never more than superficial. He was possessed of facility rather than capacity, brilliance rather than depth. Even King Louis ended by being carried away by Calonne's fine phrases, and his dazzling vision of a regenerated France. The minister appealed to the King's scientific bent by finding the money for the experiments of Lavoisier and the voyages of La Perouse. By encouraging industry he persuaded the great families with capital to invest in mines and textile industries. Foreign capitalists, especially the English, were invited to open factories in France, and within two years of peace the English had already flooded the market with cheap goods to the detriment of French manufacturers. But in the first months of Calonne's administration it seemed as if the golden age was about to return. There was enormous speculation in land, particularly in Paris, which was gradually being transformed into the city we know today. The squalid, piled-up houses along the Seine were being replaced with handsome quays and public buildings. Narrow, unlit streets made way for prosperous residential quarters. The Comte de Provence gave a home to the Théâtre Français by building a new theatre near what is now known as the Odéon. The Duc de Chartres built arcades with shops which encroached on the famous gardens of the Palais Royal. The rich were becoming richer, but little or nothing except in the form of private charity was being done for the poor.

The King himself was immensely charitable, and in the hard winter of 1784 he gave three million francs out of his private funds for distribution among the poor. He was the first of his nobles to order the trees in the royal forests to be cut down for firewood. To ingratiate himself with the Queen, Calonne offered her a million francs from the royal treasury for her to distribute in her name. The offer was proudly refused. Such charity as she could give would come out of her savings from her personal allowance. By cutting down on her expenses Marie Antoinette succeeded in giving nearly a million francs to the poor of Versailles. The King and Queen were more generous than many of their courtiers. In her descriptions of court life at Versailles, young Henrietta Dillon, the future Madame de la Tour du Pin painted an unpleasant picture of the cupidity and selfishness of the typical young aristocrat. She wrote that during the hard winters the Queen, on entering the Salle de Jeu, would be carrying a small bag and from each of her courtiers would extract a certain sum 'for the poor'. The ladies were expected to give a silver coin to the value of six francs, and the men a gold louis – a trifling amount in comparison with what was lost every night at the card tables, 'but which nevertheless aroused considerable resentment among the younger courtiers'. Although Calonne favoured the aristocracy, in later years he was heard to say that a minister of France under the old regime resembled a tree covered with caterpillars, and that these vile insects stuck to it till they had eaten every leaf. But during his first halcyon months in power everyone extolled him from the Comte d'Artois to the Polignacs, from the court bankers to the King. Only the Queen had her misgivings, of which Calonne was aware and which later made him into one of her bitterest enemies. But when the terrifying figures of the public deficit became known and, from having been the most popular, Calonne became the most hated man in France, it was the Queen who was blamed for his appointment and branded as Madame 'Déficit'.

By now the Polignacs were not so much a coterie as a cabal, and Marie Antoinette was growing aware of the harm being done to her by her friend. The Duchess's position was strengthened when her sister-in-law, Marie Louise de Polastron, became the mistress of the Comte d'Artois, who deserted the set of the Palais Royal to become the friend of Vaudreuil and *habitué* of the Salon Polignac, which was now all-powerful at Versailles, so powerful that they were able to get Beaumarchais's play produced in spite of the opposition of the King. Madame Campan describes Louis's indignation when he had the play read to him for the first time and how he told the Queen that she could rest assured he would never allow it to be performed. For all her disappointment, Marie Antoinette would have been ready to abide by his decision had it not been for the anger of her coterie, and in particular the fury of Vaudreuil who, as a friend and admirer of Beaumarchais, did not hesitate to describe him as 'a victim of tyranny and oppression'. The brilliant way in which the playwright canvassed public opinion in his favour, until all who were fashionable in Paris and Versailles talked of nothing but *Figaro*, ended in making the Queen into the most ardent of his supporters.

But the King was nothing if not obstinate. On 3 July 1783 *Le Mariage de Figaro* was due to be performed in the Salle des Menus Plaisirs at Versailles in the presence of the Baron de Breteuil, minister of His Majesty's household, whose vanity had been flattered when Beaumarchais asked him to suggest what changes in the text he considered to be necessary. The rehearsals were finished, the queues were already forming outside the ticket office with the whole of Paris and Versailles struggling to get seats when, at the eleventh hour, came the King's veto cancelling the performance.

The news brought a general explosion of indignation. Courtiers who until now had never known the meaning of liberty said that the King's veto was 'an infringement on civil liberty', and Beaumarchais' famous remark that 'it was only little people who were frightened of little writings' made the round of Versailles. The Polignacs gave no peace to the Queen until she had begged the King to reconsider his decision. Subtle and complaisant, knowing that he had public opinion on his side, Beaumarchais consented to submit to further censorship. By now he had the support of Calonne who, with his usual munificence, had handed over the money the government still owed him over his transactions with the Americans. Apart from Calonne, he already had the support of the lieutenant of police, who had helped him in some of the more shady phases of his career. As a result, the censors never even troubled to see if the offending passages had been removed from the text.

A private performance held in honour of the Comte d'Artois was given by Monsieur de Vaudreuil at his garden theatre at Gennevilliers. There were fifty chosen guests, all of whom belonged to the *Coterie Polignac* and all of whom reported to the Queen that the play was 'charming, diverting and wholly innocuous', while Artois, who delighted in teasing his royal brother, told the King that *Le Mariage de Figaro* was 'nothing but bunk from the first act to the last'. Vacillating, still unconvinced, Louis ended by giving in to the importunities of his wife and her friends. There were a few more cuts in the text, cuts which were almost instantly restored, and *Figaro*, brilliant, dangerous and irrepressible, finally appeared on the stage.

'At long last we have triumphed,' wrote Beaumarchais to his friend the famous actor Préville, who had been about to retire when he was persuaded to return to act in what was to be the greatest success of his career.

> My dear old friend, one must never despair. A great actor whom the public adores must never be allowed to retire and a courageous writer must never be put off by temporary setbacks. I have now got the approval of the King, the approval of his ministers, even the approval of the lieutenant of police. All I need now is you to turn my play into a resounding success. The play itself may not be of much importance, but to see it put on after three years of almost continual struggle is what makes it so important to me.

On 27 April 1783 *Le Mariage de Figaro ou La Folle Journée* took Paris by storm. From early morning, unprecedented crowds besieged the theatre waiting for the ticket office to open, and the King and his Chancellor were the only ones who still hoped the play was going to flop and that the cuts demanded by the censor had robbed it of its savour. 'How do you think it is going to go?' asked Louis of one of his courtiers who, not wishing to commit himself, replied, 'I can only hope it will fail, Your Majesty.' 'So do I,' said the King. But if he had gone into the dressing rooms of the Théâtre Français on the day of the performance and seen the rising excitement of the actors, or heard the bets being made in the clubs and coffee houses as to how long the play was going to run; if he had known that some of the greatest ladies of his court were humbling themselves in front of Monsieur de Beaumarchais just to get a seat in the pit, then he would have known that his hopes were vain. The court jester, who in the Middle Ages had amused his monarch with his mockery and impertinence, had been kicked into a corner when he dared to go too far. But now the jester had become more powerful than the King, and the whole of Paris and Versailles were laughing and applauding every barbed satire, every veiled insult directed against themselves. No one who was anyone dared to miss what promised to be the most fashionable event of the year. And the actors lived up to the occasion, dazzling by their virtuosity, making the most of every witty line, receiving call upon call, and Beaumarchais, who was watching from a private box, remarked to a friend, 'There is only one thing more absurd than my play and that is its success.'

Barely two months later *Figaro* received its official accolade when Marie Antoinette attended a gala performance in honour of the King of Sweden, who was on an incognito visit to Paris. That night the Queen was at her loveliest. Gone were the vapours and depressions, the lassitude and boredom from which she had suffered in the past months. Fersen was back in Paris as the King of Sweden's aide-de-camp, and all the honours paid by Marie Antoinette to this 'Count of Haga' were a tribute to the man she loved.

Nothing annoyed King Louis so much as the habit of the incognito visits made fashionable by his brother-in-law the Emperor and imitated by all his fellow sovereigns. He had been happily hunting at Rambouillet when an urgent message came from Vergennes to say that the King of Sweden had arrived in Paris and was on his way to Versailles. The disorganization of the vast palace, where '*les grandes charges*' were in the hands of incompetent courtiers, was such that the King returned to Versailles to find that his chief valet had gone off with the keys of his apartment and that none of his personal servants could be found. Such valets and pages as were available dressed him to the best of their ability, and the King of France greeted King Gustavus wearing one shoe with a red heel and a gold buckle, another with a black heel and silver buckle. But this time the Queen, who was usually so severe over his slovenly appearance, only laughed, asking him if he was going to a fancy dress party, for she was far too happy at seeing Fersen to care whether the King of France was wearing an odd pair of shoes. Neither she nor King Louis was attracted by their royal guest, whose mannerisms and affectations and endless flood of talk irritated them both. Marie Antoinette may also have resented King Gustavus keeping his aide-de-camp in close attendance for so long. His homosexual tendencies were common knowledge. The Queen of Naples is said to have written to her sister that, on an excursion to Vesuvius, the King had taken Fersen to the edge of the crater and threatened to throw himself in unless he renounced his love for the Queen of France. It was no more than a piece of Neapolitan gossip, for King Gustavus was far too ambitious to allow his private sentiments to interfere with politics, and 'le beau Fersen' at the court of Versailles was more useful to him than any ambassador.

Those six weeks of continual fêtes and balls must have been both tantalizing and frustrating for a couple who could never be alone for more than a few moments and were constantly exposed to the prying eyes of an envious court and the exacting demands of the Swedish King. Day after day Fersen was made to accompany his royal master on a vertiginous round of gaieties. 'I have to pretend to be ill, just to have the time to send you a letter,' wrote Axel to his father. 'We have already had a gala opera at Versailles as well as a fancy dress ball, without counting the numberless theatres, dinners and suppers. Tomorrow we have a fête in the Queen's garden at Trianon....
I am staying in this evening until I go to supper at Versailles.'

Supper at Versailles was held in the Queen's private apartments, newly decorated by Richard Mique in gold and turquoise. The Queen, in a gold and silver dress, sparkling with diamonds, charmed her royal guest; was sweet and affectionate to her husband, laughing at his heavy, clumsy jokes; flirted with the young pages on duty; and all for the benefit of the Swedish officer who gazed at her in such obvious adoration.

The Polignac coterie was on the alert and there were signs of the first rift with the Queen. When Marie Antoinette attended the gala performance of *Le Mariage de Figaro*, she was seen to laugh as heartily as any other member of the audience. But later Fersen, or perhaps King Gustavus, who for all his vag-

he castle of Schönbrunn: the Empress Maria Theresa's summer palace, where her children spent a happy, carefree childhood.

Versailles, the grandest palace in Europe.

The portrait of the fourteen-year-old Archduchess, Maria Antonia, painted for the King of France.

Madame du Barry, the fascinating low-born courtesan with whom Louis XV was infatuated in his last years and who contributed to the decline of the Monarchy.

Comte Mercy d'Argenteau, Maria Theresa's ambassador at the French court. He was appointed to be her daughter's mentor and at the same time the Empress's spy.

Louis XVI. A weak and well-intentioned king, who loved his people.

Emperor Joseph II of Austria, Marie Antoinette's eldest brother.

Count Axel Fersen, known as 'le beau Fersen' when he arrived in France at the age of eighteen, and met Marie Antoinette at the opera ball.

Jeanne Valois de La Motte, the illegitimat daughter of a drunken servant girl and a degen erate descendant of the Valois kings, succeede in perpetrating one of the most gigantic fraud in history.

The beautiful Yolande Gabrielle de Polignac supplanted the Princess de Lamballe in the Queen's affections. Her money, greed and extravagance made her into one of the most hated women in the country.

Pierre Augustin Caron de Beaumarchais, th creator of the immortal *Figaro*, the mockingbi which heralded the Revolution.

The temple of love in the gardens of Trianon, the Queen's private domain, where even the King came only at her invitation.

Marie Thérèse Charlotte (Madame Royale) with her brother, the elder Dauphin, who died in 1789. (Painted by Vigée-Lebrun.)

Marie Antoinette, Queen of France, in a gala dress and one of the high head-dresses of which her mother disapproved.

Marie Antoinette, wearing one of the more sober dresses in dark velvets and silks which she adopted after the birth of her children. (Painted by Vigée-Lebrun.)

The storming of the Bastille and the arrest of the governor, de Launay. This bloody event was hailed as a glorious blow for freedom and celebrated as the beginning of the Revolution in the years to come.

Gilbert de Lafayette, who hoped to lead the Revolution, failed in his efforts to become the Washington of France.

Victor Riqueti, Comte, later Marquis de Mirabeau, the most hallowed orator of his age, a renegade aristocrat who became a leader of the third estate and later tried to save the Monarchy.

Marie Antoinette, painted by Kucharski in 1791, as she must have appeared to Barnave when he accompanied her back to Paris from Varennes.

David's pen-sketch of Marie Antoinette on her way to the guillotine. She stares ahead, with the Hapsburg lips, once a pretty pout, set in a look of utter contempt.

'I appeal to the women of France.' Marie Antoinette at her trial, replying to Hébert's accusations of incest.

aries never allowed the slightest criticism from any of his subjects, remarked that the play contained dangerous and inflammable material and should never have been allowed to be produced. The Queen accepted the criticism and blamed the Polignacs for having made her influence the King against his better judgement.

Yolande de Polignac, who felt her position to be threatened by a proud young foreigner who had never troubled to pay her court, resented these aspersions and, in spite of her friendship for Marie Antoinette, made no attempt to deny the rumour linking Count Fersen with the Queen.

Stories were told of the Queen driving herself to Trianon with a single groom in attendance, of her being seen in disguise, walking through the park, accompanied by a tall stranger – ridiculous tales when Fersen was in constant duty on a jealous king and the Queen was the cynosure of a thousand eyes.

In honour of the 'Count of Haga', the Queen held a fête at Trianon – an evening of such enchantment as to win her the lifelong devotion of the impressionable King Gustavus, who wrote, 'One might have been walking in the Elysian fields with a goddess from Olympus.' The park was opened to the public. The only condition made for entry was that all the women should be dressed in white – which had become the uniform of Trianon. A performance of Marmontel's *La Dormeuse Eveillé* with music by Piccini was followed by supper in the illuminated groves. The menu served at the royal table consisted of only three kinds of entrées, one roast and four sweets, and was very modest in comparison to the 180 dishes served at the other tables. The Queen herself, who neither danced nor sat down to supper, kept continually on the move, a charming hostess with no lady in waiting in attendance. She was tonight in her own private domain, talking to everyone in turn, showing off her gardens, the English park, the hamlet with its bakery and dairy, the Chinese pavilion and the grotto; childishly pleased by the admiration of her guests. All the foreigners were singled out, and in particular the handsome Swedes of 'Count Haga's' entourage – Count Stedynk, Baron Taube, the newly appointed minister to Paris, young De Staël, and the King's aide-de-camp, Count Fersen. She passed from one to another, animated and gay; pausing for a moment in the shadow of a tree; whispering where no one could overhear; and perhaps no one would notice that it was always with Fersen that she wandered furthest from the crowds.

By the middle of July the 'Count of Haga' was on his way back to Sweden after a highly successful visit during which he had succeeded in obtaining from an impoverished France both large subsidies in money, and the possession of the West Indian island of St Barthélemy. In a new treaty of alliance signed at Versailles, France and Sweden promised one another reciprocal help in case of war. As Catherine of Russia was the most likely aggressor, it was a treaty which favoured Sweden rather than France.

King Gustavus's aide-de-camp must have been equally satisfied, but his last meeting with the Queen was a sad one. There was so much more they both wanted to say, assignations they had been unable to keep. Both promised to write, and there is no doubt these promises were kept. But such letters as survive concern only the dispatching of a large Swedish sheepdog asked for by the Queen. Some of Fersen's biographers have claimed that a series of letters written to a mysterious 'Josephine' were addressed to the Queen of France. But these letters are written to someone who bears little relation to the light-headed Queen of Trianon, whom only tragedy would make into a woman.

A t eight o'clock in the evening of 27 March 1785, King Louis wrote a note to his brother-in-law the Emperor to inform him that the Queen had been safely delivered of a second son, whom he had named the Duc de Normandie. This letter, addressed to a man whom he cordially disliked, ended: 'I trust, my dearest brother-in-law, that you will never doubt of my true feelings and affection towards you.'

For the past nine months Joseph's restless ambition had once again threatened to disrupt the balance of power in Europe. This time his quarrel was with the Dutch, whose control of the mouth of the Scheldt impeded the free flow of commerce from the Austrian Netherlands, and in particular from the port of Antwerp. The Emperor had brought the issue to a head by trying to force the passage of one of his ships, to which the Dutch had responded by firing on the Austrian flag. Infuriated at their insolence, Joseph sent troops to the frontier and enlisted the support of his ally the King of France, support which neither King Louis nor his minister Vergennes was willing to give.

The contrast between the two royal brothers-in-law was never so apparent as in their handling of domestic and foreign affairs. Louis, who was so weak and vacillating at home, showed an excellent judgement in dealing with foreign affairs. Joseph, on the contrary, was admirable at home and disastrous in his foreign policy. Austria owes him some of her greatest and most far-reaching reforms, such as compulsory public education, freedom of speech, abolition of serfdom and above all the famous edict of religious toleration, by which Jews and other dissenters were allowed to have their own prayer houses and schools, and Jews were no longer obliged to wear the humiliating yellow badge. But when it came to foreign policy, his wish to dominate and almost obsessional desire to regain for the Hapsburgs the power they had lost to the House of Brandenburg led him into one disastrous situation after the other.

In 1778 Marie Antoinette had had the whole of her first pregnancy disturbed by her brother's quarrel over Bavaria. This time it was again the question of Bavaria for, after quarrelling with the Dutch for the benefit of his Flemish subjects, Joseph was cold-bloodedly offering to exchange his provinces in the Austrian Netherlands for the greater part of Bavaria, without stopping to consult the wishes of his Flemish subjects or to consider the opposition it would arouse in Prussia and in all the smaller German states. Throughout her fourth pregnancy Marie Antoinette was beset by her brother's letters complaining of the disloyalty of King Louis and the perfidious behaviour of Vergennes. In 1781 Joseph had paid a six-day visit to Paris, during which he set out to convince the French government of the purity of his political intentions. But neither Louis nor any of his ministers was convinced, knowing that the Emperor's ambitions stopped at nothing less than establishing a Hapsburg hegemony over the whole of Germany.

The Emperor had in the end to renounce his claims to Bavaria, but he persisted in demanding either the port of Maastricht or a compensation of twelve million florins. For the sake of peace King Louis offered to mediate. Round the conference table at Fontainebleau the twelve million florins was whittled down to ten, of which the Dutch paid eight million, while France contributed the remaining two, a political gesture which was bitterly resented by the French people. They put all the blame on the Austrian Queen and this incident, exaggerated and distorted, formed one of the chief accusations brought against Marie Antoinette at the revolutionary tribunal.

The year 1785 was to be a disastrous one for Marie Antoinette, in which a succession of events combined to lose her the last vestiges of popularity. Arrogance, stupidity, a complete lack of political insight on the part of a spoilt, capricious woman, who always acted on impulse and never stopped to reason, contributed to her downfall. It was in the first year of Calonne's ministry, when the Treasury appeared to have inexhaustible funds of gold, that the King bought the Palace of St Cloud from the old Duc d'Orléans as a home for his wife and children. The extensive repairs which had to be carried out at Versailles justified the buying of another royal home. The health of the little Dauphin was beginning to cause concern and St Cloud was considered to have better air than either Versailles or Trianon. In his love and gratitude for the wife who had just given him a second son, Louis committed the blunder of buying St Cloud in the Queen's name, at a time when the expenses of Trianon were already meeting with public disapproval. The notice on the gates of St Cloud declaring it to be the private property of the Queen aroused a storm of indignation. Angry deputies stood up in the *parlements* to say that it was both 'immoral and illegal' for royal palaces to belong to the Queens of France.

When Marie Antoinette drove into Paris to attend the public celebrations for the birth of the Duc de Normandie, she was greeted in icy silence by the people. On her return to Versailles, she went sobbing to her husband, saying, 'Why should they hate me? What have I ever done to them?' This was one of the occasions when Louis might have spoken gently and firmly to his wife, telling her that it was her own foolishness and thoughtlessness, her continual meddling in affairs which were none of her concern, which had ended in angering the people who had been so ready to love her. But his wife's tears did no more than embarrass the timid King.

This year of 1785 saw the death of Choiseul, the one man who, if Louis had brought him back to power, might have succeeded in making Marie Antoinette into the kind of queen the French would have loved to have. He would have allowed her to be frivolous and extravagant, to be the arbiter of fashion and run up enormous bills with Mademoiselle Bertin. But the statesman who had created the Austrian alliance would never have allowed her to become subjected to the politics of Vienna or to have Mercy d'Argenteau as her intimate adviser. Nor would he ever have let her become the prey of the Polignacs.

Choiseul died, mourned by the Queen, who during his last illness sent twice a day to Paris to enquire after his health. The legacies left to his servants and his friends were as generous as his debts were enormous. With his customary munificence Calonne paid the debts out of the royal treasury. But Choiseul's widow, a woman of a nobility and integrity of character rarely seen in the old regime, retired to a convent with only two servants, until she had paid back to the King the whole of her husband's debts.

In the same way as Louis had been unable to forgive Choiseul the injuries done to his father, so he was now unable to forgive Beaumarchais the success of *Figaro*. It riled him to know that every ragamuffin in Paris was singing snatches of songs from *Figaro*, that every newspaper contained some reference to the greatest playwright of the century. One day an article by Beaumarchais, in which he wrote that he had had to 'conquer lions and tigers' to get his play performed, gave the King the opportunity to punish his impertinence. On the advice of Monsieur, who hated Beaumarchais for having refused to be on his pay roll, one of the most famous men in Paris was sentenced to prison – not to the Bastille, for little Monsieur Caron was not considered worthy of being a prisoner of state, but to St Lazare, a house of correction for petty criminals, for licentious pages and insubordinate younger sons, a place in which the worthy monks were permitted to inflict the salutary punishment of a sound thrashing. Even the lieutenant of police disapproved of the sentence and did everything he could to mitigate the hardships. Public opinion was on the side of Beaumarchais, from Calonne to Lafayette, from Artois to the Queen, all of whom considered him to have been a victim of Monsieur.

Once his anger had cooled, King Louis recognized his mistake and Beaumarchais stayed no more than a few days in prison. But strangely enough those few days were sufficient to break his spirit. The watchmaker's son, who was so vulnerable at heart, who made fun of the aristocrats and yet longed to be one of them, never got over the humiliation of being sent to St Lazare. He accepted his sentence with docility and dignity. But the mockingbird would not sing again as loudly and as gaily as before. To the end of his days Beaumarchais preserved that extraordinary talent for making money, whether out of commerce or out of writing. But there was never to be another *Mariage de Figaro*.

Whether out of thoughtlessness, or because she felt he had been unfairly treated, the Queen chose to act herself in *Le Barbier de Séville* at a private perfomance at Trianon. For Marie Antoinette to take part in the play by an author who earlier in the year had been sent to St Lazare was hardly likely to meet with the approval of '*les grandes charges*' of Versailles. But for once the Queen may have shown good judgement in repairing what she believed to have been an injustice.

It was early in August 1785, when she was rehearsing for the play, that Marie Antoinette first heard the extraordinary story of how the two court jewellers, Boehmer and Bassange, had sold her without her knowledge the most expensive necklace in the world. It is a story that even the imagination of Beaumarchais could never have conceived, with a villainy more vicious than any ever dreamt of by Laclos. Poets and writers from Goethe to Dumas have been fascinated by the tale of the 'Diamond Necklace', a tale which oversteps the bounds of probability.

Jeanne de St Rémy de Valois, descended from King Henry II, was the last in a long, decaying line of royal bastards. Her father was a poacher and a drunkard and her mother a debauched servant girl. A woman consumed by ambition, and hatred, knowing neither gratitude nor pity for her benefactors or her dupes, she can be compared to the legendary Mandragora, whose very roots were evil. The other leading protagonist was Cardinal Louis de Rohan, Archbishop of Strasbourg, Grand Almoner of France, a man of immense conceit, vanity and credulity, obsessed by the longing to regain favour with the Queen and attain high government office. Both characters were possessed of an element of insanity, of imaginations gone out of control.

The story of the diamond necklace has been told a hundred times, of the little beggar girl whose pathetic claim of being descended from the Valois kings attracted the notice of the benevolent Marquise de Boulainvilliers. The Marquise took Jeanne de Valois and her sister under her wing, paid for their education and, after ascertaining the truth about their royal pedigree, obtained a small pension for them from the King. A small stipend, a convent education followed by apprenticeship to a respectable dressmaking establishment in no way satisfied the ambitions of Mademoiselle de St Rémy, now grown into a pretty, beguiling young woman. In 1781 she and her little sister escaped from the convent of Longchamps to turn up at Bar-sur-Aube, where there were still the remains of the family estate, a few scattered fields and outhouses sold long ago to local peasants. Here Jeanne's pathetic story and her pretty ways aroused the compassion of the wife of a local magnate who took her and her sister into her house. But the arrival of her nephew Marc de La Motte, a young officer in the *gendarmerie*, opened her eyes to the morals of the sweet young woman who within a few weeks had enticed de La Motte into marrying her with a baby already on the way.

Turned out of the aunt's house, Monsieur and Madame de La Motte, who before long had acquired the spurious title of Count and Countess, started their married life with nothing more than his debts, the certificate of her royal pedigree, and a pension which, given their extravagant tastes, would barely keep them a couple of months. At Nancy, where they went to rejoin his regiment, they lived a life of sordid expediency, borrowing from his brother officers, buying on credit and exchanging goods at the local pawn shops. At the lowest ebb of their fortunes, Jeanne met again the benevolent Madame de Boulainvilliers, who was on her way to Alsace and, forgiving her past delin-quencies, introduced her to the Cardinal de Rohan who was living in his castle of Saverne.

This was in September 1781, and it was to take three years for a penniless adventuress to reduce one of the wealthiest princes of the Church to such a state of subjugation that he believed the tissue of lies woven by her distorted imagination. It could never have happened had Rohan been in a normal state. But he had fallen into the clutches of one of the greatest charlatans of the eighteenth century, Giuseppe Balsamo, alias Count Cagliostro, whose experiments in alchemy attracted the attentions of the greedy and the great. This extraordinary individual appears to have been possessed of certain hypnotic powers over his victims which enabled him to extort vast sums with his miraculous cures, his potions which promised beauty to ugly women, longevity and sexual potency to men. In the fifty-year-old Cardinal de Rohan he found the perfect victim, and there can be no doubt that he must have administered certain drugs that affected his brain, for the Cardinal's faithful henchman, the Abbé Georgel, recounts in his memoirs that the Prince's character deteriorated from the time that Cagliostro became a dominating influence in his life.

At Saverne Jeanne glimpsed a luxury and grandeur such as she had never dreamt of. But at their first meeting she made little impression on the Cardinal, and it was not until the following year, after months of nagging and soliciting from indifferent ministers and court officials, that Jeanne de La Motte, who was by now on the verge of destitution having mortgaged her pension, appeared at the Palais de Strasbourg in the Rue du Vieille Temple in Paris to solicit an audience of the Grand Almoner of France. She was elegant, graceful and touching in her misery, and her sad story could not fail to move the most impressionable of men. 'She had the wiles of a Circe,' wrote the Abbé Georgel. By the end of the year she had become the Cardinal's mistress, and in the following spring he was guaranteeing her a loan of 1,600 francs borrowed from a Jew in Nancy. Soon she was not only his mistress, but also his confidante, to whom he revealed his frustrated ambitions, his long-ing to become reconciled to the Queen. Every confession served as so much fuel to her already overheated imagination. She who had never seen the Queen other than in a gilded coach driving out of the gates of Versailles, now invented a story so fanciful that only someone as besotted as the Cardinal could ever have been persuaded to believe it – her story was extraordinary but given the reputation of the Queen not impossible.

In the antechambers of Versailles Jeanne had listened with avidity to every scandal, every libel whispered against Marie Antoinette: her numerous lovers, her sapphic tendencies and her friendship with Madame de Polignac, who procured young women for her pleasure. Why should not the Cardinal believe that she had become the latest favourite? And one day she came to him with shining eyes to tell him all her troubles were at an end. The Queen had interested herself on her behalf and soon her ancestral properties would be restored to her. Seeing that the Cardinal was never tired of listening to such tales, she embroidered them more and more, telling him of secret assignations, showing him letters which purported to come from the Queen – little notes on gold-edged paper and signed Marie Antoinette of France. How was it that a Rohan, whose family held half the great offices at court, should not have known that the Queen never signed herself other than as 'Marie Antoinette'? Or was he too drugged or too infatuated to care?

Before long the humble suppliant had become the valued friend who offered to intervene on his behalf, by bringing to the notice of the Queen an adoring letter in which the Grand Almoner of France begged to be forgiven for any offence he might unwittingly have given. Back came a gold-rimmed note in which the Queen professed to be glad if he could prove his innocence.

These letters had been forged by one of de La Motte's brother officers, a certain Rétaux de Villette, an amiable young man with a pretty talent for forgery which he was not averse to putting at the disposal of the charming young woman whose favours he shared with the husband and the Cardinal. But the time came when their victim was no longer satisfied with gold-edged notes and kept asking for an audience with the Queen, at which Madame de La Motte became ever more evasive, until one day in the middle of July 1784 she told him that his wishes were about to be gratified, that on that very evening he was to go disguised to Versailles and wait by the grove which was known as 'Le Bosquet de Venus'.

'La Scène au Bosquet' is one of the most famous scenes in history. A tall young woman dressed in white, who in the grace of her movements and the proud carriage of her head bore an extraordinary resemblance to the Queen, offered the bedazzled Cardinal a rose, murmuring, 'You know what this means, but continue to be discreet.' It was only a minute before a man came forward telling him to hurry away as Artois was seen to be approaching. The man whom the Cardinal took to be a servant of the Queen was none other than Rétaux de Villette.

How the accomplices must have laughed to see the great Rohan going down on his knees to kiss the hem of the robe of a certain Mademoiselle d'Oliva, whom de La Motte had seen in the gardens of the Palais Royal and, noting her amazing resemblance to the Queen, enlisted her services. In her fury and indignation Marie Antoinette was later to refer to her as '*une barboteuse des rues*'. But pretty Mademoiselle d'Oliva was rather better than a prostitute. She was just a poor young woman of easy morals ready to be seduced by the dashing Comte de La Motte with his airs of a great gentleman and his promise of a rich reward, if she would consent to impersonate a certain high-ranking personage, who could not fail to show her gratitude.

Jeanne de La Motte had triumphed. From now on the Cardinal was completely under her spell. She and her husband lived in princely state in her home town of Bar-sur-Aube on money extracted in the name of the Queen – a charity here, a charity there – money which always finished either in their pockets or in those of Cagliostro, who by now had become an ally, abetting their plans with his prophecies of a great and glorious future. Towards the end of 1784, Madame de La Motte Valois was beginning to be talked of both in Paris and Versailles. In the world which battened on the fringes of the court, people whispered of the Queen's new friend. Marie Antoinette lived so exclusively in her *société*, in the small, private world of Trianon, that Jeanne could hint of her connections in high places without running the risk of ever being discovered.

Nevertheless it is strange that someone as solid and respectable as the court jeweller Boehmer should have been sufficiently taken in by an insinuating little adventuress to approach her with regard to selling to the Queen what was the most expensive necklace in the world. Louis XV was still on the throne when the court jewellers, Boehmer and Bassange, had begun to collect the rarest and most perfect of diamonds to make a necklace of incomparable beauty for the old King to offer to La du Barry. His death came as a shattering blow, for by then the cost had far exceeded their calculations. But their hopes revived in the young Queen, who was known to be passionately fond of diamonds, and at the birth of her first child the fabulous necklace was shown to King Louis who, filled with love and gratitude for his wife, offered to buy it for her. But for once Marie Antoinette showed sense. The American war was on and the necklace cost 1,600,000 francs. The Queen refused it, which spelt ruin to the unfortunate jewellers who had overextended their credit on a necklace which was practically unsaleable. Only sovereigns could afford it at that price, and sovereigns were thin on the ground. The Hanoverian kings were not given to spending money either on their mistresses or their wives, and even Catherine of Russia preferred spending her money on wars and on her lovers. On two successive occasions Boehmer had appealed to the Queen; the last time he had gone on his knees, saying he would have to kill himself unless she saved him from bankruptcy. Marie Antoinette, justifiably irritated, told him not to be a fool. If he could not sell the necklace, then it would have to be broken up and sold in separate pieces, and he would have no difficulty in selling the stones.

Such was the situation when the unhappy Boehmer heard of the Queen's mysterious friend, who was said to have ousted Madame de Polignac, and towards the end of the year Jeanne de Valois, who only a few years before had been soliciting alms at the doors of the great, was giving audience to the court jeweller, who asked her to intercede on his behalf. The sight of the necklace – blazing with a hundred peerless stones – seems to have aroused the element of insanity which was latent in the character of a woman who until then had confined herself to petty larceny, swindling, and lying, but who now evolved a scheme so mad that it had no possibility of success and could only end in bringing ruin on everyone concerned.

Two circumstances were in her favour. The first was that neither Boehmer nor Bassange had been in the Queen's confidence and they knew nothing of her bad relations with the Cardinal. The second was that the Cardinal, who could have heard of it from any of his relations at court, knew nothing of the King having offered to buy the necklace for his wife. All he knew was what was told him by Madame de La Motte, that the Queen coveted the necklace and was prepared to buy it, but for the time being wanted to keep it a secret from the King. If the Cardinal helped her to acquire it, he would earn both her gratitude and friendship. All he had to do was to buy the necklace in his name and draw up a contract with the jeweller, who only at the eleventh hour would be told it was for the Queen. Her Majesty would pledge herself to pay it in four instalments of 400,000 francs, the first of which was to be paid before August 1785.

Jeanne de Valois must certainly have possessed 'the wiles of a Circe', for neither the Cardinal nor the jewellers appear to have questioned the extraordinary nature of the deal. On 1 February 1785 the necklace was delivered by Boehmer to the Hôtel de Strasbourg, and the delighted jeweller received the deed of acquisition with each paragraph signed 'Marie Antoinette de France'. He was also shown an extract of a gold-rimmed note on which was written: 'It is not customary for me to transact business with my jewellers in this fashion. So keep this note and do whatever you think is best.' That same evening the Cardinal set out with the necklace for Versailles where Madame de La Motte was staying in a hotel. He had no sooner handed it over to her when a man arrived whom he recognized to be the Queen's servant whom he had already seen that night in the garden, and who was none other than Rétaux de Villette. This was the last that was ever seen of the legendary necklace which had brought its creators to the verge of ruin. Within a few days it had already been broken up, smuggled by Monsieur de La Motte to London, and sold piece by piece in the jewel markets of the city.

In the following months the Cardinal waited for a sign of approbation from the Queen, who continued to treat him with the same frozen indifference. Feast day followed upon feast day without the Queen ever wearing the diamond necklace, and by July Rohan was beginning to have doubts of his mistress's good faith. The time was drawing near for the payment of the first instalment and Boehmer was becoming anxious. The only one to remain as cool and self-confident as ever was Jeanne de La Motte, who now dictated a letter to Rétaux in which the Queen complained of having been over-charged for the necklace and demanding a reduction of 200,000 francs, offering by way of compensation to pay 700,000 francs by 1 October. Pressed by their creditors, the jewellers did not dare to refuse, and on Rohan's advice Boehmer addressed a fulsome and obsequious letter to Marie Antoinette, stating that his zeal and respect for Her Majesty was such that he was ready to accept the terms, happy to think that the most beautiful necklace in existence would be adorning the greatest and best of queens.

Small wonder that this letter was totally incomprehensible to the Queen, who saw it as yet another proof that the poor jeweller had gone out of his mind. She threw it away without giving it another thought, until on 9 August, when she was in the middle of a rehearsal for *Le Barbier de Séville*, which was claiming all her attention at the time, she was suddenly interrupted by Madame Campan, who had been visited by Boehmer and told of a gigantic swindle in which the Cardinal de Rohan had not hesitated to implicate his Queen.

It was Monday 15 August and Versailles was full for the feast of the Assumption, which was also the feast day of the Queen. In spite of her growing unpopularity, Marie Antoinette could still draw the crowds from Paris to stand in queues in the Gallery of Mirrors, to see her pass on her way to mass. But this morning mass was late. Dressed in his pontifical robes of purple silk, carrying his jewelled crozier, the Grand Almoner was waiting to lead the royal procession to the chapel, when he was suddenly called by one of the King's guards to accompany him to His Majesty's study. Here he found the King and Queen and three of the ministers, Breteuil, Vergennes and Miromesnil. Louis, who was always a man of few words, went straight to the point. 'Who was it who commissioned you to buy a diamond necklace from Boehmer?' And the Cardinal, who had grown visibly paler, replied, 'A lady called the Comtesse de La Motte Valois, who showed me a letter from the Queen.' At this moment the Queen, who was obviously having difficulty in controlling herself, burst out, 'How could you have thought that I, who have not addressed a word to you for eight years, would ever have chosen you to act on my behalf and with a woman of that kind!'

Seeing the cold fury on the Queen's face, Rohan must have known that he was lost and he answered, stammering from nerves, 'I see now that I have been cruelly duped. I am ready to pay for the necklace. I was so anxious to do a favour to Your Majesty that I completely lost my head and thought I was acting in good faith.' Whereupon he handed over the forged letter which Madame de La Motte had given him as coming from the Queen. The King, who in spite of his outward calm was almost as angry as his wife, gave one glance at the letter and threw it on the ground saying, 'This is not the Queen's handwriting nor her signature. Is it possible that a prince of the House of Rohan, who is also Grand Almoner of France, does not know that the Queen never signs herself other than by her Christian name? As for the handwriting, it is as false as the signature.' Then, proceeding in a gentler tone, he added, 'The whole thing is inexplicable. I would like you to justify yourself as I do not want to find you guilty. But you must explain the meaning of all these strange dealings with Boehmer, these promises and letters.' Seeing that the Cardinal was finding difficulty in replying, Louis told him to go into an adjoining room, where he would find ink and paper, and to sit down and transcribe everything he had to say.

Meanwhile there was mounting tension in the royal study. The King was outraged not only on account of the insult to his wife, but because of the slur which the Cardinal's behaviour had cast on the Church. Breteuil, who had succeeded Rohan as ambassador in Vienna, where he had been a failure following on the popular Prince, was only too ready to find him guilty, whereas Vergennes and Miromesnil were both inclined to moderation, realizing that the arrest of a prince of the Church would entail endless complications. But in view of the Queen's fury, the tears she could no longer control, neither dared to say a word in the Cardinal's defence. When Rohan came back into the room, the King, speaking in the same gentle tone, told him he had no other choice than to place him under arrest. This was the moment when Rohan, fatuous, foolish and debauched, showed he could still behave like a *grand seigneur*, accepting the news with dignity and calm, only asking not to be exposed to the shame of a public arrest in front of the whole court; asking it not so much for himself but out of regard for the pontifical robes he was wearing. And only the Queen's tears prevented Louis from acceding to his request.

Quiet and composed, looking neither to right nor left, Rohan walked slowly through the Gallery of Mirrors, where no one dared to speak above a whisper, until suddenly Breteuil's stentorian voice called out, 'Have the Cardinal arrested,' and there followed a moment of shocked silence in which even the captain of the guards appeared to hesitate before daring to lay hands on a Rohan. That moment of hesitation was sufficient for the Cardinal who, acting with a surprising presence of mind, bent down, ostensibly to adjust the buckle of a shoe, and scribbled a note for his Vicar-General, the Abbé Georgel, telling him to destroy all the letters addressed to him from Madame de La Motte. That same evening he was taken to the Bastille, and the most despicable and contemptible of men, a disgrace to his name and to the Church, became a martyr overnight.

Versailles was in a state of ferment. With the exception of Breteuil, who was openly gloating over Rohan's arrest, the rest of the ministers were regretting the King's decision – a decision which was intended as a show of strength, but was no more than weakness in giving way to the tantrums of his wife. Madame Campan writes in her memoirs that Breteuil and the Abbé Vermond influenced the Queen's behaviour. But in a letter to the Emperor written four days after the Cardinal's arrest, Marie Antoinette said:

> Everything was arranged between the King and myself. The ministers knew nothing up to the moment when the King summoned the Cardinal to appear in the presence of the Lord Chancellor and Baron de Breteuil. I was also there, and I was really touched by the good sense and the firmness which the King displayed in this unpleasant affair. When the Cardinal implored the King not to have him arrested he replied that, both as a king and as a husband, it was impossible for him to do otherwise.... I hope everything will soon be settled. One does not know yet whether he will be judged by Parliament, or if his family

will throw themselves on the mercy of the King. But all I want is for the whole of this horrible business to be shown up in front of the whole world.

Impulsive, honest and innocent, the Queen ignored the appalling repercussions that Rohan's arrest was going to have both on the court and on the general public. She could not imagine that someone as vile as Jeanne de La Motte would be able to drag the name of the Queen of France in the mud. She wrote to her brother:

The Cardinal believes to have bought in my name a necklace for the sum of 1,600,000 francs. He makes out that he has been swindled by a certain Madame de La Motte Valois. This creature of the lowest kind, who does not even belong here and whom I have never set eyes on, was put in the Bastille two days ago. Though she admits to have been on intimate terms with the Cardinal, she firmly denies having had any part in the buying of the necklace.

The adventuress had been arrested at Bar-sur-Aube, where she had been living in great state on the fruits of her ill-gotten gains. Cornered by the police, she had turned like a viper on the man who had been her lover and protector. Her accomplices having escaped, she still believed she could maintain her innocence at the Cardinal's expense. But before the trial had opened Rétaux de Villette had been discovered living under an assumed name in Geneva, and poor Mademoiselle d'Oliva had been brought back from her hiding place in Brussels. Both had confessed to everything at the very first interrogation.

Once again the Rohans rose as one man to defend their kith and kin, in the same way as they had upheld the Prince de Guéménée at the time of his bankruptcy. The King's former governess Madame de Marsan, whose influence had obtained for her nephew the post of Grand Almoner, now went on her knees before the Queen whom she detested, imploring her to have pity on the Cardinal. But Marie Antoinette turned away without a word. Behind the Rohans were the King's aunts, only too ready to believe that their niece had been involved in a nefarious intrigue. Together with Mesdames was the Prince de Condé, the most anti-Austrian of all the princes of the blood, the Queen's old enemy the Duc d'Aiguillon, and all those who at some time or other had been rebuffed and ignored and divested of some hereditary post in favour of the Polignacs. Not only the nobility but also the clergy now rose to protest against a prince of the Church being tried by secular law, maintaining that only the Pope could sit in judgement on a cardinal. But Louis made the mistake of allowing Rohan to be tried by Parliament, a fractious body of men who were constantly challenging the royal authority.

Meanwhile Marie Antoinette continued to behave with an incredible insouciance, performing in Beaumarchais's *Barbier de Séville* only four days after the Cardinal had been condemned to the Bastille. From all accounts she appears to have been an adorable Rosine, while Artois surpassed himself in the role of Figaro. But did it make no impression on either of them to hear Beaumarchais's famous indictment against calumny, 'which starts as quietly and as softly as the wings of a swallow, skimming the ground before a storm, spreading little by little, gradually growing in force till it develops into a tempest'?

In the Paris streets, the campaign of calumny against the Queen was growing in volume daily. People were openly accusing her of having connived with the Cardinal into swindling the jewellers. Proud and apparently indifferent, Marie Antoinette continued to ignore the rumours, writing to her brother on 19 September:

> The Cardinal took my name like a vulgar, clumsy cheat. He was probably short of money and thought he could repay the jeweller at the date he had fixed without anything being discovered. I am delighted not to hear anything more about it. It cannot come up for trial before December. I shall never forget the King's wonderful behaviour towards me. He did not let his ministers influence him in the slightest, though some of them had connections with the Cardinal and others with his relatives.

Alas! it would have been better had the wise and prudent Vergennes been able to prevent his monarch from making the disastrous mistake of having the Cardinal tried. What the Queen believed to be the end of the affair was only the beginning. Axel Fersen, who was back in France serving with his regiment at the garrison town of Landrecies, appreciated the gravity of the situation, informing King Gustavus that

> The stories which are being repeated, particularly in the provinces, are quite appalling. People refuse to believe that the buying of the necklace and the forged letters are the real reasons for the Cardinal's disgrace. They persist in imagining that there is some political motive behind it; which is certainly not the case. Even in Paris they are saying that the Queen made use of the Cardinal for her own purposes, that she only pretended to hate him while on the contrary, she was on the best of terms with him, got him to buy the necklace and passed the money on to her brother.

When Fersen returned to Paris in the autumn of 1785, the Queen had already gone to Fontainebleau, where she was far more interested in completing the new decorations for her apartments than in the approaching trial. The season at Fontainebleau had never been more brilliant. The King spent his days out hunting and the Queen, who was at the beginning of another pregnancy, was in excellent health and the best of spirits. The Emperor's long-drawn-out negotiations over the Netherlands had come to a satisfactory conclusion, with France supplying the two million florins to make up the ten million demanded by Joseph as indemnity. What was a wise move on the part of Vergennes appeared to the general public as the theft of millions by the Queen to finance her brother's wars. Five years later, when the King and Queen were already prisoners in the Tuileries, Joseph wrote to his brother Leopold: 'The French are obsessed by the idea that our sister has secretly sent me millions, whereas I don't know why or how I could ever have asked for them, nor how she could ever have been able to procure them for me. Actually I have never received a sou from France. It is a horrible calumny.' Joseph was speaking the truth. The two million florins supplied by France were part of a treaty between the French and the Dutch which was highly advantageous to France. But from 1786 right up to the time when she stood on trial before the revolutionary tribunal, Marie Antoinette was to be accused of having acted against the interests of her country. And this at a time when Joseph was berating her for having become completely 'Frenchified', that all she retained of Germany was the face and figure. Torn between two allegiances, having inherited from her mother the conviction that the Austro-French alliance was vital to the future of their two countries, poor Marie Antoinette, who understood so little of politics, ended in pleasing no one.

While the Cardinal was languishing in the Bastille and his lawyers were preparing his defence, during the interrogations at which Jeanne de La Motte, with an incredible effrontery, continued to assert her innocence and public opinion was daily mounting in the prisoners' favour, the court revolved round a series of balls, one more magnificent than the next. The halcyon days of Calonne's administration were drawing to an end in a last outburst of fireworks. In 1786 the Queen's bills from Mademoiselle Bertin were so astronomical as to give sleepless nights to her mistress of the robes, who dared to ask for a detailed account from the arrogant and impertinent milliner. Even the Queen took fright on hearing that she had spent the sum of 87,594 livres in a single year, which did not include the bills of the court dressmaker Madame Eloffe, nor the 31,000 francs spent on the riding habits ordered from her English tailor. At thirty, Marie Antoinette was obsessed by the fear that she was growing old. She was putting on weight, and conscious of her ample bosom, her increasing *embonpoint*, she no longer wanted to wear the exaggerated fashions of her youth. 'No more flowers and feathers,' she told Mademoiselle Bertin, 'no more extravaganzas.' But she still retained all her elegance and grace, the gliding walk, the proud carriage of the head, and in Fersen's eyes she was still the most beautiful woman at her court.

To please the Swedish King, and incidentally Count Fersen, both the King and Queen of France signed the marriage contract of the wedding which took place in the chapel of the Swedish Embassy between the new ambassador, Baron de Staël-Holstein, and Necker's daughter Germaine, who brought to her husband one of the biggest dowries in France. Two weeks later, on 31 January 1786, the young ambassadress was presented at Versailles where, to quote her own words, 'The Queen received me with a graciousness which never let one forget that she was Queen, yet managed to persuade one that she had forgotten it.' The twenty-year-old Germaine, who was gauche, clumsy and unused to the complicated etiquette of Versailles, tore her train while making her curtsey. The palace ladies tittered behind their fans, but Marie Antoinette was sweet and sympathetic, immediately sending for a serving maid to repair the damage, a kindness which Germaine was never to forget.

King Gustavus had gained a brilliant correspondent in his young ambassadress, who supplemented her husband's diplomatic dispatches with vivid descriptions of life at Versailles in the last years of the old regime. In between her accounts of the puerilities and trivialities of court life, of extravagant balls in which the gardens of Trianon, with its fountains, trees and statues, were faithfully reproduced in the Salle de Spectacle, she wrote of 'the poor Cardinal suffering from asthma in his damp narrow room at the Bastille'. For Germaine, like most of the fashionable young women in Paris, was in sympathy with the unfortunate Rohan, duped by his mistress and victimized by the court. At the races at Longchamps it was smart to wear hats '*à la Cardinal*' and ribbons in red and yellow – *couleur Cardinal sur paille* ('colour of the Cardinal on straw').

The long-drawn-out trial, of which the preliminaries had lasted for over nine months, finally came to an end on 31 May 1786. In the last ten days the accused had been confronted with one another in front of the judges – the Cardinal calm and dignified, Jeanne de La Motte spitting out spite and venom, losing herself in a tangled web of lies. By the morning of the 31st unprecedented crowds had gathered along the Seine, outside the Conciergerie and the Quai des Tournelles. When the Cardinal entered the chamber he was treated not as a prisoner but as a *grand seigneur*, all the councillors and magistrates rose to their feet, after which he was invited to sit down. At the entrance to the chamber stood a solid phalanx of Rohans, all dressed in black, headed by Madame de Marsan who, on the arrival of the judges, called out 'Messieurs, you have come to judge us all.' It was common knowledge that several of those supposedly incorruptible men had already been won over by bribes from the family.

The Attorney General was fair but severe, declaring the Cardinal to be guilty of *lèse-majesté* in having dared to presume that the Queen of France would demean herself in secret dealings and assignations. But he had barely time to finish his speech before he was interrupted by violent remonstrances on the part of the Cardinal's supporters, some of whom did not hesitate to call him 'the victim of court intrigues'. And though no one as yet dared to name the Queen, the very violence of their protests were aspersions on her honour. Rohan was acquitted. Not only was he acquitted, but all the accusations brought against him at the time of his arrest were proved to be null and void, showing that the *parlement* of Paris dared to challenge the authority of the Crown. The judgement of the courts condemned *in absentia* the Comte de La Motte to be sent to the galleys, Rétaux de Villette to be banished in perpetuity, and Cagliostro to be deported from the country. Mademoiselle d'Oliva, who had impressed the judges with her innocence, was declared to be free of all blame. But Jeanne de La Motte was to pay in full the punishment for her crimes, sentenced to be publicly whipped and branded with hot irons with a 'V' (*voleuse*), before being given a life imprisonment in the notorious prison of La Salpêtrière – a sentence so savage as to cause a sudden hush in the crowded courtroom. Yet not even her lawyer could find a word to say in her defence.

There was widespread jubilation over the Cardinal's acquittal. The *poissardes* crowned the magistrates with flowers, and in the streets of Paris they chanted

Le Saint Père l'a rougi	The Holy Father made him red
Le Roi et la Reine l'ont noirci	The King and Queen made him black
Le Parlement l'a blanchi	Parliament has made him white
Allelujah.	Hallelujah.

Rohan returned to the brilliantly illuminated Hôtel de Strasbourg as a hero and a martyr, while the woman who had been his mistress for the past three years was having the first part of her sentence carried out in the courtyard of the Conciergerie. So violent were her struggles that it required four men to hold her down, and she bit one of them so fiercely on the hand that the iron slipped and branded her breast instead of her shoulder, after which she fainted and was carried unconscious to La Salpêtrière. But even now she had not yet lost her power for evil. The Queen's enemies and even some of her friends, such as the compassionate Madame de Lamballe, were shocked at the severity of a sentence which condemned the last descendant of the Valois kings to be branded as a common thief. Chartres, who by his father's death had become Duc d'Orléans, launched a fund to finance an appeal; great ladies brought gifts to her in prison. On 2 June 1787 the gates of La Salpêtrière, one of the most heavily guarded of the state prisons, mysteriously opened; and Jeanne de La Motte, disguised as a boy, escaped to England, where she published memoir after memoir of accumulated venom, attacking both her former lover and the Queen, accusing Marie Antoinette of every natural and unnatural vice, saying that both she and the Cardinal were her lovers; memoirs which the British government made no attempt to have suppressed and which, when smuggled back to France, did terrible harm to the already unpopular Queen.

Jeanne de La Motte's good fortune did not last for long. The insanity which had always been latent in her character gradually gained the upper hand, sinking her ever deeper into debauchery, until one day she was found dead in a London street, having fallen or been thrown out of the window of a house of ill fame. But by then the harm had been done. To quote one of the judges, 'Sufficient mud had been thrown to besmirch both the crozier and the crown.'

The Cardinal had been acquitted, and though no one would have expected the King and Queen ever to receive him at court, or to allow him to keep his position as Grand Almoner of France, Louis nevertheless made a fatal mistake in condemning him by *lettre de cachet* to exile in a monastery in the Auvergne. For the *lettre de cachet* was one of the most odious and the most hated of all the symbols of despotism. But Louis, who was usually so calm and apathetic, had been so outraged by the behaviour of Parliament, so convinced of the Cardinal's guilt and so full of commiseration for the Queen, that he had allowed himself to be influenced by the personal animosity of the minister of his household, the Baron de Breteuil.

No one dared to be the first to break the news of the Cardinal's acquittal to the Queen, who was in the last months of her pregnancy, and she is said to have heard of it eventually from a young page who had just returned from Paris. Madame Campan found her lying sobbing on her bed, crying out, 'Come and pity your Queen, in whom you see a victim of conspiracy and lies. But I pity you even more, my poor Campan, for belonging to a country where there is no justice and where even the judges are corrupt.' They were bitter words, from a queen of France who no longer loved her country.

ever had Marie Antoinette felt so lonely and unhappy as in the early summer of 1786. She who in the past had laughed so carelessly at the slanders of Versailles and written to her mother of 'my charming subjects who accuse me of having lovers – both men and women', now saw for the first time what calumny could achieve when there were members of the Parliament of Paris ready to believe that she, a Hapsburg and a Queen of France, would consort with a woman of the type of Jeanne de La Motte. And just at the time when she needed him most, the King, acting on the advice of Calonne, had left for Cherbourg on the first journey he had ever taken outside the Ile de France. It had been kept a secret from her until the last moment, for the ministers had feared she would want the visit to be postponed until after her confinement, when she could accompany her husband on the tour. It was the general opinion that she might jeopardize its success for the scandal of the diamond necklace had spread even to the provinces.

Nearly ten years had passed since the Emperor had advised his brother-in-law to travel in his country and see for himself the conditions under which the people lived. Louis's constitutional apathy, his inability to come to a decision, allied to his natural timidity and diffidence, led him to believe his brothers were better at representing the Crown. In contrast to his brothers, whose extravagance and ostentation alienated the people, Louis travelled with a small suite and very little show. Those who accompanied him all belonged to the '*Société de la Reine*', for Louis was a man with neither friends nor favourites of his own. Now for the first time, among the farmers of Normandy, in the naval barracks and docks of Cherbourg, he was to meet with a friendliness and warmth he had never known at Versailles. His retinue, who until now had never heard him talk of anything but hunting, were amazed at the extent of his knowledge on naval science and strategy, and the pleasure with which he talked to the officers and engineers. Gone was the timidity which so often made him seem gauche and rude; the farmers' wives of Caen found the King to be the most jovial and amiable of men, complimenting them on their excellent fare when he sat down to share one of their simple meals. For all his embroidered coats and glittering orders, he might have been one of themselves. The enthusiasm he aroused was tremendous. And there is no doubt that, if Louis had acted earlier on his brother-in-law's advice, he might have been the most popular of kings. But he was the slave of

Versailles and of an antiquated class system, binding him with chains he was not strong enough to break.

Those few days in Normandy were among the happiest of his life, and he wrote to his wife, 'The love of my people has gone straight to my heart. Judge for yourself if I am not the most fortunate of monarchs.' But his state of euphoria had vanished by the time he returned to Versailles, where the atmosphere was still heavy with the echoes of the scandal of the diamond necklace which, being a man of little imagination, he had almost forgotten. The Queen, who was in the last stages of her pregnancy, was querulous and tearful. Fersen had returned to Sweden, and Versailles was full of bored and discontented courtiers. The Rohans, starting with the old Prince de Soubise, had handed in their resignations, the King's aunts had shown their sympathy by retiring to Bellevue, and the Polignacs had quarrelled with the Queen over Calonne, whom they persisted in supporting despite his growing unpopularity. Marie Antoinette's almost morbid depression told on her health, and the baby girl born in July 1786 was delicate and malformed, dying a year later from a tubercular complaint which was to affect both her brothers. But again, as at the birth of the Duc de Normandie, the Queen's enemies persisted in saying that Fersen was the father, and if the child was malformed it was the fault of the Queen for having insisted on tight lacing.

The Prince de Ligne, who returned to Paris in the summer of 1786 after an absence of several years, was shocked at the growing spirit of discontent, the change for the worse both in manners and in customs. 'There was no more amiability, no more elegance or grace, no more gallantry or wish to please. The men were neglected in appearance and the women were badly dressed. Wherever one went, people were both boring and bored.' And what he regarded as the sure sign of a coming revolution was that the very classes in whose interest it was to support the government did nothing but criticize it, while members of the parliaments boasted openly of their impertinent attacks on the Crown. He was shocked at the way in which morals and behaviour were being affected by a growing anglomania; at the pretty women who neglected their toilette in order to read the works of the encyclopaedists and to inveigh from morning to night against the very abuses which nourished their families, thus making without realizing it propaganda for a republic. 'They have spoilt my Versailles,' wrote the Prince, who felt nothing but foreboding for the future. But he could not bring himself to admit that the Queen, whom he had always loved and admired, was largely to blame.

Resentful at what she regarded as the disloyalty of her courtiers, disillusioned with the Polignacs, Marie Antoinette encouraged the anglomania he condemned. She had made a new friend in the British ambassador, the young Duke of Dorset, frivolous, handsome and enormously rich, who created a scandal by being seen at one of the opera balls in the company of his Italian mistress, who was wearing his order of the garter on her forehead. But the Queen found him amusing. The smart world of London flocked to Paris for the parties of an ambassador who spent what was then the enormous sum of £11,000 a year on entertaining. Georgiana Devonshire, who was one of his intimate friends, was invited to Versailles, and among the criticisms brought against the Queen of France was that she enjoyed dancing Scottish reels with young Lord Strathavon, who was attached to the embassy – anything to be distracted from her loneliness, to make her forget her beloved Fersen, who had returned to Sweden to serve his King in the war against Russia. Gossip numbered the Duke of Dorset among her lovers, but he was never more than a friend, a friend of the kind she could never have in a Frenchman. Georgiana Devonshire regarded him as 'the most dangerous of men, who with that beauty of his was so unaffected and had a simplicity and persuasion in his manner that made it easy to account for the number of women who had been in love with him'. Marie Antoinette on the other hand described him somewhat unflatteringly as '*une bonne femme*', what in German she would have described as '*gemütlich*' – 'cosy'. She exchanged with him countless letters, chiefly about trivialities, asking him to procure her the latest novelties from London – such as an ivory-handled billiard cue, for billiards had become the fashion at Versailles. 'The French are *aimable, si vous voulez*, but capricious and inconsistent, especially the women. In fact I have no friend but Mrs B.,' wrote the Duke to Georgiana Devonshire. Mrs B. (Mrs Brown) was his code name for the Queen. At the time of the Cardinal's acquittal he wrote,

> Mrs B. and I had a great deal of talk about this business the other day. I happened to say that the Parliament was just. The Cardinal had to be acquitted. Mrs B. was of another opinion and thought him censorable. Her prejudice against him has always been kept up by the Baron de Breteuil, whom Mrs B. has been led by in the whole of the affair. Now her eyes are opened, I hope to God she will treat him with the contempt he deserves. You have no notion how Mrs B. has hurt herself in the opinion of the public by supporting such a tyrannical and haughty minister.

Marie Antoinette continued to support Breteuil even when Calonne persuaded the King to get rid of him. It was said that the Duchesse de Polignac had had a hand in his dismissal, because he had refused to give his immensely wealthy granddaughter in marriage to her son. But whatever may have been the reason, the Queen should never have discussed her husband's ministers with the British ambassador, a matter on which Calonne had every right to complain.

In a year when even a foreign visitor like the Prince de Ligne spoke of revolution, when even a seventeen-year-old bride like the future Marquise de La Tour du Pin, newly arrived in court, noted that 'The spirit of revolt was rampant in all classes of society', the British ambassador was writing complacently to his government, 'It is hardly possible to conceive a moment of more perfect tranquility than the present. The French government, free from the late causes of its anxiety, appears entirely bent on improving the benefits of peace.' This was written only a few weeks before Calonne broke the news to the King that the country was in debt for well over 100 million francs, that it was impossible to raise any further loans, and that fundamental and drastic economies were necessary to save both France and the monarchy from complete collapse.

Calonne now realized what Turgot and Necker had realized before him, that no country could survive in which certain regions were more privileged than others, and in which the upper classes, both the nobility and clergy, were practically exempt from taxation, of which the whole burden fell on the working classes and the peasants. To put an end to this injustice, Calonne presented the King with a detailed programme in which taxes such as the *taille* and the *corvée*, both of which were borne by the poorer sections of the population, were either lightened or abolished, and a land tax was to be imposed on the upper classes and above all on the clergy, who owned one tenth of the country's lands. Knowing how bitterly these measures would be opposed by those who until now had been his supporters, and by the *parlements* which were always ready to uphold the nobility against the Crown, Calonne suggested that the land tax should be presented for approval to an assembly of notables, made up of leading citizens. Once these measures had been approved, Parliament would have no other choice than to register them, or if necessary be forced to do so by a *lit de justice*.

Assemblies of notables had been resorted to in the past by Henry IV and Richelieu, whose powerful personalities had cowed them into submission. But Louis was no Henry IV and Calonne was no Richelieu. When Louis returned from his tour of Normandy, his minister's proposal came as a bombshell for the King. 'This is pure Necker,' he shouted, so furious that he broke a chair in his rage.

Yet he made no attempt to cancel the autumn journey to Fontainebleau, the most costly of all the royal journeys, for which no less than two thousand horses were commandeered, not counting those required for the transport of the heavy baggage. This was to be the last visit to Fontainebleau, visits which in the past Comte Mercy had always dreaded for his young Queen, in whom the autumn rains combined with boredom to encourage gambling and dissipation. Marie Antoinette no longer played for high stakes and now led a far quieter life, devoting herself to her children, particularly to her little girl, who was at last beginning to respond to her affection. She had become very religious in the past year, going regularly to confession and spending many hours in prayer. But court life remained as empty and as futile as ever. The insipid comedies staged at enormous expense, the endless card playing and billiards, the childish games of lotto and of *tric-trac* had nothing to attract the younger courtiers. Rain or fine, the King went out hunting every day, returning in the evening in such a state of exhaustion that four lackeys had to carry him upstairs to bed. And all during these weeks he appears to have kept Calonne's projects a secret from the Queen.

The winter season opened at Versailles with the usual round of balls and entertainments, the Sunday courts, the weekly *Grand Couvert*, of which the memoirs of Madame de La Tour du Pin give such a vivid picture. She shows Marie Antoinette with her frailties and faults, redeemed by an all-embracing charm, 'always greeting the King with a delightful air of pleasure and of deference, stopping on the way to mass to speak to the foreign ladies who had been presented to her in private, singling out by an inclination of the head, a gracious smile, some artist or writer she had noted in the crowd'. Yet the Queen was never able to conquer her dislike of *Le Grand Couvert*. 'While the King ate heartily, the Queen never removed her gloves or opened her napkin, which was a big mistake,' wrote the young lady-in-waiting. The sightseers who had come down from Paris to watch the *Grand Couvert* returned disappointed and angered at the Queen's haughtiness and indifference. But the King's gluttony must have irritated someone as innately fastidious as Marie Antoinette. She must have hated seeing him wolf down his food and drink in public, and perhaps already knew that her enemies were spreading the tale 'that the King had taken to drink encouraged by his wife'. The gay young woman, who gave the impression of being enchanted with life, had changed into a sad, mature-looking matron. Her long-drawn-out adolescence had finally come to an end, leaving her alone in a hostile world, faced with problems she did not begin to understand.

Outwardly life at Versailles remained the same, but the atmosphere of disintegration was apparent to any intelligent observer. 'It was the fashion to complain of everything,' wrote Madame de La Tour du Pin. 'One was bored being in attendance at court. The officers of the *Garde de Corps*, who were lodged in the château when on duty, bemoaned having to wear uniform all day; the ladies of the household could not bear to miss going to supper in Paris during the eight days of their attendance at Versailles. It was the height of *bon ton* to complain of their duties at court, profiting from them none the less. All the ties were being loosened, and alas it was the upper classes which led the way.'

While Versailles was becoming fossilized in antiquated ceremonies and obsolete traditions, Paris was seething with excitement. In salons, clubs and coffee houses, people were speaking of nothing but politics. The young men who had returned from America talked of the Bill of Rights and of the need for a constitution. Noblemen like the Noailles and the La Rochefoucaulds fraternized with the bourgeoisie in the masonic lodges that had become the fashion. Even women belonged, women as empty-headed as Marie Thérèse de Lamballe, who presided over the *Loge de la Candeur* and described some of the strange ceremonies to the Queen, who was always fascinated by any novelty.

It was in a masonic lodge that the young Vicomte de Noailles met Choderlos de Laclos and introduced him to his friend the Duc d'Orléans, who before long had appointed him as his *secrétaire de commandement*, so that with the blessing of the masonic lodges, the author of *Les Liaisons Dangereuses* became the *éminence grise* of the Palais Royal.

Sedition was in the air. Not even the 144 notables chosen for their integrity and loyalty to the Crown could be relied on, for the majority, and in particular the richer members of the clergy, thought of themselves rather than of their country.

In January 1787, the death of Vergennes was a shattering blow both for the government and the King. He was not only the ablest of Louis's ministers, he was also the only one whom the King liked and trusted. Now he was lost and rudderless, asking everyone's advice and never coming to any definite decision. Rumours even accused Marie Antoinette of having had him poisoned to revenge herself on his anti-Austrian policy. It was not a story that was generally believed, but it nevertheless helped to swell the tide of slander against the Queen.

On Mercy's advice, Marie Antoinette had abstained from becoming involved in the convocation of the notables, of which she had only been told the day it was announced to the public. More sceptical than the King, she had little faith in the patriotism of his nobles. Postponed by the death of Vergennes, the assembly's meeting at the end of February took place in an atmosphere charged with mistrust of a minister who, for all his plausibility and brilliance, could not reconcile the notables to the deficit of 112 million francs, for which they were being called upon to sacrifice some of their age-old privileges. Calonne was no longer the polished, urbane courtier, but a man hollow-eyed from lack of sleep, haunted by the spectre of bankruptcy, turning like an animal at bay to attack his predecessors and to hold them responsible. In particular he blamed Necker, who had burdened the treasury with foreign loans which had to be repaid. But to most of the notables Necker was still the financial wizard who during his term of office had never called on them to make the slightest sacrifice, and they resented these aspersions coming from a man who in the previous month had encouraged the King to reimburse the Polignacs for the expenses they claimed to have incurred in entertaining the Queen at Fontainebleau. Apart from a few liberal-minded young aristocrats, the notables refused to accept the reforms proposed by Calonne, who, infuriated by their attitude, published his famous *avertissement* (warning), which to the selfish courtiers at Versailles sounded like nothing less than an incitement to revolution.

In it he declared: 'Someone will have to pay more. But who? Those who have not paid enough will now have to pay what they should, in just proportion to their means. No one will suffer, but privileges will have to be sacrificed. Justice requires it, necessity demands it. Is it fairer to add to the taxes of those who are already overburdened – that is the general public? There will be an outcry, but that is to be expected. One cannot work for the general good without coming up against private interests. Is it possible to carry out reforms without giving rise to complaints?' This inflammatory pamphlet brought about the downfall of Calonne. It alarmed the King, angered the Queen and infuriated both the notables and the *parlements*. Only the Polignacs, dominated by Vaudreuil whom Calonne still subsidized in private, continued to uphold him.

A last-minute attempt to gain the support of Marie Antoinette ended in failure. Acting on her advice, the King dismissed the minister who until now had dazzled him with his plausibility. The Queen had never liked Calonne and now blamed the Polignacs for having got her to support him in the beginning. When she complained of them to her brother, Joseph replied with his usual scepticism.

> What you write on Madame de Polignac and her friends is perfectly true. But I am not sufficiently kind to think they have been mistaken on the subject of Calonne. On the contrary, they have judged him very well, obtaining all sorts of concessions and advantages as the price of their support, knowing him to be a man who was ready to sacrifice everything to his own convenience. Do you remember, my dear sister, the last time I had the pleasure of seeing you, when we were sitting together on a stone in the avenue at Trianon and I brought up the subject of this '*soi-disante société*'. And I cannot help repeating that if you want to assure yourself that these good people are really attached to you, or if they are only fond of themselves, all you have to do is occasionally to say *no* to one of their demands – then you will be able to see how much their attachment is worth and distinguish those who really care for your honour and reputation from those who care only for their own advantage, trimming their sails to any favourable wind.

Despite her final rejection of him, the general public linked the Queen's name with that of Calonne, and in the streets of Paris they hummed the latest ditty:

Ce n'est pas Calonne que j'aime	It is not Calonne I like,
Mais l'or qu'il n'épargne pas	But the gold he will not spare.
Quand je suis dans quelque embarras	When I am in need,
Alors je m'addresse a lui-même	I tell him.
Et ma favorite fait de même	My favourite does the same.
Et puis nous rions tout bas, tout bas, tout bas.	Then we laugh quietly to ourselves.

When Calonne's effigy was burnt in front of the Palais Royal, poisonous attacks against Madame Déficit were pinned to his clothes. Exiled by the King to his estates in Lorraine, the minister eventually retired to England, to add to the number of the Queen's enemies already there. More loyal to Calonne than to her mistress, Madame de Polignac threatened to resign from her position as governess to the royal children, and on the plea of ill health travelled to England to take the waters at Bath. She appears to have been in sufficiently good health to attend the dinners of the French Embassy in

London, where her wistful beauty and sad complaints won her the sympathetic admiration of all the chivalrous Englishmen who were only too ready to take the part of a dethroned favourite. 'Poor little thing! Don't you feel pity for her?' wrote the Duke of Dorset to Georgiana Devonshire. 'Mrs B. continues to treat her with kindness but her heart tells her she has lost Mrs B.'s confidence and no attentions can console her.'

The Emperor Joseph took a less sentimental view when writing to his brother the Grand Duke Leopold of Tuscany. 'Madame de Polignac is about to resign as royal governess, supposedly for health reasons. She has feathered her nest and one only hopes that the next one will be less rapacious.' But Marie Antoinette was to have no more favourites. From now on, her only friend was Axel Fersen, a foreigner, who wanted nothing for himself and was ready to place his life and fortune at her service.

It was not until the death of Vergennes that Marie Antoinette began to play an active part in politics. Both he and Maurepas before him had encouraged King Louis in his diffidence and distrust of his Austrian queen. For all her efforts on behalf of her brother, she herself admitted that she had very little influence over her husband, who always tried to keep affairs of state a secret from her. In the correspondence between Comte Mercy, the Emperor and Prince Kaunitz, there were endless complaints of her negligible efforts in furthering Austrian interests. Her husband's ministers had never found the Queen more than a tiresome liability, whose constant nagging to promote one or the other of her favourites – a military command for the one, an ambassadorship for the other – led to many a threatened resignation. But even the fall of Turgot, for which Marie Antoinette has so often been held responsible, would never have come about had not Maurepas wanted to rid himself of an uncomfortable colleague. Even the acquittal of the Duc de Guines was not so much the work of the Queen as that of the friends of the Duc de Choiseul.

Vergennes' death left the King so lost and bewildered by events that involuntarily he turned to his wife as the only person whom he really loved, a love which had matured slowly over the years, inspiring both confidence and trust. Marie Antoinette had neither taste nor talent for politics. According to Madame Campan she regarded them as an inevitable burden imposed on her by the weakness and irresolution of the King. One day the Queen even went so far as to tell her lady-in-waiting with a certain sadness, 'My happy days are over since they have made me into an *intrigante*.' When Madame Campan objected to the word *intrigante*, she insisted, 'A woman who meddles in matters of which she has neither knowledge nor experience is no more than an *intrigante*.' But having accepted the challenge, she threw herself into the role with all her usual ardour and impulsiveness.

Loménie de Brienne, Archbishop of Toulouse, who succeeded Calonne as director of finance, had been the friend of Choiseul who had recommended the Abbé Vermond as tutor to the young Dauphine. Those who hated Vermond and looked upon him as a sinister influence over the Queen held them both responsible for the Archbishop's appointment and ultimate failure. Marie Antoinette was not the only person to admire Loménie de Brienne. At the beginning of the reign, Turgot had wanted to have him in the government. On his first visit to Paris the Emperor Joseph had met him and been so impressed by his talents that he had praised him to the King. Louis, however, had such an antipathy for what he called '*les prêtres philosophes*' that when Loménie's name came up for nomination as Archbishop of Paris he turned him down on the grounds that an archbishop of Paris 'has at least to believe in God'. But though the Archbishop of Toulouse might have little faith in God, he had an implicit faith in himself and, backed by the Queen, was sufficiently persuasive to override the King's objections and get himself nominated to a post he had been coveting for years. However, the situation for the new director of finance was so desperate that he had no other choice than to try to enforce the reforms already proposed by Calonne, and he met with the same opposition from a recalcitrant assembly and a mutinous parliament.

The only reforms that were greeted with universal approval were the cuts in the expenses of the royal household – handsome salaries for court favourites vanished overnight. Regiments whose functions were purely decorative were abolished. The Duc de Polignac forfeited his job with an income of 50,000 francs a year. Monsieur de Vaudreuil was no longer grand falconer, while obsolete hunting packs like those of the wolf and boar hunts were sacrificed in the general drive for economy. Both Choisy and La Muette, two of the royal family's favourite *maisons de plaisir*, were put up for auction.

The Queen was the first to set an example. There were to be no more balls at Versailles, no more gambling at court. The expenses of her table were reduced, and Mademoiselle Bertin's bills were halved. 'How could I know the country was in such a state?' said Marie Antoinette. 'Whenever I asked for money, I was always handed twice as much as I had asked for.' But her example was in no way followed by her courtiers. The Duc de Coigny, master of the horse, who had hitherto been regarded as the most loyal of courtiers, was so incensed when the greater and lesser stables were joined into one and he no longer had a regiment of horses at his disposal that he dared to lose his temper in front of the King. When Marie Antoinette complained of his behaviour to the Baron de Besenval, he had the impertinence to reply that it was terrible to live in a country where one could become dispossessed overnight. 'It was the kind of thing which usually only happened in places like Turkey.'

Courtiers who had hardly dared to whisper in the days of the Roi Soleil were now openly impertinent; the *parlements* which Louis XV had crushed attacked the sacred person of the King in refusing to register his edicts; society no longer looked up to the King and Queen as the centre of their world, and twenty million people struggled to be heard for the first time. But neither Louis nor Loménie de Brienne could see that the whole feudal system was beginning to crack. Only one man, the old philosopher-statesman Malesherbes, whom the Archbishop had brought back into the government, had the courage to give King Louis advice which, if he had taken it, might have saved him his throne. 'Sire,' he said, 'a king who submits to a constitution feels himself to be degraded. But a king who proposes a constitution adds to the glory of his reign and earns the eternal gratitude of his people. Create the constitution of your country. Take your place in the world, and do not be frightened of founding it on the rights of the people. In order to control great events one has to create them oneself.'

Louis was incapable of following his advice. For all his weakness and timidity, he was convinced of his divine right to rule and unable to see himself in any other role than that of a benevolent despot – the father of his people, but of a people who had no right to challenge his authority. His other conviction, one which was completely incompatible with the role of a despot on the eve of revolution, was never to shed the blood of a single Frenchman other than in time of war. It was a vow he had made at his coronation at Rheims and he was determined to keep it. These two conflicting convictions doomed him from the beginning. He who might have made an admirable king in times of peace was unable to cope with events beyond his comprehension. His obesity, which in the last years had increased at an alarming rate, tended to make him lethargic. Like all the Bourbons, he had always had an enormous appetite, but by now he had become almost a compulsive eater, which affected his health, making him unnaturally somnolent so that he would fall asleep in the middle of a cabinet meeting.

Her husband's inadequacy drew Marie Antoinette more and more into the vortex of politics. But her unpopularity was such that she did more harm than good. His ministers were shocked when the King, unable to come to a decision on his own, would leave the room to consult with the Queen. They were still more shocked when she appeared at a meeting of the Grand Council, for in the past hundred years the Queens of France had kept modestly in the background. The news seeped through to the general public who, not content in labelling Marie Antoinette as a Messalina, now compared her to Frédégonde and Isabeau de Bavière, the most hated and most vicious Queens of France.

When Madame Vigée-Lebrun's celebrated portrait of the Queen and her children was due to be shown at the opening of the Salon du Louvre, the directors decided to postpone the showing for fear of unpleasant demonstrations due to the unpopularity of the Queen and of her favourite artist, who was known to have been the mistress of Calonne. The frame was already hung without the picture when a Parisian wit made the famous remark, 'Here is the portrait of Madame Déficit.'

But in 1787 French taste was not yet entirely warped by politics, and when the picture was finally exhibited it was generally acclaimed to be the artist's finest work. It is interesting to note that Vigée-Lebrun, who until now had never been commissioned for such an important family group, consulted her friend David, who advised her to study the compositions of Raphael. A man who was later to become the most virulent of Jacobins and who drew the cruel and bitter sketch of Marie Antoinette on her way to the scaffold was in 1787 advising his young colleague to base her royal portrait on Raphael's sketches of the Holy Family.

Axel Fersen, who had returned to France in the summer of 1787 and divided his time between Paris and his regiment quartered at Valenciennes, wrote home to his father, 'The Queen is generally detested. The King as weak and as distrustful as ever. He has confidence only in the Queen and she appears to be running everything. The ministers come and see her and make a point of keeping her informed. Since everyone in Paris is obsessed with anglomania, Versailles has become more deserted than ever.'

Axel Fersen was not the most perspicacious of observers. His outlook and mentality were as superficial as those of the average young man at court. Bored with his military duties, he took every opportunity of coming to Paris, where he rented a small house in the elegant Rue Matignon, keeping ten servants and a stable with nine horses, never moving without a cook, two valets and a groom – an extravagant way of life, bitterly disapproved of by his father. Most of his time was spent with the Queen at Versailles. Marie Antoinette was a miserably unhappy woman, unhappy both as a queen and as a mother. In the summer of 1787 she lost her baby girl. The Dauphin was already showing signs of having tuberculosis of the spine and his body was becoming crooked and deformed. Sorrow now marked the Queen's charming face, which had once been so full of laughter, and there was a nervous irritability Fersen had never known before. But for the romantic Northerner the sad young woman was far more touching than the sparkling hostess of Versailles.

In his memoirs, the Comte de St Priest wrote that Fersen went riding two or three times a week near Trianon where the Queen came to meet him alone, and that this caused a lot of scandal in spite of Fersen's modest and circumspect behaviour. But St Priest's account is open to doubt, for his wife, who was in love with the handsome Swede and at some time or other had been his mistress, resented his devotion to the Queen and was only too ready to make mischief. She may even have been the author of the letters which were handed to the King one day when he was hunting in the forest of Rambouillet, and which contained circumstantial evidence of the Queen's intimate relations with Count Fersen. It was on this occasion that an equerry came across the King sitting sobbing under a tree. So distraught was he that he had to be carried into his carriage and brought back to the palace.

That Fersen not only went to Versailles but actually stayed there is evident from letters addressed to his sister. Behind the state apartments was a warren of small rooms and secret staircases. Besenval was the first to note the existence of these secret rooms when he was once summoned to a private audience by the Queen and was sufficiently indiscreet to suggest that Marie Antoinette may have had an intimate life unsuspected by her court. In recent years the

archivists of Versailles have compared certain notes in Fersen's correspondence with details of the work carried out during these years at Versailles,
details which included the installing of a Swedish stove in one of the inner
rooms.

But in spite of all the evidence one is inclined to doubt that Fersen and
Marie Antoinette were lovers in these crucial years of 1787–9, when the
situation was deteriorating so rapidly that it needed all the Queen's energy
and willpower to support a vacillating king and a supine archbishop, the
friend of Choiseul to whom she persisted in remaining foolishly and touch-
ingly loyal. Under pressure from an empty treasury, Loménie de Brienne had
nothing else to offer than the watered-down remedies already proposed by
his predecessor.

The notables who refused to collaborate were dismissed in the hopes that
the *parlement* of Paris would prove more amenable. But the magistrates, who
had never forgiven the King for overriding their judgement on the
Cardinal's acquittal in exiling Rohan by a *lettre de cachet*, were now out to
humiliate the throne. A few minor reforms, such as the abolition of the
corvée and the doing away with internal customs barriers, were passed without difficulty. But every member, whether lawyer, magistrate or noble, was
determined to dispute the passing of the stamp duty and the land tax. Those
who were most vehement declared that no one had the right to introduce such
taxes without the consent of the Estates General, a consultative body of the
clergy, nobles and commoners which had not met since the beginning of the
previous century. Neither the King nor the Queen understood the meaning
of the Estates General. All that Marie Antoinette could understand was that
the King was being challenged in his royal prerogatives, and it was largely on
her incentive that *parlement* was exiled to Troyes.

This was a political mistake, for neither the King nor the Archbishop had
the strength to stand up to the riots and demonstrations which broke out all
over Paris and the provinces. And within a month the *parlement* was back, its
members more arrogant and fractious than before. Young nobles who in the
past had made up the Queen's quadrilles at Versailles now called for a
constitution; unknown lawyers from the country declared that the nation had
the right to control government expenditure. To frighten the deputies into
submission, the Archbishop produced the staggering figures of the deficit
and announced the raising of an emergency loan, which led to angry scenes
in the *parlement*, the arrest of two of the more unruly deputies, and the
unexpected appearance of Philippe, Duc d'Orléans, in the role of the people's
champion. Rehearsed by Choderlos de Laclos, impelled by his hatred of the
Queen, the Prince stood up to defy the King. It was hardly an edifying
spectacle to see the two Bourbon cousins, the one blushing and stammering
with embarrassment, conquering his natural timidity to assert that the issue
of such a loan was illegal, the other almost apopleptic with rage, shouting, 'It

is legal, because I say so.' Neither the exile of the Duc d'Orléans to one of his country estates by order of the Queen, nor the arrest of two more deputies could control the rebellious *parlement*. The Duke, who had hitherto been looked upon as a frivolous libertine, became the hero of the Paris mob, the two imprisoned deputies were acclaimed as martyrs in the cause of liberty, while the Queen, more hated than ever, was blamed for the sudden show of strength on the part of the government. One of the deputies even went so far as to tell the King, 'Sire, we realize that such measures do not come from your heart. Such principles are foreign to your nature and derive from another source.'

This was a deliberate attack on the Queen, who had brought the Archbishop into the government and, at a time when he had already proved his incompetence, had persuaded the King to appoint him as Prime Minister, a post to which even Maurepas had never aspired. Both the Maréchal de Castres and the Maréchal de Ségur, two of the oldest and most trusted members of the government, resigned in protest.

If the Queen remained loyal to Loménie de Brienne it is because he gave her her first real taste of power. Like all Maria Theresa's daughters, she had a latent wish to dominate, and the fact that her husband had such a deep aversion to the supple and hypocritical prelate made it all the more necessary for her to spare him his presence. While Louis sought escape in hunting and other violent exercise, the Queen spent hours closeted with the Archbishop trying in vain to understand the meaning of a rising deficit and the rising anger of the people.

To one of her few friends, the Hungarian Count Esterhazy, she confided 'how unhappy I am to have chosen a prime minister who, in spite of his talents, is so generally reviled, and how cruel it is that I myself should be so hated, when all I have ever wanted was the good of my country. Surely I don't deserve to be so unfortunate.'

But even Esterhazy did not dare to tell her that much of her unhappiness might have been spared her if she had been content with her role as queen instead of trying to act the king. Feeling herself to be superior to her husband, she thought she could dominate him and, blinded by her pride, believed she could control the machine of state, which was far beyond her powers.

By the spring of 1788 the situation had become so alarming that the government had no other choice than to resort to force. And on 8 May, in a solemn *lit de justice* held at Versailles with all the pomp and panoply of state, the King invoked his right to carry through the edicts without the consent of the *parlements*. Troops were sent to clear the Palais de Justice, and both the *parlement* of Paris and the twelve provincial *parlements* were suspended and deprived of their powers. An extraordinary situation arose in which the government, which was trying to enforce a fairer system of taxation and a land tax to benefit the poorer classes, found itself opposed both by the nobility and the *parlements* who were supposed to be 'the fathers of the people'. For the first time in history the *noblesse d'epée* and the *noblesse de robe* acted together. Even the clergy joined them – not the impoverished country *curés*, but the rich bishops – reacting, not out of patriotism, but out of egotism to prevent the passing of a law which would deprive them of the one tenth of the land still in their hands.

In this first year of revolution the people themselves played very little part. The revolts which broke out all over the country, in the Dauphiné, Provence and Brittany, were led by the local nobility allied to the local *parlements*. In Paris there was rioting in the streets and the Archbishop was burnt in effigy in front of the Palais de Justice. A report suppressed by the minister of police said that troops had acted just in time to prevent the burning of the effigy of the Queen. After she was publicly hissed at the theatre, Marie Antoinette was advised to stay away from the capital.

She was wrongly advised, for, accompanied by her children, she was still sufficiently appealing to be cheered by the fickle and changeable Parisians. But calumny had destroyed her faith in the people she had wanted to love her, and she shut herself up in Versailles. The diaries of courtiers there make curious reading in contrast to the exciting accounts of day-to-day events in Paris. The diaries of the Marquis de Bombelles describe the power still held by the Duchesse de Polignac, whom the Queen would visit of an afternoon, not so much out of pleasure as out of habit, to play a game of *tric-trac* or listen to some music, or occasionally join in the singing of a duet, which even when out of tune was always performed with great charm and aplomb. She was still a young woman, essentially frivolous and Viennese, who until the last year had never had a serious idea in her head, who had always lived in terror of being bored and was now trying to escape from her unhappiness. But the French, who had never understood her, understood her even less when they saw her carried away by the music, jumping up to dance with one of the guests. 'I could have wished there had been fewer witnesses, and Madame de Polignac was of the same opinion,' wrote the Marquis de Bombelles, schooled in the rigid etiquette of Versailles.

It was not considered *bon ton* to talk of politics at Madame de Polignac's parties, but in Paris one talked of nothing else. Axel Fersen, who had returned in the last months of 1788, wrote to his father, 'Everyone here is in a great state of excitement. There is talk of nothing but of a constitution, and the women are the worst of all. You know what an influence they have in this country. Everyone has suddenly become an administrator and speaks of nothing but "progress". In the anterooms the valets pass their time reading the ten or twelve pamphlets which appear every day. And one is surprised there are sufficient printing presses to produce them all.' Most of these printing presses were to be found in the precincts of the Palais Royal, the centre of anti-government propaganda, where the Duc d'Orléans's agents were using his vast wealth to encourage sedition. Deprived of their *parlement*, out-of-work deputies aired their grievances in the crowded cafés. Political meetings overflowed into the gardens. And the government did not make the slightest attempt either to seize the printing presses or break up the meetings.

By now Loménie de Brienne was visibly cracking under the strain. The coffers were empty. Even the reserves intended for use in the hospitals and public charities had been expropriated. The Archbishop had no other choice than to announce the convocation of the Estates General in the following spring of 1789, but the country refused to accept it. Still clinging to power, Brienne offered to bring Necker into the government as Controller General, but the Swiss banker refused to associate himself with anyone as discredited as the Archbishop.

By the middle of August, a tearful Queen had to summon her favourite minister and ask for his resignation, which was only obtained at the price of a cardinal's hat. Necker was waiting in the wings, a man whom the King disliked even more than he disliked the Archbishop, but who in the eyes of the general public was the financial wizard who would bring back prosperity to France. On the advice of the Austrian ambassador, Marie Antoinette succeeded in persuading Louis to accept as his Prime Minister someone who was physically so repellent to him that involuntarily he trembled whenever he came near him. The Queen on the contrary had always been on good terms with Necker and even tolerated his starchy and pedantic wife. Now she confessed to Mercy that she felt afraid: 'Forgive me this weakness, but as I am responsible for bringing back Mr Necker and my fate is to bring bad luck, I feel that, should some infernal combinations be once more at work to make him fail, then the King's authority will suffer and I will be even more detested than before.'

Necker's return to power was hailed with enthusiasm both in Paris and Versailles. When he was seen coming out of the Queen's apartments everyone who was on duty at Versailles rushed to the Oeil de Bœuf to be the first to congratulate the idol of the day. Looking smug and self-satisfied, convinced he could still be the saviour of his country, Necker accepted the acclamations as his due. In Madame Necker's influential salon the philosophers were singing his praises, and from the Swedish Embassy his daughter, Germaine de Staël, was writing to King Gustavus of Paris exploding with joy over her father's return. King Louis, however, was far from joyful and his first words on greeting his new Prime Minister were, 'Ah, Monsieur, for many years now I have not known one moment of happiness,' to which Necker replied, 'Sire, in a little while you will not have to talk like that any more.'

For the moment it seemed as if his optimism was justified. Such was his prestige that, no sooner was he in office than government bonds rose by thirty per cent. Bankers who had had no faith in his predecessor were ready to subscribe to his emergency loans. But the political situation was still in a state of ferment, and the terrible drought which had decimated the countryside in the summer of 1788, followed by a hailstorm of such dimensions as to have destroyed a large part of the crops, had brought the price of bread to double that of the previous years, adding to the sufferings of the poor.

Paris was full of beggars, evil-looking, importunate beggars, ready to join in any riot for the price of a few *sous*. The scenes of joy that had heralded Necker's return to power, accompanied by the burning in effigy of unpopular ministers, had caused disorders of a sufficiently serious nature to bring out the Gardes Français. The riots were quelled by force. But there was a new spirit abroad – a people who had hitherto been cowed and submissive now showed for the first time their hatred of '*les privilégiés*'. Noblemen's carriages were stoned, well-dressed women insulted in the streets, a page of the Comte d'Artois attacked and robbed in full daylight. In this uneasy atmosphere Necker, true to his democratic principles, advised the King to reinstate the *parlements*, in the hope that they would be able to settle the thorny question as to how the Estates General were to be composed and how they were going to vote.

The Queen did all in her power to prevent the return of the *parlements*. But the King, still clinging to the old traditions, remembered being told by

Maurepas that it was impossible to govern France without the *parlements*, and the 'fathers of the people' made a triumphal return into an illuminated city. But their popularity did not last for long. One of the first conditions they laid down was that the Estates General should be in no way different from when it last met in 1614, with the clergy, the nobility and the third estate, the commoners, all having the same number of delegates. This meant that if each order voted separately the clergy and nobility could always combine to obtain a majority over the third estate.

The Queen showed a better judgement than either the King or his ministers in suggesting that the Estates General should meet in one of the provincial towns such as Orléans or Rouen, where they could work undisturbed by the explosive atmosphere of Paris. But Necker, who valued his own popularity more than that of the King, believed he could dominate the Paris mob and earn its undying gratitude as 'father of the constitution'. The King favoured Versailles, because there at least he could be at home and might still find time for a day's hunting, when he was not being forced to listen to the haranguing of insolent magistrates telling him how to rule his country. What really concerned him was the plight of the poor in this terrible winter, when bread was soaring in price. The sums he gave in charity were enormous, buying on his own account no less than 1½ million hundredweight of wheat abroad. But there was no Choderlos de Laclos, no brilliant press officer at Versailles to sing the praises of the 'best of kings', while the whole of Paris talked of the generosity of the Duc d'Orléans, who had put his finest pictures up for sale and donated the eight million francs they fetched to the 'hungry people of Paris'. No one was by temperament less suited to be the 'people's idol'. Fastidious, nervous of crowds, loathing the smell of the unwashed masses, Philippe d'Orléans was being forced into a position in which he was only sustained by his hatred of the Queen and his resentment of his royal cousin, who had consistently refused him the honours he considered his due.

The quarrels over the claims of the third estate had spread even to the royal family, where Monsieur and the Queen were for once in agreement in supporting Necker over the doubling of the representatives of the third estate. The *révolte nobiliaire* of the previous summer and the egotism displayed by the notables had led Marie Antoinette to feel there might be more loyalty to be found among the bourgeoisie, while Monsieur hoped to further his personal ambitions in posing as a liberal prince. Artois on the contrary upheld the rights and privileges of the aristocracy, joining with the Prince de Conti and the Prince de Condé in signing a petition to the King denouncing Necker and his works and asking him to 'protect the country from those writers and philosophers who with little or no experience try to set themselves up as legislators and lead France into a democracy more dangerous than any despotism'. Such language was applauded by the courtiers of Versailles.

'One cannot admire sufficiently the behaviour of the Comte d'Artois. He expresses himself as a loyal brother of the King, a good Frenchman and an excellent citizen,' wrote that stiff-necked diplomat the Marquis de Bombelles. But in his haughtiness and intransigence, his indifference to public opinion and his refusal to make concessions to a changing world, Artois had forfeited his popularity in Paris, and from having been the best loved of all the royal princes was now no less hated than the Queen.

But he and Marie Antoinette had come to a parting of their ways. They had quarrelled over Calonne, to whom Artois was to remain loyal throughout his years of exile. And, to make matters worse, the Polignacs associated themselves with Artois. The memoirs and diaries written during the last years at Versailles time and again contain insinuating, softly-worded attacks directed against the Queen, written by those who owed her their very existence. A party of deputies approached Madame de Polignac with a view to presenting the Queen with the conditions on which they would be prepared to support the Crown, upon which the Duchess sadly regretted that she was unable to comply, for whatever she suggested would immediately be rejected by the Abbé Vermond, thus deliberately accusing the Abbé of being the power behind the throne and influencing the Queen against the interests of her country. If such had been the case, Vergennes, who had always been anti-Austrian, would have had no difficulty in getting the Abbé dismissed by the King, who personally had always disliked Vermond as '*un prêtre philosophe*' and the choice of Choiseul. But Louis recognized the Abbé as being fundamentally honest, a loyal servant who had done his best to restrain Marie Antoinette in her follies and extravagances. So Vermond stayed on, putting up with the envy and the backbiting of the humble Campans, the rudeness and arrogance of the *société* Polignac.

In this unhappy winter of 1788–9, when the Dauphin was slowly dying and the Queen was ashamed for her poor disfigured child to be seen in public, she found the woman who had been her dearest friend gradually turning against her, siding with those whom she regarded as her enemies. With the strange insight of the sick, the little Dauphin had taken against his beautiful governess and could not bear having her in the room, complaining that the perfume she used made him feel sick. In default of the governess the Queen spent whatever time she could spare by the bedside of her dying son.

But the relentless ritual of court life went on unchanged. 'Never had people been so pleasure-seeking as in this spring of 1789 before the opening of the Estates General. For the poor the winter had been very hard, but there was no concern for the misery of the people,' wrote Madame de La Tour du Pin describing the life of the 'smart set'. 'We laughed and danced over the yawning precipice, thinking people were content just to talk of abolishing all the abuses. France, they said, was about to be reborn. The word "revolution" was never uttered. Had anyone dared to use it, he would have been considered mad.' Writing in her old age, the Marquise notes all the terrible mistakes committed by the unfortunate young King and Queen, so weak in themselves, so badly advised. 'The people of Paris hardly saw the Queen and her children and the King even less. Hidden away at Versailles or hunting in the nearby forests, he suspected nothing, saw nothing and listened to nothing he was told.'

Both Louis and Marie Antoinette dreaded the opening of the Estates General, the hordes of people converging on Versailles, where the humblest room above a stable was being rented at an enormous sum. Filled with anxiety, Marie Antoinette questioned Necker as to the possible outcome. Would the Estates General end in ruling the King or would the King succeed in remaining in control? Necker, who was as nervous as they were, was at a loss for an answer.

There were 1,200 delegates from all over France, of whom 610 belonged to the third estate. Idealists and opportunists, theorists and rationalists, none of them were as yet republican. All of them were monarchists, even the renegade aristocrat the Comte de Mirabeau. Rejected by his own class, he had elected to stand for the third estate and had been returned by both Marseilles and Aix. Socially an outcast, venal and immoral, a slave to his sexual appetites, Mirabeau had spent the best part of his life in prison, the victim of *lettres de cachet*, condemned more than once on charges of immorality. Now at long last he had found a forum in which his talents could shine with a meteoric brilliance, the most dangerous and the most persuasive of the electors converging on Versailles.

On 4 May, a cloudless spring day, the first assembly of the Estates General for 175 years opened at Versailles with a great procession through streets hung with tapestries and banners, from the church of Notre Dame to the cathedral of St Louis. It was a glittering parade, displaying for the last time all the pomp and pageantry of the old regime, with trumpeters and standard bearers, pages and halberdiers in their blue and gold uniforms embroidered with fleurs-de-lis. The King in cloth of gold with the famous Pitt diamond in his hat, the Queen in silver tissue, her hair interwoven with flowers and pearls, walked behind the Holy Sacraments carried under a dais, the cords of which were held by the four royal princes, Provence, Artois and his two young sons, Angoulême and Berry. The bishops wore their red and purple robes, the nobles their plumed hats and satin suits with lace ruffles, but the 610 deputies of the third estate, many of whom had never seen Versailles before, wore plain black suits with white cambric ruffles and unadorned tricornes.

All Paris had come to Versailles. Not a window or roof was free. There was an air of optimism, an air of hope among the cheering, laughing crowds. There were cheers for the King, cheers for the young Marquis de Lafayette, elected as one of the nobles of Auvergne, and the loudest cheers of all for the

Duc d'Orléans who, dissociating himself from his peers, walked with the third estate. But there was not a single acclamation when the Queen went by with her graceful, gliding walk, looking so elegant and proud, until a fish-wife screamed in her face, 'Long live the Duc d'Orléans!' For a moment she faltered and seemed about to faint. But supported by the Princesse de Lamballe she recovered and walked on with a pale face which showed nothing but contempt. Only once did her expression soften, when passing by the stables, where the Dauphin lay propped up on cushions watching the procession from a balcony. She suddenly looked up and gave him the saddest of smiles.

The Bishop of Nancy, famous for his oratory, delivered the address, dwelling on the sufferings of the poor, inveighing against the luxury of the court. Many interpreted this as a deliberate attack on the Queen. But the King smiled amiably on coming out of church. Having slept through most of the sermon, he had not heard the strictures on his court. Again there were shouts of '*Vive le Roi!*' but the same sinister silence greeted the Queen. The Marquis de Bombelles noted in his diary: 'Never has there been a queen of France less loved and yet she cannot be reproached for a single wicked deed. We are certainly unfair towards her and much too hard in judging what are only faults of frivolity and thoughtlessness.' How heavily Marie Antoinette was being made to pay for the follies and extravagances of her youth, the light-hearted mockery, the childish insouciance. At a time when the Dauphin lay dying, she was being forced to act as hostess at Versailles to people she knew detested her. The gardens of Versailles and Trianon were thrown open to the delegates. Some were to insist on visiting the pavilion, which was the Queen's own private domain, penetrating into every corner in the hopes of finding some signs of the extravagant orgies which were part of the legend of Trianon. Its exquisite simplicity was far removed from the fantastic description which had reached the provinces, of floors inlaid with gold and columns encrusted with diamonds. The Swiss Guard who acted as guide was at a loss to satisfy the curiosity of those who had heard these tales. But when they reached the ears of King Louis, he remembered that in his grandfather's day there had once been a theatrical performance at Fontainebleau in which the setting for an eastern drama had included columns made out of composite diamonds. Such was the way in which calumny did its work.

When Marie Antoinette arrived for the opening of the Estates General, the Comte de Mirabeau, who was among the most virulent of her attackers, whispered to a neighbour, '*Voilà la victime.*' On this occasion she was wearing what was to be the last of the grand gala dresses, ordered from Mademoiselle Bertin, a dress of purple satin over a white skirt embroidered with diamonds and paillettes. And in her hair, which was already growing thin from worry, a bandeau of diamonds with a single heron's feather. Beautiful and majestic, she took her place in an armchair slightly below the King's throne. But all her beauty did not arouse a single cheer from the crowded gallery of spectators. The Philadelphia banker Gouverneur Morris, who was among them, would have liked to show his sympathy, but as a foreigner thought it wiser to abstain. The King on the contrary, a singularly uninspiring figure in spite of his magnificent golden robes and plumed hat, was loudly cheered on his arrival, and his speech, delivered in a strong clear voice, in which he welcomed the representatives of the nation to cooperate with him for the good of the state, was heard in respectful silence.

The setting and decor were of an unparalleled magnificence. In spite of an empty treasury, the Salle des Menus Plaisirs, which only a few months before had housed the assembly of notables, had now been entirely redecorated to resemble a Greek temple. To the right of the throne sat the clergy, to the left the nobles, and facing the King the serried ranks of the delegates of the third estate, those who in the words of the Abbé Sieyès 'were nothing for the moment, but who aspired to become the future rulers of the nation'. Some were already as notorious as the Comte de Mirabeau, others were no more than provincial lawyers and advocates such as Danton and Robespierre. Seated among the Queen's ladies, Madame de La Tour du Pin observed how the Queen kept scrutinizing the faces which hitherto had never entered into her world and how, for all her outward calm, the way in which she kept playing with her fan betrayed her agitation.

Necker's speech was of an interminable length, delivered in a flat, mono-tonous voice, punctuated by the King's snores. The sight of their monarch sleeping throughout a historic speech was not calculated to inspire enthusi-asm. Speaking as a banker rather than a statesman, Necker treated his audi-ence to a flood of figures and statistics to explain the deficit, while barely touching on vital problems such as the concessions the Crown was willing to make or the principles it was determined to adhere to. Above all there was no mention of a constitution, and at the end of the session no one was satisfied. Nevertheless the King was cheered and this time even the Queen had a share in the cheers, which she acknowledged with a curtsey, thereby drawing further cheers to which she responded with another curtsey.

By the end of the month the third estate had succeeded in disrupting the clergy by persuading some of the lower orders such as the parish priests to join their ranks. The nobles remained firm in defending their privileges, but a liberal minority represented by the Duc d'Orléans and the Marquis de Lafayette were ready to forfeit their privileges for a constitution on the English model.

Meanwhile the doctors gathered round the sick-bed of the seven-year-old Dauphin had given up all hopes of his recovery. The King and Queen were in despair. Etiquette decreed that the child's new governor, the Duc d'Harcourt, took his orders from the doctors rather than the parents, and there were times when Marie Antoinette was denied access to her own child. Bombelles gives a touching picture of the King sitting outside the sickroom of his dying son, with the Queen kneeling beside him sobbing into his lap. On 3 June there were public prayers in all the churches and the sacraments were exposed on the altar. And on the following evening of 4 June the little Dauphin died in his mother's arms. Brought together in their grief, Louis and Marie Antoinette kept vigil all night by their dead son. But the rigid rules of court etiquette denied them the right of attending the funeral at St Denis. On that same day Necker had the tactlessness to insist on the King receiving a deputation of the third estate demanding his arbitration on the rules of procedure. 'Are there no fathers among these gentlemen?' asked the indignant King.

The death of the child whose birth had been heralded with such enthusiasm and joy passed almost unnoticed in the growing struggle for power. 'My son is dead,' said Marie Antoinette, 'and nobody seems to care.'

While the King and Queen remained at Marly in mourning for their son, stormy debates were taking place in the Salle des Menus Plaisirs. On 17 June the Abbé Sieyès introduced the historic motion that the Estates General, which represented ninety-six per cent of the nation, should from now on be known as 'the National Assembly'. The King and Queen returned to find a government unable to control a situation which was rapidly drifting towards anarchy, with Necker still advocating a policy of conciliation, urging the King to accept the National Assembly which represented the will of the nation, and to modify the existing constitution by having two chambers based on the English model. This policy was bitterly opposed by the royal princes, the majority of the aristocracy, and most of all by the Queen, who now regretted having supported Necker over his claims for the third estate. Harassed on every side and still grieving for his son, the unhappy monarch made a brief show of strength in ordering the assembly hall to be closed till 23 June, when he himself would preside over a *séance royale*. Finding the doors closed against them, the indignant deputies took possession of a neighbouring building, which somewhat incongruously happened to be the royal tennis courts. Here, in a bare hall under a ceiling decorated with the *fleurs-de-lis*, they took the oath never to separate until a constitution with or without the royal consent was established on solid foundations. Such was the enthusiasm of the moment that only one deputy had the courage to abstain, an action which later was to bring him to the scaffold, though in the summer of 1789 liberty of conscience was still allowed. The meeting in the Salle de Jeu de Paume came to an end when, with characteristic frivolity, the Comte d'Artois booked the courts for a game of tennis. Undaunted, the deputies moved to the church of St Louis, opened up for them by a sympathetic *curé*.

Meanwhile confusion reigned at the palace, with Louis listening first to his ministers, then to his family. While Necker and his colleagues kept nagging him not to alienate the third estate which was the mouthpiece of the nation, his brothers were loud in their condemnation of a policy which would put them at the mercy of the populace. Monsieur, who together with the Queen had been in favour of double representation for the third estate, was now in favour of dissolving the assembly. Artois went even further and demanded that troops be brought in from the provinces to restore order in the capital. The most intransigent of all was the Queen who, having hoped that the third estate might defend the Crown against the *révolte nobiliaire*, now felt she had been deceived by a minister more concerned for his own popularity than for the prestige of the Crown.

The speech prepared by Necker for the King to deliver at the *séance royale* was at the last moment so changed and distorted, largely owing to the influence of the Queen and of Artois, that the minister publicly disassociated himself by not appearing at the meeting. He thereby failed in what Marie Antoinette considered to be his duty to the King, and paralysed a government of which he was still a member. She never forgave him for what she regarded as his cowardly behaviour, and from then on looked upon him as an enemy.

The *séance royale*, which opened on 23 June with all the pomp and circumstance of a *lit de justice*, bore no relation to the events of the past weeks. The trumpets and fanfares which heralded the arrival of the King and the master of ceremonies, who in his glittering uniform threw open the doors to introduce the clergy and nobility, while the third estate were left waiting outside in the rain, were measures calculated to irritate men who in the last few days had become conscious of their power.

The King's speech, delivered with neither energy nor feeling, as if Louis himself had little faith in his words, was both paternal and despotic. It promised reforms, the abolishing of the more burdensome taxations and the assurance that none would be levied in the future without the consent of the Estates General, but it nevertheless insisted on the three orders continuing to vote each in their separate chambers, and refused to allow the name 'Estates General' to be changed to that of 'National Assembly'. His speech ended with the words, 'Should the third estate refuse to cooperate in my efforts to improve the lot of my people – a misfortune I hope will never come to pass – then I shall have no other choice than to continue my labours alone, for it is I alone who am the true representative of France.' It was the speech of a benevolent despot rather than of a constitutional monarch. And Mirabeau drew attention to this in his reply when, speaking for the third estate, he declared, 'Gentlemen, we have just heard words which may well bring about the salvation of our country, if the presence of despotism were not always open to suspicion.'

The King rose to declare the session at an end and for the three orders to repair to their separate chambers. Artois looked on in triumph, for it was he who had insisted that the separate orders should be maintained. Louis left, followed by the clergy and the nobility. But when asked to leave, the third estate remained firmly in their seats. The master of ceremonies was young and inexperienced. Intimidated by the flashing eyes, the huge pock-marked face and compelling voice of Mirabeau, he hurried away for further instructions. The King raged and stormed, but ended by giving way. 'Damn it, then let them stay!': the first of a series of humiliating capitulations which was to place the throne at the mercy of the third estate.

By now almost all of the clergy and fifty of the more liberal-minded nobles, such as the Noailles, the Montmorencys and the Rochefoucaulds, had gone over to the majority. Among these was the young Marquis de Lafayette, who felt the time had come for him to play a historic role, and the Duc d'Orléans, whom the Paris mob acclaimed as King. Only the more reactionary elements were left behind, loud in their protests but with very little power. The Marquis de Bombelles noted sadly in his diary, 'We have lived for too long an easy life and no longer have the energy and resolution of our forefathers. The long wars waged against the enemies of our country, even the civil wars, combined to keep up the spirit of chivalry. But now luxury and *le douceur de vivre* have succeeded in corrupting us. The word honour is always on our lips, but it is not sufficiently graven in our hearts to dictate our actions.'

Necker handed in his resignation following the *séance royale*, but was persuaded to stay on for fear of the public reaction to his dismissal. He kept urging the King to let the three orders vote together, for the Parisians were threatening to march on Versailles. Again King Louis capitulated, to the fury and disgust of the Queen and the despair of those members of the nobility who had remained loyal to the Crown. In Paris the streets were illuminated to celebrate the people's victory, and in the National Assembly the President, Jean Sylvain Bailly, announced in triumph, 'Now our victory is complete.' But it was an uneasy victory, and many of the more peace-loving citizens, among them the electors who had selected the Parisian deputies, were beginning to fear for their properties and their lives. Shops were being pillaged and riots were almost a daily occurrence, while the Gardes Français, sent to keep order in the capital, were themselves in a state of mutiny.

Still the social life of Paris, the races, supper parties and operas, went on undisturbed by the violence in the streets. The Devonshires visited Paris on the eve of the taking of the Bastille, and the Duchess and Lady Elizabeth Foster dined with the Queen at Versailles on 27 June. This was the very day the King surrendered to the National Assembly, when the President of the nobility, the Duc de Luxembourg, had spent hours in trying to convince him that he was bringing ruin on himself and the monarchy in sacrificing the one class which was ready to defend him. The Queen, who had spent the previous day in tears after failing in her efforts to persuade the King to dissolve the assembly, now welcomed her English friends as if she did not have a care in the world. 'I found her sadly altered,' wrote Georgiana Devonshire to her mother, 'her belly quite big, and no hair at all, but she still has a great deal of éclat.'

Three days later the Devonshires were again at Versailles, this time with the Duke. They attended a state dinner, which proceeded in all its formal splendour in spite of the populace invading the courtyards and having to be driven back by the Swiss Guards. They also attended *La Messe du Roi*, and had a private meeting with Marie Antoinette. One wonders what two women so essentially frivolous as Marie Antoinette and Georgiana Devonshire, whose friendship in the past had been based on the trivialities of fashion, a love of gaming and of masquerades, found to say to one another on the eve of revolution, of which neither had any understanding. The Whig Duchess heralded it as 'the greatest of events', but for Marie Antoinette it spelt the end of her world. Georgiana Devonshire found nothing incongruous in supporting the Revolution and being at the same time the friend of the Queen. In spite of the violence in the streets, the screaming and shouting at the Palais Royal, she wrote home to London that she was enjoying herself in Paris.

For the Queen there was nothing but disillusion and disgust. The throne was in peril, but it was only at the eleventh hour that the King could be persuaded to resort to force and summon Maréchal Broglie, a veteran of the Seven Years' War, back from his command in Alsace to bring in reinforcements of troops to protect the capital against further disorders. Most of these regiments were foreign mercenaries, the only ones whose loyalty could be fully relied on. But their presence in the suburbs only served to aggravate the situation. The wildest rumours were abroad. The National Assembly was to be dissolved, the deputies assassinated or imprisoned, and Paris delivered into the hands of foreigners. The deputies took fright, and a delegation was sent to the palace to ask why a king who was loved by twenty-five million people should want to surround himself at great expense with several thousand mercenaries, to which Louis replied in all good faith that the troops were there to protect his people and not to overawe them.

It was the dismissal of Necker that ignited the flame. By order of the King, the minister had left secretly by night and his departure was not known until the following morning, when all hell broke out in the capital with hysterical crowds screaming for his recall. Busts of Necker, of the Duc d'Orléans and of Lafayette, the new idols of the day, were carried through the streets and anyone who refused to applaud them was insulted and molested. Bakers' shops were pillaged, banks shut down, and the stock exchange was closed. Two companies of Gardes Français, confined for insubordination, broke out of prison and joined in with the rioters, while loyal troops of the Royal Allemand, defending the Tuileries, were attacked and stoned. A cavalry charge led by the Prince de Lambesc, which dispersed the mob with very little loss of life, was immediately denounced as a massacre. The fact that it was led by a prince of Lorraine and a relative of the Queen was sufficient to label him as a murderer. In the gardens of the Palais Royal, agitators paid by Laclos were inciting the people into a frenzy of hatred. An unknown young lawyer by the name of Camille Desmoulins called on the people to arm themselves against those who were out to destroy them and a desperate search for arms now spread to every quarter of the city.

Left without orders from Versailles, the Baron de Besenval, in charge of the troops in the Plaine de Grenelle, was powerless to intervene. The King's principal concern was that there should be no loss of life, and the cavalry charge in the Tuileries had been carried out against his orders. For Louis still persisted in believing that the duties of the army should be confined to policing the city, but never to attack, and that the presence of Maréchal Broglie would be sufficient to restore order.

On the night of 14 July, the King went quietly to bed, probably the only person in the great palace who was sleeping soundly, when he was woken up at dawn by the Duc de la Rochefoucauld to be told that the Bastille had been captured by a mob, the governor and his staff assassinated and their heads, mounted on pikes, were being paraded through the streets. Still half asleep, the King cried out, 'But this is a revolt!', to which the Duke replied, 'Sire, it is a revolution' – celebrated words which were to come down to history.

Unlike her husband, Marie Antoinette had hardly slept in the past weeks. But for the last twenty-four hours she had been reassured by the presence of Breteuil, who had taken over the government at a time when only someone of his vanity and ambition would have accepted such a post. Breteuil was a strong man whom she had always liked and trusted. The fact that he was hated by the opposition, who had never forgiven him for the part he had played in the arrest of Cardinal de Rohan, was a matter of complete indifference to a queen who had never taken public opinion into account. As ambassador to Vienna, Breteuil had been approved of by Maria Theresa, and what was even more important to her daughter was the friendship he had shown to the young Count Fersen on his first arrival in France. Axel was with his regiment at Valenciennes. In his absence the Queen welcomed Breteuil as one of the few friends she had in France. At a meeting of the Grand Council the previous day, he had called on the King to dissolve the National Assembly and to put himself at the head of his troops, a motion backed by the royal princes and by the Prince de Condé. Marie Antoinette woke to a day she hoped would see the restoration of royal prestige, instead of which she was to witness its dissolution.

On hearing the news from Paris, the King, who had never lacked physical courage, went straight to the National Assembly. He went unguarded and on foot, accompanied only by his two brothers. It was a brave gesture, and braver still on the part of Artois, who was publicly insulted on the way with cries of 'Take care, Monseigneur, we know it is you who give evil counsels to our King!'

Unconvinced and unconvincing, Louis capitulated yet again, declaring that he never had any intention of using force and that orders were being given for the troops to withdraw from Paris. He invited the gentlemen of the National Assembly to convey this news to the capital. The more moderate of the deputies cheered his speech. Others, like Mirabeau, had little faith in words spoken under duress. But the crowds milling outside the palace were won over by the simplicity of the King walking home alone with neither retinue nor guards, and cheered him with enthusiasm. Even the Queen was called out upon the balcony. When she appeared together with her children, the sight of the new little Dauphin, a beautiful child of four, drew enormous enthusiasm. For the first time, on the Queen's orders, the royal governess had been asked to stay away. For Marie Antoinette no longer dared to show her children in public with the hated Polignacs. That very morning her faithful attendant, Madame Campan, had been walking in the gardens and heard ugly threats uttered against the Queen's favourite.

The shouting and cheering grew louder as the King returned to the palace, and a faint flush rose to the Queen's cheeks as she turned to acknowledge the cheers, with a smile as dazzling as ever and the head still held as proudly, thought at heart she knew that the cheers were neither for her nor for her children, but to celebrate the King's capitulation to the nation.

The news of the fall of the Bastille spread like wildfire across Europe. The derelict fortress, already due for demolition, had been empty for years, but was still regarded as a monument of tyranny and oppression. It recalled the dreaded *lettres de cachet*, which sent men to prison for years without ever bringing them to trial. On the day of its capture the Bastille contained no more than seven prisoners, while the governor, de Launay, who was to fall a victim to mob violence, was a kindly, ineffectual man, quite incapable of defending his fortress. Hailed as a glorious event in the history of mankind, the fall of the Bastille was largely the result of muddle and inefficiency on the one hand and, on the other, of hatred instigated by fear.

The British ambassador, Lord Dorset, wrote in a rapturous letter to London: 'The greatest revolution that we know of has been effected with, comparatively speaking, the loss of very few lives. From this moment we may consider France as a free country, the King as a very limited monarch, and the nobility as reduced to a level with the rest of the nation.' This may have been the natural reaction on the part of an ambassador whose country was a traditional enemy of France. But we hear of Philippe de Ségur, King Louis's ambassador to Russia, expressing the same sentiments in conversation with that uncompromising autocrat the Empress Catherine. While his cousin, the young Marquis de Lafayette, did not allow the spectacle of de Launay's severed head transfixed upon a pike to deter him from his ambition to play the part of a French Washington in this 'most wonderful of revolutions'. When King Louis visited the National Assembly on the morning of 15 July, Lafayette, who was the only one of the deputies with any experience of revolution, had been chosen to receive him and to head the delegation which was to convey the King's message to the capital.

At the Hôtel de Ville, terrified officials welcomed Lafayette as a saviour. Still wearing the King's uniform, he was unanimously elected to command the new citizen's militia, composed mostly of shopkeepers and the professional classes, all anxious to put an end to mob violence. Those drunken crowds, those terrifying women with bloodshot eyes and gnashing teeth, uttering foul curses against the Queen, were far removed from the orderly American citizens raising the standard of liberty outside the courthouse of Philadelphia, and there may have been times when even young men as self-confident as Lafayette and his friends must have wondered how they were going to close the Pandora's box they had opened with such enthusiasm.

The whole of Paris was given over to an explosion of joy. This mood of hysteria was to prove highly profitable to the professional stonemasons who had been called in to complete the demolition of the Bastille and who sold the stones for large sums to fashionable jewellers, who polished them and set them in gold to be worn by smart Parisians as the latest craze, jewels *à la constitution*.

Meanwhile abortive discussions were taking place at Versailles, where the King's inability to come to any decision was driving the Queen to despair. The Prince de Condé, the one real soldier in the family, had come from Chantilly to offer his services to his royal cousin in the hopes of leading an army against the rebels. Both the Queen and Artois were in favour of resistance. Marie Antoinette had already destroyed her papers and packed her diamonds in preparation for the court to leave for the security of a frontier town from where, with the help of loyal troops, Paris could be reconquered. But the King refused to contemplate the possibility of a civil war, and Maréchal Broglie, newly appointed minister of war, introduced a still more depressing note by saying that, given the state of the army, of which over half the soldiers were disaffected, there could be no question of marching on Paris. The greater part of France was in the throes of rebellion. Travelling from Alsace, he had passed by pillaged farms, and châteaux and manor houses in flames. In such conditions he could not even guarantee a safe conduct for the royal family and the court to reach either Metz or any other frontier town. And once they had arrived there, what would they do?

The Duc de Liancourt arrived from Paris, bringing news of fresh out-breaks of violence. The populace was screaming for the recall of Necker. Their bloodlust had been aroused. They were shouting 'Death to Artois and to the Polignacs', who, had they been in Paris, would have immediately been put to death. The gilded salons of Versailles were filled with frightened courtiers, the favourites of yesterday now saw an abyss opening at their feet. In this atmosphere of disintegration, the Comte de Provence was one of the few to remain calm and controlled, refusing to envisage the possibility of abdication, insisting that the King's duty was to stay and weather the storm, to make the necessary sacrifices, recall Necker and get rid of the Polignacs. To ensure his own personal safety and the future of the monarchy, both Artois and his sons should leave the country. There was little need to convince Artois, for the insults and threats to which he had been exposed that morning at Versailles had robbed him of a courage which was never more than skin-deep. Even the King, who loved his younger brother, now ordered him to leave. On the night of 16 July, the Comte d'Artois, accompanied by his friend Vaudreuil, left Versailles on horseback without waiting for either carriages or escort. With the confidence of those who had always had money, horses and carriages at their command, they counted on finding faithful subjects to provide hospitality on the way. And the first shock came when, only a few leagues from Versailles, they arrived at the château of an old marquis, grown rich in the previous reign, to find the gates barred and the owner too frightened to let them in. Artois's two sons, the Duc d'Angoulême and the Duc de Berry, set off the same evening, travelling by carriage with their tutor, who brought them in safety to the Austrian Netherlands. Before leaving, there had been touching farewells between the young cousins, with Madame Royale in tears at saying goodbye to Angoulême, whom she already regarded as her fiancé.

But for Marie Antoinette the hardest of all was to part with Yolande de Polignac. Whatever differences they may have had in the past years, whatever moments of jealousy and presumed ingratitude, all was forgotten in a great surge of tenderness for the woman who in a cold and formal court had helped her to forget she was a queen. It was unbearable for her to think of someone as spoilt and fragile as Yolande having to endure the dangers and hardships of the journey, the bitterness of exile, just because she had been her friend. Yolande herself was begging to be allowed to stay, whether from devotion or from fear of what awaited her outside the walls of Versailles. But the Queen was more realistic. The King had finally decided to stay and there was no end to the sacrifices he would be called upon to make. 'It was not his decision,' she told Madame Campan. 'He allowed himself to be persuaded by the family. They wanted him to stay, and only the future will tell whether they were right.' By staying on he was putting himself at the mercy of the rabble, and to save her he might even end by sacrificing her friends. Today she could still send the Polignacs to safety and provide money and transport for the journey; tomorrow it might already be too late.

That night saw the departure of all the Polignacs, with the Duchess disguised as a maid sitting on top of the coach. There was an unpleasant moment at Sens, when she was recognized by a postilion. Had it not been for his loyalty, she might well have been torn to pieces by the mob. On mounting the coach she had received a last message from the Queen: 'Farewell, my dearest of friends. What a dreadful word, farewell. But, alas, it is necessary. I have not sufficient strength to embrace you for a last time.' Enclosed was the sum of five hundred golden louis, the last and perhaps the most appreciated of all the royal gifts which had made Yolande de Polignac hated throughout the country.

Some of the greatest names in France left the country that night, including the Prince de Condé who, having been cold-shouldered by the King, and seeing that the situation was deteriorating hour by hour and that his own town of Chantilly was already in a state of revolt, left hastily for the frontier together with his entire family, including his mistress.

The flight of the Bourbon princes made a tremendous impression abroad.

The Emperor Joseph wrote in horror to his brother, Leopold of Tuscany, of the appalling news from Paris and the terrible role played by the King. 'I have just heard that the Comte d'Artois with his children, the Prince de Condé with his children, and the Prince de Conti have escaped to the Netherlands practically without their shirts. I am deeply distressed for the Queen, who will suffer a lot from the shame and *avilissement*.' The proud Hapsburg had no sympathy for the brother-in-law who was ready to put up with endless humiliations rather than spill the blood of a single Frenchman.

The Parisians were threatening to march on Versailles if the King did not come to Paris. And on the morning of 17 July Louis, with a courage which was almost sublime, set out for what the deputies still referred to as 'the good town of Paris' – a dirty, neglected, stinking town, with rubbish piled up in the streets, which in the general excitement of the past days no one had troubled to remove. Before leaving Versailles, the King took communion with the Queen, made his will, and appointed the Comte de Provence as lieutenant of the kingdom, in case he should fail to return. Marie Antoinette, who was convinced he was going to be murdered or taken prisoner, went on her knees begging him not to go. But the King turned away for fear she might see his tears.

Accompanied by four devoted courtiers, men with courage equal to his own, Louis set out on the twelve-mile journey to Paris, during which he did not speak a word. From now on his safety depended entirely on General Lafayette and his untrained, undisciplined citizen militia, known as the National Guard. Though he was virtually a prisoner there was still the farce of receiving him as King with Bailly, the newly elected mayor of Paris, waiting at the city gates to present him with the keys of the city placed on a gilded salver. There was even a throne prepared for him in the Hôtel de Ville. But the crowds which lined the streets, many of whom were armed, were tense and almost hostile. And there were only cries of '*Vive la Nation*' and none of '*Vive le Roi*', while all the cheering was for General Lafayette. The British ambassador, Lord Dorset, wrote home in a dispatch that 'His Majesty was treated more like a captive than a king, being led along like a tame bear.'

It is hard to forgive Lafayette for his behaviour to the King, to whom he owed his loyalty, if not his devotion. Even the American republican Gouverneur Morris was shocked at his boasting 'how on that day he had given orders to 100,000 men and promenaded the King through the streets, just as he pleased, even to deciding on the amount of applause he was to receive. In fact he could have kept the King a prisoner had he chosen to.' Gouverneur Morris was discreet and Lafayette's confidences got no further than his diaries. But there is no doubt that the General's letters to his mistress, Adelaide de Simiane, made the rounds of Versailles and probably ended in reaching the ears of the Queen, which may account for Marie Antoinette's almost pathological dislike of Lafayette.

Jean Sylvain Bailly, now mayor of Paris but an astronomer by profession, appears to have been far more tactful in dealing with the King. In his memoirs he admitted to a certain hesitation and embarrassment when, on arriving at the Hôtel de Ville, the King was presented with the tricolour, the symbol of the Revolution. 'I did not know quite how the King would like it and whether there was not something improper in giving it to him.' But Louis never hesitated, accepting it without protest and straight away pinning it in his hat. From the moment he stepped out on the balcony wearing the tricolour, the mood of the people changed and there was a great outburst of cheering, of frenzied shouts of '*Vive le Roi!*' 'All eyes, filled with tears, turned towards him; everyone held out their hands,' writes Bailly, 'and when he was placed on the throne which had been prepared for him, a voice from the back of the wall uttered a heartfelt cry of "Our King, our father", which served to double the applause and the shouts of "*Vive le Roi!*" The Parisians were now ready to love the "King of the third estate".' But they were acclaiming their own victory rather than their monarch, and the Austrian ambassador, who was present, wrote, 'The people of Paris now play the part of King.' Louis himself had no illusions, and he returned to Versailles as silent as when he set out.

Meanwhile the Queen was in an agony of apprehension. Fearing the King might not return, she had ordered the carriages to be ready to take her and her family to the National Assembly, where she planned putting herself at the mercy of the deputies, even going so far as to prepare a speech begging them not to separate a union which had been made in heaven. Madame Campan wrote that she kept repeating these words every now and then, breaking down in tears, saying, 'I know he is not coming back.' But at six in the evening a page arrived on horseback from Paris to say that the King was returning. And four hours later Louis, with his clothes covered in dust, his face dripping with sweat, came back to his half-deserted palace, from where so many had already fled and where those who had remained were so frightened they had put padlocks on their doors.

A loving, anxious family was awaiting his arrival. Marie Antoinette was already halfway down the great staircase when he came in from the marble court. A second later she was in his arms, when she caught sight of the tricolour cockade and instinctively recoiled. But there is no proof of her having said the cruel words which have sometimes been attributed to her: 'I thought I had married a king of France and I find I am married to a commoner.' It was not in her nature to denigrate their father in front of the children who adored him. He was a good, weak man, whose religion meant more to him than his crown, and now all he could find to say was, 'Thank God there was no bloodshed.'

But neither Louis's capitulation nor General Lafayette riding through the streets on his white horse could slake the Parisians' thirst for blood. Five days after the fall of the Bastille, the seventy-year-old Foulon, a member of the interim government, together with his son-in-law Berthier de Sauvigny, were foully murdered, having been quite wrongly accused of speculating in grain. Foulon's and Berthier's murders went unpunished, and though Lafayette resigned from his post in protest against the crime, the tears and prayers of the Paris electors soon persuaded him to return. The theatres reopened and, inured to daily violence, the Parisians resumed their ordinary lives. But the news from France made a tremendous impact abroad. The Emperor Joseph wrote to his brother Leopold, 'The news from France continues to be almost unbelievable, and one wonders how it will end. I have at last received a letter from the Queen, who is deeply unhappy over all the humiliations her husband has had to undergo.'

Even someone as complacent as the Duke of Dorset was sufficiently alarmed to advise his government that, 'In view of the events some public caution should be given to put on their guard those who may propose to visit this part of the continent'. The emotional King of Sweden was horrified: 'I keep seeing the head of Foulon, which those monsters gave his son-in-law to kiss. To think that this is the charming Paris where the whole of Europe came to distract themselves and to forget their worries. What horrible people.'

Paris that summer seemed to be full of 'horrible people'. The ever-recurring violence appears to have affected the population with a curious form of drunkenness. In the National Assembly, a left-wing deputy from the Dauphiné, called Antoine Barnave, defended Foulon's murder with the words: 'Why all this fuss? Is Foulon's blood so pure?' And as the worst example of bad taste, a certain fashionable milliner, not Mademoiselle Bertin, launched a new ribbon in *couleur du sang de Foulon* ('colour of the blood of Foulon'). While Paris accepted the violence, Versailles continued to ignore it. Only three days after a member of his government had been assassinated in the streets of his capital, the King went hunting in the forest of Rambouillet.

In that long hot summer of 1789 revolution spread to every corner of France. And at the end of July occurred what historically became known as the 'Great Fear' when, on a given day and hour, mysterious horsemen appeared in various towns and villages, terrorizing the population by announcing that armies of bandits were on the march, that foreign powers were planning to invade the country to restore the King's lost power and that the Emperor's troops, summoned by the Queen, were pouring in from the Austrian Netherlands. A systematic campaign of hatred inciting the people against the 'aristos', the peasants against their masters, was sweeping across the countryside. Good and bad landlords suffered alike at the hands of their frightened tenants, who believed that foreign mercenaries were coming to shoot them down. There was no longer any central authority, the King's administrators had abandoned their offices, his soldiers were fraternizing with the rebels, and attempts to raise local militia to protect property failed as the majority either joined in with the demonstrators or were too frightened to resist.

The mysterious horsemen and the raising of a fictitious panic was only a passing phenomenon. But it was sufficient for every landlord and châtelaine to realize they could no longer sleep peacefully in their beds. In the province of Dauphiné alone, seventy châteaux were burnt down in one month, most of them belonging to nobles who in 1788 had distinguished themselves in defending the privileges and rights of the *parlements* against the government. In the days of the 'Great Fear' the liberal-minded Marquis de Ferrières, who had always been hostile to the court of Versailles and was to remain in France and survive the Terror, saw clearly into the future when he wrote to his wife:

> The revolt against the nobility is widespread. Among the deputies are people who hate us without knowing why. Their hate is all the stronger and more active for having no definite cause. They do not stop to think that they will end in being the victims of the troubles they have provoked, that the people they work up against us will end in turning against them with an even greater force.

When the Neckers were recalled to France they were appalled by the devastation of the countryside, which confirmed Madame Necker in the opinion that it would have been far better for her husband to remain in Coppet rather than become Prime Minister of a country in circumstances which could only end in tarnishing his reputation. But Necker like Lafayette still believed his charisma to be sufficient to control '*les enragés*' and that his financial talents could bring back prosperity to France. The gloomy atmosphere of Versailles soon served to dispel these illusions. Those of his colleagues who had already arrived were despondent over the apathy shown by the King, who had completely dissociated himself from politics, while the Queen spent most of her days with her children at Trianon. In the National Assembly the majority of the deputies were so frightened of offending the people that the few who dared to denounce the excesses committed in Paris and the burning down of châteaux and ill treatment of their owners were promptly shouted down.

The King, who had gone out hunting, was not at Versailles to receive Necker on his arrival. Having been forced to recall him against his will, he saw no reason to deprive himself of a day's sport. The Queen, however, who had learnt to dissemble in the past months, managed to give him a gracious welcome, but it was a welcome still voiced in the grand manner, which was hardly in keeping with the times, 'calling on his loyalty to the King, the gratitude he owed in having been recalled'. Necker somewhat tactlessly replied 'that it was his duty to be loyal to the King, but he saw no reason to be grateful'. The Queen bit her lip and flushed, then turned away to say a few obliging words to Madame Necker, who by now was wishing she was a thousand miles from Versailles.

Among those who left France on the same day as Yolande de Polignac was the Abbé Vermond, whose departure, advised and abetted by Comte Mercy d'Argenteauil, was almost as great a loss to Marie Antoinette as that of her 'dearest friend'. Vermond had been her first contact with France, her first link with Choiseul. And though many a time in her frivolous years she had both neglected and forgotten him, he had always remained in the background, unfailingly loyal and never betraying a confidence. But Vermond's support of the hated Loménie de Brienne had rendered him as unpopular as the Polignacs. And the Austrian ambassador, who now deemed it wiser to limit his own visits to Versailles, arranged for the Abbé, whom many accused of being an Austrian agent, to leave the country as quickly and as unobtrusively as possible.

'The Queen is well and takes the only possible line of living in retirement, looking after her children,' wrote the Emperor to his brother Leopold. And in the oft-quoted letter addressed to their new governess, Madame de Tourzel, Marie Antoinette analysed her children's characters, revealing a hitherto unsuspected judgement and perception: 'I have always accustomed my children to trust me completely and when they have done wrong to tell me so themselves. When I scold them I try to give them the impression that I am more hurt than angry. I have made them understand that if I say yes or no it is irrevocable, but I always try to give them a good reason for my decision.'

In her description of the four-year-old Dauphin, whom she calls her '*chou d'amour*', we already see the traits which were going to turn the poor, distracted child so easily into a foul-tongued little Jacobin. 'He is very indiscreet and is apt to repeat whatever he has heard, and often, without actually wanting to lie, he adds according to his fantasy. It is his biggest fault and one which must be corrected.' Her children were her only joy, the one thing which brought her and Louis together and helped her to forgive his blunders and mistakes. In one of her first letters to Madame de Polignac, who was now safely in Switzerland, she wrote:

> My dear Heart, I was so touched by reading your letters. Don't think that I can ever forget you ... your friendship and my children are my only consolation. I will never give up on account of my son, and I will endure my sad existence to its bitter end. It is only misfortune which makes one aware of oneself and of the blood which flows in one's veins and which never lets one down. Here we are more likely to perish through the weaknesses and faults of our so-called friends than through the machinations of our enemies.

But Marie Antoinette had never learnt to distinguish her enemies from her friends. So many times she could have won over a loyal and devoted partisan if she had not been blinded by prejudice and pride. Many years later in describing the events of that last summer at Versailles, Madame de la Tour du Pin recalled certain occasions when Marie Antoinette forfeited her last chances of regaining her lost popularity.

She wrote:

> On the day of the feast of St Louis it is the tradition for the magistrates and municipal authorities of Paris to come to Versailles to offer their good wishes to the King. This year the National Guard wanted to share the privilege and Monsieur Lafayette brought his entire staff to be presented. The Queen received them in state. She was seated on the throne, blazing with diamonds, the duchesses, seated on their tabourets to her left and right, were all in court dress, while her entire household of ladies and gentlemen, excluding the few who had already fled the country, stood behind her. The usher announced 'The city of Paris', and the Queen waited for Monsieur Bailly to pay the customary homage of going down on one knee, instead of which he only made a very low bow, and she replied with a brief inclination of the head, which was not sufficiently friendly. When Lafayette came to present the officers of his staff, the Queen was seen to flush, as if under the stress of a deep emotion. Then, stammering a few words, in a shaking voice she dismissed them with a curt nod. They all left very annoyed with the Queen.

This was one of the many occasions when Marie Antoinette, who could charm so easily, might have won the hearts of those impressionable young officers, instead of letting herself be dominated by her dislike of Lafayette. As daughter-in-law of the minister of war in Necker's new government, the Marquise de la Tour du Pin played a leading role in the strange social life of that last summer at Versailles. At a time when many of her class were already being murdered in their homes and others had taken the road to exile, she could still write that she had very little in common with the wife of the minister who belonged to the *noblesse de robe*, which had never frequented Versailles. A new world, however, was already forcing its way through the gilded gates of the Sun King's palace. Presiding as hostess at the dinner parties held at the ministry of war, Madame de la Tour du Pin entertained deputies of the third estate, and her memoirs contain one of the first descriptions of Robespierre, formally attired 'in an apple green coat with his thick white hair wonderfully dressed'. And she adds the curious detail that 'Mirabeau was the only one of the deputies who never called on any of the ministers, and was therefore never invited.'

Necker's return came too late to improve the situation. The shortage of food brought on by the bad harvests of 1788 and the pillaging of granaries and farms became ever more acute, and subversive agencies spread rumours that the government was cornering the grain. All over France people were marching on the town halls, crying out for bread. Riots were an everyday occurrence. Anarchy was rampant, and in the space of one month 6,000 passports were issued to Frenchmen wishing to leave the country. But there was still talk of the 'glorious revolution'. And young men who had fought in the American War of Independence still upheld the ideals of 'Liberty, Equality, Fraternity' and consulted with Mr Jefferson, the American minister in Paris, over the drafting of the new consitution.

The fourth of August saw the extraordinary spectacle of a voluntary renunciation of feudal privileges by the deputies of the nobility. In a stirring speech Lafayette's brother-in-law, the young Vicomte de Noailles, who as a younger son had very little to lose, managed to inspire his fellow nobles to adopt measures which practically spelt their ruin. In what can only be described as a mood of mass hysteria, peers and prelates vied with one another in renouncing tithes and tolls, manorial rights and dues. It is significant that neither Mirabeau nor the Abbé Sieyès, the two most intelligent members of the assembly, attended the session, which claimed to have destroyed in one night the whole of the feudal system, but which the cold light of day revealed to be subject to many revisions and modifications and which above all could not become valid without the King's consent.

Louis for once was firm, writing to the Archbishop of Arles, 'Never will I consent to the spoliation of my clergy and nobility or sanction any decree which deprives them in any way.' The Declaration of the Rights of Man, giving civil equality to all and proclaiming the absolute sovereignty of the nation, brought the King into direct opposition both with the National Assembly and his own government, where Necker was in secret agreement with the leaders of the left. Faced by his passive resistance, the revolutionaries felt the time had come to stage another *coup d'état*. But this time their target was to be the Palace of Versailles.

In view of the disturbing rumours of a march on Versailles, the minister of the King's household, acting in conjunction with the town authorities, decided that additional troops should be brought in to reinforce the local garrison, which consisted of 300 men of the King's bodyguard, 200 *Chasseurs de Lorraine*, and the newly formed National Guard.

The arrival of the Flanders regiment, which was to spark off the disastrous events of 5 and 6 October, took place in a friendly atmosphere with the various regiments, including the National Guard, united in their loyalty to the crown. Versailles was calm, and Marie Antoinette wrote to Yolande de Polignac, 'Things seem to have taken a turn for the better. I am discovering all kinds of truly and sincerely attached people, of whom I have never even thought.' Her optimism may also have been due to the fact that Axel Fersen was back from Valenciennes, where his regiment had distinguished itself in suppressing a mutiny. But certain deputies in the National Assembly were already trying to abolish the foreign regiments, and Fersen was now on leave, riding out every day to Trianon, the perfect knight errant for an unhappy queen, but unfortunately the most incompetent of counsellors.

In the last days of September all Versailles was *en fête* to celebrate the arrival of the Flanders regiment, and on the evening of Thursday 1 October the King's bodyguard followed the usual custom of holding a banquet in honour of the incoming regiment. The King had given his consent for it to be held in the palace theatre, which was sometimes used for balls, and it was here, in Gabriel's beautiful blue and gold theatre inaugurated on her wedding day, that Marie Antoinette was to attend her last public ceremony at Versailles.

She had not wanted to be present and only at the last moment had been persuaded by a young lady-in-waiting on the grounds that it would amuse the Dauphin. She had suffered so much from the illness of her eldest son that she enjoyed showing off this beautiful, healthy child, a happy little extrovert who loved applause. The King, who had just returned from hunting, accompanied his family to a railed-off box facing the stage, where two hundred officers dined on a horseshoe table.

A tremendous ovation greeted their arrival and the hall resounded to the shouts of 'Long live the King! Long live the Queen! And long live Monsieur le Dauphin!' The orchestra struck up an air by Grétry, the Queen's favourite composer, '*O Richard, O mon Roi, l'univers t'abandonne, sur cet terre il ny'a que moi qui s'interesse à ta personne*'. The atmosphere was charged with emotion, and in a moment of enthusiasm the royal family came down onto the stage. A Swiss Guard lifted the Dauphin onto the dining table, and he walked the whole length of it without spilling a single glass. The cheering grew ever louder and the King and Queen left with the cheers still ringing in their ears – a warm demonstration of loyalty such as they had not known for months, but which the gutter press of Paris soon turned into an orgy. There may have been a lot of drinking after they had left. Some foolish things may have been said; a pretty palace lady in one of the boxes may have been sufficiently imprudent to make her ribbons into white cockades to replace the tricolour. At another dinner, held two days later in the royal riding school, the company may have been still less restrained, the drinking even heavier. Toasts were drunk and words were said which the Marats and Desmoulins, the scavengers paid to stir up trouble, were only too ready to distort. 'The tricolour has been trampled underfoot. The Queen herself has distributed white cockades, as the sign of a counter-revolution. And on Saturday night at the riding school officers of the King's bodyguard have threatened to march on the Assembly.' By Monday all Paris was in an uproar and the stage was set for the march of the women on Versailles.

That morning there was no bread to be had in Paris. The bakers' shops were closed and a famine cunningly contrived. Large crowds of women were gathering in the central markets and in the poorer quarters of St Antoine. Fishwives and prostitutes, side by side with well-dressed women with powdered hair, all clamouring for bread. By half past nine in the morning they had stormed the Hôtel de Ville, and terrified the municipality into sounding the tocsin, which served to spread the alarm. The hundreds grew into thousands, many of them armed with pikes and scythes, even with axes, and among them were men in disguise – *agents provocateurs*, who afterwards were said to have been in the pay of the Duc d'Orléans. Was it all the work of Laclos with his brilliant, embittered mind, or were other subterranean forces at work to bring the King to Paris and keep him as a prisoner of the Revolution?

Now it was not only the women but elements of the National Guard, composed of the disaffected Gardes Français, who asked to march on Versailles to revenge the insult to the tricolour, and all Lafayette's vaunted charisma was powerless to dissuade them. Threatened and insulted, yesterday's idol, the hero of two worlds, was instructed by the municipal authorities to accompany two of their delegates to Versailles and to bring the King back to Paris. It can hardly have been a pleasant experience for the elegant young Marquis to lead his rebellious troops in the van of a horde of drunken women, straggling along the road, raiding the wine shops, terrifying the villages they passed, shouting foul-mouthed obscenities against the Queen. He had been the first to warn the government that some of the rebellious soldiers of the Gardes Français were planning to march on Versailles and that there was a plot to assassinate the Queen. With supreme self-confidence, he had assured ministers that there was no need to worry as he was in complete control of his troops. But the glorious general and his troops did not present a very heroic picture preceded by a crowd of harridans who, with frightful laughter, threatened to 'slit Antoinette's pretty throat, to fry her livers and make lace out of her entrails'.

Only a twelve-mile journey from Paris, Versailles was another world. On the morning of 4 October the King had gone hunting at Meudon and the Queen remained at Trianon discussing with her gardeners the laying out of the flowerbeds for the following spring. The clouds were gathering, but Trianon had never looked more lovely with the last of the summer roses still in bloom and the leaves already beginning to turn. The Queen was resting in a grotto beside a stream when a breathless page came running across the lawn bringing her a message from the Comte de St Priest telling her that an army of women was marching on the palace.

From all accounts, Marie Antoinette was alone at Trianon, but Fersen, who was in Paris and anxious for her safety, had followed on horseback the first party of women leaving for Versailles. Outdistancing them *en route*, he must have arrived at Trianon in time to warn the Queen, and for the next two days he appears to have been among that small group of faithful courtiers hovering round the Oeil de Bœuf – a silent figure in the background, playing what for him must have been a very frustrating role. Later he wrote to his father, 'I was witness to it all.'

Of the eight ministers waiting on the King's return, St Priest was the only one with a definite plan which, if it had been carried out, might well have saved the monarchy. It consisted in having the bridges over the Seine at Sèvres and St Cloud guarded by battalions of the Flanders Regiment, posting the Swiss Guards at Neuilly, and sending the Queen and her children under strong escort to Rambouillet where there was a garrison of loyal troops. Meanwhile the King, with the rest of his army and the 800 men of his bodyguard, would go out and meet the Parisians and order them to retire. Should they fail to do so, a few cavalry charges should be sufficient to disperse them. Or at the worst there would still be time for the King to ride to Rambouillet at the head of his army. Three colleagues, including the new minister of war, approved the plan to which Necker was bitterly opposed, telling St Priest that anyone who gave advice of this kind ran the risk of losing his head, to which the latter replied that a minister who was not prepared to risk his head in a crisis had no right to be in the government. But the one who dismissed the plan from the very beginning was the Queen, who refused to be separated from the King, saying, 'I know they have come from Paris to demand my head, but I learnt from my mother not to fear death and I will wait beside my husband for whatever comes.'

By three in the afternoon the King was back from Meudon. The conspirators had guessed that he would refuse to use the army against a band of women. This explained their using hundreds of men disguised in women's clothes who, armed with cutlasses and knives, were descending on Versailles in pouring rain, invading the National Assembly, striking terror in all but the most violent of demagogues, threatening and embracing them in turn, hanging up their skirts to dry in the galleries, many of them drunk and vomiting on the benches, making lewd gestures, singing filthy songs. Mounier, the president of the Assembly and one of the more moderate democrats, managed to escape to the palace to beg the King to reconsider his decision of opposing his sanction to the Declaration of the Rights of Man, but he was kept waiting while Louis received a deputation of six market women presenting a petition. The women were young and pretty and the King spoke to them with so much kindness and comprehension that one of them fainted from emotion or fatigue, and all of them left shouting, 'Long live the King!' to the fury of their companions waiting outside in the rain. Troops of the Flanders regiment were still lined up in the Place d'Armes and could have protected the palace and covered the King's departure but precious time was wasted with the King refusing to give any definite orders or to come to any decision. The meeting of the ministerial council was interrupted while the King sat down to dinner, eating with his usual hearty appetite while the Queen maintained an extraordinary dignity and calm, never showing the slightest sign of exasperation with her husband who, in reply to the entreaties of St Priest, kept muttering, 'I do not want to be a fugitive.' At eight o'clock in the evening came the news that Lafayette was marching on Versailles with 30,000 troops of the National Guard, including the former soldiers of the Gardes Français. In grandiloquent words the general assured the King that there would be no disorders. St Priest, who had little faith in Lafayette's command over his men, advised an instant removal to Rambouillet and, acting on his own initiative, ordered the great gilded gates of Versailles to be closed for the first time in history.

By now it was too late to act on the advice of St Priest. When the orders were finally given for the carriages to be brought out of the stables, they were immediately surrounded by a mob of Parisians shouting, 'The King is leaving! We must stop him!' Cutting the reins, they overpowered the drivers and frightened away the horses, while the army, still waiting for orders from the King, was powerless to act. Both St Priest and La Tour du Pin, the new minister of war, offered their own carriages to bring the royal family to safety, but the King refused and kept saying, 'I cannot be a fugitive.' The Queen, who had been prepared to pack, retired to her apartments together with the royal princesses, while her frightened ladies sat whispering among themselves in the dimly lit Salle de Jeu. People kept coming and going, bringing contradictory reports. The local National Guards were said to be firing on their officers. The household troops were being attacked with stones and bottles. Fearing for their safety rather than his own, and acting largely on Necker's advice, the King took the extraordinary decision of ordering both the royal bodyguard and the Flanders regiment to leave their posts and go and bivouac in the park. Except for a few of his personal bodyguard, the whole of the great palace was to rely for its defence entirely on the untrained National Guard of Versailles and the former Gardes Français commanded by Lafayette.

It was nearly midnight when Lafayette arrived, exhausted and bespattered with mud, having ridden for seven hours in the pouring rain. Leaving his men in the Place d'Armes, he went straight to the King, walking across the Oeil de Bœuf, still crowded with people, one of whom murmured, 'Here comes Cromwell.' Overhearing these words, the general replied, 'Cromwell would not have come alone.' Forgetting the sorry role he had played earlier in the day, he addressed the King in the heroic manner: 'Sire, I have brought you my head to save that of Your Majesty. If my blood must flow, let it be in service of my King rather than strung up on a lamppost in the Place de Grèves.' Louis, who had little use for heroic phrases, was not impressed. But he was nevertheless prepared to believe in Lafayette's assurances that the former Gardes Français asked for nothing better than to take part in the defence of the palace. It was now long past midnight, and both King and general were utterly exhausted and longing to go to bed. With a mass of murderous hooligans camped outside the gates screaming, 'Death to the Austrian whore!' and bands of armed ruffians prowling round the town,

Louis, to quote the words of the journalist Rivarol, 'left everything to a general who was sure of nothing'. At one o'clock in the morning, Lafayette left the King's apartment and announced that His Majesty was retiring for the night and that he advised everyone else to do the same. He then made a last tour of inspection and, succumbing to fatigue, took the fatal decision of leaving the palace for his quarters in the nearby Hôtel de Noailles, which was to earn him from Rivarol the sobriquet of 'General Morpheus'.

Not many were able to sleep that night. In his rooms overlooking the court of the ministers, St Priest lay wide awake listening to the menacing noises outside. At dawn he got up and went out on the balcony, from where he suddenly saw one of the gates opening and a horde of armed bandits pouring into the courtyards and running at full speed in the direction of the court of the princes, from where a staircase led straight into the royal apartments. He wrote, 'They passed under my windows without seeing me. I stayed there for a while and they returned dragging with them a dozen of the King's bodyguards whom they were intending to massacre, when General Lafayette, raised from his slumbers, fortunately appeared accompanied by a body of grenadiers of the former Gardes Francais who succeeded in rescuing them. But not before two of the sentinels on guard at the entrance to the royal apartments had been seized and decapitated by the most savage of the bandits, while the drunken viragos gathering round bathed their hands in their blood.'

St Priest was watching all this from his window, one of the many eyewitnesses to this day of horror, when the Queen, who had managed to snatch a few hours sleep, was roused by two of her women whose courage and initiative probably saved her life. Disobeying her orders to go to bed, they had barricaded her doors and spent all night sitting outside her room. It was six o'clock in the morning when they first heard the incoming rush of feet and the menacing shouts of the bandits coming up the marble staircase in search of the Queen. A heroic young bodyguard, who tried to bar the way, was struck down with the butt of a gun and, with his face all covered with blood, had just time to call out, 'Save the Queen! They are out to kill her,' before he fainted away. With immense presence of mind the two young women bolted the door and ran to the Queen, begging her not to stop to dress but to go straight to the King. Leaping out of bed, throwing on a shift and petticoat with a cloak around her shoulders and with her stockings in her hand, Marie Antoinette, followed by her women, ran barefoot down the secret passage which connected her bedroom to the Oeil de Boeuf and the King's apartments, only to find that the door was locked on the inside. Screaming for help, she battered on the door and after what must have seemed an eternity but was probably no more than a few minutes, it was opened by a frightened valet who told her the King had gone to look for her. Woken by the noise, Louis' first thought had been for his wife. Taking another of the many subterranean passages which passed under the Oeil de Bœuf (passages made in happier times with a view to bringing the shy young King into closer contact with his wife), he ran to her apartments, only to find her gone. But a few moments later the whole family was united in the King's apartment. In their rooms overlooking the gardens, the royal children had been peacefully asleep, when their governess was woken by one of the guards to tell her that the palace had been invaded. Following the instructions given her by the Queen, Madame de Tourzel had taken her charges at once to the King. Bathed in tears, with her husband's arms around her and the terrified children clinging to her knees, Marie Antoinette heard the menacing cries coming nearer and nearer, and the hammering against the doors of the Oeil de Bœuf – until, suddenly, the sounds changed to the stampede of feet running away, of isolated shots and the shouts of officers rallying their men. Lafayette's extraordinary charisma had triumphed and the grenadiers of the Gardes Français had joined forces with the loyal bodyguards in clearing the palace.

The Queen returned to her room, which according to many accounts had been desecrated by the mob who, baulked of their prey, had vented their fury by plunging their pikes into her bed and ripping the brocaded curtains. This was denied by Madame Campan who, though not present that night, left one of the most explicit accounts of the morning of 6 October, describing how the beleaguered guardsmen sought refuge in the Queen's bedroom and protected it from the bandits. As she was still wearing only her cloak and shift, one of her women brought the Queen a dressing gown, a charming, feminine garment in white and yellow stripes, of the kind she usually wore in the early morning to receive the first visit from the King, but curiously unsuited to this occasion when, with pale face and disordered hair, she entered the Oeil de Bœuf, by now crowded with people, many of whom, living in other parts of the palace, had known nothing until now. Among these were Madame Elisabeth and the Comte and Comtesse de Provence; Monsieur's elegant, unruffled appearance must have been particularly irritating for those who, like Axel Fersen, had kept vigil all night in the vicinity of the royal apartments.

The palace was cleared. But the courtyards were a seething mass of angry, frustrated people – people more like beasts than human beings. Somewhere they had found a cannon which they had dragged into the Place d'Armes and pointed menacingly in the direction of the palace. Others were parading in triumph the heads of the murdered guardsmen, transfixed on pikes, and among the crowds agitators dressed in women's clothes with their pockets full of Orléanist gold were inciting their comrades to turn on Lafayette, who had betrayed them to the King. There were those who later claimed to have seen the Duc d'Orléans himself mingling with the people. Others went so far as to say that he had directed the assault on the Queen's room. But the final evidence proved him to have spent all night at the Palais Royal and to have arrived at Versailles later in the morning, when he appeared to be intimidated and embarrassed by the enthusiasm he evoked among the populace.

Whatever may have been the faults of Lafayette, he was certainly courageous. With a confidence he must have been far from feeling, he walked straight into the King's council chamber and told Louis and his ministers – none of whom, not even Necker, had any advice to give – that order could only be restored if His Majesty went out on to the balcony and spoke to the people. The balcony gave out from the state bedroom, where the whole of the royal family, including the old aunts, were gathered together. Marie Antoinette stood at the window looking out with sad eyes at a people who had learnt to hate her. Beside her were her daughter and Madame Elisabeth, while the little Dauphin, who was standing on a chair playing with his sister's curls, kept complaining that he was hungry. All she could do was to embrace him and to tell him he would have to wait till the tumult had died down. But would it ever die down? The King, who was always ready to sacrifice himself rather than any of his subjects, went out onto the balcony, where he was greeted with a few isolated cheers. He tried to speak, but his voice was drowned by reiterated cries of, 'To Paris! To Paris! We want our King in Paris!' Other cries more ominous and more insistent kept calling out, 'Show us the Queen. We want to see the Queen!'

Everyone in the state rooms held their breath. Even Lafayette grew pale. But Marie Antoinette never faltered. With hair undressed and face devoid of rouge, her little head held high, she had never looked more truly magnificent than when, holding her children by the hand, she stepped out on to the balcony to face the Paris mob. 'No children!' screamed the crowd, and she turned quietly to hand the children back to their governess before going back on to the balcony. For two minutes she remained completely immobile while muskets already loaded were aimed at her head and the viragos screamed abuse. But such was her magnetism, the effect that her presence had on the crowd, that one by one the muskets were lowered, the cries died down. And suddenly one heard cheers of '*Vive la Reine!*', to which the Queen, with a gesture that not even her heroic mother could have equalled, dropped a deep curtsey in reply. 'How strange,' writes Rivarol, 'that this woman, so unpopular and so vilely calumniated, is able by the sheer magic of her presence to reconquer her prestige and evoke admiration from the moment she finds herself face to face with the masses.' Then Lafayette, who could never resist a dramatic occasion, stepped out on to the balcony and kissed her hand. And those who had been ready to assassinate their Queen and to consider Lafayette to be a traitor now joined in shouting, '*Vive la Reine!*' and '*Vive Monsieur de Lafayette!*'

There were tears in the Queen's eyes, she who a moment ago had been so calm and composed. They were neither tears of fear nor tears of sorrow, simply tears of anger. In all her life Marie Antoinette had never hated anyone as much as she now hated Lafayette, who had dared to humiliate his King and was taking them to Paris as prisoners of the people. He had asked her, 'What are your intentions, madame?' to which she had replied, 'Whatever may be my fate, my duty is to die at the King's feet with my children in my arms.' And she broke down only when she came back into her room and, in a voice strangled with sobs, turned to Madame Necker saying, 'They are going to force us to go to Paris, preceded by the heads of our murdered bodyguards.'

Twenty-four hours before, St Priest had warned King Louis that to go to Paris meant losing his throne. But now there was no alternative, and at half past one in the afternoon the tragic procession set out from Versailles. And perhaps the most tragic of all was that the town which for the past 150 years had battened on the court and benefited by the generosity of the present King, now celebrated his departure with an indecent display of joy. From every balcony and rooftop came the cries of '*Vive la Nation*!' and never one of '*Vive le Roi*!'

Labouring under the shock of the recent events, the King and Queen were too shattered to take the slightest initiative, and all the arrangements were left to Lafayette. The son of the minister of war was put in command of two battalions, one of the Swiss Guards, the other of the National Guard, which were to remain behind and prevent looting in the palace. And the only time the King showed any emotion was before getting into the carriage, when he turned to the young officer and said, 'You are now in charge. Try to save for me my poor Versailles.'

There have been numberless accounts of what for the King and Queen must have been a nightmare drive. The royal coach was preceded by wagon-loads of flour rifled from the stores of Versailles, guarded by soldiers of the National Guard, and by hundreds of market women, brandishing the heads of the murdered guardsmen, laughing and singing as if they were taking part in some hideous bacchanal; others, half naked, riding astride the cannons, jumping onto the soldiers' backs, knocking off their caps, making them lewd advances, and shouting to the crowds who lined the roads, 'We are bringing back the baker and the baker's wife and the little baker's boy.' On his white horse, Lafayette did little to control the rabble, and the grenadiers who followed in the rear of the royal coach had no orders to protect the King from their insults, while the loyal bodyguards, many of them wounded and still wearing their bloodstained shirts, were disarmed and helpless. At the end of the cortège came a long trail of carriages – the debris of the greatest court of Europe, followed by one hundred deputies of the National Assembly, which from now on was to hold its sessions in Paris.

Riding beside the royal coach, a symbol of loyalty to the past, was the oldest of the bodyguards, who throughout the drive kept one hand firmly on the door, while on the other side rode the Comte d'Artois' Scottish gardener, now in the employment of the Queen, the only one who had the courage to protest when some drunken ruffian fired a musket over their heads. Despite the many contradictory accounts, these were the only two people outside the coach to whom the Queen addressed a word throughout the whole of the six-hour drive. Sitting at the bottom of the coach with the Dauphin on her knees, to whom she kept whispering words of comfort and endearment, Marie Antoinette appeared neither to see nor hear what was going on outside.

The rain had stopped. It was a lovely autumn evening by the time the long unwieldy cortège had reached the outskirts of Paris, and the trees of the Bois de Boulogne were bathed in a golden haze. At Auteuil the streets were empty, as if the inhabitants had no wish to view the humiliation of their King. But on the terrace of a house in Passy stood the Duc d'Orléans with his children and their governess, obviously delighted to see how well Laclos had been spending his money, yet at the same time embarrassed by the cheers. King Louis saw his cousin standing on the terrace and looked away in disgust. Lafayette saw him too, and if there was one thing he and Marie Antoinette had in common it was their hatred of the Duc d'Orléans. That day he swore he would make him pay for the excesses of Versailles.

The mayor of Paris was waiting to receive his sovereigns at the barrier of Chaillot, though it was hardly the occasion for an official welcome. However brilliant as an academician and famous as an astronomer, Bailly appears on this occasion to have been singularly inept in choosing his words. If she had not been so outraged, Marie Antoinette might have laughed at the absurdity of his saying, 'What a beautiful day it is which has brought His Majesty and his august consort to take up residence in the capital, together with the little Prince who will grow to be as noble and as just as Louis XVI'. But Louis replied in his direct and kindly fashion, 'I only trust that my coming to Paris will put an end to lawlessness and bring back peace and order to the city.' They had hoped to go straight to the Tuileries, but they had still to face the ordeal of another welcome at the Hôtel de Ville. When the Queen pleaded that she and her children might be allowed to go direct to the palace, she was told quite bluntly that it was safer for her to remain with the King.

The scene changed in the Place de Grèves, which was crowded with decent, well-dressed people, all genuinely happy to see their King in Paris. Gone were the drunken harridans who, worn out with their own excesses, had retreated to their lairs, the armed ruffians who, having earned their wages, had gone to spend them in the wine shops. At the end of an appalling day, Louis and Marie Antoinette heard again the heartening cheers of '*Vive le Roi!*' and even '*Vive la Reine!*'

It was ten o'clock when they got to the Tuileries, the vast, dilapidated palace where no king of France had resided since Louis XV had lived there as a boy, where Louis XVI had never spent a night, but where Marie Antoinette had always kept a small apartment for her occasional visits to the theatre. Here the royal family camped for the first night, while all around was chaos and confusion, with ministers, courtiers and ladies-in-waiting disputing among themselves the possession of a bed, a couch, or even a table on which to sleep. But in the midst of this chaos someone had thought of preparing an excellent supper to which the King and his famished courtiers did full justice, and after which Louis was heard to make the extraordinary statement: 'Make yourselves as comfortable as best you can. I personally am content.'

'The papers will have told you all that has happened at Versailles. On the Monday and Tuesday, 5 and 6 October, I saw it all and returned to Paris in one of the court carriages. The journey took six and a half hours. God preserve me from another such agonizing experience,' wrote Axel Fersen to his father two days after the events. He had not only made the journey from Versailles to Paris but had been waiting for the sovereigns to arrive at the Tuileries. Wrapped in a dark cloak, he might have escaped detection had it not been for the sharp eyes of the Comte de St Priest, who had an uncontrollable aversion to the handsome, conceited Swede. Fersen had not only been his wife's lover, but was presumed to be the lover or *cicisbeo* of the Queen; it mattered little which, except that his presence in itself was compromising her. Unhappy and humiliated for the King he had been unable to save, St Priest vented his ill temper on Fersen, whom he told quite bluntly that if he had any respect for Her Majesty then it would be wiser for him to stay away. But in the next few weeks before he returned to his regiment at Valenciennes Axel was always near the Queen, helping her to endure the endless frustration of what was virtually a prison, albeit a very gilded prison. Even Fersen was surprised at the luxury of her apartments. From the first day an army of workmen had been commandeered to make the necessary alterations. Elderly courtiers who had been lodged in 'grace and favour' apartments were hastily evicted. Wagonloads of furniture, pictures and tapestries were brought from Versailles. And within a few days the former palace of the Bourbon Kings was again functioning as a court with all the old ceremonies revived – *Le Lever, Le Coucher, La Messe du Roi* and *Le Grand Couvert* all taking place under the eyes of Lafayette's National Guard, mostly decent, well-intentioned bourgeois, replacing the faithful bodyguard whom the King, always only too ready to think of the safety of others, had dismissed rather than have them risk their lives in his defence. The '*grandes charges*' were back on duty; the foreign ambassadors came to court on the usual days, and liberal-minded aristocrats, who 'believed' in the new order but were still monarchists, were assiduous in paying their respects. Loyal courtiers rallied round the Crown, and the first to arrive was Marie Thérèse de Lamballe. This fragile, nervous little woman, who fainted if she saw a dead bird, had the courage to return to Paris after the events of 6 October and to take up her duties as superintendent of the Queen's household. Unfortunately she was still as foolish and as frivolous as ever, and neither she nor

Fersen, the Queen's two most intimate friends, was sufficiently intelligent to be of any real help at a time when there might still have been a chance of saving the monarchy.

For the time being the fickle, volatile Parisians appeared to be delighted to have their King and Queen in residence at the Tuileries. When Marie Antoinette awoke on the morning of 7 October and heard the people shouting outside her windows, she could hardly believe that the shouts were friendly rather than menacing. After all she had gone through she still had the spirit to give thought to her toilette, choosing one of her prettiest dresses and most elaborate hats in which to face the crowds, hoping to disarm them with her gentleness and charm. Soon their very accusations were interspersed with laughter, and the same women who the day before had wanted to kill her were now shouting '*Vive la Reine!*' and begging for a ribbon from her hair, a flower from her corsage. With an infinite patience, Marie Antoinette took off her hat and distributed her ribbons, and everyone saw that there were streaks of white in her golden hair, white not due to powder but to the horrors she had witnessed in the past two days.

Later that morning she wrote to Comte Mercy, 'Things look better this morning. Don't worry, I am quite all right. And if one could forget where we are and how we came here we should be quite pleased with the way the people are behaving.' But Mercy, who was less of an optimist, reported to the Emperor that 'The Paris rabble is now the master of France.'

The worst of all was not having a moment's privacy, for the Tuileries gardens were open all day to an indiscreet and curious public who peered into the windows, calling out both obscene and complimentary remarks. 'You are still very pretty,' the Queen was told on more than one occasion. During the first weeks she made every effort to conciliate the people: 'We now give our hands to everyone. It is very strange,' she wrote in one of her letters to Madame de Polignac. Even Madame Elisabeth, who was not always an admirer of her sister-in-law, admitted that 'No one could have shown more amiability and more courage than the Queen has shown in the past eight days.' The little Dauphin was taught to make friends with the guards on duty and to wave to the crowds. But all this enforced amiability was completely alien to Marie Antoinette, of whom the young Madame de la Tour du Pin wrote with a considerable discernment, 'This ill-starred princess either did not know how to consider people's feelings or was not prepared to do so. When she was displeased she allowed it to be evident, regardless of the consequences. And this did great harm to the King's cause. She was gifted with a very great courage, but very little intelligence, absolutely no tact, and the worst of all a mistrust always misplaced in those who were most willing to serve her.' But one can hardly blame her if she did not believe in the words of welcome offered by Bailly and Lafayette, or in the rhetorical addresses of the numberless deputations that came to pay homage to a captive king.

When, only a few days after their arrival, a delegation from the Paris municipality spoke of the joy it would give the people to see their Queen more often
at the theatre, she replied very politely that she would have great pleasure in
accepting their invitation, but it would need some time before she was sufficiently recovered from the painful experiences which had caused her so
much suffering. Nor was it encouraging to go to the theatre, where André
Chénier's *Charles IX*, a violent attack on royalty which would never have been
produced except for the weakness of Bailly, was drawing rapturous crowds at
the Théâtre Français. In the words of Beaumarchais, '*Figaro* destroyed the
aristocracy, but *Charles IX* has destroyed the monarchy.'

Yet there were still people who thought that the Revolution had burnt itself
out. The National Assembly, which had followed the King to Paris and
which now held its sessions in the Manège, the riding school adjoining the
Tuileries, was far more orderly than it had been at Versailles. But there was
also little opposition to all the radical measures brought forward by the left.
The government of which Necker was still the Prime Minister was powerless
or unwilling to intervene, while many of the more moderate members, in
protest against their colleagues' attitude to mob violence, had ended in
resigning their seats and in leaving for the country. Such monarchists as
remained had very little influence and took little part in the debates.

During those first months at the Tuileries, the King appeared to be no
more than a passive spectator while his country was falling apart. Though he
was in no way forbidden to hunt, he took no pleasure in going out into the
woods with a National Guardsman at his elbow. Deprived of the violent
exercise which was necessary for his health, and still a compulsive eater,
Louis became fatter, more lethargic and more exasperating to his wife, whom
he constantly consulted but whose advice he rarely took. Monsieur, who was
now living in the Luxembourg Palace, where he was almost as closely
guarded as the King, complained that to get his brother to come to a decision
was 'like trying to get three oiled billiard balls to move together'. Still firmly
convinced of the divine right of kings and unable to adapt himself to the role
of a constitutional monarch, Louis took the dangerous path of paying lip-
service to the reforms of the National Assembly, while secretly encouraging
the counter-revolution. As a Bourbon prince he adhered to the family pact.
Such confidences as he made were given to the King of Spain rather than to
his Hapsburg brother-in-law, of whose reforming zeal and sympathy with
the *Philosophes* he had always disapproved. In a secret letter addressed to
King Charles IV, Louis wrote, 'I owe it to myself, I owe it to my family and to
the House of Bourbon not to degrade the sacred prerogatives which over the
centuries have belonged to our dynasty. I choose Your Majesty, as the head of
the junior branch of our family, to convey my solemn protestations against all
the illegal edicts to which unwillingly I have been forced to adhere since July
15th of this year.'

But there was little point in such a letter coming from a king who would not allow his most devoted subjects to draw a sword in his defence. With a show of strength, a little firmness, he might still have saved the throne, for even in the ranks of the National Assembly and in the most unexpected quarters there were still men willing to help him rather than see their country fall into a state of dissolution.

The strangest of all the political friendships, which in this year of 1789 brought the most divergent elements together, was that of Auguste, Prince d'Arenberg, Comte de La Marck, prince of the Holy Roman Empire and grandee of Spain, companion of Marie Antoinette in her youth and a *habitué* of Trianon, though never belonging to the Clan Polignac. The other was Comte Honoré Riqueti, now Marquis de Mirabeau who, having lit the first flames of revolution, was beginning to realize that it was easier to kindle the fire than to put it out. Disgusted by the excesses of 5 October, excesses for which he was unjustly considered to be responsible, and seeing that '*La Revolution Bourgeoise*' was in danger of foundering into anarchy, Mirabeau succeeded in convincing the Comte de La Marck of his genuine desire to support the King. In his own words, the ship of state was foundering and there was no one at the helm. But how could one make the King, and still more the Queen, believe that this venal opportunist, accused of rape and incest in his youth, was really genuine in his intentions. Marie Antoinette was still labouring under the shock of the recent events. Her dreams were haunted by the heads of the murdered guardsmen brandished as trophies by bloodthirsty harpies. And all she replied to the first overtures made by de La Marck was, 'I hope we will never be so unfortunate as to need the help of Monsieur de Mirabeau.' If only Fersen, the only man whom she really trusted and who, in spite of the warnings of St Priest and the guards of Lafayette, appears to have had easy access to the palace, could have given more intelligent advice. But unfortunately the proud and intransigent Swede considered it impossible for his 'pure and angelic queen' to have any dealings with a scoundrel like Mirabeau, who asked money for his services.

After a few weeks spent with his regiment at Valenciennes, one of the many foreign regiments which the Assembly was planning to disband, Fersen returned to Paris in January 1790 entrusted with a secret mission from King Gustavus, who no longer trusted his official ambassador de Staël, a weak man completely dominated by his wife. Fersen remained in Paris throughout the following year, a year which saw the full flowering of his amatory relations with the Queen. There can be little doubt that they became lovers. In the Tuileries Marie Antoinette looked upon herself as a prisoner who had the right to seize every opportunity for freedom. What as Queen of France she might have denied herself at Versailles would in her eyes have been permissible at the Tuileries. Fersen appears to have had no difficulty in going in and out of the palace at all hours of the day and night. In April 1790 he wrote to his favourite sister, Countess Sophie Piper, 'I am a little happier, for from time to time I am able to see her quite freely in her apartments, and this consoles us slightly for all the unpleasantness she has to put up with.' Naturally there was gossip. The Comte de St Priest thought it his duty to tell the Queen that a guard had seen Count Fersen leaving the palace at three in the morning, and had been about to arrest him. 'The Count should be warned that his continual visits to the palace will end in getting him into trouble.' But all that Marie Antoinette replied was, 'Tell him if you must. Personally I could not care less.' And the visits continued as before.

The Queen had fallen in love for the first time and was desperately snatching at a few hours of happiness. She was to love Axel to the end of her life, sending him that last pathetic message from prison '*Tutto a te mi guida.*' Axel's romantically-minded sister compared them to Tristan and Iseult, but neither was capable of an all-absorbing passion. Marie Antoinette was inexperienced, and frigid by nature. Fersen was a full-blooded sensualist, 'a volcano covered by an iceberg', a man who had had innumerable affairs with women of every class and kind. But it was always he who had been pursued, the others who made the efforts. And those by whom he was sexually attracted were usually women with the talents of a courtesan. Poor Marie Antoinette had no such talents. She was a simple German woman sentimentally in love, but surrounded by a nimbus of royalty which caused Fersen, who looked upon Hapsburgs and Bourbons as races apart, superior to other mortals, to think of her as 'the most perfect creature I have ever known', 'an angel of goodness', 'the very epitome of courage'. He adored and worshipped her as the Queen of France, but he was never physically in love with her as he was with Eleanor Sullivan.

The unsuspecting Marie Antoinette had as a rival the daughter of a theatrical costumier from Lucca. Eleanor Franchi, who at one time had had a brief but passionate affair with the young Emperor Joseph, began her career as the mistress of the reigning Duke of Württemberg by whom she had two children. She had since wandered all over Europe until she came to Paris and met an Irish officer, Captain Sullivan, sufficiently idealistic to marry her and to take her with him to India. Here she soon abandoned him for Quentin Crawford, known as the Nabob of Manila, who, while still in his early twenties, had amassed a vast fortune in the Philippines. Having made his money he retired to live in Paris, taking with him Eleanor Sullivan. There her opulent beauty adorned by Crawford's diamonds made her the perfect hostess to the brilliant circle which met in his splendid mansion in the Rue de Clichy. From all accounts Eleanor Sullivan had an extraordinary fascination, one of those chameleon women who could be anything to any man, a gift she appears to have handed down to her grandson, the celebrated dandy the Comte d'Orsay.

Fersen's devoted sister was shocked at her brother's deviations and, thinking of Marie Antoinette, wrote, 'I pray she never knows of this for it would cause her so much pain.' But Axel, who has come down to history as the '*chevalier sans peur et sans reproche*', had no hesitation in becoming the friend of Quentin Crawford and the lover of his mistress, and later in enlisting their help in what was to culminate in the ill-fated flight to Varennes.

By the beginning of 1790, Marie Antoinette was finding life at the Tuileries so intolerable that she was ready to contemplate any form of escape. All those who still upheld the monarchy knew it could never survive in Paris. Men whose views were as diametrically opposite as Fersen and Mirabeau realized that the King would have to leave the capital. But whereas Fersen thought in terms of flight, a furtive escape across the frontier, Mirabeau's plan was at once bolder and more dangerous and, had it succeeded, it could have saved the throne. Mirabeau believed that all men could be bought. His plan was for the King to buy political support in the Assembly, beginning with Mirabeau's own; to finance an efficient propaganda campaign in his favour and, when the time seemed propitious, to leave openly for a tour of the provinces. Once installed in a loyal town like Rouen, he could dissolve the Assembly and appeal to the country as a whole. The plan was not impossible, for there were large areas of France where the people were still attached to the King and disgusted with the excesses committed in Paris and the revolutionary measures rushed through by the Assembly. Nevertheless it entailed the risk of civil war, something to which King Louis would never consent.

During the whole of his first winter at the Tuileries, Louis remained in a state of apathy, accepting without protest the changes in his status, to rule by law rather than by divine right, to be called 'King of the French' rather than 'His Christian Majesty, King of France and of Navarre'. He did not even attempt to prevent the publication of the famous *Livre des Comptes*, the red book listing all the court expenses, going back over the years with the details of the various emoluments and gifts handed out to the Polignacs and their circle. The one stipulation he made was in defence of his grandfather's memory in preventing the publication of the sums squandered by Louis xv on his favourites. The King's exaggerated reverence for his grandfather and the indifference with which he allowed the list of her personal gifts to her friends to be seized on by the gutter press infuriated the Queen, who was now subjected to a fresh campaign of calumny and defamation. Hurt and unhappy, she shut herself up in her apartment, seeing no one but her children, denying access even to Count Fersen, whose name figured in the red book as the recipient of royal favour in the free grant of the command of a regiment.

Shortly after the publication of the red book came the news of the Emperor Joseph's death. For the past year he had been suffering from an inflammation of the lungs, slowly wasting away, still trying to cope with the running of an empire he no longer had the strength to rule. One reversal had followed on another. All his reforms had come to nothing, all his wars had ended in disaster. In his own strange way he had loved his sister, and the fact that he felt himself powerless to help her added to his humiliations and aggravated his disease.

Philippe de Ségur, on his way back to Paris from St Petersburg, painted a pathetic picture of the dying Emperor. When Ségur told him that Marie Antoinette was in a critical situation and asked him for a letter to his sister, the Emperor replied, 'Me? How can I give you a letter for her? Everywhere the people are in arms, everywhere there are brigands – at the slightest suspicion a traveller is arrested. If one found on you a letter from me, I do not know what would happen to you.' What about a verbal message? asked Ségur. But the sick man replied brusquely, 'What advice can I give? What do you want me to say? I commiserate with them, but from this distance I cannot think of any means to extricate them from so bad a situation other than to show both prudence and firmness. If they have both, then everything will perhaps arrange itself. If they lack them, then I have nothing more to say.' They were harsh words coming from a man who had lost faith in himself, and Ségur did not have the courage to repeat them to Marie Antoinette, to whom Joseph had always been the heroic figure who at the ultimate hour would come to rescue her. The new Emperor Leopold was a stranger whom she had not seen since he had left for Florence to govern Tuscany when she was a little girl.

CHAPTER

32

In February 1790 the Emperor Leopold wrote to his sister, giving her the
news of their brother's death,

> I can picture your grief, all the greater as his late majesty was particularly
> attached to you and had your interests so very much at heart. Though I
> know such a loss is irreparable, I hope you will find in me a friendship and
> attachment and a real and sincere interest in everything that concerns you, which
> will be in no way less than that of our late brother. Please give me the same
> friendship, the same confidence in return, and I flatter myself that I will in every
> way deserve it.

Unfortunately Leopold was to reign as emperor for barely two years before
he died at the age of forty-nine. He was the cleverest of the Hapsburgs, and
after 200 years is still remembered in republican Tuscany as the wisest and
most enlightened of rulers. To stamp out rebellion in Brabant (the Austrian
Netherlands), pacify Hungary, make peace with Turkey and win back the
confidence of the Austrian Church and aristocracy, alarmed by Joseph's
radical reforms, were the priorities which claimed his attention, rather than
the cause of France. He is reported to have said, 'I have a sister in France, but
France is not my sister.'

Marie Antoinette was to blame her brother for not having lived up to the
promises made in his first letter. Axel Fersen, who thought the Emperor
should mobilize all his forces to come to the aid of his unhappy sister,
dismissed him as 'a complete Italian, a real Machiavelli who always remained
a little duke of Tuscany'. But Leopold, who had as poor an opinion of Louis
XVI as his brother Joseph, must have found it hard to think of assisting a
monarch who accepted without question the decrees of the National
Assembly and the tutelage of Lafayette. He must have had an even poorer
opinion of the émigrés who kept pouring into his dominions and who were
for the most part both conceited and disloyal, many of them filled with so
much hatred of the Queen that Marie Christine, Regent of the Netherlands,
complained that in her own park in Brussels the French were repeating such
slanderous libels about her sister that she would like to send the whole lot of
them packing across the frontier. Small wonder if Marie Antoinette in her
first letter to the new Emperor wrote, 'The most sincere of all my wishes is
that you should never meet with disloyalty and ingratitude, for in my own sad
experience I know that this is the bitterest thing of all.'

Never consciously cruel or unkind, generous to a fault, too ready to give

posts and pensions to those who were often unworthy, Marie Antoinette
may have been stupid and careless, but these were hardly qualities to justify
the wave of hatred passing through France. Her ladies-in-waiting and all
those who lived in her intimacy were devoted to her. Many of them came
back from exile to serve her to the end, frivolous young women of fashion
ready to become martyrs out of love for their Queen. Those who were more
critical noted her failings. Lafayette and Madame de la Tour du Pin agreed
that, 'Though the Queen has everything that is needed to gain the heart of
the Parisians, a pride and bad temper she does not know how to control end
in alienating them.' The diamond necklace affair had destroyed her faith in
her subjects, and she had since found it impossible to trust a Frenchman.
By nature she was frank and open, and it was an effort for her to dissemble
and be charming to people she disliked like Lafayette, though he had
earned her gratitude in getting rid of the Duc d'Orléans. Fearing the
results of a commission set up to enquire into the excesses committed at
Versailles on the night of 5 October, Philippe d'Orléans had allowed
himself to be intimidated by Lafayette into leaving for England on a
trumped-up mission intended to save his face. Left without a leader, the
Orléanist party lost much of its prestige.

Throughout the whole of 1790, Lafayette occupied a precarious pedestal
as ruler of Paris. Gouverneur Morris, who in common with Mr Jefferson
had little admiration for 'the hero of two worlds', wrote, 'Unfortunately for
himself and for his country he has not the talent the situation requires.' By
now the Assembly had succeeded in securing legislative, executive and
judiciary powers and the King and his ministers were virtually impotent.
Madame Necker had been right in prophesying that her husband would
tarnish his reputation in accepting a third term of office. For in the past year
the great banker, the idol of France, had shown himself to be a man of
straw, trying to bolster a bankrupt economy with the introduction of paper
money, the famous *assignats*, the currency of the Revolution. Subjected to
the scathing attacks of Mirabeau, distrusted by the King and Queen, and
alarmed by the growing state of anarchy, Necker resigned from office
before the end of the year, leaving the two rivals, Lafayette and Mirabeau,
to try and control a revolution they had been the first to encourage. However much they might dislike one another, both were agreed that by now it
had gone far enough. During the whole of the winter of 1790 Mirabeau
tried in vain to make contact with the court. His first approach was
to the Comte de Provence, but Monsieur had no intention of seconding
a plan which might help the brother whom he had always hoped to
replace.

Cold-shouldered by Monsieur, Mirabeau turned in despair to his friend
de La Marck, telling him, 'What are these people thinking about? Don't they
see that they are walking on an abyss, that unless they listen to me they will

perish miserably and the people will stamp on their corpses. They do not understand the danger of the situation.' But how could de La Marck persuade either the King or Queen that a man whose notorious immorality filled them with horror, and whose violent diatribes against the monarchy had shown him to be one of their most dangerous enemies, had suddenly been converted to their cause? Unable to convince them of Mirabeau's sincerity, Comte de La Marck left for his estates in the Low Countries, from where he was recalled after a few months by Comte Mercy d'Argenteau. After all these years, the Austrian ambassador was still Marie Antoinette's wisest and most experienced counsellor, who succeeded in prevailing on the Queen to conquer her prejudices and accept the services of the greatest orator in the Assembly. These services were expensive, for not only had the court to pay Mirabeau's enormous debts but at the same time to guarantee him a monthly salary of 6,000 livres.

Freed of the creditors who had been harassing him for years, Mirabeau indulged in a mood of euphoria, convinced that he could save the monarchy, and attributing to the Queen qualities she was far from possessing. Dismissing the King as a nullity, he placed all his hopes in Marie Antoinette, 'a worthy daughter of the great Maria Theresa'. But though she may have inherited her mother's courage and moral standards, Marie Antoinette lacked both her political acumen and her ability to compromise. And it was only when the nationalization of Church property and the threat of a legal constitution for the clergy roused the King from his habitual lethargy into active opposition to the Assembly that the Queen finally consented to give an interview to Mirabeau.

The interview took place early one morning in the gardens of St Cloud where, largely through the influence of Lafayette, the court had been allowed to spend the summer holidays of 1790. The meeting was strictly secret. All its success depended on the fact that Mirabeau must never be known to be an agent of the Crown. Later Marie Antoinette confessed to de La Marck that she was so overcome with revulsion at the sight of that huge, pock-marked face and leonine head that she almost fainted. But in her carefully worded greeting, which one suspects may have been dictated by Comte Mercy, she flattered the vanity of a man who until now had been ostracized by his own class. 'It would hardly be my place to see a man who time and again has spoken against the monarchy, without stopping to think how much a king contributes to the happiness of his people. But one has to make an exception for a Mirabeau.' The cynical politician, the experienced statesman was conquered by the ineffable charm, the extraordinary dignity of a woman who in spite of misfortune had kept all her powers of seduction. That neither of them trusted one another is shown by the fact that Mirabeau gave the nephew who drove him to the castle a letter to be handed to the National Assembly in case he fell a victim to the perfidy of the court. But they were mutually impressed, and by the end of their meeting each believed the other to be sincere. With that natural spontaneity which was part of her fascination, Marie Antoinette gave her hand to kiss to a man whom only a few weeks ago she had believed to be one of the instigators of the October riots. And Mirabeau, who had thundered against her in the Assembly, went down on his knees before her and with tears of emotion told her, 'Madame, I swear the monarchy will be saved.'

It was the only time they ever met, but though Marie Antoinette recognized in Mirabeau the one man with sufficient power to help them, she was at the same time appalled at his cynicism and as frightened as the King at the prospect of civil war. He earned his salary by condemning the flood of revolutionary measures which kept pouring out of the Assembly. He even joined the newly formed club which met in the Convent of the Jacobins and which was frequented by the deputies of the extreme left. But he joined in order to restrain the tide of revolution rather than to promote it, and he went so far as to advise the King to take one of its members into his government, 'for a Jacobin minister does not always remain a Jacobin'. But a man of Louis' temperament would never understand advice of this kind. And the memorials which Mirabeau sent month after month to instruct the King as to how to deal with the current political situation contained advice which neither Louis nor Marie Antoinette was capable of following.

That summer there was every chance of carrying out the plans made by Mirabeau. At St Cloud surveillance was relaxed and the King went hunting again, accompanied only by one of the General's aides-de-camp. The Queen and her children went picnicking in the woods, sometimes driving as far as Meudon. Monsieur and Madame, who had rented a small house in the neighbourhood, drove over for supper, and family life resumed its quiet, even tenor. Louis' health benefited by the violent exercise so necessary for one of his lethargic constitution, and Marie Antoinette regained some of her lost youth in the company of a few chosen friends, Marie Thérèse de Lamballe, the Duchesse de Fitz-James and the Princesse de Tarente, women who were not afraid to advertise their loyalty to the Queen. Foreign visitors still came to St Cloud. Strange as it sounds, Georgiana Devonshire, accompanied by her mother, Lady Spencer, came to Paris in the middle of a revolution in order to have a baby without awkward questions being asked at Devonshire House.

Madame Elisabeth wrote to a friend in exile, 'Paris looks far better when seen at a distance. Here at least we are spared from being in constant contact with those dreadful people who, not content with being always at our gates, intrude into the gardens so that we have to listen to their horrible obscenities.' No mention is made in her letters of the presence of Count Fersen, whose friendship with the Queen she bitterly resented. But from his correspondence with his sister we know that Axel was living near by, staying with Valentine Esterhazy at his house at Auteuil. Esterhazy, whose intimacy with the young Queen had been disapproved of by her mother, had proved to be one of her staunchest friends. Referring to Fersen as *'le chose'* (the thing), he protected his relationship with the Queen, and throughout the summer there were frequent nocturnal visits to St Cloud. In one of Fersen's letters to his sister he confided, 'I am writing this from her house.' But in the following one he made a point of saying, 'I have not been to St Cloud.' However, there were plenty of eyewitnesses to note the constant comings and goings of the handsome Swede on whom Marie Antoinette was beginning to rely to a dangerous degree, and to whose advice she listened rather than to that of Mirabeau. His description of the Fête de la Fédération, one of the few dissenting voices in a general chorus of praise, shows only too clearly that Fersen was completely out of touch with the spirit of the times.

For this fête to celebrate the fall of the Bastille was one of the happiest events of the Revolution, in which all classes joined in a genuine outburst of patriotism, and the words *'Liberté, Egalité, Fraternité'* acquired a real meaning. For weeks an army of workmen, assisted by volunteers from every walk of life, had been labouring to transform the wide open spaces in front of the Ecole Militaire into a great grass amphitheatre. Elegant ladies and porters from the Halles together pushed barrows of earth. Talleyrand wrote that the Duchesse de Montmorency had a wheelbarrow designed by Jacob made out of mahogany with silver fittings. Fishwives and knights of St Louis, priests and prostitutes all worked happily together, singing *'Ça Ira'*, the theme song of the Revolution. The *fédérés* who marched into Paris under the banners of the eighty-three departments of France were all given hospitality in private houses in a spontaneous demonstration of friendship and good will.

Both patriots and monarchists had viewed with apprehension the approach of 14 July, the patriots because they feared the court might profit by the enthusiasm of the *fédérés* to stage a *coup d'état*, the court because they feared a recurrence of violence on the part of the populace. 'One has to take part, but how I dread it,' wrote the Queen to Comte Mercy. 'One is required to have an almost superhuman courage at this moment. And Lafayette is continually making us do the wrong thing. One gives in more and more. And it only ends in making those monsters still more insolent, while making decent people feel ashamed.' The Queen could hardly be expected to welcome celebrations which saw the apotheosis of Lafayette, and mass being celebrated on the high altar erected in the middle of the amphitheatre by no less a person than the notorious Bishop of Autun, who had been the first to vote for the spoliation of the clergy. The appointment of the young Charles Maurice de Talleyrand-Périgord to the bishopric of Autun had been one of the last scandals of the old regime when family patronage was still sufficiently powerful to secure a bishopric for the most dissolute of priests.

Contrary to all expectations, the Fête de la Fédération took place in a spirit of amity and good will. Even the rain failed to damp the euphoria of the 300,000 spectators who cheered Lafayette, the *fédérés*, the deputies, the King and even the Queen. Marie Antoinette, her children and the rest of the royal family watched from a window in the Ecole Militaire, while the King sat on a throne on an elevated stand reserved for the ambassadors and members of the National Assembly. Louis had wanted the Queen to share his throne, and both blamed Lafayette for refusing her this honour. Chivalrous as always, Louis stayed till the last moment at the window with the Queen. Marie Antoinette had gone to the lengths of wearing tricolour ribbons in her hair and of dressing the poor little Dauphin in the uniform of the National Guard. But for all her attempts to win favour with the public, those who were familiar with her various expressions noted that she was making a tremendous effort to hide her ill humour, and that the sight of Lafayette, mounted on a superb horse, directing the troops and receiving the lion's share of the applause, was almost more than she could bear.

The most moving moment was when the King rose from his throne to take the oath, 'I, King of the French, accept and swear to employ the power delegated to me in maintaining the constitution decreed by the National Assembly.' And in the enthusiasm of the moment almost every person present believed him to be sincere. It was now the Queen's turn to play her part in what she never regarded as more than a theatrical performance. Leaning out of the window, holding the Dauphin in her arms, she cried, 'Here is my son. He and I both swear to abide by the constitution.' And the outburst of cheering which greeted these words showed that the mystique of royalty was still alive in France, and that the monarchy was still sacred and inviolate.

Such was the ovation received by the King that Antoine Barnave, one of the most radical members of the Assembly, was later to admit that if Louis had known how to profit by the enthusiasm of those days the revolution would have failed. But a king who knew nothing of his country beyond the Ile de France was incapable of appreciating the spirit of patriotism that was struggling to be born. Like Fersen, he regarded the festival as 'an indecent bacchanal, devoid of dignity, a pagan ceremony celebrated by a renegade priest'. If only he had been able to act on the advice of Mirabeau and in those first days of popular rejoicing left openly for the provinces, which, given the mood of the moment, neither Lafayette nor the National Assembly would have dared to prevent. Loyal courtiers, like the Duc de Villeguier, the Duchesse de Luynes, the Comte d'Hinnisdal, all had carefully laid plans for the royal family to escape from captivity in Paris. But the King was not a man to mount his horse at the head of his loyal troops and run the risk of civil war. And Marie Antoinette, who for months had been urging him to leave, had to submit to his excuses. The one she must have found the hardest to accept was his saying it was impossible to go while the old aunts remained behind at the mercy of a revengeful mob.

By the end of the summer it was too late. The *fédérés*, when entertained in Paris, had been subjected to subversive influences. Agitators in the Palais Royal had undermined their loyalty, and only a few weeks after the day of the *Fédération* the minister of war, the Comte de la Tour du Pin, was reporting that army discipline was being undermined. A mutiny of the Swiss Guards stationed at Nancy, which on the orders of Lafayette had been harshly and efficiently repressed by General Bouillé, brought about a fresh outbreak of violence and a new campaign of hatred launched by Marat's *Ami du Peuple*, in which the Queen was accused of having ordered the execution of the ringleaders. Paris was again the scene of internecine strife: a duel between two hot-headed young aristocrats, one of them, Charles de Lameth, belonging to the extreme left, the other the son of the Duc de Castries, in which the former received a slight wound, resulted in the burning down of the Hôtel de Castries, an act of vandalism which Lafayette and his National Guards were either unwilling or unable to prevent.

Louis was ready to face every danger and put up with every humiliation until it came to his religious convictions. Though not a bigot like his father – for several laws benefiting non-Catholics had been passed in his reign – he was nevertheless extremely pious, and the civil constitution of the clergy, which followed on the confiscation of the vast tax-free church properties, affected him more than any of the other decrees introduced by the Assembly. From now on all the administration of church affairs, even to the appointment of bishops, was to come under the jurisdiction of the National Assembly. Independent of Rome, every member of the clergy was to become a salaried servant of the state, which was to take charge of all the schools, hospitals and charitable foundations formerly looked after by the church. Mirabeau had never shown himself more brilliant and more devious than in making an impassioned speech urging the Assembly to prosecute all priests who refused to take the oath to the constitution. At the same time, in one of his private memorials to the King, he advised Louis to sanction a decree which in most parts of the country would be so unpopular as to unite all malcontents behind the crown in resistance to the Assembly. The King was shocked by such bare-faced cynicism and only sanctioned the decree because he had no other alternative with angry crowds demonstrating against the clergy at the gates of his palace. But he signed with a heavy heart in fear of a schism with Rome and the anger of the Pope.

The first reaction to the decree came from the old aunts. In the middle of winter, Mesdames, travelling with a large retinue, left for Rome rather than stay in a country where they could no longer practise their religion in freedom. They had only got as far as Burgundy when they were arrested by units of the National Guard, who would have forced them back to Paris had it not been for the eloquence of Mirabeau, who succeeded in persuading a reluctant Assembly to let them go in peace. The proud Madame Adelaide would hardly have enjoyed hearing Mirabeau taunting his colleagues and telling them not to make themselves ridiculous by arresting 'a couple of useless old maids'.

It was one of the last services Mirabeau was able to render to the royal family, for two months later, in April 1781, he was dead, his powerful constitution ravaged by his own excesses. Drinking and whoring to the end, his last words on his deathbed were, 'You can now wear mourning for the monarchy, for I am carrying the last shreds of it into my grave.'

Marie Antoinette wept when she heard of his death. For all the harm he had done them in the past, she realized they had lost in Mirabeau the only friend they had in the Assembly who was sufficiently powerful to save them.

'*Liberté, Egalité, Fraternité*', the favourite slogan of the Revolution, the basis of the Declaration of the Rights of Man and of the as yet unfinished constitution, applied to everyone in the country other than the King. When the royal family tried to leave the Tuileries, to celebrate the Easter festival in St Cloud and take communion from a non-juring priest, they were stopped by an angry mob who, ever since the departure of the old princesses, had suspected the King of planning to escape from Paris. When Louis leant out of his carriage window to reason with the demonstrators, saying in a loud, firm voice that it was strange that, after having given his country its liberty, he should not be free to move himself, he was met with nothing but insults. And neither Bailly nor Lafayette could persuade the crowds to let him go, while the National Guards refused to intervene. After two hours of remaining besieged in their carriages, the royal family had no other choice but to return to their palace. It was a somewhat shamefaced Lafayette who helped the Queen out of the carriage and whom she addressed in an icy voice, 'Now, Monsieur, you will have to admit that we are no longer free.'

In a way Marie Antoinette had welcomed the incident, for it served to convince Louis that they would have to escape from Paris. Ever since December, she had been planning and plotting with Axel Fersen as to the best way of getting away. General Bouillé, who was in command at Metz, had been taken into the secret and chosen to conduct the operation which was to take the royal family to the small fortified town of Montmédy, the headquarters of the Royal Allemand, one of the foreign regiments not yet disbanded and still loyal to the King. From Montmédy Louis could rally support to his cause, and if all else failed the frontier was within easy distance.

A man of Bouillé's experience must have been shocked to find that the arrangements for the King's escape should be entrusted to a foreigner who was generally considered to be the lover of the Queen. There were many Frenchmen in Paris still willing to sacrifice their lives and fortunes for their King. Only a few weeks before, when the departure of the old princesses had directed the anger of the mob against the Tuileries, a few hundred nobles, armed with swords, pistols and even hunting knives, had rushed to the palace to defend their King. No sooner was this known to Lafayette than he appeared on the scene and forced the King publicly to disavow their action by making them hand over their arms, which were subsequently pillaged. It was a sad story, and yet another proof of Louis's refusal to allow a single sword to be drawn in his defence. Contemptuously referred to by Lafayette as '*les chevaliers du poignard*', these nobles either took the road to exile or stayed on in Paris to die by the guillotine.

The humiliations he had suffered at Versailles in the early years of his marriage had given Louis a dislike of his courtiers, so that he preferred to trust a foreigner like Fersen with the arrangements of a journey which Mirabeau had intended as an open gesture of defiance against the excesses of the National Assembly, but which by now had degenerated into a flight. Ill-starred and ill-conceived, it was a tragic adventure containing the elements of farce, with the King of France relying on his wife's lover to bring him to safety; with one of Fersen's ex-mistresses, a certain Madame de Korff, the wealthy Swedish widow of a Russian officer, not only supplying the passports, but paying for the luxurious *berline*, a vehicle far too heavy and too slow for a journey in which speed was one of the vital elements for success; with Fersen's current mistress, Eleanor Sullivan, and her Scottish lover, Quentin Crawford, giving financial assistance and hiding the showy *berline* in the stables of their mansion in the Rue de Clichy. Never were so many futilities treated as priorities as on this unfortunate journey. We find Marie Antoinette spending hours with Fersen in choosing the taffeta for the cushions and the white Utrecht velvet which was to line the green and yellow coach – a coach so ostentatious as to attract attention in every village. More time was wasted in ordering a *nécessaire de voyage*, which can still be seen in the Louvre, an exquisite object containing everything from a vermeil manicure set to a teaset in the finest Sèvres porcelain, but so large it had to be sent on ahead, ostensibly as a present for the Queen's sister, the Archduchess Marie Christine, who had only just returned to Brussels, and in the still troubled state of the country was bound to arouse suspicion on the frontier. Even the admiring Madame Campan ventured to question her mistress on the advisability of ordering a large trousseau of dresses and lingerie for herself and her children, 'For surely a queen of France would be able to procure whatever she needed wherever she went.'

But the most foolish of all was to entrust the court hairdresser, Leonard, with the Queen's jewellery, which he was to take either to Montmédy or across the frontier. The only possible reason for choosing a creature as hysterical, effeminate and totally unreliable as the fashionable hairdresser was that Marie Antoinette still wished to appear as the queen of fashion when she and Louis received the acclamations of their loyal troops at Montmédy or visited her sister's court at Brussels, where the Emperor was due to arrive on a tour of inspection of his subjugated provinces. To the very end she counted on the Emperor's help, on the 10,000 Austrian troops which were already in Luxembourg and which were to be kept in readiness on the frontier. But Leopold procrastinated. In the famous letter written by Comte Mercy to the

Queen, later produced at her trial, the experienced old diplomat tried to dissipate Marie Antoinette's illusions by telling her quite bluntly that the great powers were only ready to help if it was to their own advantage. The Emperor was the only one who could be counted on to help without an ulterior motive. But he would have to do so without arousing the opposition of Prussia, who was hand-in-glove with England. The most important thing of all, which had to be secured at any price, was the neutrality of England.

It was a chastening letter to receive for a queen who still believed that all the Kings of Europe would rush to the defence of their fellow monarch. Neither she nor her husband had taken into account the hostility of England, who had never forgiven Louis for the part he had played in the American war and who was only too ready to witness the humiliation of the Bourbons. Neither did they realize the envy which the arrogance of the Bourbons had aroused in all those European courts which imitated their manners and copied their palaces, but hated them at heart. Of all the *confrérie* of kings, the romantic Gustavus of Sweden was the only one who was prepared to lead a crusade in their defence. But his wild extravagance had left him with no money to pay his troops.

For the first time in their lives the King and Queen of France were desperately short of funds. So as not to attract the attention of the ministry of war, General Bouillé had suggested that the expenses of the operation should be paid for by the King. The movements of troops, the payment of horses and forage, of postmasters and postilions, could come to well over a million francs, and Louis like most kings was without private resources. His expenses at Versailles had been paid for by the treasury, and at the Tuileries the superintendent of his household was allocated the sums necessary for the maintenance of the court. Apart from a few shares in a water company which had been discreetly sold and sent abroad, he had nothing of his own, while all that Marie Antoinette possessed were her jewels, which could not be sold without arousing suspicion. In another of his depressing letters, Mercy had told the Queen that it was difficult if not impossible to raise funds, for all the courts of Europe except the English were heavily in debt and no more loans were being granted by the banking houses of Amsterdam.

After the death of Mirabeau Mercy had written, 'Everything goes against us. There is no fighting against such bad luck.' And for Marie Antoinette the worst luck of all was when the Emperor recalled his ambassador to Brussels to help pacify his rebellious provinces. The Queen no longer had a wise and experienced mentor to counsel prudence and prevent her from putting herself entirely in the hands of a foreigner like Fersen, however honourable and dedicated he might be. Apart from Fersen, the only person in whom both Louis and Marie Antoinette had confidence was Fersen's friend and protector, the Baron de Breteuil, who had emigrated in the first year of the Revolution and as Louis's roving ambassador abroad did more harm than good.

Neither he nor Comte Mercy was able to raise the necessary funds for the journey, and in the end Fersen mortgaged part of his inheritance and got his past and present mistresses to pay the rest.

Again it was Fersen who on the night of 20 June 1791, after endless procrastinations and delays, finally got the royal family safely out of the Tuileries, with the royal governess playing the part of the wealthy Madame de Korff travelling with her children, the King dressed as her steward and the Queen as the governess. But while Louis, wearing a plain brown suit with a round hat, looked perfect in the role of the solid, honest factotum, the Queen in her grey silk dress and wide-brimmed hat and veil looked far too elegant. Six people were packed into the *berline*, which Fersen drove himself as far as the first relay station at Bondy. There were the King and Queen and their two children, with the two extra places which, according to General Bouillé, should have been taken by two experienced officers who would know how to deal with an emergency, being occupied by two useless women, Madame Elisabeth and the royal governess, who could have travelled with the two maids in the carriage which preceded the coach. But court etiquette still prevailed. A Bourbon princess could not travel with her servants, while Madame de Tourzel, a typical product of the old regime, had insisted that it was her prerogative as *gouvernante des enfants de France* never to be separated from her charges.

General Bouillé's original plan had been for the royal family to be divided and to travel in two light carriages, a plan followed by the Comte and Comtesse de Provence who left Paris on the same evening and reached the frontier without the slightest difficulty. But the Queen and Fersen had insisted on the *berline* being fitted with every comfort for the children, from the tanned leather chamber-pots to the elaborate picnic basket, which Fersen's loving foresight had filled with every conceivable delicacy from roasted pigeon, cold veal and *boeuf à la mode* to a supply of wine and orangeade. For his part, the King had insisted on packing the heavy, gold-embroidered uniform he intended wearing when he inspected his loyal troops at Montmédy and presented General Bouillé with a marshal's baton, which also found a place in the luggage rack.

Of all that has been written on this unfortunate and ill-timed flight, what remains unaccountable to this day is why the King refused to let Count Fersen accompany the party any further than the first relay station at Bondy. The only possible explanation is that he did not wish to arrive at Bouillé's headquarters travelling under the protection of a foreigner generally considered to be the lover of his wife. With all the obduracy of the weak, he persisted in his refusal when, before leaving, Fersen begged to be allowed to continue the journey to Montmédy. For a man like Fersen, a king's command was irrefutable. But instead of taking the northern road to Mons, why did he not ride secretly ahead of the *berline* and warn the troops which, beyond

Chalons, in the area of General Bouillé's command, were posted at various relay stations along the route? He could then have given the vital information that the *berline* was travelling with several hours' delay, and the young Duc de Choiseul would not have deserted his post or sent the fatal message by Leonard to say that the so-called 'treasure' would not be passing that day. It was a mistake which was to haunt Fersen for the rest of his life and for which posterity has never forgiven him. He left the royal family, who had never travelled further than Fontainebleau, utterly defenceless except for their three bodyguards, one driving the coach, another on the box and a third as an outrider, all honest and devoted men but utterly unqualified to be in charge of what Fersen himself had called 'that delicate operation'.

It must have been agonizing for Marie Antoinette to part from the man she loved and to whom, in his disguise as coachman, she could not even say goodbye. The King's thanks, on the contrary, were so effusive as to surprise the postmaster at Bondy. He would have been still more surprised had he known that in the coachman's pocket was a note signed by Louis King of France bequeathing to him the sum of the 1,500,000 francs Fersen had handed over to General Bouillé to defray the eventual cost of military movements along the frontier.

In spite of his gratitude to the man who had delivered him and his family from captivity, Louis's spirits rose from the moment Fersen had gone. In a pathetic attempt to assert his manhood, he said to his wife, 'I will be another man when I have my bum in the saddle again.' And Marie Antoinette made a brave attempt to smile. Regardless of the fact that they were already three hours behind schedule and that by early morning the whole of Paris would be in a state of ferment, neither the King nor the Queen seemed to think there was any need to hurry. One can hardly bear to read of Louis getting out to talk to the local farmers gathered round the post-houses, discussing the prospects for the harvest, as if he were back in those happy days in Normandy. Enjoying the beauty of the countryside, both he and the Queen got out to stretch their legs and follow the *berline* on foot, while the children went chasing for butterflies.

While the slow, heavy vehicle driven by six horses rumbled along the sun-drenched roads of Champagne into the valley of the Marne, Paris had woken to the news that the King had fled. At an emergency session of the National Assembly, a young lawyer called Danton was accusing Lafayette, calling on him to bring back the King or to pay with his head. Madame Roland, one of the new heroines of the Revolution, who hated the general, was writing: 'It is now open war. There can be little doubt that Lafayette must have connived at the flight.' And for all his courage, the former idol of Paris saw himself already strung up on a lamppost. Secretly he may have wanted the royal family to escape, but he had no other choice than to send out messengers in pursuit, one of them an aide-de-camp armed with a warrant to arrest the King, but worded in such a way as to exonerate him from responsibility: 'The King having been removed by the enemies of the Revolution, the bearer is instructed to impart the fact to all good citizens who are commanded to take him out of their hands and bring him back to the keeping of the National Assembly.'

At Chaintry, which lay halfway along the route, the King was recognized, and the homage accorded him by the royalist postmaster was such that Marie Antoinette graciously accepted his hospitality and thereby caused further delay. At Chalons, where politics were divided and there was already a Jacobin club, Louis was sufficiently foolish as to lean out of the window, and again he was recognized. Nevertheless, they were allowed to drive peacefully through the town. And for the first time the Queen relaxed and said, 'At last we are safe,' when every mile was bringing them nearer to disaster. But how could she know that the peasants of the Argonne were at loggerheads with the militia and had behaved in such a threatening way that the young Duc de Choiseul, with only forty-eight men at his command, had deemed it wiser to leave his post at Somme-Vesle? How could she know that an ambitious young postmaster called Drouet was furious because the detachment of Hussars stationed at Ste Menehould had put up at a rival establishment instead of at the newly opened *Relais de Poste*; and that Leonard's garbled, hysterical messages, passed along the route, had ended in convincing General Bouillé that the *berline* would not be passing that day? While Lafayette's agents were gaining on them every hour and the ostentatious coach with its mysterious occupants was the subject of heated discussion in every village they had passed, the royal family, lulled into a false sense of security, were peacefully asleep when with a heavy lurch the *berline* suddenly came to a halt at the bridge of the little town of Varennes. The vindictive postmaster, who had laid a trap, thinking he had recognized the King, had succeeded in convincing the town procurator, an honest decent man called Sauce, that it was his duty to prevent the coach from going ahead till the identity of the passengers had been verified.

Again an element of farce is introduced into this tragic story, with the last act of the Bourbon monarchy being staged in a stuffy bedroom smelling of dried goods and tallow candles at the back of Monsieur Sauce's grocery shop. There was the fatal appearance of the man who had lived at Versailles and identified the King, falling on his knees and addressing him as 'Sire' – a loyal, harmless little man whom Victor Hugo described as one of the villains of the drama of Varennes. Louis, who still believed he was loved by his people, admitted he was indeed their King. A great wave of emotion passed through the overcrowded room, with the King embracing Monsieur Sauce and all the other municipal officers of Varennes, telling them the reason he had been forced to flee was that the knives and bayonets of the Paris factions were threatening the lives of both him and his family.

Meanwhile the Queen sat frozen with horror to see her husband embracing a grocer. But Louis was at his best with people of this kind, addressing them with such honesty and simplicity that for the moment it seemed as if even the vindictiveness of Drouet could not prevent the well-intentioned Monsieur Sauce from wishing his sovereigns good luck and helping them on their way.

But everything changed with the arrival of the officers from Paris, and the friendly, festive crowd which had gathered in the street, delighted at having their King in their midst, suddenly turned into dangerous, frightened animals ready to bite the hand they had been so ready to kiss. Lafayette's aide-de-camp, Monsieur de Romeuf, a chivalrous young man with a romantic attachment for Marie Antoinette, had tears in his eyes when he presented the King with the warrant. But his companion Bayon, an ambitious, unpleasant man of the same type as Drouet, was thinking only of the reward he would earn on bringing the King back to Paris. Louis gave one glance at the warrant and, throwing it on the bed where his children lay asleep, said, 'There is no longer a king in France.' Marie Antoinette leapt from her chair. Looking with scorn at the unfortunate Romeuf, she snatched the warrant from the bed and, throwing it on the ground, cried, 'I will not let my children be contaminated by this thing!'

By a strange twist of fate, the officer who tactfully bent down to retrieve the document was the young Duc de Choiseul who, after having lost his way in the forest of Argonne, had arrived in Varennes with his forty-eight Hussars, and with incredible courage had forced his way through the crowd and into Monsieur Sauce's bedroom to offer the King a last chance of escape. There were fresh horses outside for the royal family, and by cutting a way through the crowd he and his Hussars could get them to Montmédy. The Queen would have been only too ready to trust herself and her children to someone with the name of Choiseul, but the King replied that it would be monstrous to risk his family's lives and to murder innocent people. Playing for time, he still believed that Bouillé's troops would be coming to rescue them, while Drouet and Bayon were whipping up the crowds into a frenzy of hatred and fear, telling them that if Bouillé's German mercenaries arrived before the King had left they would have their crops destroyed, their houses razed to the ground. By now every national guardsman in the district was converging on Varennes. Ten thousand people in the streets were screaming, 'The King to Paris! The King to Paris!' and even the loyal Monsieur Sauce lost courage when a man cried out, 'To Paris, or I will shoot them all!'

It was seven thirty in the morning when, after nine hours spent in Monsieur Sauce's bedroom, the royal family walked out of the grocer's shop to face a hostile crowd. Choiseul helped the Queen into the coach, and with tears in her eyes she found time to whisper, 'Do you think Monsieur Fersen is safe?' The officer, who can have had little opinion of the Queen's friend, replied, 'I am sure of it.' 'Don't leave us,' she pleaded. But at that moment one of the national guardsmen struck him to the ground. And the last words she heard on leaving Varennes were: 'Arrest Monsieur de Choiseul!'

34

Under leaden skies in one of the worst heatwaves of the year, the royal family, exposed to every indignity and insult, started out on the nightmare journey back to Paris. The cruellest irony of all was that General Bouillé and his troops arrived only a few moments after the King had left. From the heights above the town on the other side of the river, the General could see the melancholy cortège leaving Varennes, with the coach so surrounded that any attempt at rescue would have been hopeless and the whole of the royal family could have been murdered long before he had reached them. Stricken with grief, feeling he had failed his King, Bouillé turned his horse's head and rode off into exile at the head of his loyal troops, leaving a country where nothing awaited him other than the scaffold.

No one spoke in the closed, stuffy coach. The King looked dazed, as if he were in a state of shock. The children had cried themselves to sleep. And, suffering from utter exhaustion, the Queen had fallen into a fitful slumber when she was suddenly awoken by horrible shouts. One of the local gentry, the old Comte de Dampierre, who had approached the coach wanting to pay homage to his sovereigns, had been struck down and decapitated by one of the guards. When the Queen asked the reason for the noise, the only answer she got was that 'a madman' had been killed. In some places the inhabitants were openly hostile; in others, as in Chalons, the local authorities, who were still royalist at heart, did everything in their power to honour their captive King, even going to the lengths of presenting him with the keys of the city and lodging him at the *intendance*, where twenty years ago the young Dauphine had spent one of her first nights in France. For all their sympathy, no one now dared to cheer. And Marie Antoinette had to be grateful when a few young girls had the courage to bring her flowers.

The morning brought a rude awakening. To royalist Chalons came a band of republicans from Rheims made up of the dregs of the city, screaming insults against the Queen. They erupted into the courtyard of the *intendance* while the royal family were at mass, celebrating the *Fête Dieu*. In fear of a fresh outbreak of violence and a fight between the republicans and the decent people of Chalons, the authorities hurried on the King's departure, but not before Marie Antoinette, with her inimitable grace and charm, had thanked her hosts for the warmth of their hospitality, 'regretting that circumstances prevent us from staying a little longer among our loyal subjects of Chalons'.

A very different welcome awaited them at Epernay, where only a young officer who had served at Versailles and who was in command of a local troop of National Guards, managed to save their wretched bodyguards, sitting handcuffed on the box, from being lynched by the mob. The violence of the demonstrators was such that the Queen's dress was torn when they got out to dine at the inn, and had to be sewn up by the innkeeper's daughter. The spectacle of the King of France, dirty and sweating in his dusty brown suit, served to rouse the people to a fury of resentment, as if they were unable to forgive him for having destroyed his own image and torn the last shreds of the nimbus of royalty which until now had rendered him inviolate. At Epernay a man spat in his face, and for once Louis broke down and tears rolled down his cheeks. To protect her husband the Queen went to the window of the coach with her son in her arms, but a man in the crowd called out, 'Don't show us the brat. Everyone knows it has not been sired by that fat pig.'

After the horrors of Epernay, Marie Antoinette lived in terror of what awaited them further along the road and the arrival of the three deputies sent by the Assembly to escort them back to Paris was welcomed with an almost hysterical relief. The Queen opened the coach door and both she and Madame Elisabeth, in a nervous, overwrought manner, begged the gentlemen to protect the wretched bodyguards who had nearly been massacred at Epernay. This concern for her servants came as a surprise to Pétion and Barnave, both of whom belonged to the left and who had been indoctrinated to think of the Queen as 'a heartless wanton who thought of no one but herself'. Both Pétion and Madame de Tourzel have left detailed accounts of the two-day journey to Paris, made in conditions of appalling heat, in which the clouds of dust churned up by the crowds which gathered in every town and village made it impossible even to open a window. Eight people, including two children who had to be taken on the knee, were crowded into the airless coach, where the austere Barnave was embarrassed by the heady scent of the Queen's perfume, which she sprinkled liberally to purify the air. Pétion, a fussy, conceited bureaucrat, enormously pleased with his appearance, was chiefly concerned with the impression he was making on Madame Elisabeth, whom he found utterly charming: 'Our arms touched, a current of sympathy passed between us, which in other circumstances might have developed into something more.'

Madame de Tourzel rejected these insinuations with a pious horror, but described how the Princess did most of the talking, explaining in detail the circumstances which had forced the King to retire to Montmédy. And from Madame Elisabeth's own account, in a letter to a friend in exile, it would seem as if the journey had not been such a nightmare as Madame de Tourzel would have us believe: 'You may think it was all terrible, but the deputies were really quite pleasant and Monsieur Barnave in particular behaved extremely well.' This high-spirited young woman of twenty-seven, who till now had lived in the cloistered atmosphere of a household composed entirely of women, to which even the husbands of her friends were invited only on formal occasions, may well have looked upon the journey as an adventure rather than an ordeal.

The Queen spoke very little on that first day. When Pétion had the misfortune to ask her the name of the foreigner who had driven the coach as far as Bondy, she replied that she was not in the habit of knowing any of her coachmen's names and, pulling down her veil, put an end to all further conversation. Pétion's companion, Antoine Barnave, was as silent as the Queen. The young deputy from the Dauphiné was one of the most ardent and dedicated of revolutionaries. Protestant by birth, he came from a good bourgeois family and as a boy had had the humiliating experience of seeing his mother turned out of her box at the theatre of Grenoble to make room for a party of local aristocrats. He had grown up with a hatred of the aristocracy and of the court, and he now found himself shut up for two days in the company of a woman he had been taught to abhor, but whom he found to be a simple, loving mother fussing over the comfort of her children, handing her little son over to the King to be put on his chamber-pot. It was the Dauphin who broke the silence by wishing to show off his cleverness in spelling out the letters of the words engraved on the buttons of Barnave's coat: '*Vivre libre ou mourir.*' The young deputy flushed with embarrassment and the Queen smiled one of those entrancing smiles which lit up the whole of her pale, tired face.

Many of her contemporaries assert that by now Marie Antoinette had lost much of her beauty and that there was little left of the radiant and somewhat vapid young woman painted so often by Vigée-Lebrun against the backgrounds of Versailles and Trianon. The Polish artist Kucharski, who in this year of 1791 was admitted to the Tuileries, painted a very different Marie Antoinette – a woman looking older than her thirty-six years but still infinitely appealing and infinitely seductive. The mouth is proud and contemptuous, but the eyes beneath their dark, arched brows have a puzzled, questioning look as if trying to understand the reason for the hatred she inspires. 'What have I ever done to deserve it?' is the question she seems to ask, the question she was later to ask Barnave when, on approaching Meaux, a howling band of hooligans attacked a humble *curé* who was trying to approach the coach and who would have suffered the same fate as the old Count at Ste Menehould had not Barnave leant out of the carriage and called out in a loud clear voice, 'Frenchmen, you who consider yourselves to be brave, do you want to degenerate into a nation of assassins!' Such was the strength of his personality that the crowds parted and the *curé* was allowed to depart in peace. And in spite of her unhappiness and fear Marie Antoinette knew that this shy young revolutionary was ready to become her champion.

That evening, in the gardens of the bishopric of Meaux, the King and

Queen had a talk with Barnave. Louis spoke little and retired early to his apartment. But the Queen stayed far into the night talking to the young deputy, who expounded his views with a fervour such as no one had dared to express in front of her before. And she who was usually so proud and so uncompromising admitted that evidently she and the King had been mistaken in believing that the whole country outside of Paris was on their side and that the journey to Varennes had shown them what subversive propaganda could achieve.

The last day of their journey from Meaux to Paris was one of unmitigated horror, and not even Barnave's chivalry could protect Marie Antoinette from the insults of the crowds, which, as they approached the capital, became ever larger and more hostile. When one of the military escort complained of hunger and the Queen in her kindness offered him a piece of beef which remained of the provisions provided by Fersen, a woman called out, 'Don't touch it! She has probably poisoned it.' The Queen's eyes filled with tears, and without saying a word she gave the beef to the Dauphin to eat. All through a day of scorching heat and pulverizing dust, the carriage blinds had to be left open so that the crowds could feast on the humiliation of their King, and horrible faces which terrified the children kept peering into the windows. The feeling in Paris, whipped up by the Republican press, was so violent that the municipal authorities had decided that the coach should go by the outer boulevards, thereby avoiding the popular quarters of St Denis, and placards had been put up all along the route to say that whoever insulted the King would be flogged and whoever cheered him would be hanged. Though every rooftop and window along the Champs Elysées was packed with faces, every man kept on his hat and the only shouts to be heard were '*Vive la nation!*'

Lafayette was at the entrance to the Tuileries celebrating his precarious triumph as the idol and the hostage of the mob, who today were willing to adore him and yesterday had been ready to string him up on a lamppost. By him were his brother-in-law, the Vicomte de Noailles, and the young Duc d'Aiguillon, both of them fervent converts to the new order and officers in the Parisian militia. By a curious twist of fate, it was a Choiseul who had helped Marie Antoinette into the carriage at Varennes, and the son of her old enemy d'Aiguillon who now rushed to protect her from being attacked by a band of hooligans and to carry her in his arms into the palace. In their attitude to the Queen, the Parisians showed that they considered her to be chiefly responsible for the flight to Varennes. Her children on the contrary were welcomed with good humour, even with endearments, while a deputy who tried to insult the King was immediately shouted down. Louis mounted the steps of his palace in silence, and in the words of Pétion, 'he looked as calm and unruffled as if he had come in from a day's hunting'.

The whole of the Tuileries was brilliantly illuminated. From all outward appearances the royal family might never have left. The palace ladies made their respectful curtseys to the dusty, dishevelled Queen. The *'grandes charges'* prostrated themselves before a king still wearing the uniform of Madame de Korff's factotum. The kitchen had excelled itself in the preparation of an exquisite supper. But in every room, even in the Queen's bedchamber, a national guardsman was on duty. And when Lafayette, holding his plumed hat under his arm, asked His Majesty for his orders, Louis replied with the plain common sense which never deserted him, 'It seems to me, Monsieur de Lafayette, that it is you who are giving the orders.'

The Queen's reactions were very different. The exasperation and the fury, above all the humiliation she had kept under control throughout the journey, now vented itself in a blind hatred of Lafayette. Sweeping past him without addressing him a word, she entered her apartments and immediately ordered a bath. But even here she found a guard posted at the door. Later that night, safe behind the curtains of her bed, she wrote a few lines to Fersen: 'Reassure yourself. We are still alive.'

Ever since he had left the royal family at Bondy, Fersen had been living in an agony of apprehension. The journey went smoothly, almost too smoothly, and by nightfall he was already across the frontier at Mons, pushing on towards Arlon where he hoped to have news of the safe arrival at Montmédy. But on that same day he ran into General Bouillé with the whole of his staff, and the despair on the General's face made words unnecessary. In a grief too deep for recriminations, neither blamed the other, though the arrival of the Comte de Provence, who, travelling in a light carriage with a single companion, had succeeded in reaching Mons without any difficulty, showed all too plainly the terrible mistake Fersen had made in ordering the slow and ostentatious *berline*. Monsieur's ill-concealed ambition was too well known for Fersen to have any illusion as to his secret delight at having his brother powerless and discredited in the hands of the Assembly, leaving him to take on the role of lieutenant-general of the realm, to which Louis had appointed him by letter when he left for Paris the day after the storming of the Bastille. That Louis had never endorsed that title and was never to do so was immaterial to a prince who saw himself as the real ruler of France.

The Archduchess Marie Christine, who had taken a violent dislike to all those French *émigrés*, welcomed the Swedish Count as a model of chivalry and rectitude. In a letter to her brother she recommends him as 'one of our sister's only disinterested friends'. Unfortunately the Emperor and Fersen were too dissimilar in character ever to be in sympathy. Axel thought only of his beloved Queen and made no allowances for the multiple problems which confronted Leopold in his heterogeneous empire. He blamed him for not displaying the ardour and enthusiasm shown by his own romantically-minded King. But whereas Gustavus envisaged life as a charade, with himself as another Perseus going out to destroy the Gorgon's head of Revolution, Leopold was a cautious, clear-headed politician who, had the flight to Montmédy succeeded, would have done all in his power to help the French sovereigns, but, as they were captives in the Tuileries, he could do little to help without the cooperation of the other powers.

He was in Italy at the time of the flight, and the first news received was that the operation had been successful and that Marie Antoinette had arrived safely in Luxembourg. His letter, written to her on 5 July when he still believed her to be free, is that of a loving brother delighted at the news:

> I have given orders both to our sister and to Comte Mercy to carry out your wishes in every way. I flatter myself you realize that being with me is like being in your own home and that you will not stand on ceremony with a brother who is as deeply attached and loves you as tenderly as I do. As to your affairs, I can only repeat that I have already written to the King. Everything that is mine is yours, money, troops, whatever you may want.

Her brother's letter took many weeks to reach the captive Queen, adding to her bitterness and disillusion. Though he was working day and night on her behalf, the first two months brought her no word from Fersen. With his cautious nature he may have been afraid of compromising her still further and of thereby adding to her difficulties. But his silence hurt her more than all the humiliations of those first weeks when she did not even dare to venture out into the garden for fear of the insults of the mob. Left without Fersen, she turned to Barnave, whose behaviour on the journey had inspired her with confidence and trust. Her woman's instinct told her that she had made a conquest of the shy young deputy from the Dauphiné, who for the time being was one of the most powerful men in France, representing with Alexandre Lameth and Adrien Duport what was known as the 'triumvirate', who still believed that a king was necessary for the working of the constitution in which they placed their hopes in an effort to combat the rising power of the Jacobins.

In those first weeks which followed on their return to the Tuileries, when a large section of the Parisian public was screaming for a republic and the King was too apathetic, too sunk in despondency to make the slightest effort, Marie Antoinette played a leading role in politics – a woman without any talent or experience, desperately fighting to save the throne for her son.

Marie Antoinette saw in the idealistic revolutionary Barnave the only means of alleviating the terrible conditions in which they were living at the moment. She had no constructive policy and, with no trust or faith in the French, believed that help could only come from outside.

Republican feeling in France was growing day by day. On 17 July a giant rally held at the Champs de Mars, calling for the abolition of the monarchy and the proclamation of a republic, which started as a peaceful gathering, ended in bloodshed. Two men discovered hiding behind the altar of liberty were immediately seized on by an inflammable crowd and accused of trying to set fire to the high altar and assassinate the republican delegates. The appearance of Lafayette at the head of a detachment of cavalry only led to further disturbances. A man in the crowd took a shot at the General, and for the first time in two years the forces of order fired on the mob. Fifty men were killed, the rest dispersed and fled, and for the time being the Jacobin leaders went into hiding. But Lafayette lost his popularity overnight, and in the following municipal election Bailly, a man of moderate opinions, was replaced by the left-wing Pétion.

Lafayette, Barnave and the two other members of the triumvirate, Duport and Alexandre Lameth, men who had hitherto hated one another, came together in an uneasy alliance to support the constitution which they considered to be the panacea of all evils. And as the constitution required a King, Louis was to be exonerated for the part he had played in the flight to Varennes. The declaration he had made on leaving Paris stating the reasons for his flight was ignored and he was officially declared to have been the victim of a royalist plot and taken away against his will. General Bouillé encouraged this story in writing to the Assembly, taking upon himself the entire blame for the expedition. Fortunately the General was safely across the frontier, but the three bodyguards, as well as the Marquis de Coquelat and the Duc de Choiseul, who had been in command of the Hussars at Ste Menehould, were all thrown into prison.

The King was made to understand that his whole future depended on his acceptance of the constitution, which he recognized from the very first to be unworkable. The Crown was so discredited that only a few men as loyal and disinterested as the foreign minister, the Marquis de Montmorin, were prepared to remain in office, where they were constantly criticized both by constitutionalists and republicans. The weakness of his ministers and Louis's own apathy and despondency were such as to force the Queen to take the initiative, and her first letter to Barnave, written early in July, was sent through an intermediary, the General de Jarjayes, whose wife was in service of the Queen. The loyalty of this young couple stands out as a touching example of devotion to a woman who was all too often let down, even by those she loved the most. Jarjayes was later to find his way into the Temple Prison, which even Fersen never tried to do.

Marie Antoinette wrote to Barnave, asking almost humbly for advice: 'I desire to know from you what is the best for us to do in the present situation.' Barnave was delighted, only too ready to put his trust in a woman who had subjugated him on the last day of their journey to Paris. His partners in the triumvirate were inclined to be more sceptical, judging Marie Antoinette to be too shallow and frivolous to be taken seriously. But politically they were losing ground and needed the Queen's help over two vital matters, one of which was to persuade the King to write to his brothers, and in particular to the Comte de Provence, ordering them to return to France and to break up the camps of *émigrés* near the frontier, which were forcing the country to keep 100,000 national guardsmen under arms. Even more important was for the Queen to use her influence with her brother the Emperor in getting him to accept the constitution as the true and lawful government of France, carried out with the King's full consent and cooperation.

The situation had changed so radically in the past year that Barnave and his friends now represented the moderate side of the Assembly. Pitted against the ever-growing power of the Jacobins, of men such as Danton and Robespierre, they were anxious to establish the legality of the constitution by gaining the support and financial aid of the foreign powers and renewing the family pact with Vienna, Naples and Madrid. Even the old princesses in Rome could be made to play a part in persuading the Vatican to recognize the civil constitution of the clergy. But Marie Antoinette had little faith either in the constitution or the words of a brother she had hardly ever seen. She had inherited neither the subtlety nor the diplomatic skill of her brilliant mother, and with her frank, impulsive character floundered hopelessly in a sea of intrigue and double-dealing.

The declaration of Pillnitz, signed by the King of Prussia and the Emperor, called on their fellow sovereigns to help in restoring the monarchy in France. But though both may have been inspired by the purest of motives, a short phrase inserted at the instigation of Prince Kaunitz was sufficient to rob it of its meaning: 'Their Majesties were only prepared to act should the other monarchs be prepared to join in the crusade.' '*Alors et dans ce cas*' was the fatal phrase which pulled the teeth out of the dragon's mouth and reduced the most menacing of documents into a puff of smoke. The Comte de Provence deliberately eliminated it from the manifesto which he had printed and distributed all over France, and which only served to incite the French people still further against the machinations of the Austrian Queen.

Marie Antoinette was in despair. Who were the worst, the *enragés* (madmen) or the *émigrés* who ignored the King's orders to return and acted as if they were the only legitimate power in France? 'My existence is an inferno,' she wrote on one of those stifling summer days when she did not even dare to venture out into the Dauphin's garden for fear of hearing the insults of the crowds outside. Shut up with a husband who barely spoke and who spent most of the day either reading in his room or working at an improvised forge with his favourite locksmith, Gamain; at loggerheads with her sister-in-law, who had only stayed behind out of loyalty to the King but who with her ardent, passionate nature was heart and soul with her brothers in Coblenz; without any of the friends whose company had been so necessary to her in the past, there were times when Marie Antoinette felt she could no longer stand the strain. 'It is simply not possible to go on living in this way. One runs the risk of quarrelling all the time. My sister-in-law is so indiscreet that one cannot trust her with the smallest secret,' she wrote in one of her pathetic letters to Mercy, who in the safety of Brussels appeared to have no idea of the appalling conditions under which they were living. They had no choice other than to accept the constitution which at least would give them the illusion of freedom. The guards would be removed from the Tuileries, for Europe must be led to believe that the King had accepted it of his own free will. A general amnesty would liberate all those who had been implicated in the flight to Varennes, and the King would again be given a bodyguard of his own with the faithful old Duc de Brissac in command. 'No doubt it would have been more honourable to refuse, but in our position what could we do?'

Throughout their negotiations, Barnave was the more sincere. Like Mirabeau, he endowed the Queen with qualities she was far from possessing. All she had was an indomitable courage, a blind belief in the divine right of kings, and a determination to preserve her husband's inheritance for her son. She recognized the noble qualities in Barnave, writing to Fersen: 'It would be unjust to deny that though he and his friends hold fast to their opinions, I have always found them to be extremely frank, strong-willed and inspired with a genuine desire to restore order by reinstating the royal authority. But whatever may be their good intentions, their ideas are too extravagant for us ever to accept them.' No doubt she was touched by the idealistic young revolutionary who had fallen in love with her half against his will, and who lectured her in the tone of a hectoring schoolmaster rather than a courtier. But the thought that she was deceiving him never seems to have worried her. That he risked the scaffold for her sake was of secondary importance in her heroic struggle to save the throne. Her sole aim in accepting the constitution was to gain time while waiting for help to come.

Meanwhile she let Barnave direct her actions, even to the lengths of dictating a letter from her to the Emperor in which she asked Leopold to recognize the constitutional monarchy in France and to make every effort to restrain the activities of the *émigrés*. It was a letter which suited Leopold's temporizing policy far better than the hysterical pleas for help she kept sending him through Comte Mercy. But the day after she had sent it, she was already writing to his ambassador denying the contents of a letter written under duress. 'You must have recognized at once, it was not at all my style. The fraud would be too humiliating if I did not hope that my brother would realize that in my present condition I have to do as I am told.'

The one person who made no allowances for her position was Axel Fersen, who for the past two months had been travelling across Europe trying to enlist help from kings and politicians who, with the exception of King Gustavus of Sweden, were increasingly reluctant to come to the aid of a King who did so little to help himself. As Catherine of Russia wrote: 'What can one do for people who do not know what they want and are continually championing two conflicting outlooks?'

The news that his adored, unhappy Queen was negotiating with Barnave infuriated Fersen, who looked upon himself as Marie Antoinette's appointed champion. Both in Stockholm and in Brussels they were saying quite openly that her relationship with the handsome revolutionary was not entirely platonic. In a mood of jealous pique the Count noted in his diary: 'Things are going very badly. The Queen is sleeping with Barnave and allows herself to be dictated to by him. She restrains the Emperor from taking any definite action and is against the princes.' It was time to break his two-month self-imposed silence. And the poor Queen, who had been sending him loving messages, most of which had never reached him, received a short, angry note: 'It may be necessary for you to accept the constitution. But how far do you intend to go? Do you really want to identify yourself with the Revolution, or do you still want help from outside? Have you a fixed plan as to what you intend to do? I only pray you have not been taken in by those scoundrels, who can do nothing for you. You must never trust them, only use them if you must.' He spoke of Barnave in the same way as he had spoken of Mirabeau, for in his overwhelming conceit and possessive jealousy he resented the Queen having any other champions than himself.

This cruel, unsympathetic note stands out in contrast to the sad, loving letter which Marie Antoinette wrote him on 4 July and which never seems to have reached him. Expressing all her frustrated passion for the most loved and loving of men, she begged him let her know where he could be found, for she was 'unable to live without writing to him'. It was sad that she found it necessary to excuse herself with Fersen by making a scapegoat of Barnave. The young lawyer from the Dauphiné, who was risking his life on her behalf, deserved more gratitude. 'You can rest assured I am not letting myself in with those *enragés*. If I see them and am in touch with some of them, it is only in order to make use of them. They inspire too much horror for me to be taken in by them.'

Barnave and his friends kept their promises. On 3 September, the day on which the King was presented with the constitution and ten days before the official acceptance, the restrictions were lifted from the Tuileries and the gardens were once more open to the public. In the Assembly, a stirring speech by Barnave resulted in a majority vote for the restoration of royal authority, the inviolability of the King, and a general amnesty which included the release of all those who had been implicated in the King's flight. The generous mood of the Assembly spread into the streets, and cheers for the royal family were included in the general outburst of joy. For the first time in many months, Marie Antoinette heard the cries of '*Vive la Reine!*' Royalists who had not dared to show their faces appeared again at court, and the Sunday mass held in the chapel of the Tuileries had never been more brilliant. Acting on the instructions of Barnave, who was always stressing the necessity of regaining popularity, the Queen appeared again in public and made a brave attempt to smile at those who only yesterday would have been ready to kill her. One evening, driving with her children through the illuminated streets, she turned to their governess saying, 'It's all so beautiful and all so sad when one knows that on the slightest provocation they would be ready to start again on the same atrocities.'

Nevertheless it was pleasant to have those few hours of freedom, to drive out into the forest of Meudon and enjoy the fresh air in the gardens of St Cloud. And poor fat Louis, who was in such need of exercise, was able to go riding again in the Bois de Boulogne. It was pleasant to go to the theatre and the opera and to be cheered by enthusiastic audiences. The one really happy event came when Marie Thérèse de Lamballe returned to the Tuileries. That this nervous, hysterical little woman should have come back to revolutionary Paris to be with her beloved Queen showed such a selfless devotion that at first Marie Antoinette did not dare to accept. In the past year she had sent her to England on a fruitless mission to William Pitt. No one was less likely to impress the cold English Prime Minister than the frivolous Princess, whom Fersen met in the same year at Aix and found 'as stupid and as gossipy as ever'. But her love and loyalty towards Marie Antoinette transformed her into a heroine.

> Don't come back, my dear Lamballe. Stay away in the country with your father-in-law .... You would weep too much over our misfortunes. The race of tigers who now abound in this country would be cruelly delighted to see how much we are suffering. But the acceptance of the constitution, which has become inevitable, will at least give us a few moments of respite.

Marie Thérèse ignored the Queen's advice to stay away, and by the beginning of September was back in Paris, lodged in the Pavilion des Flores and accompanying Marie Antoinette on every public occasion. As always, the

Queen tended to be too exclusive in her friendships, ignoring Barnave's advice to invite the wives of some of the deputies to the palace and to set up a court, since the Assembly had voted an adequate sum for a civil establishment. But what was the point of a court when all honours were to be abolished, when there were to be no *chevaliers* or *dames d'honneur*, and when even the Duchesse de Duras, one of the most faithful of her 'palace ladies', had resigned rather than give up her right to the *tabouret*. From now on it was forbidden for anyone to wear the order of the Saint Esprit other than the King, and so Louis decided he would not wear it himself. Barnave complained that Louis did nothing to make himself popular, that the people were on his side and would have liked to have seen their sovereign glittering with orders. But he kept away from them, only heard them spoken of by their enemies and never noticed if they were there.

The few aristocrats who still had seats in the Assembly did nothing to help their unfortunate sovereigns. Bitterly opposed to the constitutionalists who had robbed them of their privileges, they were more inclined to side with their open enemies, the Jacobins, than support men like Barnave and Lafayette. Abstaining from voting, they left the field free for the triumph of the Girondists, a republican party to the left of the constitutionalists, who took their name from the Gironde, the province to which most of them belonged. The spirit which was to dominate the new Assembly was already evident from the first day, when the King on arriving to take his oath found himself seated in an armchair in a line with that of the president. When he stood up to speak, all the deputies remained seated, and neither the applause nor the cheers which greeted his words could compensate for what he regarded as a public humiliation, depriving him of his divine rights by putting him on the level with a bourgeois president.

Madame Campan relates how on their return to the palace the King followed the Queen straight into her apartments, flinging himself down on a chair and putting his handkerchief to his eyes, saying in a voice strangled in tears, 'Everything is lost. And you, Madame, had to come to France to witness the humiliation of the monarchy.' Whereupon Marie Antoinette fell on her knees and took her husband in her arms, while the unfortunate waiting women remained rooted on the spot, not daring to move, till the Queen called out in a desperate voice: 'Get out! Get out!'

Later that night Marie Antoinette sent a confidential messenger to Vienna with yet another cry for help. But there was little Leopold could do. Pillnitz had been a failure. Prince Kaunitz was advising him to look after his interests nearer home. Russia and Prussia were planning yet another partition of Poland, and Austria must have a share of the spoils. For the time being it was better to recognize the French constitution and send an official letter of congratulation to King Louis. In the whole of Europe, King Gustavus of Sweden was the only monarch still ready to come to their defence, and in collaboration with Axel Fersen was planning yet another way of escape.

At the beginning of February 1792, disguised in a brown wig, travelling on a false passport as the servant of his orderly, the Swedish Count set out with the blessing of his King on a secret mission in which discovery meant death.

Marie Antoinette had begged him not to come. She who was so brave herself trembled for the man she loved: 'Your coming would risk our happiness, I am convinced of it, though at the same time I am longing to see you.' Fersen ignored the protests and after a comparatively uneventful journey arrived in Paris on the afternoon of 13 February. By five o'clock he was at the Tuileries. The door leading to the Queen's private apartments was unguarded and he entered with his own key. His morbid imagination had pictured her in a kind of prison and he was surprised at a luxury reminiscent of Versailles. The room where she was waiting for him was dimly lit, as if she did not want him to see the ravages of the past months, the white hair, the red-rimmed eyes worn out by tears and the endless deciphering of letters written in a complicated code for which she had often to call on the help of the clever Madame Campan. It is not recorded whether there were witnesses to their meeting. But whoever was there appears to have preserved an exemplary discretion.

Fersen wrote two accounts, one of them an official report to the King of Sweden, in which he referred throughout to 'Their Majesties, whom I saw on the evening of my arrival and again on the following evening'. But in his private diary, the famous *Dagbok*, he admitted to having spent twenty-four hours alone with the Queen and that King Louis joined them only on the following evening – yet another proof of the separate lives that Louis and Marie Antoinette succeeded in leading in the limited freedom of the Tuileries. Even those who persist in believing Marie Antoinette's relations with Axel Fersen to have been entirely platonic cannot really think that those twenty-four hours were entirely devoted to conversation. That laconic phrase '*resté là*', which one of Fersen's strait-laced descendants was at such pains to eradicate but which the untiring efforts of historians have succeeded in deciphering, is the key to a relationship which the Swedish nobleman was at such pains to hide, but which a woman as frustrated, as passionately in love and also as naturally indiscreet as Marie Antoinette never seems to have made any attempt to deny either in her letters to Comte Mercy or to Valentine Esterhazy. Much of the time must have been devoted to a detailed account of what had happened at Varennes. Tears must have been shed in recounting the humiliations of that terrible débâcle, for which Fersen blamed himself while the Queen blamed no one, only her unhappy destiny. She was heart and soul given over to Axel, who in those twenty-four hours succeeded in convincing her that he alone had the right to dictate her future policy and to act as guardian of her interests.

Fersen revealed his official mission, producing King Gustavus's plan for escape, which was discussed in all its aspects. It was a wild, desperate scheme involving a flight to England, coinciding with a descent on Normandy by Swedish and Russian naval forces. For twenty-four hours Axel and Marie Antoinette were again the bold, adventurous lovers, pinning their last hopes on a plan which held no future. On the following evening at six o'clock the conspirators were joined by the King. Whether Louis was unaware of what went on in his own palace or accepted Fersen on his face value as an official envoy of the Swedish King, he appears to have given him a warm welcome and spoken to him with an unusual frankness: 'I know the people tar me with weakness and irresolution. But no one has ever found himself in such a difficult situation. I had one chance of escape and I missed it. That was over two years ago after the fourteenth of July. Such a chance never came again. And now the whole world has abandoned me.' Fersen pleaded the loyalty of his royal master and his genuine desire to help. But Louis rejected his proposals as being too dangerous, not only for his family but for all those who would be involved in the operation. Also he had given his solemn promise to the Assembly to make no further attempt to escape. The Swede respected his decision as being 'that of a true man of honour'.

Ten o'clock was approaching, the hour when the night guards were doubled. The King returned to his apartments after bidding the Queen goodnight with his usual formal politeness. The lovers were left alone, but they had barely time for a last embrace before they heard the heavy tramp of the sentries changing guard. Fersen slipped out into the winter night, to start on what the Queen believed to be a long and hazardous journey, but was in reality less than a mile to Quentin Crawford's luxurious mansion in the Rue de Clichy, where a beautiful and voluptuous mistress was waiting for him with open arms. This is not an edifying episode in the story of the romantic knight errant, and it is hard to forgive the cold sensuality of a man who was capable of going straight from the Queen's bed to that of Eleanor Sullivan and of betraying King, Queen, and his friend Quentin Crawford all at the same time. Admittedly Eleanor Sullivan appears to have been the warmest and most sympathetic of women with whom he could luxuriate in misery, and would listen to him for hours talking of his unhappy Queen. Unknown to Crawford, who appears to have been absent for some of the time, Axel remained hidden in the attics of the Rue de Clichy for over a week, waited on by servants who believed him to be Eleanor's son by the Duke of Württemberg and whose arrival had to be kept a secret from their master. Eleanor divided her days between two lovers.

One evening after returning from the Théâtre des Italiens she described to Fersen the scene she had witnessed at a performance of Grétry's *Les Evéne-*

ments Imprévus. Acting on the advice of Barnave, the Queen, her daughter and Madame Elisabeth were in the royal box, and the management had ensured that most of the boxes were occupied by royalist sympathizers. Madame Dugazon, who played the role of a soubrette and was a passionate royalist, was sufficiently imprudent, when singing the aria '*O comme j'aime ma maîtresse*', to curtsey to the Queen. This gave rise to a storm of catcalls from the pit, and shouts of 'No mistresses!', 'No masters!' and 'Long live liberty!' Those in the boxes responded with cries of 'Long live the Queen!' and before long the audience had come to blows. The royalists being the more numerous, the Jacobins had the worst of the fray, 'and tufts of their long unpowdered hair were flying about the theatre'.

Fersen took pleasure in recounting this royalist triumph in his *Dagbok*; but the only result of the episode was to inflame passion still further against the Queen, who never went again to the theatre or acted on the advice of Barnave. Two days later Axel Fersen left Paris in the snow without making any further attempt to see the Queen. In his terse, laconic style he noted in his *Dagbok*: 'I told Crawford the same story as I told her regarding my imaginary journey.' It was not a pretty confession on the part of a man whom the nineteenth-century romantics have made into a hero.

Meanwhile in Paris the Constitutionalists were daily losing ground to the Jacobins and the Girondists. Neither the King nor Queen had known how to make use of their transient popularity. Unqualified to sit in the new Assembly, Barnave had left for Grenoble to canvass votes and be returned for the next Assembly. Before leaving he had a secret interview with Marie Antoinette. Fersen's lamentable influence had estranged the Queen from a young man who, touched by her misfortunes and by those he foresaw for his country, had genuinely desired to serve her, but who in the past weeks had noted with sorrow that her inborn prejudices and innate frivolity prevented her from following his advice. There had been futile arguments over the colours of the uniforms of the King's Household Troops, now known as the Constitutional Guards. Both Louis and Marie Antoinette had insisted on retaining the Duc de Brissac and the former members of his staff, whose very names were anathema to the members of the National Assembly. The result was that in the next few weeks the Constitutional Guards were disbanded and replaced by the National Guards, chosen from all walks of life.

Barnave wrote in a letter to the Queen shortly before their meeting at the Tuileries:

> I see that my advice does not correspond to the views of Your Majesties. I am afraid I place little hope in the success of the plan you now follow. You are too far away from any outside help, and you will be lost long before it can reach you. I only pray that I may be mistaken in my gloomy presentiments. I myself have no

doubt that I will pay with my head for the interest I have shown in your misfortunes. All I ask in recompense is the honour to kiss your hand.

During their last tragic interview, Marie Antoinette's eyes were bathed in tears. Both knew that they were doomed and the Queen had realized too late that the young Protestant lawyer was the noblest of all her champions.

Other champions came forward to defend her, but none as idealistic as Barnave. They were for the most part brave, dashing adventurers ready to stake a last gamble in their struggle for power. One of them was Louis de Narbonne, who in his youth had been protected by Madame Adelaide and was now the lover of Germaine de Staël and one of the few aristocrats who had given himself heart and soul to the Revolution, hoping thereby to satisfy an ambition frustrated at Versailles. The Queen had never liked him and had tried to prevent his appointment as minister of war. Now he aspired to even greater heights and in a dramatic interview announced that, given the post of Prime Minister, he would be able to save the country, whereupon Marie Antoinette laughed in his face with that clear, mocking laughter which had made her so many enemies in her youth. And Narbonne left the palace discomfited and angry.

The Queen made an even bigger mistake in refusing the services of General Dumouriez, a brilliant, complex man of many parts who at one time in his chequered career had been a secret agent of King Louis xv and served a term in the Bastille following the fall of Choiseul. Now he had attached his fortunes to the Girondists and was nominated as foreign minister in a government consisting almost entirely of members of their party. Of all the ministers who in the past years had been forced on the unhappy King, Dumouriez, whom the spiteful Madame Roland (wife of the new minister of the interior) describes as 'a witty rake', appears to have been the only one who obtained a certain influence over Louis and was able to rouse him from his apathy. But the Queen was never won over to his charm and all his attempts to ingratiate himself ended in failure. Madame Campan relates how on one occasion he went so far as to deny his revolutionary past, throwing himself at the Queen's feet, covering her hands with kisses and imploring her, 'Madame, let yourself be saved.' But Marie Antoinette remained quite unmoved, and when he had gone she told her waiting woman 'that she had never put her trust in traitors'. It was a decision she may have regretted when Dumouriez resigned from the government to resume his military career and lead the young armies of the Republic to victory at Valmy and Jemappes.

The spring of 1792 brought a series of disasters. On 1 March the Emperor Leopold died after a two-day illness, suspected of having been poisoned. His son Francis, a cold, unimaginative young man with none of his brilliance, had little interest in an aunt he had never seen. But the military training he had received from his uncle Joseph made him more bellicose than his father, and he had no hesitation in accepting the challenge when the French sent an ultimatum to the Elector of Treves, which was a fief of the Holy Roman Empire.

Two weeks after the Emperor's death, the French sovereigns lost the bravest and most ardent of their allies when King Gustavus of Sweden was assassinated by one of his officers in the middle of a masked ball. In Paris his murderer was acclaimed as another Brutus and publicly cheered outside the windows of the Tuileries while the Queen was writing to console her lover on the loss of 'the noblest of kings and the most devoted of friends'. It was a bitter blow for Fersen, who since his earliest youth had been a privileged favourite at court and now had little to expect from Gustavus's successor, a fourteen-year-old boy under the tutelage of his uncle, the Regent, who had always looked on the arrogant Fersens with disfavour and saw in Axel nothing but a liability to be placated with empty titles and assiduously kept away from his nephew's entourage.

'Since the death of our King, war remains our only hope.' For once Fersen, the Queen and the Girondists were all on the same side. Only King Louis resisted to the end, finally compelled to give way to the war fever which was spreading across the country. On 29 April 1792 he dragged himself to the Assembly to announce in a tired, subdued voice that having done all in his power to preserve peace, as he was in duty bound to do, he would now resort to war rather than see the dignity of his people insulted any longer. It was a sad little speech, vociferously cheered by an audience who wanted war to keep themselves in power and distract the people from the difficulties at home, the rising cost of living, the serious food shortages and growing unemployment.

War would provide an outlet for these people, an incitement to hate their enemies both within and outside the country, while giving them at the same time an opportunity for glory. No sooner had King Louis proclaimed war against the King of Hungary – for Francis had not yet been elected as Emperor at Frankfurt – than a campaign of vicious hatred was launched against the Austrian Queen and what was called '*Le Comité Autrichien*', which was supposed to meet in the apartments of the Princesse de Lamballe. From the assembly rooms in the former riding school, not a stone's throw from the Tuileries, the Girondists made thinly veiled attacks against the Queen. One of them, delivered by a brilliant orator named Vergniaud, was particularly virulent. Pointing a finger at the palace he cried,

> Terror and dread have often gone forth from this place.... Let all those who still live there know that the King alone is inviolate and that the law will, without distinction of persons, overtake the guilty sheltered there, so that there is not a single head which, once found guilty of crime, can escape its knife.

And the Queen, who was usually so courageous, felt afraid for the first time. 'Any kind of action would be preferable than letting ourselves be murdered in our beds,' she wrote to the Comte Mercy. But not all her letters to him were confined to cries for help. The sweet young Queen who had been so ready to love her adopted country, and who in one of her early letters to her mother wrote, 'When one is so well treated by people who have so little to be grateful for one feels oneself more than ever obliged to try to make them happy,' was now filled with disgust and contempt for those she called '*les queux*' (the rascals), who had turned against her. France to her meant no more than her son's inheritance, to be fought for to the end, even if it should lead to treason. There are royalists, and there are many of them, who would make a saint out of the martyred Queen and would have us forget the black page of her history, when Marie Antoinette deliberately betrayed her country in sending Comte Mercy the details of the French plan of campaign she had succeeded in obtaining from Dumouriez. But the Queen was not responsible for the disastrous defeats at the beginning of the war.

As the news from the front grew worse, the campaign of hatred against the King and Queen redoubled in violence. The few foreigners still left in Paris reported that outside the Tuileries the news vendors were selling obscene pamphlets on '*La Vie Scandaleuse de Marie Antoinette*', while in the precincts of the Assembly the King's name aroused catcalls and laughter, which the Girondist ministers did nothing to prevent. Roland, the new minister of the interior, whose ambitious wife now held a salon in the beautiful apartments where Calonne had formerly entertained the princes of the blood, was particularly aggressive in his behaviour to the King. Republican at heart, he and his colleagues were only waiting for an opportunity to depose the monarch. And now they tried to force him to accept a decree by which all refractory priests, when denounced by twenty citizens, could be deported. This decree, which affected his conscience, was impossible for Louis to accept. More ready to be a martyr than a king, he refused to sanction it, making use of the veto granted by the constitution. The Queen has been accused of having encouraged her husband to stand firm on the one occasion when it was dangerous to resist a popular measure. But it was the King, and the King alone, who, dictated to by his religious scruples, had the courage to defy the Assembly and dismiss his Girondist ministers, after Roland, in a particularly objectionable letter read out in full council, had accused him of going against the wishes of the nation.

The Parisians' reply to the King's veto was the manifestation of 20 June. Starting as a peaceful demonstration with the planting of a tree of liberty in the gardens of the Tuileries, it ended with the storming of the palace. A crowd of over 8,000 – shopkeepers, artisans, porters and market women, all armed with hatchets, scythes and pikes – came pouring out of the *faubourgs*, shouting, 'Long live the Girondists and down with the veto!' Not one of the soldiers on guard outside the palace made any move to disperse the crowds who, finding one of the side gates unlocked, rushed up the stairs, dragging a cannon and breaking down the doors.

The King was in an antechamber together with his sister, and there was a dangerous moment for her when she was mistaken for the Queen. Fortunately Marie Antoinette, who had tried to join her husband, had been prevented from doing so by some loyal officers who barricaded her and her children behind a large table in the council chamber. For over two hours the royal family had to submit to the insults of the crowds, while across the way the Assembly was in full session and the banners were flying from the Hôtel de Ville. It was not until evening that the mayor made his appearance, with the improbable excuse that he had only just heard of the attack on the palace. But the courage shown by the King, who throughout the ordeal had remained calm and imperturbable, listening to the harangues, accepting a glass of wine from a butcher, and even going so far as to try to put the Phrygian cap of liberty on his head, which was much too big for it, ended in impressing the mob. The Queen was even more heroic, standing barricaded behind a table, while the brewer, Santerre, one of the most popular leaders of the *faubourgs*, showed her off to the hostile crowd as if she were a wild beast in a circus. Once again her magic asserted itself, and many who had begun in abusing her ended by weeping in remorse. But when the last of the insurgents had left and Louis and Marie Antoinette remained alone in their desecrated palace, they realized that 20 June had only been the dress rehearsal and that there was worse to come.

'By a miracle I still exist. The day of 20 June was a nightmare. It is no longer only me whom they are against. They are also plotting to assassinate the King and they do not attempt to hide it. He showed such strength and courage that for the moment it has done some good. But the horrors could repeat themselves at any time.' This is only one of the many letters addressed to Fersen by a despairing woman who saw no hope in the future unless the allies arrived in time.

The events of 20 June had been followed by a brief reaction in favour of the King. Deputations had arrived from the provinces to protest against the invasion of the Tuileries. The more moderate members of the Assembly like Maurice de Talleyrand and the Duc de La Rochefoucauld Liancourt stood up to denounce the treatment of the King. Lafayette left his command at the front to make a courageous and impassioned speech in the King's defence. For a moment it seemed as if his former power had reasserted itself, and his speech was acclaimed by the majority. But his triumph was shortlived. With their pens steeped in vitriol, Marat and Hébert, the editor of the scurrilous newsheet *Père Duchesne*, were working up the people into a frenzy of hatred. Lafayette, the one-time idol of Paris, knew that he had lost his hold, but he could still make one heroic gesture by saving the royal family from disaster. The anniversary of 14 July was to be commemorated with the usual festival of the Champs de Mars. The King and Queen were to be present, as was General Lafayette at the head of a detachment of cavalry. The General's plan was to surround the sovereigns with his troops and in the ensuing confusion to bring them safely out of Paris. It was a bold scheme but one which might have worked, for the cavalry was still loyal to its General. But he reckoned without the chief protagonists. The King gave him a cold reception when he visited him in his palace, still full of splintered glass and with shattered doors. The Queen was even colder, for neither could forget or forgive the harm that Lafayette had done them. Now at the eleventh hour, when his own star was setting, he dared to propose himself in the role of saviour. 'Better to perish than be saved by Monsieur Lafayette,' was Marie Antoinette's proud reply.

Contrary to expectations, the celebrations of 14 July were comparatively peaceful. Having been alerted of a plot to assassinate the King, Marie Antoinette had persuaded her husband to wear a bullet-proof waistcoat. She herself had refused to wear one. Both her courage and her vanity recoiled from wearing such a bulky and disfiguring garment in public. As Lafayette commented with a certain bitterness, 'The Queen was always more concerned in appearing beautiful when in peril than of making any attempt to avert it.' But the celebrations in the Champs de Mars had none of the spontaneity and joy of 1790. And the *fédérés* who passed in parade beneath the balcony of the royal palace were very different from the happy, laughing men who in that year had cheered their King. In every town and province political agitators had been at work, corrupting and disseminating false news of royalists plotting a counter-revolution, of the King being in league with the enemy. And in all that vast gathering there was barely a cheer of '*Vive le Roi*!' Louis appeared even in the eyes of his sympathizers to be a pitiable figure in his embroidered clothes and carefully powdered hair, a relic from another age, cast out by his subjects.

The *fédérés*, who were supposed to leave Paris after the celebrations, stayed on at the invitation of the various clubs, entertained with copious supplies of wine and propaganda. Last to arrive were the Marseillais, marching through the streets, brandishing their swords to the strains of the song which Rouget de Lisle had composed for the army of the Rhine and which they had made into their own. Within a few days all Paris was singing the stirring words of the '*Marseillaise*', calling on all Frenchmen to rise against the enemy, '*Aux armes, citoyens*' – the enemy who was not only at the frontier but still within the Tuileries.

'The band of assassins is being continually swelled by fresh recruits. Tomorrow eight hundred are expected from Marseilles, and it is said that in a week they will have sufficient force to carry out their plans.' In one of her last despairing letters to her lover, Marie Antoinette made it clear that by now she had lost all hope. But she was not prepared for the final blow of the Brunswick Manifesto which reached Paris in the last days of July. Signed by the commander-in-chief of the allied armies, it was couched in such insulting terms as to unite Frenchmen of every creed and class against the enemy. How and why it should have been composed by Fersen remains a mystery. Axel could not have rendered a greater disservice to his mistress than in composing such an idiotic manifesto. Nothing is so indicative of the lack of cohesion and of leadership in the allied armies than that the Duke of Brunswick, known for his liberal sympathies, should have put his signature to this hysterical and ill-judged document written by a man who had no official status in his army.

Filled with hatred against the French, of whom Fersen with his intolerable conceit had the poorest opinion, it reflected all the emotional frustration of a man burning for revenge against those who had humiliated his beloved Queen. Time and again Marie Antoinette had asked for a manifesto to be drawn up by the allied powers, one which however was careful to draw a distinction between the Jacobins and the French nation as a whole, and to avoid any attempt to interfere in the internal affairs of France or to give too much importance to supporting the King. Every one of these instructions had been ignored. The Brunswick Manifesto threatened Paris with total destruction if the royal family were not protected or the Tuileries were again invaded. The French troops who did not go over to their legitimate sovereign, King Louis, as soon as the allied armies entered the country were liable to be shot and have their houses razed to the ground – an extraordinary manifesto for a general to sign who had not yet won a single battle, and which in later years the Duke himself would bitterly regret.

But Axel Fersen was delighted with it. 'By now you will have received the manifesto and you will be very pleased with it,' he wrote. At last the armies were on the march and it would only be a question of days before they were in Paris. In his unfounded optimism he was telling the Queen that on no account must she leave the city, that should there be another attack on the Tuileries she could always seek safety in the cellars of the Louvre. Marie Antoinette's faithful servants cannot have had a very high opinion of the knight errant who sent such absurd advice from the safety of Brussels, at a time when the republican leaders were demanding the abolition of the monarchy and the *faubourgs* were already under arms; when beneath the windows of the Tuileries the mob was chanting, '*Madame Veto avait promi . . . d'égorger tout Paris*'; when Marie Antoinette was spending sleepless nights waiting for the tocsin to give the alarm for the attack for which 20 June had been no more than the dress rehearsal. At that time Axel Fersen was already seeing himself in the role of Prime Minister, asking King Louis to delegate him the authority to choose a government when the allies entered Paris. In a tragic last letter received by Fersen when she was already in prison and no longer Queen of France, Marie Antoinette wrote, 'It is difficult to think of the choice of ministers when one is trying to avoid being assassinated.'

In the year to come, she was often to regret that she had not been assassinated on 10 August when 20,000 Parisians stormed the Tuileries. Even so, the palace could have been defended. There were 900 brave and dedicated Swiss brought in from their barracks at the Porte Maillot, supported by 2,000 national guardsmen, some suspected of being disaffected but others who under strong leadership would have remained loyal to their King. 'A brave man on horseback could have saved the day,' was the opinion of a young out-of-work lieutenant who, with the eyes of a great tactician, noted the failures and mistakes of defenders left without orders; of a fundamentally good-natured crowd turned within an hour into a horde of wild beasts thirsty with blood lust. Watching from a nearby window, Napoleon Bonaparte wrote to his brother, 'The King had only to appear and he would have won the day.' The Queen was of the same opinion as she waited surrounded by a few loyal friends, among them the poor little Princesse de Lamballe who, though shaking with terror, refused to desert her and kept saying to Madame de Tourzel, 'I am sure she is doomed.'

The night before, it had been decided to turn the palace into an armed camp and to defend it to the end. The Marquis de Mandat, a capable officer of the old school who commanded the National Guard, was in charge of the defence. But the revolutionaries recognized his qualities and early that morning had summoned him to the Hôtel de Ville, where an insurrectionary commune had seized control. Acting against the wishes of his wife, Louis had let him go, and within an hour he was decapitated and his body sent floating down the Seine.

The Assembly was in session, hesitant, frightened, many of the deputies still innately conservative, but having already lost control to the radical elements in the town. Of the 2,000 nobles still known to be in Paris and who had been summoned to take part in the defence of the palace, no more than 150 had complied, for the most part elderly men, survivors of another age, ready to die in fighting for a king many no longer believed in. The King himself, a pitiable figure in a crumpled purple suit and flattened wig, kept wandering listlessly from room to room, unable to come to a decision. Yesterday the Tuileries were to be defended to the last man. Now he was assailed by doubts and hesitations. The courage he had shown on 20 June had gone. In the worst crisis of his reign he appeared unable to act or think coherently. The Queen on the contrary was an inspiration to everyone, handing out food and drinks to the defenders, urging her husband to go out among them and make a stirring speech pledging himself to fight to the end. But the words she would have found so easily, the words with which the young Maria Theresa had once rallied the Hungarian nobles to her side, were not in Louis's vocabulary. With his wobbling walk and short-sighted look, he went around like someone who already knew his cause was lost, murmuring a few uncertain words to men who no longer had any faith in him either as a leader or a king. There were some shouts of '*Vive le Roi!*' but many more of '*Vive la Nation!*' and '*A bas le veto!*' His very presence seemed to spread the disaffection. By the time he had reached the battalion of gunners stationed at the drawbridge, the men were already fraternizing with the crowds outside and the few cheers had turned to insults: 'Down with the fat pig!' Some were even showing him their fists. 'Good God! they are booing the King,' cried a minister watching from a window. Marie Antoinette was also watching and, with tears of anger in her eyes, turned to Madame Campan saying, 'It is no use. He has done more harm than good.' She could not help but despise this heavy, inert creature who, on returning to the palace, flopped into an armchair breathing heavily, 'I have given my orders. No one is to fire until the assailants have fired first.'

By seven in the morning, the first of the insurgents had reached the

Tuileries, advancing in the hundreds and thousands from along the Seine, down the Champs Elysées and through the narrow streets of the *faubourgs* – a motley, disorderly crowd drawn from every walk of life, some of ferocious aspect, armed with cutlasses and pikes, those horrible weapons made famous by the Revolution; others decent, ordinary citizens, small shopkeepers and artisans, with a sprinkling of lawyers and professors, all of them united in their grim determination to abolish the monarchy. By now they had reached the Place du Carrousel, and their singing and shouting could be heard all over the palace. The loudest and most threatening of all were the strains of the '*Marseillaise*', with 600 *fédérés* shouting in chorus, '*Aux armes, citoyens!*'

Marie Antoinette was not afraid to die. Life without a throne had little meaning for her. When it was suggested that the royal family should seek asylum in the National Assembly, her instinctive reaction was to refuse. 'I would rather be nailed to the walls of the palace than to seek the protection of those who have behaved so badly towards us and desert those who are ready to defend us.' The public prosecutor, the Comte de Roederer, an honest man of royalist sympathies, had fought his way through hostile crowds to urge on his sovereigns the necessity to leave before the palace was invaded. His pleas were useless when confronted by a vacillating king and a furious queen whose will to resist increased as the situation became more menacing. An hour later he returned when the mob was already battering at the gates, and this time he addressed the King directly: 'Sire, there is not a minute to lose. The only place you will be safe is in the Assembly.' Whereupon the Queen broke in: 'We have a considerable force ready to defend us. We cannot leave our loyal nobles and our gallant Swiss to die without us.' And Roederer replied: 'Madame, you are hopelessly outnumbered. They are still coming in by the thousands. In staying you are endangering the lives of your husband and your children.' The courtiers who had been brave enough to remain looked first at the King, then at the Queen, who could no longer control her tears. For a moment there was silence. Then Louis put up his hand, as if to prevent any further discussion, and said, 'Let us go.' Marie Antoinette had no other choice than to obey. Taking her children by the hand, accompanied by their governess and the Princesse de Lamballe, she followed the King who had allowed his throne to be lost so easily. Defiant to the end, she called out to the stricken courtiers, 'We will be back soon.' But she knew that no one believed her, and that even the soldiers were contemptuous of a king who refused to fight. Louis never spoke a word until he reached the colonnade at the bottom of the great staircase, when he turned to Roederer and asked, 'What is going to happen to all those who are left behind?' and Roederer could only reply, 'Sire, they are not in sufficient numbers to resist for long.' And Louis, who was too honourable to let others die in his defence, gave orders for the Swiss to lay down their arms. These orders seem to have gone astray, and the Swiss, brave, disciplined and unimaginative, kept to their first orders, remaining immobile at their posts till the assailants attacked. Then, with the deadly accuracy of a first-class fighting force, they opened fire, and it was only a question of minutes before the courtyards were cleared of the rabble and the ground littered with bodies.

By now the royal family had reached the riding school, their guards having to force a way through a furious mob who covered them with insults and tried to prevent the Queen from entering the hall. The crowds were so dense that in order to protect the Dauphin one of the guards lifted him up in his arms. The Queen screamed, thinking he was about to be kidnapped. But it was the only time she showed the slightest sign of nerves, accepting with a stony composure all the insults and abuse. The pompous speech of welcome delivered by the president, Vergniaud, who only a few days before had vituperated against 'the traitors still sheltered in the Tuileries', bore little relation to the prevalent mood among the deputies, which was one of embarrassment and fear – a fear which turned to panic when there was suddenly the sound of gunfire and a few stray bullets flew through the open windows. The King shouted above the general uproar, 'I assure you I have forbidden the Swiss to fire,' and a deputation was sent to the palace to repeat his orders. But it had barely left when a horde of insurgents burst into the hall, reducing the deputies to such a state of abject terror that, thinking of themselves rather than of the King, they gave in to all the demands of the people, shouting together, 'Liberty and Equality forever!' The Monarch, whose person according to the constitution was still inviolate, had become their prisoner. The only protection they afforded was to confine the whole of the royal family, together with the children's governess and the Princesse de Lamballe, into the recorder's box, a small room barely ten feet square, below the public gallery and separated from the main hall by an iron railing which was removed so that, in case of necessity, the King and his family could seek shelter in the midst of the Assembly. Louis, who was a man of exceptional strength, removed some of the bars himself. During the first session, lasting for over fifteen hours in almost tropical heat, the unfortunate sovereigns had to listen to long, wordy speeches of delegates anxious to appease the members of the insurrectionary commune seated in the public gallery and without a thought as to the feelings of their humiliated King.

From outside the noise became more deafening, the screams more horrible as the *fédérés* gave themselves over to an orgy of killing. The first wave of insurgents had been repulsed, the palace cleared, when the Swiss received the fatal order to surrender. Used to honourable warfare, the officers laid down their arms, only to find themselves overwhelmed by a horde of wild beasts. Screaming *'Mort aux traîtres!'*, the Marseillais stormed into the palace, filled with a mad lust to murder. No one was spared from the oldest of the nobles to the youngest of the palace servants, many of them Jacobins at heart who thought they had nothing to fear. Those who tried to escape through the galleries to the Louvre were tracked down, their bodies flung out of the windows. Others were impaled on the trees in the gardens, until the statues were bespattered with blood. Even the women joined in this carnival of death, women from the dregs of the Paris streets mutilating the dead bodies with their own hands, gloating over the murders they had committed. Over 1,000 people perished; 500 of the Swiss guards were slaughtered in the palace and another sixty taken prisoner and brought before the insurrectionary commune at the Hôtel de Ville, where there was a general massacre. Four hundred insurgents lost their lives. The rest were innocent victims, palace servants, elderly courtiers who had only their court swords to defend themselves. The reign of a king who at Rheims had sworn never to shed the blood of a single Frenchman ended in a holocaust of murder.

Shut up in a stifling room, the unfortunate sovereigns had to listen during three interminable days to the new rulers of France arguing and quarrelling among themselves. Unable to say a word in their own defence, they heard every fact distorted, every lie believed. They and their terrified children had to see their faithful Swiss, covered in wounds, come rushing into the Assembly, begging for protection, pursued by men still howling for blood. They had to hear the deputies, supposedly educated men, praise the brigands who were bringing in the loot from the palace, piles of assignats, jewels and silverware, exquisite enamels and miniatures all thrown pell-mell onto the president's table. Worn out with crying, the children had fallen asleep. Even the King, overcome by the heat, was seen heavily snoring, to the disgust of the Queen who for fifteen hours remained almost immobile, now and then wetting her handkerchief to wipe the sweat off her forehead. Throughout the day not a single deputy as much as offered them a glass of water. Only a kindly doorkeeper came with some wine and biscuits bought out of his own money.

It was nearly two o'clock in the morning when they were finally taken to rest in the convent of the Feuillants, where four cells had been improvised as bedrooms. Here they were joined by a few faithful attendants who came at the risk of their lives. Madame Campan, who had had her house razed to the ground for no other reason than that she was known to be a confidante of the Queen, has left a moving account of her last visit to Marie Antoinette, whom she found in a dismal, green-painted cell, lying crying on a truckle bed, crying not so much over her own misfortunes as over the sufferings she had brought on others. Without clothes or money, for everything even to her purse and watch had been lost in the Tuileries, she had to depend on the charity of friends. The British ambassadress Lady Sutherland, who had a son of the same age as the Dauphin, had sent them clothes and linen; a former minister of the same size as the King had provided him with a suit of clothes. The Queen was even reduced to borrowing twenty-five louis from one of her waiting maids.

Three nights were spent in the cells of the Feuillants, where the singing and dancing in the streets outside prevented any proper sleep. Every morning at ten o'clock they were brought back under guard to the Assembly, for by now it had been made quite clear that they were prisoners. The deputies no longer made any secret of the fact. The King whom the 'glorious constitution' had declared to be inviolate had been deprived of his functions; the measures to which he had applied his veto had become the law of the land; and he and his family had been placed under what was somewhat erroneously called '*la sauvegarde de la nation*'. On the first day the deputies would have been satisfied to have confined them in the Luxembourg Palace. But the Commune, the new revolutionary government which had come into existence on the night of 10 August, declared that it was too easy to escape from a palace like the Luxembourg, and that for their own safety the 'illustrious captives' should be sent to the Temple, the medieval fortress of the Knights Templar, situated in the heart of the Marais and said to be impregnable.

At six o'clock on the evening of Monday 13 August, the royal family, travelling for the last time in one of the court carriages and accompanied by Monsieur Pétion, set out for the Marais. It was a long drive, for the coachmen had been told to go slowly, so that the people in the streets could enjoy the spectacle of their King on his way to prison.

The Paris headquarters of the Knights Templar was a medieval fortress built in a quadrangle surrounded by gardens enclosed by high walls. It included two towers and an elegant little palace which in former times, when the Prince de Conti was grand prior, had been the centre of the artistic life of the capital, where the young Mozart had entertained the guests and the exquisite Madame de Boufflers had acted as hostess. The last of the grand priors had been the Comte d'Artois, and the Queen had often attended his glittering and extravagant fêtes. It must have been a traumatic experience for her to return to the Temple as a prisoner and to find it brilliantly illuminated to celebrate the people's victory. A splendid meal awaited them in the hall of mirrors, and no one doubted that they were to live in the palace. Louis in a sudden outburst of energy was already allotting the various rooms for his suite, when Pétion informed them with a certain embarrassment that they were to be lodged in the big tower, which was being prepared for their accommodation and would not be ready for several weeks. Meanwhile they were to live in the little tower, where the archivist had been turned out of his apartment. The space was restricted but the rooms were well furnished and comfortable, for the archivist was a man of taste. But even Pétion must have had misgivings as to how the news would be received by the Queen, who nevertheless maintained the same icy composure she had shown throughout the day.

The tears were kept for later when on the evening of 11 August two officers arrived from the Commune with the orders to remove all persons other than the members of the royal family, leaving them only one valet in attendance. All the other servants – the six waiting women, the children's governess, Madame de Tourzel, her young daughter, and last of all the Princesse de Lamballe – were to be taken to prison. Marie Antoinette was in despair. Forgetting her dignity and pride, she implored Pétion to spare the Princess, who was not only a relation but in such delicate health that she would never stand up to the hardships of the women's prison of La Force. Madame de Tourzel, who together with her daughter was to survive by a miracle the horrors of the September massacres, left an account of the Queen's touching concern for the friend of whose weakness and foolishness she was only too well aware: 'Take care of my dear Lamballe. Try to prevent her from having to reply to awkward and embarrassing questions.' But Marie Antoinette underestimated the courage of the heroic Princess who, when submitted to the brutal interrogation of the tribunal made up of murderers, refused to say a word against her beloved Queen.

The royal family was now alone except for Cléry, who had formerly been attached to the Dauphin and who left a detailed account of life in the Temple. But the guards were not as insolent as Cléry would have us believe, nor were the commissioners as inhuman. The brewer Santerre, the hero of the *faubourgs*, and Simon the failed cobbler may have been vulgar and illiterate, but they were rarely cruel. The Dauphin was usually allowed to play in the gardens and Simon was even ready to do errands for the Queen. In the first months the Commune did its best to make the prisoners comfortable. Having lost their entire wardrobe in the sack of the Tuileries, the Queen, her sister-in-law and daughter were allowed to buy a whole new trousseau of clothes – dresses for the various seasons, large supplies of cambric lace-trimmed underwear, taffeta mantelets in the latest fashion, ribbons and bonnets and fichus of linen and gauze, fans and high-heeled shoes. One marvels that a government on the verge of bankruptcy should have been willing to pay such extravagant bills, and that the Queen in her condition should still have shown so much interest in fashion.

The meals served at the King's table were on the same lavish scale, and we read of a choice of soups, entrées and roasts followed by dessert being served at dinner together with champagne, claret and madeira, to which the King did full justice, while the Queen only picked at her food. But her desires were catered for too, and the special type of mineral water she had always drunk at Versailles was provided for her in the Temple and, what is even more surprising, continued to be supplied later at the Conciergerie.

Life in the archivist's apartment was not uncomfortable. The rooms, with their sky-blue walls, blue and white striped velvet chairs and mildly improper prints, had very little of a prison. There was even an excellent library of several hundred volumes which pleased the King, and before long both he and his sister had settled down in piety and resignation to the monotony of their restricted life. But Marie Antoinette was of another fibre. Every instinct reacted against the insolence of the guards, the familiarity of the commissioners who visited them three or four times a day, and at the beginning she would barely reply when asked as to whether she had any complaints or demands. Someone had had the imagination to produce a clavichord, and in the morning, while Louis, who would have made an excellent professor, taught history and geography to their son, she and her sister-in-law gave drawing and music lessons to Marie Thérèse. At times she would try to amuse the children by singing them some of the simple songs she remembered from her Austrian childhood. But the memories of her happy, carefree life too often reduced her to tears. At other times the guards on duty in the passages would gather outside her room to hear the erstwhile Queen of France playing an air by Grétry. But she was not often inclined to sing, and most of the day was spent in embroidering tapestries of flowers and heraldic emblems, a piece of which later came into the possession of the Italian poet Manzoni, who treasured it as a precious relic of the martyred Queen.

The days dragged on, infinitely boring. Hours were spent in playing chess or backgammon with the King, in trying to find means of amusing a high-spirited little boy who chafed at the restrictions and whose one pleasure was to go out into the gardens and fly his kite with his father, or play ball with the valet Cléry. No news or papers from the outside world reached them in this impregnable fortress. But sympathetic newsvendors would occasionally be bribed to shout loudly under their walls; and on 19 August Cléry, who was allowed to receive visits from his wife, came to tell them that Verdun had fallen to the allies. Hope dawned again, for it could be only a question of days before Brunswick's troops arrived in Paris, and the Queen had difficulty in concealing her satisfaction from the guards.

There was panic in the capital. Roland, the minister of the interior, who was still in power, was already talking of evacuating the government to Rouen. Girondists and Jacobins were accusing one another of treachery, and the insurrectionary Commune was far more effectual than the government. At the front the soldiers were turning against their officers and rumours were coming in of a royalist rising in the Vendée. Revolted by the excesses of a revolution he had been the first to encourage, Lafayette had deserted to the enemy and was now the inmate of an Austrian prison. In Paris no 'aristo' was safe. Those who had not yet left went into hiding or tried to escape, only to find the city gates closed against them, their carriages and horses commandeered for the army. A general witch-hunt, organized by the Commune to placate the angry populace, was directed against priests and aristocrats and all others suspected of royalist sympathies. Whole families including children were thrown indiscriminately into the already overcrowded prisons. And in this atmosphere of terror Georges Danton stood out as the one strong man in France, 'the Mirabeau of the mob', who with his stirring call to arms – '*De l'audace, et encore de l'audace et toujours de l'audace!*' – roused the public to a frenzy of patriotism. But to his everlasting shame he condoned the September massacres – an action taken advantage of by psychopaths like Marat and Hébert, who declared that the only way to fight the counter-revolution was by 'making the blood of all traitors flow'.

The September massacres, which began as an organized attack on the prisons and in which 1,400 persons were murdered, would only have been possible in the hysterical, overwrought atmosphere of a town dominated by fear. The assassins were few in number, and there is little doubt but that there were decent, honest workmen among them who, thanks to propaganda, genuinely believed that they were only doing their duty in protecting their families from the fury of the counter-revolution. Had the Temple been less well guarded and the commandant less efficient, the royal family might well have been among the first victims. They only knew that something was afoot from the pale, excited faces of their guards, who were suddenly doubled in number, and the fact that they were forbidden to go out into the gardens. From over the walls they heard the ringing of the tocsin and the cries of a rabble out of control. Then suddenly all hell broke loose. Some of the assassins had succeeded in penetrating into the outer courtyards, bringing with them the grisly trophy of the head of Marie de Lamballe transfixed on a pike, her face twisted into a terrible grimace, her blonde curls bespattered with blood. Others dragged her mutilated trunk, on which the most horrible outrages had been committed. 'What is the matter?' asked the King, and one of the guards replied, 'They have brought the Queen the head of Madame de Lamballe, so she can kiss her dearest friend. I suggest you show yourself at the window if you do not want them to come up here.' Marie Antoinette, who heard these words, gave a stifled moan and fell into a dead faint. In later years her daughter recalled, 'It was the only time I ever saw my mother lose control.' Meanwhile Cléry rushed to the windows to close the curtains, while below in the courtyard the commanding officer of the Temple guards, who was utterly disgusted by the display of bestiality, succeeded with consider-able presence of mind in persuading the drunken mob to go and parade their horrible trophy in the gardens of the Palais Royal, where they would find a larger audience to applaud them.

No one had been kinder and more generous to the poor than Marie Thérèse de Lamballe, now chosen to be one of their first victims. She and her father-in-law, the Duc de Penthièvre, had devoted half of their vast fortune to looking after the old and the sick. But in the scurrilous pages of *Père Duchesne* she was labelled as the Queen's lesbian friend, a coryphée of 'the orgies of Trianon'. Yolande de Polignac having escaped from their clutches, the gutter press accused of every vile obscenity a harmless little woman who had never committed an unkind action in her life.

By the middle of September Brunswick's armies had entered the forests of the Argonne, and the prisoners of the Temple were beginning to hope and to await the sound of the allied guns. From Brussels Fersen was writing to the Duke that the iniquitous town of Varennes should be razed to the ground for having betrayed its sovereigns. The Prussian army was less than 140 miles away from Paris, when suddenly the tide turned, the inexplicable and unpredictable happened. On 20 September at the mill of Valmy, the well-trained Prussian soldiers, led by veterans who had fought under the great Frederick, were turned back by the young army of the republic, going into battle for the first time in history to the shouts of '*Vive la nation!*' The combination of their excellent artillery and the reckless enthusiasm of their ready-to-die patriotism took the Prussians completely by surprise. Goethe, who was present in the Duke of Brunswick's camp, saw the utter consterna-tion which reigned there at the end of the day and noted in his journal, 'From today dates a new epoch in the history of mankind, the epoch of armed nations.'

Valmy was not a great victory, but it saved France. Instead of reassembling his troops and marching on to Paris, the Duke of Brunswick turned back and recrossed the frontier. The brutal truth which the *émigrés* could not forgive was that Prussia's and Austria's real interests lay on the other side of Europe, where the Empress Catherine was planning yet another partition of Poland.

Valmy can claim to have been the first victory of the new republic, for the battle was not yet over and the dead were not yet buried when the newly elected members of the National Convention, which had replaced the Legislative Assembly, voted for the abolition of the monarchy. The delegates from the provinces, mostly middle-aged men of moderate views who had sat in previous assemblies, were now completely dominated by the Jacobins, who held all the key positions in the capital, and among whom there was hardly one who did not want to see the King put up for trial.

On 21 September the royal family were still hoping to hear of a Prussian victory when at four in the afternoon they heard the sound of trumpets, followed by frenzied cheers and a stentorian voice proclaiming the abolition of the monarchy and the establishment of a republic. The valet Cléry described the superb indifference with which the King and Queen received the news. The municipal officer who happened to be on duty that evening was the foul-tongued Hébert, and Cléry observed him watching with a perfidious smile on his lips to see how the King reacted. But Louis never looked up from the book he was reading, while Marie Antoinette quietly went on with her tapestry. They expressed far more concern when they were told on the same day that their faithful old friend the Duc de Brissac, together with other royalist prisoners, had been massacred at Versailles.

Louis, His Christian Majesty of France and of Navarre, was from now on to be known as Louis Capet. The pettiness of the Convention went to the lengths of refusing any request made in the name of the King and of demanding the destruction of any garment embroidered with a crown. By the middle of September the alterations in the big tower were completed and the King was made to move into his apartments when the paint was barely dry, with the result that both he and the Dauphin fell seriously ill, and it was only after considerable delay that Cléry was allowed to send for the royal doctor. The Queen and Madame Elisabeth spent all their days in nursing the invalids, and when Cléry in his turn fell ill they looked after him in the same way. Three weeks later they had also moved into the tower, and though Cléry, who wrote his memoirs in the full tide of the monarchist revival, would have us believe that the Temple was a barred and gloomy prison, this does not appear to have been entirely true. Admittedly the furniture, of which some can still be seen in the Musée Carnavalet, was hardly of the standard of Versailles. But the Queen's bedroom had a pretty blue and green striped paper, a green damask bed, green and white upholstered chairs and a rosewood chest of drawers. Above all it had the luxury of a bathroom with one of those sabot baths Madame Campan described the Queen using at Versailles.

The Paris Commune prided itself that the Temple was impregnable. Adjoining buildings had been pulled down, new walls had been built, and six guarded gates had to be passed before entering the precincts. But there was not one of the guards who was not corruptible. Those who looked the fiercest and behaved the most brutally were often those who were amenable to bribery. Faithful servants had succeeded in infiltrating themselves among the Temple staff, of whom the most cunning and the most courageous was a scullion boy called Turgy, who had escaped the massacre at the Tuileries. and was now employed in bringing the meals from the kitchens which were at some distance from the tower. In a language of signs and gestures practised by him and Madame Elisabeth, who was not as closely watched as her brother and sister-in-law, he succeeded in conveying to the royal family the events of the outside world – the recall of the British ambassador, the Duke of Brunswick's defeat, the progress of a revolt in the Vendée. Though a commissioner or municipal authority was always present at their meals, even going to the lengths of cutting the bread to see if it contained any secret messages, the resourcefulness of a Parisian kitchen hand succeeded in outwitting them.

Summer turned to autumn and the airless rooms in the tower, which had been stiflingly hot in August, became cold and damp. The stoves smoked, and to add to the Queen's depression the first days of November brought news that Dumouriez had beaten the Austrian army at Jemappes and had invaded Belgium, where the republican troops were being welcomed as liberators. Her sister the Archduchess Marie Christine and her husband were in flight from Brussels, followed by a panic-stricken crowd of refugees. Where was Fersen? Marie Antoinette's first thoughts were always with her lover, though she might not have cared to know that he was still in the company of Eleanor Sullivan and of Quentin Crawford, and had escaped from Brussels in the comfortable coach of the Russian ambassador, who shared the favours of the lovely Eleanor.

The prisoners in the tower were now supplied with daily newspapers in which they could read of the triumphs of the Republic, of the capture of Nice, the annexation of Monaco, of Savoy becoming the eighty-fourth department of France. The end of November brought news more dangerous to their future. The locksmith Gamain, patronized by the King who had treated him almost as a friend and with whom he had worked in his smithy at Versailles, came forward to denounce his former benefactor, telling of how, in May of that year, Louis Capet had ordered a strong box to be built into the walls of the Tuileries. Despicable characters like Gamain, who lived in fear of being arrested on account of their royalist past, were now the most fervent of Jacobins. The famous strong box, which when opened revealed all of Louis's secret correspondence – his letters to the King of Spain and to the Emperor, his correspondence with Barnave and Mirabeau – provided the devastating proof that ever since 1789 Louis had been playing a double game, giving lip-service to a constitution to which he was always opposed. This correspondence, which sent Barnave to the scaffold and caused the bones of Mirabeau to be disinterred from the Panthéon and thrown into a ditch, provided the King's enemies with all the necessary evidence to put him up for trial. In the eyes of men like Robespierre and his henchman, the beautiful and pitiless St Just, not even a trial was necessary, for Louis had already been proved guilty as a king.

New commissioners came to the tower. The regulations became even more severe. There were no longer any newspapers, and one day a commissioner arrived to confiscate all articles such as knives and forks, scissors and razors with which the prisoners might inflict bodily injury on themselves. This was the one occasion when the King showed his indignation with those who thought he could be so cowardly as to attempt to take his life.

By 3 December, all Paris knew the King was to be tried – all except the prisoners in the Temple, to whom Cléry tried to break the news as gently as he could. The Queen had no illusions. For the past weeks she had been harbouring gloomy presentiments, hardly eating or sleeping, with the result that she had grown so thin that the Commune had given permission for a dressmaker to come into the tower to alter her clothes and had ordered a 'medicinal broth' to give her strength. The pale, fragile woman with the red-rimmed eyes bore little resemblance to the exuberant young Queen or the stately matron portrayed in a hundred canvases. Already she looked far older than her thirty-seven years. But the charisma was still there, that extraordinary quality which made foul-tongued beasts like Hébert become humble and obsequious in her presence.

By 11 December her gloomy presentiments had become reality. At five in the morning cannons were posted outside the Temple, a detachment of cavalry stationed in the gardens. When the King and the Dauphin came up as usual at nine o'clock to breakfast in the Queen's room, they found so many guards on duty that they were unable to speak or even to communicate with Cléry. An hour later they went downstairs for the Dauphin's daily lesson. But barely half an hour after that Cléry came back to the Queen, bringing her the Dauphin, telling her that the King had been summoned to the Convention where his trial was about to begin. Marie Antoinette was not to see her husband again until six weeks later, on the evening before his execution. Throughout the trial, even before he was condemned, Louis was not allowed to communicate with his family other than by messages carried to and fro by his faithful valet. Night after night the hapless Queen was to hear her husband's heavy tread moving around his room on the floor below, without being able to bring him a single word of comfort.

It was hatred of the Queen rather than of the King which dictated this inhuman measure. As a refinement of cruelty Louis was offered the choice of having his children with him, providing they did not see either their mother or their aunt, and he was far too kind and selfless to accept a sacrifice which might prove fatal to the Queen's health. All during those lonely, unhappy weeks Louis displayed an inner strength, an almost superhuman courage of which he himself may not have been aware. He had no belief in the clemency of his judges and from the first day of his trial prepared himself for death. Hume's *History of England* provided his favourite reading, and he told the priest who accompanied him to the scaffold that he had found in the account of the execution of Charles I a lesson on how to die. Even the horrible Hébert admitted that Louis was noble and composed when confronted by his judges, and that the dignity of his behaviour and his language made him want to cry with rage.

Those tragic weeks also brought consolation. In republican France there were still men sufficiently brave to risk their lives in defending their sovereign. Louis's former minister Malesherbes came out of his retirement to act as counsel for his King. When asked by a member of the Convention why he should choose to speak in favour of those who were proscribed, he made the admirable reply, 'Because I care for you all as little as I care for life.' When Malesherbes arrived at the Temple to offer his services, even Louis's imperturbability gave way and he embraced the old man in tears. Malesherbes was not the only one who came forward to defend his king. Louis de Narbonne, Charles de Lameth and Lally-Tollendal, none of whom had ever been favourites of Versailles, came back from the safety of England to try to save their King. The young advocate de Séze endangered his career by making an eloquent and impassioned speech in his defence. But when it came to his turn to speak, the King himself had little to say.

His lawyers had done their best. What they had spoken had been the truth. He was innocent and his conscience was clear. Malesherbes himself was struck by his indifference, as if he was already living in another world. His chief concern was for his family, and he would spend hours in talking of the Queen, who had been so calumniated and so misunderstood. 'If only the people realized how great she had become in her misfortunes, they would revere and cherish her instead of believing all the wicked lies made up by her enemies.' Malesherbes wrote that in one of their last interviews the King was still speaking of 'that poor Princess to whom our marriage promised a throne. She was a child when she came to France and had no one to help her, not even my own relatives.' It was the first time the King had admitted that the bitterest calumnies against the Queen had originated in the drawing rooms of Mesdames Tantes.

While the King prepared himself to die with a serene and Christian resignation, the Queen was going through weeks of miserable uncertainty. Though innately religious, she lacked the unquestioning faith which helped her sister-in-law to surmount every vexation and humiliation with angelic fortitude. Her unhappiness made even the guards compassionate and they would try to cheer her with charitable lies, telling her there was to be a referendum and that the people of France would never allow the King to die.

On 15 January the Convention declared Louis Capet to be guilty of treason against the state. And two days later, after an all-night session in which the Girondists made a last attempt to save the King, a small majority voted for the death penalty. Louis accepted the verdict with the same stoical resignation he had shown throughout. The only time he showed emotion was when he heard that his cousin, Philippe d'Orléans, now known as Philippe Egalité, had voted for the death sentence.

The last lonely Christmas Day was spent in writing his testament, a nobler document than any to which he had ever put his signature as king, in which he forgave his enemies and asked that none of his descendants should ever seek revenge. He was granted his two last wishes, one of which was to be allowed to take leave of his family in private; the other was to confess to a priest of his own choice. The non-juring priest was an Irishman called Henry Essex Edgeworth, who had once been confessor to his sister. To the credit of Garat, the new minister of justice, he himself went to fetch the Abbé and brought him in his own carriage to the Temple, after assuring the King that he would take him under his protection and make sure that no reprisals were taken against him.

Cléry, who was still in attendance on the King, was forbidden to communicate with the Queen, who on the morning of 20 January heard the verdict shouted by the newsvendors below. On that evening at eight o'clock, Louis saw his family for the last time. The Convention had voted they should be left alone, but in their mean and spiteful way the Commune had insisted on four municipal authorities watching from behind a glass door. The scene was evidently so poignant that these men, most of whom were family fathers, had the decency to look away. We know little of what was said between the tears and the embraces. In Madame Royale's emotional account, written long after the event – and one must remember that she was only fourteen at the time – we are told that the King spoke to her mother of the trial, then, taking her brother on his knees, made him solemnly swear to forgive their enemies. His daughter wrote, 'My father cried on account of us, but not out of fear of death.'

Marie Antoinette wanted to spend the last night with her husband, but Louis refused. He needed quiet to prepare himself for the following day. But she insisted with such vehemence that he ended by giving way and telling the family they could come back before he left in the morning. No sooner had they gone than he told the guards to prevent them from coming down, as it would cause them too much pain. We do not know how much of this is true, for Marie Thérèse, who adored her father, had fainted on saying goodbye. Abbé Edgeworth related that after his family had gone the King turned to him and sighed, 'It is hard to love so much on earth and to be so much loved in return. But now one's thoughts and affections must go only to God.'

Marie Antoinette did not sleep that night. Lying on her bed in her white dress, the sign of mourning for a queen of France, she thought of the man who had been her husband for over twenty years and whom she had never known or understood, but whose death now filled her with a cold despair. Day dawned, a dank, foggy winter's day, and she waited trembling for the call which never came. There was the tramp of soldiers marching up the stairs, the mustering of cavalry in the street below, the grinding of the wheels of the carriage to take the King to his execution. Then silence – a terrible hollow silence for those for whom there was nothing left but tears.

The execution of the King of France shocked the whole civilized world, shaking England out of her neutrality and uniting the monarchies of Europe against a country whose triumphal armies threatened to introduce the sequestration of property, the abolition of feudalism and the introduction of practically valueless *assignats* into all the conquered territories. A month after the King's death, the Convention found itself at war with almost every major power. England, Spain and Holland now ranked among its enemies. Austria and Prussia, alarmed at Danton's declaration of his country's right to expand her natural frontiers 'to the sea, the Rhine, the Alps and the Pyrenees', turned their acquisitive eyes from Poland to join forces under the Prince of Coburg in a new spring offensive 'against those murderers in Paris'. The fate of the prisoners in the Temple was itself of little interest to the courts and chancelleries of Europe, and the few who cared were shocked by the indifference of Marie Antoinette's relations in Vienna.

Axel Fersen, who was in Düsseldorf when he heard of the King's death, could think of nothing but the unhappy Queen, and he drove from court to court, sending petition after petition soliciting for help. In a pathetic letter to his sister he wrote, 'If only I could do something to bring about her liberation, then I think the agony would be less. I find it terrible that my sole resource is to go round begging others to help.' Coburg at that moment was negotiating with Dumouriez who, having suffered reverses in the Low Countries, and knowing the fate the Convention reserved for unsuccessful generals, was planning to defect with the whole of his army, to march on Paris, dissolve the Convention and proclaim the Dauphin as the constitutional King of France. It was a bold, adventurous plan typical of a bold adventurer like Dumouriez. But he presumed too much on the loyalty of his men and the glamour of his reputation. To the new armies of the Republic, La Patrie meant more than a general. They refused to obey and Dumouriez had no other choice than to escape to the Austrian camp at Mons, taking with him the whole of his staff.

Neither Mercy nor La Marck, both of whom regarded the Prince of Coburg as a fool, had ever had any faith in these negotiations. But Fersen, the romantic idealist, allowed his imagination to run riot. The Republic had been abandoned by its greatest general. It could only be a question of days before Dumouriez was in Paris and there would be nothing more to fear for the Queen and her children. Now was the time to protect her interests from the ambitions of Monsieur and the pretensions of a victorious general. In a long and fatuous letter addressed to Marie Antoinette, which fortunately for his reputation never reached her, Fersen tells her in detail what should be her future policy and to what courts she should address herself. It is hard to believe that even someone as loving as Marie Antoinette would have had much faith in a man who wrote as if Dumouriez was at the gates of Paris, when four days later the news of the General's defection was being shouted by the newsvendors under her windows.

While Fersen continued to dream his hopeless dreams, others were ready to risk their lives for the prisoners in the Temple. The bravest and most resolute of all was the Chevalier de Jarjayes, still hiding in revolutionary Paris, hoping to render service to the Queen. Supervision at the Temple had relaxed since the King's death, as if even those who had condemned him were ashamed of what they had done, and in the first weeks were trying to make amends to the Queen, now known as the 'Widow Capet'. Her desire to wear mourning was immediately and generously complied with, and she was even given a fan. As the clothes fitted badly, permission was given for a serving woman formerly attached to Marie Thérèse's household to come into the Temple to do the alterations. When the little Princess, who was inconsolable over her father's death, fell ill with an ulcerous leg, the royal physician Dr Brunier was allowed to attend on her. Though the devoted Cléry was sorely missed and the couple named Tison, who now looked after the royal family, were ready to spy on their slightest movement, new friends had been found among the guards. The most surprising of them all was a young soldier from the south, an ardent republican called Toulon, who proudly displayed the medal he had earned for the part he had played in the storming of the Tuileries. But beneath the ferocious aspect and the rough language was a compassionate, chivalrous nature, touched by the sorrows of the prisoners in his charge: the Queen, who no longer went out into the gardens as she could not bear to pass by her husband's room; the sick girl and the poor little boy deprived of air and exercise.

It was Toulon who found a way of introducing Jarjayes into the Temple, disguised as a lamplighter, and with the help of another friendly guard, a former schoolmaster named Lepitre, conceived the audacious plan of smuggling the royal family out of the Temple. Lepitre, who was a member of the Commune, was able to furnish forged passports. A former banker of the Queen, who was known to Jarjayes, supplied the funds to bribe the officials and provide the carriages which were to take them to the coast. All was arranged when Lepitre, the most intelligent but also the most timid of the conspirators, lost his nerve. It was a dangerous moment to try to get out of Paris. The bad news from the front had caused fresh disturbances, the issuing of passports had been suspended and the city barriers closed. In the

Temple, the Tisons were more than usually alert in spying on the prisoners, and Lepitre ended in persuading Marie Antoinette that it was dangerous if not impossible to get the children out of Paris. Both Jarjayes and Toulon were still determined to help the Queen escape. But no pleas or persuasion could induce Marie Antoinette to leave her children. For a moment she let herself be tempted by the vision of freedom, of escaping from all the humiliations and miseries of the past years, of meeting again with Fersen. Her saintly sister begged her to go, promising to act as mother to her children. She might have left Marie Thérèse in the care of an aunt who loved her. But she could not bring herself to leave her son, her *'chou d'amour'*, for whom she was ready to make every sacrifice and who, with the unthinking cruelty of a child, was to end in destroying her. Her mind was made up. She would not leave him, and she wrote to Jarjayes:

> We have dreamt a pleasant dream, that is all. But I have gained much in being given yet another proof of your wholehearted devotion. My trust in you has no limits.... But my son is all that matters to me. However wonderful might be the thought of freedom, of getting away from here, I could not bring myself to part from him. I know you have my interests at heart and that the chance we are now missing may never come again. But I should never have a moment's happiness if I abandoned my children. And therefore I have no regret.

Before leaving Paris, Jarjayes was able to render a last service. The King's signet ring and seal, which Louis XVI had handed to his valet before mounting the scaffold, had been impounded by the Commune. As a guardian of the Temple, Toulon with his usual daring had succeeded in getting possession of them and handing them over to the Queen. Fearing that they might be taken away from her and regarding them as heirlooms of the crown of France, Marie Antoinette decided to send them by Jarjayes to her brother-in-law in Coblenz. One suspects that her sister-in-law Elisabeth, who was devoted to her brothers, may have influenced this decision, for Marie Antoinette, who was not forgiving by nature, had always looked upon Provence as an enemy rather than a friend. It was too dangerous for Jarjayes to carry a letter to Fersen. Instead she entrusted him with a signet ring which her lover had given her at their last meeting in return for one of her own, engraved with the *fleur-de-lis*. All she had to tell Jarjayes was 'to hand over the enclosed ring to the person whom you know to have come from Brussels to visit me last year, and to whom you will say that the words on the device have never been truer than now'. The inscription on Fersen's ring, which Marie Antoinette wore every day in prison and was still wearing in the Conciergerie, consisted of five words in Italian: *'Tutto a te mi guida'*.

Jarjayes had left. Toulon and Lepitre had been dismissed, having been denounced by the woman Tison. The regulations were tightened and outwardly it seemed as if there was no longer any chance of escape. But very few of the republican guards, and even some of the staunchest members of the

Commune, were immune to bribery. In a city policed by the vigilante societies, where no one was safe from the denunciations of his neighbour, there flourished an extraordinary character called Baron de Batz, immensely wealthy, utterly reckless, courting danger for its own sake – a character who may well have been the original of Baroness Orczy's Scarlet Pimpernel, the scourge of men like Robespierre, who referred to him as 'that infamous Batz', who remained in Paris throughout the terror, saving hundreds of lives from the guillotine and always evading capture.

The most audacious of his schemes was to rescue the royal family from the Temple, and he very nearly succeeded. For such was his wealth that he was able to bribe not only the underlings, but the military commandant, the inspector of the prisons and all his officers down to the sentries at the gates. Country houses rented under false names in various parts of France were to shelter the royal family until the propitious moment came to get them out of the country. All might have gone well had there not been on duty that night one of those rigid, incorruptible republicans in the mould of Robespierre who, suspecting a conspiracy to be on foot, reported it to the shoemaker Simon, a loyal member of the Commune. Simon hurried hotfoot to the Hôtel de Ville to report to his fellow councillors, who were not impressed, however, for hardly a day passed without false denunciations coming in from all parts of the town. It was impossible to believe that the Temple, guarded by some of the most trustworthy officers in the Commune, could be open to subversion. Simon, who liked his wine, had probably taken a drop too much. But they allowed so loyal a member to go and inspect for himself.

The conspirators knew they had been betrayed the minute he appeared. For a mad moment Baron de Batz, who was disguised as a private soldier, thought of shooting Simon. But the sound of a shot would have alerted every guard inside and outside the Temple, not all of whom had been bribed. And it would only have endangered the prisoners' lives. There was nothing to do but to get out of the Temple all those whom Baron de Batz had brought in in disguise, and both Cortey, the commandant, and Michonis, the prison inspector, carried this out so efficiently that all escaped to safety. No one was arrested and no one was dismissed. Only the prisoners suffered. But rumours spread that Baron de Batz was again in Paris dispensing millions, and the very thought that some of their officers might be open to corruption embittered the Commune still more against the Austrian Queen. When the Dauphin fell ill the royal physician was no longer allowed to attend him. The prison doctor was considered good enough for the son of the Widow Capet. Luckily the doctor was a brave and honest man. The little boy had hurt a testicle when playing with a stick and, suffering from a lack of fresh air and exercise, had failed to respond to treatment. Unknown to the authorities, the doctor consulted with the royal physician, who having attended the child since birth was able to prescribe the right medicines. The Dauphin got over his illness, but he never recovered the robust health he had enjoyed as a small child, and his mother saw with horror the first signs of the disease which had afflicted her eldest son.

It may well have been the doctor's medical report which gave Hébert the idea for the fiendish accusations he was to bring against the Queen at her trial. The Dauphin had had pain in his testicle, and the doctor may have recommended that special care should be taken to prevent the boy from indulging in masturbation. He may also have dwelt on his unhealthy life, deprived of air and exercise. Ever since his father's death and the departure of Cléry, the poor little boy had never gone out into the gardens and had remained shut up all day in the company of three sad women, who added to the boredom of his life by treating him as King, insisting on having him served first at meals and constantly telling him that he must be worthy of his inheritance.

A year before, the then Legislative Assembly had already discussed the necessity of providing the boy with a tutor. The name then suggested had been that of the famous mathematician and philosopher the former Marquis de Condorcet. So low had the Convention fallen in the past months that they now proposed the shoemaker Simon as guardian for the little Louis Charles Capet – a man who in their opinion was eminently suited to bring a descendant of *Le Roi Soleil* to the level of a *sans culotte*. Though Simon was not the sadistic brute of royalist legend, and on the contrary had on more than one occasion earned from the Queen the epithet of 'Le Bon Simon', he was nevertheless a deplorable choice as guardian to a precocious, intelligent boy of eight. Those who like Hébert had an almost abnormal hatred of the Queen could not have dealt her a crueller blow than in depriving her of her child, who was to go on living on the floor below but was not allowed to have any communication with any member of his family.

It was late in the evening on 1 July, when the little boy was already in bed, that six officers of the Commune, without giving any previous warning, came into the Queen's sitting room to announce that the newly formed committee of public safety had decreed that she was to lose the custody of her son. The Queen's pleas and entreaties were so heartrending as to embarrass the republican officers who in their official report wrote that 'the separation was carried out with all the kindness and consideration proper to the circumstances'. On the other hand, the little King's sister, who must have been in a highly emotional state at the time, recalls her mother bathed in tears, begging the officers to kill her rather than to take away her son, and them threatening to kill both her children if she continued to oppose their orders. Neither of these reports can be believed.

When Marie Antoinette heard of the fatal decision, she knew that neither prayers nor protests could prevail against the pathological hatred of a Hébert. The sight of her sobbing child being carried away in the arms of the republican guards broke her proud spirit. From now on her sole interest in life lay in the few moments a day when she would climb up the spiral staircase to the third floor, where through one of the window slats in the tower she could look out over a courtyard where the little King would sometimes come to play. For the first days he was miserably unhappy and she would hear him crying in his room downstairs, calling for his mother. The guards and commissioners, who were for the most part young men with families of their own, did their best to comfort him, and before long he had adapted himself quite happily to his new life. It was far more amusing to play in the gardens with the soldiers than to recite his prayers and catechism with his pious aunt. He enjoyed hearing the revolutionary songs, and was soon singing the '*Marseillaise*' and the '*Ça Ira*' at the top of his voice. In 1789, when he was only four, the Queen had written to his governess, Madame de Tourzel, to warn her that her son's worst fault was his extreme indiscretion and his readiness to repeat whatever he overheard, and often, without any intention to lie, to embroider it in his imagination. Unfortunately the lives of the royal family ever since that time had consisted of nothing but subterfuge and deceit, of having to pay lip-service to a revolution they hated and a constitution they never believed in. Whether at a feast of the *Fédération* or the proclamation of the constitution, the little Dauphin had always to appear in public with his parents to swear an oath of loyalty to the Revolution he knew that neither of them believed in. And in his child's mind he had already learnt that one had to dissemble in order to survive.

Even now Hébert was not content, and in the filthy pages of *Le Père Duchesne*, which appealed to the lowest dregs of the populace, he repeated that it was 'time for the Austrian whore to try on Sanson's necktie'. Sanson was the dreaded executioner, whose prowess at the guillotine was watched day after day by an audience mostly of women, the so-called '*tricoteuses*', who took a morbid pleasure in seeing the heads of aristos and unsuccessful generals serve as fodder for the guillotine, which had now been moved from the prison in the Conciergerie to a place of honour in the former Place Louis xv, renamed the Place de la Révolution. A lost battle and the grievances of a subordinate officer were sufficient for a general to be sent to the scaffold. Left without leadership, the untrained armies of the Republic suffered defeat after defeat. The Prince of Coburg had retaken Valenciennes, the Austrians had cleared the French out of the Low Countries. Revolts had broken out all over France, pursued with an increasing savagery by the peasants of the Vendée, led by naval officers at Toulon who had proclaimed Louis xvii as king and opened the port to English and Spanish warships. Meanwhile in Paris the murder of Marat, the people's idol, by a young royalist woman called Charlotte Corday had inaugurated a reign of terror. The extremists were clamouring for vengeance and the predestined victim was the Austrian queen, who was to be handed over to be tried by the revolutionary tribunal.

At two o'clock in the morning on 2 August four police officers arrived at the

Temple to get the Queen out of bed and in the name of the Convention to take her to the prison of the Conciergerie. All she was allowed to bring with her was a small bundle of clothes and a bottle of smelling salts; by one of those curious anomalies which one occasionally finds in the Convention's treatment of the Queen, the little dog which had been brought to her from England by Marie de Lamballe and had come with her from the Tuileries to the Temple was now allowed to accompany her to the Conciergerie, where it remained with her to the end. Some say it was a pug, others a Scotch terrier. Being an English dog, the latter is more likely. His name was Odin, the name which Fersen had given his pet dog, the inseparable companion of his travels.

The Queen listened quietly to a decree which she knew could end only in death. She made no attempt to either argue or resist. There were a few tears on parting from her daughter and sister-in-law. But she was quite calm and composed when, walking unassisted down the stairs, she passed by her husband's room for the first time since his death. Unseeing and unhearing, frozen with grief, she knocked her head against the low stone archway of the entrance gate. One of the police officers, showing a genuine concern, asked her whether she had hurt herself, and she replied, 'No, for nothing can hurt me now.'

The seventy days which Marie Antoinette spent in the Conciergerie are obscured in the mist of royalist legend. Such information as we have rests mainly on the ghost-written memoirs of an uneducated country girl called Rosalie Lamorlière, a maid in the service of the governor's wife. Both Madame Richard and her maid seem to have done all they could to alleviate the discomforts of prison life in the damp and miserable cell, where by order of the Convention the Queen of France was condemned to spend her last days.

A visit to that grim prison on the Ile de la Cité still fills one with a sense of doom. When Marie Antoinette came to the Conciergerie, 300 people, priests, aristocrats, hairdressers and generals, were all incarcerated in what was known as 'the antechamber to the guillotine'. The governor and his wife were a kindly couple, but all that the municipal authorities allowed them to provide for the former mistress of Versailles was an iron bedstead, two straw mattresses, a cane armchair, two chairs, a table and a washbasin with a ewer. But Madame Richard had the Queen's bed made up with the finest and whitest of sheets from her own linen chest, and the food she provided was the best she could find in the markets. Both she and Rosalie were excellent cooks, and though the dishes were only pewter, the little maid polished them till they shone like silver. In her dark cell at the Conciergerie Marie Antoinette found a disinterested kindness and affection such as she had never known at Versailles. Frail and shabby in her widow's weeds, she still retained the mystique of majesty. When Madame Richard went shopping the market, women, some of whom may have been the same who had joined in the march on Versailles, produced their plumpest chickens, their finest fruit '*pour notre bonne reine*, who will see that we are not all like those monsters at the Hôtel de Ville'. Even the gendarmes on duty felt compassion for the tired, sad woman who never complained, and they would go out and buy her flowers and try to refrain from smoking in her presence.

Marie Antoinette was isolated in her cell, but she was in the midst of prison life. Michonis had kept his job as inspector and in memory of Baron de Batz's millions was always ready to render some little service, giving her news of her children, and on one occasion bringing her a parcel from Madame Elisabeth containing garments she had left behind – a white wrapper, some cambric lace-trimmed chemises, silk stockings, linen fichus and caps, and a pair of high-heeled satin shoes she was to wear on going to the scaffold. On receiving this precious parcel, the woman who had been Mademoiselle Bertin's most extravagant client wept with pleasure like a child. We hear of the Queen being dressed in rags, of her shoes being covered with mildew from the damp of the stone floors. And it is true that such was the spite of the municipal authorities that she was allowed to have her chemises laundered only every ten days, while Madame Richard would never have dared to procure her a new dress. But small parcels of fine underwear were constantly being smuggled into the Conciergerie, and under her shabby clothes the queen still wore exquisite chemises, carefully washed by Rosalie. Bribery was rampant, and the amiable and venal Michonis was prepared to introduce into her cell anyone who was ready to pay for the privilege. There was a mad Englishwoman called Lady Atkins, full of extravagant schemes to rescue the Queen, none of which ever materialized, and to whom she never addressed a word when Michonis brought her into her cell. There was the unknown artist who painted the last picture we have of the Queen, which is still to be seen in the Musée Carnavalet, a picture devoid of talent, showing a woman with pallid cheeks and lifeless eyes, who has already lost all hope.

But there was a moment when Marie Antoinette dared again to hope, when in the last days of August Michonis came into her cell with a young man wearing two carnations in his buttonhole, whom she recognized as the Chevalier de Rougeville, a brave officer who on 20 June had protected her from the fury of the mob. All that we know for certain of what is called '*l'affaire des oeillets*', which later Alexandre Dumas was to turn into a novel, is that de Rougeville with the help of Michonis was planning to get the Queen out of the Conciergerie. Though penniless, he appears to have had sufficient funds to offer her several hundred louis with which to bribe the guards. A note wrapped round a carnation, which he dropped on his first visit, told her of his plans. On his second visit he brought her the money, and she appears to have been sufficiently foolish or sufficiently desperate to attempt to bribe one of her guards who, however well-intentioned, was not prepared to lose his job, still less his head, helping her escape. The conspiracy was denounced. De Rougeville fled, Michonis was arrested and Madame Richard and her husband transferred to another prison. But the one who suffered most was the Queen. Such privileges as she had had were curtailed. She was moved to what was regarded as a safer prison, the former dispensary, which smelt unpleasantly of medicines and had one barred window giving out over the women's exercise yard. At night she was not even allowed a candle and, now that the days were drawing in, would spend long hours in the dark, the only illumination coming from a dim lantern in the yard. But the worst of all was the lack of privacy, for she was guarded night and day by policemen watching from behind the grilled window. Fortunately her new jailor, a former governor of the prison of La Force, was a man of character and standing who did not allow himself to be bullied by the municipal authorities and did his best to see that the Queen was treated with humanity. When Hébert told him that the ordinary prison food was good enough for the woman Capet, Bault replied that he alone was responsible for his prisoner's health and that in her present state of weakness she had to be given decent food. When he was refused a second blanket for the Queen's bed, he got his wife to supply her with a soft wool mattress, and when the public prosecutor, Fouquier-Tinville, threatened him with the guillotine for having dared to put an old piece of tapestry behind the Queen's bed to protect her from the damp wall, he was sufficiently ingenious to reply that he had done so in order to prevent her from overhearing messages which might be passed from the prison yard. Deprived of writing materials, forbidden to embroider or to knit, the Queen must have passed days as endless as her nights, and for the first time in her life she asked to be given books to read. Madame Bault tells us that what she preferred were tales of adventure and of violent action, and that *The Voyages of Captain Cook* and *The Stories of Famous Shipwrecks* were among her favourites. Many years ago her brother Joseph had told her that she would never have any satisfaction in life unless she learnt to read. How little she had listened either to him or to the Abbé Vermond when he begged her to dedicate at least one hour a day to serious reading. Life had seemed too full and glittering to waste her time in reading. But now she had nothing left to do but to read and pray and sometimes, when her eyes were too tired to read, to sit and watch the soldiers playing at cards. These men, many of them devout Catholics, at heart felt sympathy for a young woman condemned to die, for they knew it was only a question of weeks, perhaps of days, before she came up for trial before the revolutionary tribunal.

There were reports of large sums having been offered for her ransom, of Fersen having employed the dancing master Noverre to bribe members of the committee of public safety, of even Danton having allowed himself to be corrupted. But it was all too late. The extremists were clamouring for her death, and the only delay was in finding sufficient evidence to justify the death penalty.

The treason of which Marie Antoinette was irrefutably guilty, and of which the proofs are to be found in the Vienna archives and in Fersen's memoirs, was not known at the time of her trial. What was called *Le Comité Autrichien* was suspected of having been in communication with the enemy. But nothing was known of the French military plans sent by the Queen to Comte Mercy at the beginning of the war. The accusations against her rested on the same old stories: the millions she had taken out of France to give to the Emperor Joseph; the millions she had squandered on her favourites and on the building of Le Trianon; the deplorable manner in which she had corrupted the King, encouraging him to drink and leading him into a policy of lying and deceit, influencing him in his decision to escape and in exercising his veto against the wish of the people.

The filthy libels of a Jeanne de La Motte, the obscene pamphlets which had come long ago from the printing presses of the Luxembourg Palace and the Palais Royal – all served as evidence against a woman described as 'a scourge of her country and a dishonour to her sex'. But it was the foul-minded Hébert who produced the most infamous of accusations ever brought against a mother, to which her eight-year-old son was made to sign his name.

The little King had been caught out by Simon the shoemaker in the act of self-abuse, and in order to save himself from punishment he said he had been initiated in these practices by his mother and his aunt. It was a naughty and impudent lie on the part of a child who had already learnt to protect himself through deceit, and Simon, who was an avid reader of *Père Duchesne*, had seized on it as yet another proof of Marie Antoinette's depravity. He went straight to Hébert, with the result that six municipal councillors headed by the mayor arrived at the Temple to interrogate the little King. Intimidated by their presence, not daring to contradict himself, the boy repeated the lie, and encouraged by Hébert went so far as to say that his mother and his aunt had amused themselves by taking him into their beds and watching him perform. Royalist apologists would have us believe that the wretched child had been bullied and beaten by his tormentors who had forced him into telling that terrible lie. But unbiased witnesses claim that he appeared to be quite cheerful and unconcerned, and that he persisted in his lies, even when confronted with his sister and his aunt. Marie Thérèse, a shy and nervous girl who was terrified by the severe-looking men, insisted that she had seen nothing and did not understand what they were talking about. But her aunt, who was a mature woman of twenty-nine of strong religious principles, was so disgusted that she called out half involuntarily, 'The little monster!' Fortunately Marie Antoinette was spared the knowledge of these accusations till the day before her death.

The seventy days in the Conciergerie destroyed the Queen's once-splendid constitution. Though barely thirty-eight, she was already suffering from the menopause and had severe menstrual pains and haemorrhages which weakened her resistance. It was an old woman, a ghost of her former self who at eight o'clock on the morning of 14 October was brought from her cell through long corridors and courtyards to the great hall of the Palais de Justice, formerly the home of the *parlement* of Paris where in the old days she had accompanied the King for the ceremonies of the *lit de justice*. The tapestries had gone, the golden *fleurs-de-lis* had been defaced and replaced by a crude allegorical painting of the Declaration of the Rights of Man. Gone were the gilded thrones, the Aubusson carpets. Now there was nothing but hard cane chairs, a wooden table and a bare stone floor. She had already had to submit to a preliminary interrogation before she was even given a counsel to defend her, and the judges were impressed by her courage and strength, a strength in which she had been helped by prayer, for in the past few weeks non-juring priests imprisoned in the Conciergerie had, with the connivance of the prison governor, been introduced into her cell, where on more than one occasion they had celebrated mass and heard her confession.

In her last letter addressed to her sister-in-law and written only a few hours before her death, Marie Antoinette categorically denied having received any form of spiritual consolation. Fearing quite rightly that her letter might never reach its destination, for later it was found among the papers of Robespierre, she deliberately refrained from saying anything which might implicate either Bault and his family or any of those heroic priests who had helped her in those last days. By some miraculous chance all of them survived the Revolution.

The two lawyers who were to defend the Queen were only notified twenty-four hours before the trial was due to begin, and a request for a three-day adjournment in which to prepare their briefs was summarily dismissed. The two lawyers and in particular Chauveau-Lagarde were dedicated and brave, when one considers that Malesherbes' eloquence in defending the King had cost him his life. Neither they nor their client can have had any illusions as to the outcome of a trial in which not a single member of the jury would have dared to vote for an acquittal.

For two long days, in sessions lasting over fifteen hours, Marie Antoinette had to defend herself against a rigged court and a perjured jury, defending not only her life but her honour as a woman, clearing her name for posterity, determined not to go down in history as the guilty queen who had been the ruin of her country, but as the wife of Louis XVI who, in her own words, 'had done nothing but comply with his wishes'. Forty-one witnesses were called one after the other, each with some miserable lie, some ridiculous invention – maidservants and pages, hairdressers and tradesmen, all of whom had once battened on the court, and were now vying with each other to discredit the Queen they had formerly professed to adore.

Their tales were becoming tedious. Even the *tricoteuses* were beginning to lose interest, when Hébert stepped forward to make his filthy allegations. At first it seemed as if the Queen, who sat pale and frozen in her chair, had barely heard. Then one of the jury, whom Herman the president would willingly have silenced, insisted on 'Antoinette' replying to the charges. And suddenly she came to life. Her cheeks flushed red, her tired eyes blazed in anger, and rising to her feet she answered: 'If I did not reply it was simply because human nature cannot answer such a charge against a mother.' And turning to the women in the gallery she cried: 'I appeal to all the mothers in the room!' There was a moment of stunned silence, of consternation among the judges, who saw that the accusation had boomeranged against the accuser. The women in the gallery were now applauding the Queen and screaming against Hébert. The more emotional among them had fainted. Marie Antoinette had triumphed, her extraordinary charisma had asserted itself for the last time, and for the moment the *tricoteuses* were on her side. Herman the president rang the bell to restore order in the court. Witnesses followed one another in quick succession. But at the end of the day judges and jurymen were looking equally worried. That night, at supper in his favourite restaurant, Robespierre denounced Hébert as a fool whose revolting allegations had only served as a victory for the Queen: 'Was it not sufficient for her to be a Messalina instead of trying to make her into an Agrippina as well?'

At eleven o'clock the worn-out Queen was back in her cell, but she had still to face another day. Suffering from agonizing menstrual pains, unable to take any nourishment other than a little soup, she had still to listen to more irrelevant witnesses dwelling on her extravagances and intrigues. Even the president of the court appears to have realized the futility of some of the evidence, for he barely referred to it in his summing up, concentrating on her relations with the enemies of the republic, her efforts to spread civil war in France and to encourage the King in a policy contrary to the interests of his country.

It was three in the morning when the jury left the hall, and the Queen, half fainting from fatigue, had remained in the dock for nearly fifteen hours listening to speeches first from the public prosecutor, then from her counsel, who had spoken for over two hours bravely and eloquently in her defence. 'How tired you must be, Monsieur Chauveau, and how I appreciate all the trouble you have taken on my behalf.' Her smile and thanks were sufficient for the lawyer to be placed under arrest.

The jury's deliberations lasted for one hour, while outside in the streets people waited anxiously for news, royalists came out of hiding, still hoping against hope that the verdict would be commuted to deportation. But none of the twelve jurors were heroes. If they stayed out an hour it was only to give an appearance of legality to what was already a foregone conclusion. The verdict was unanimous. Marie Antoinette de Lorraine d'Autriche, widow of Louis Capet, was judged guilty on all counts and was to be executed on that same morning. The news was no sooner known than crowds were already converging on the Place de la Révolution to secure their seats for what was to be the greatest spectacle of the year.

Marie Antoinette listened unmoved to the verdict. The president's last question remained unanswered. There was utter stillness when she left the hall, looking to neither left nor right. For all her weakness and fatigue, she moved with the same light step with which she had formerly crossed the Gallery of Mirrors at Versailles. But she was so tired she could hardly see and would have fallen on going down the steps leading to the cells had it not been for a young officer in the gendarmerie who caught her in his arms. It was the same young officer who had been the only one in court to offer her a glass of water and to take off his hat in her presence. These small courtesies were sufficient to have him denounced by one of his colleagues. On this night there were lighted candles on the table in her cell, a supper of roast chicken, despite the lateness of the hour, and as a special concession pen and paper with which to send her last messages.

By now the Queen was crying, not so much for herself as for the children whom she would never see again and for whose future she was so afraid, and the last letter addressed to her sister-in-law was watered with those tears. Every biographer of Marie Antoinette has quoted this letter, which never reached its destination but was stolen by Robespierre and discovered twenty years later. It is a letter which speaks only of love and never of revenge, and where, in what for the Queen must have been the most painful thing of all, she asks forgiveness for her son: 'I know how much my little boy must have made you suffer. Forgive him, my dear sister. Remember how young he is and how easy it is to make a child say whatever one wants, to put words into his mouth he does not understand. I hope the day will come when he will grasp the full nature of your kindness and the affection you have shown to both my children.'

In the end it becomes not so much a letter as a testament expressing her inner thoughts: 'I had friends. The thought of being separated from them and their distress is one of my greatest regrets in dying. Let them know at least that to the very last they were always in my mind.' These words can only refer to Fersen, to whom she did not dare to write but whom she thought of at every hour of the day. Even her little dog was named in memory of Fersen's, and Odin was still with her on that last night, snuggling up to her when she lay exhausted and still fully dressed upon her bed.

On the morning of 16 October 1793, 30,000 men, the whole armed force of the capital, had been mobilized to guard one woman on her way to the guillotine. Even now at the eleventh hour the committee of public safety still feared there might be demonstrations in her favour. Policemen and vigilantes were disseminated among the crowds – a gay holiday crowd with whom the sellers of lemonade and sweetmeats, the hawkers of pornographic pamphlets on the private life of the licentious Queen were doing a roaring trade. The day was fine and a pale autumnal sun shone over the Seine. At eleven o'clock in the morning the gates of the Conciergerie opened to the sound of drums, and a tall, pale woman in a white gown came out blinking in the unaccustomed sunlight. There was a shocked silence when she was seen to have her hands tied by a cord, led by the executioner. The sight of a former queen of France tethered like an animal to a cart gave even the most hardened of revolutionaries an involuntary sense of guilt. And not a single voice was raised against her.

Marie Antoinette had been praying when Bault came early into her room. She asked for a cup of chocolate and a bread called a *mignonette* which was brought in from a neighbouring café. It was the governor's wife, not Rosalie, who helped to dress her on this last morning, and in all the years at Versailles she had never dressed with so much ease. Her white wrapper, starched and ironed, was put over a black underskirt. The finest of muslin fichus and caps were chosen for what was to be her last public appearance, and she wore her best black satin shoes. She would have liked to cut her hair before it was mangled by Sanson's shears, but not even the kindly Bault dared to lend her a pair of scissors. A priest arrived, one of those constitutional priests who were still employed by the Convention to accompany their victims to the guillotine. But both Marie Antoinette and Louis had always despised all constitutional priests. When the Abbé Gérard, who was a good man at heart, offered her his services, she politely refused, saying, 'God in His mercy has already provided them,' and she showed the same polite indifference when he offered to accompany her to the guillotine. There was a moment when she faltered on seeing the rubbish cart with the muddy wheels drawn by two old nags which was to take her across Paris. Louis had been allowed to go to his death in a closed carriage, but for her they had reserved this final humiliation. She was terrorized to think that the rabble might pull her down from the cart and tear her to pieces. Her terror brought on a sudden loosening of the bowels, and Sanson had to untie her hands for her to go and relieve herself in a corner behind a wall. But five minutes later she had recovered her composure, and for the whole of the long drive she remained almost immobile, seated on a wooden plank. Even her enemies paid tribute to her courage. 'The whore was bold and insolent to the end,' wrote *Père Duchesne*. The majority of the crowd was curiously silent until she reached the Rue St Honoré, where the stalwarts of the Revolution, the worst of the *poissardes*, were waiting to gloat over her fall. A low-class actor called Grammont was strutting around on horseback, brandishing a sword and shouting, 'Here goes the wicked Antoinette! She is finally finished with, my friends.' And here stood David, a great artist but a despicable human being, a regicide who now licked the boots of Robespierre and was later to pay homage to Bonaparte. In those few short moments he sketched that memorable and cruel likeness of a shattered woman, all beauty gone, with nothing left but pride and a grim determination to die in a manner worthy of her ancestors. She stares ahead, with the Hapsburg lips, which were once a pretty pout, set in a look of utter contempt.

The only time she showed some life was on reaching the Tuileries, when she turned to look at the palace which held so many memories. Did she think of that fatal August day when Louis's indecision had lost them their throne? Or did her thoughts go back to a spring day so many years ago, when as a young Dauphine she had stood on the terrace looking out over a sea of cheering faces, and the Duc de Brissac had told her, 'Madame, you have 200,000 lovers waiting to adore you'?

Now there were 200,000 people waiting to see her die. The cart came with a jolt to a halt. The Place Louis xv was sadly altered. Where was the old King's equestrian statue, and what was that hideous monument covered with garlands and inscriptions erected in its place? Abbé Gérard, still clutching his ivory crucifix, told her it was 'the statue of Liberty'. How ugly it all was – everywhere slogans and tricolours, and dominating all the stark silhouette of the guillotine outlined against the sky. Sanson offered her an arm to assist her from the cart, but she refused and got quickly down, and with the same light step mounted to the scaffold. She moved so swiftly that it almost seemed as if she was in a hurry to die. Inadvertently she trod with her high heels on Sanson's foot. The huge man let out an oath. She turned and said to him in a voice that was still so young and held just a hint of mockery, 'Forgive me, monsieur, I did not do it on purpose.'

BIBLIOGRAPHY

Almeras, Henri de, *Les Amoureux de la Reine Marie Antoinette* (Paris, 1907).

Arneth, Ritter von (ed.) *Correspondance Secrète entre Marie Antoinette, Marie Thérèse et Mercy d'Argenteau*, 3 vols (Paris 1868).

　Joseph II und Leopold von Toskana Brief Wechsel (Vienna, 1872).

　Marie Antoinette, Joseph II und Leopold II, der Brief Wechsel (Leipzig, 1868).

Baillio, Joseph, *Marie Antoinette et Vigée-Lebrun, L'Œuil* no. 308 (March, 1981).

Belloc, Hilaire, *Marie Antoinette* (London, 1910).

Bernier, Olivier, *Lafayette, Hero of Two Worlds* (New York, 1983).

Besenval, P.J.V., Baron de, *Mémoires*, 4 vols (Paris, 1805).

Bombelles, Marc, Marquis de, *Journal*, 2 vols (Geneva, 1982).

Burke, Edmund, *Reflections on the Revolution in France* (London, 1790).

　A letter from Mr Burke to a member of the National Assembly (London, 1791).

Campan, J.L.H. de, *Mémoires sur la Vie Privée de la Reine Marie Antoinette* (Paris, 1823).

Castelot, André, *Marie Antoinette* (Paris, 1953).

Cléry, J.B., *Journal de ce que c'est passé à la tour du Temple pendant la captivité de Louis XVI, Roi de France*, including *Les Dernières Heures de Louis XVI* by Abbé Edgeworth, *Mémoires* by Marie Thérèse Charlotte de France (Mercure de France, Paris, 1983).

Coigny, Aimée de, *Textes Inédites*, 2 vols (Paris, 1981).

Condorcet, Marquis de, *Mémoires sur le Règne de Louis XVI et la Révolution*, 2 vols (Paris, 1862).

Coquelat, Baron, *Mémoires* (Paris, 1829).

Crankshaw, Edward, *Maria Theresa* (London, 1969).

Cronin, Vincent, *Louis and Antoinette* (London, 1974).

Croy, Duc de, *Journal Inédit 1718–1784*, 3 vols (Paris, 1906).

Dard, Emil, *Un Rival de Fersen, Quentin Crawford* (Paris, 1947).

Deffand, Marie, Marquise du, *Lettres de la Marquise du Deffand à Horace Walpole 1766–1780*, 3 vols (trans. London, 1912).

Diesbach, Ghislain de, *L'Histoire de l'Emigration 1789–1814* (Paris, 1975).

Dorset, Duke of, *Dispatches from Paris 1784–1790* (ed. Oscar Browning, London).

　History of the Sackville Family, Earls and Dukes of Dorset, 2 vols (ed. Charles Phillips, London).

Fay, Bernard, *Louis XVI ou la Fin d'un Monde* (Paris, 1981).

Fejtö, Joseph, *Joseph II* (Paris, 1953).

Ferrières, Marquis de, *Mémoires* (Paris, 1822).

Flaissier, Sabine, *Marie Antoinette et l'Accusation* (Paris, 1967).

Friedrichs, Otto, *Marie Antoinette Calomniée* (Paris, 1948).

Frischauer, Paul, *Beaumarchais, an Adventurer in a Century of Women* (London, 1936).

Fuinck-Brentano, F., *L'Affaire du Collier* (Paris, 1901).

　La Mort de la Reine (Paris, 1901).

Gaxotte, Pierre, *Le Siècle de Louis XV* (Paris, 1933).

Geffroy, A., *Gustav III et la Cour de France*, 2 vols (Paris, 1867).

Genlis, Madame de, *Mémoires* (Paris, 1925).

Georgel, Abbé de, *Mémoires pour Servir à l'Histoire des Evénéments de la Fin du Dix-Huitième Siècle, 1760, 1810*, 6 vols (Paris, 1817).

Girard, Georges (ed.), *Correspondance entre Marie Thérèse et Marie Antoinette* (Paris, 1933).

Goncourt, Edmond et Jules de, *Histoire de Marie Antoinette* 2 vols (Paris, 1858).

Gooch, G.P., *The Monarchy in Decline* (London, 1956).

Gower, Ronald, Lord, *The Last Days of Marie Antoinette* (Paris, 1885).

Hearsey, John, *Marie Antoinette* (London, 1972).

Heidenstam, O. G. von, *Correspondance Secrète de Marie Antoinette, Fersen et Barnave* (Paris, 1913; trans. 1926).

Hibbert, Christopher, *The French Revolution* (Penguin Books, 1982).

Hüe, François, Baron, *Dernières Années du Regne de Vie de Louis XVI* (Paris, 1816).

Kerima, Françoise, *Hans Axel de Fersen* (Paris, 1985).

Klinckowström, Rin de, Baron, *Le Comte de Fersen et la Cour de France*, 2 vols (Paris, 1877).

Kunstler, Charles, *Le Secret de Fersen* (Paris).

La Marck, Prince Auguste d'Arenberg, Comte de, *Correspondance avec Mirabeau Pendant les Années 1789–1791* (Paris, 1851).

La Rocheterrie, Maxime de, *Histoire de Marie Antoinette*, 2 vols (Paris, 1905).

La Tour du Pin Gouvernet, Marquise de, *Journal d'une Femme de Cinquante Ans* (Paris, 1913).

Langlade, Emil, *La Marchande de Robes de Marie Antoinette, Rose Bertin* (Paris, 1911).

Lauzun, Gontaut-Biron, Duc de, *Mémoires*, 2 vols (Paris, 1822).

Le Nôtre, G., *La Captivité et la Mort de Marie Antoinette* (Paris, 1897).

Lescure, Adolphe, *Correspondance Secrète Inédite sur Louis XVI, Marie Antoinette, la Cour et la Ville*, 2 vols (Paris, 1866).

Lever, Evelyne, *Louis XVI* (Paris, 1982).

Ligne, C.J.E., Prince de, *Memoirs and Letters of the Prince de Ligne*, (trans. by Katherine Prescott Wormsley, London).

Loomis, Stanley, *Du Barry* (London, 1962).
    The Fatal Friendship (London, 1972).
    Paris Under the Terror (New York, 1969).

Manceron, Claude, *Les Hommes de la Liberté*, 3 vols: Vol. 1, *Les Vingts Ans du Roi* (1972), Vol. 2, *Le Vent d'Amerique* (1974), Vol. 3, *Le Bon Plaisir* (1976).

Mansel, Philip, *Louis XVIII* (London, 1983).

Maxwell, Constantia, *The English Travellers in France, 1781–1795* (London, 1932).

Morris, Gouverneur, *Diary of the French Revolution, Diary and Letters*, 2 vols (ed. Anne Cary Morris, 1889).

Nolhac, Pierre de, *Trianon, La Maison de Marie Antoinette* (Paris, 1914).
    La Reine Marie Antoinette (Paris, 1890).
    Marie Antoinette, Dauphine (Paris, 1897).
    Autour de la Reine (Paris, 1926)

Oberkirch, Baronne de, *Mémoires*, 2 vols (Paris, 1835).

Orieux, Jean, *Talleyrand* (Paris, 1970).

Padover, J.K., *Joseph II, the Revolutionary Emperor* (London, 1934).

Rignault, Henri, *Les Enfants de Louis XV: La Descendance Illégitime* (Paris, 1953).

Saint Armand, Robert de, *The Duchesse d'Angoulême and the Restoration* (London, 1892).

Saint Beuve, *Portraits Litéraires*, 3 vols (Paris, 1937).

Saint-Priest, Comte de, *Mémoires Publiés par le Baron de Barente* (Paris, 1929).

Ségur, Philippe, Comte de, *Mémoires et Anecdotes*, 3 vols (Paris, 1894–95).

Ségur, P.M.M.H., Marquis de, *Marie Antoinette* (trans. London, 1927).

Seward, Desmond, *Marie Antoinette* (London, 1981).

Söderhjelm, Alma, *Fersen et Marie Antoinette: Journal et Correspondance de Comte Axel Fersen* (Paris, 1930).

Sorel, Albert, *L'Europe et la Révolution Française*, 8 vols (Paris, 1885).

Staël-Holstein, Baronne de, *Oeuvres Complètes* (London, 1820).

Stryienski, Casimir, *Le Dixhuitième Siècle* (Paris, 1909).

    Mesdames de France: Les Filles de Louis XV (Paris, 1910).

Talleyrand, Charles Maurice de, *Mémoires*, 2 vols (Paris, 1957).

Tilly, Alexandre, Comte de, *Mémoires*, 3 vols (Paris, 1929).

Tourzel, Duchesse de, *Mémoires* (Paris, 1883).

Toynbee (ed.), *The Letters of Horace Walpole*, 9 vols (Oxford, 1903).

Valloton, *Marie Antoinette et Fersen* (Paris/Geneva, 1952).

Vigée-Lebrun, Marie Anne, *Souvenirs* (trans. London, 1904).

Zweig, Stefan, *Marie Antoinette* (London, 1933).

INDEX